Essential

All Colour
Vegetarian

Cookbook

Essential
All Colour
Vegetarian
Cookbook

hamlyn

First published in 2000 by Hamlyn, an imprint of
Octopus Publishing Group Limited
2-4 Heron Quays
London E14 4JP

Copyright © 2000 Octopus Publishing Group Limited

ISBN 0 600 602516

A CIP catalogue record for this book is available from the British Library

Produced by Toppan

Printed in China

The recipes in this book have previously appeared in *The Hamlyn All Colour
Vegetarian Cookbook* and the *Hamlyn New All Colour Vegetarian Cookbook*.

The publishers would like to thank the following for supplying photographs:
Batchelors, Edward Billington (Sugar) Ltd, Birds Eye Wall's Limited, British
Cheese, Butter Information Council, California Raisin Advisory Board, Egg
Marketing, Fresh Fruit and Vegetable Information Bureau, The Kellog
Company of Great Britain Ltd, Mushroom Growers' Association, Pasta
Information Centre, Potato Marketing Board, Sun Pat Peanut Butter, Tabasco,
Twining's Information Service, U.S. Rice Council, U.S.A. Peanuts Information
Service, John West Foods.

All other photographs from the Octopus Publishing Group Picture Library.

NOTES
Both metric and imperial measurements have been given in all recipes.
Use one set of measurements only and not a mixture of both.

Standard level spoon measurements are used in all recipes.
1 tablespoon = one 15 ml spoon
1 teaspoon = one 5 ml spoon

Eggs should be medium unless otherwise stated
The Department of Health advises that eggs should not be consumed raw.
This book contains dishes made with raw or lightly cooked eggs. It is prudent
for more vulnerable people such as pregnant and nursing mothers, invalids,
the elderly, babies and young children to avoid uncooked or lightly cooked
dishes made with eggs. Once prepared, these dishes should be kept
refrigerated and used promptly.

Do not re-freeze a cooked dish that has been frozen previously.

Milk should be full fat unless otherwise stated.

Nut and Nut derivatives
This book includes dishes made with nuts and nut derivatives. It is advisable
for customers with known allergic reactions to nuts and nut derivatives and
those who may be potentially vulnerable to these allergies, such as pregnant
and nursing mothers, invalids, the elderly, babies and young children, to
avoid dishes made with nuts and nut oils. It is also prudent to check the
labels of pre-prepared ingredients for the possible inclusion of nut
derivatives.

Pepper should be freshly ground black pepper unless otherwise stated.

Fresh herbs should be used, unless otherwise stated. If unavailable, use dried
herbs as an alternative but halve the quantities stated.

Measurements for canned food have been given as a standard metric
equivalent.

Ovens should be preheated to the specified temperature – if using a
fan-assisted oven, follow the manufacturer's instructions for adjusting
the time and temperature.

contents

soups

*Choose a soup to complement the courses
which follow, in both texture and flavour..
Light, tangy Mulligatawny Soup or delicately
flavoured Tomato and Carrot Soup make good
appetizers for a substantial main course. If the
course to follow is light, consider serving a
protein and fibre-rich pulse-based soup, such
as Bean and Pasta soup. But don't confine soup
to a permanent position of first course – extend
its status to that of a nourishing snack or lunch.*

leek and chickpea chowder

Preparation time 10 minutes	*125 g (4 oz) leeks, sliced* *1 small onion, chopped*
Cooking time 25 minutes	*2 tablespoons oil* *1 teaspoon ground cumin*
Serves 4	*1 teaspoon ground coriander* *375 g (12 oz) potatoes, diced*
Calories 325 per portion	*1 x 425 g (14 oz) can chickpeas* *750 ml (1½ pints) vegetable stock* * or water* *salt and pepper*

Sauté the leeks and onion in the oil until soft. Sprinkle over the cumin and coriander and cook for a further minute. Add the potatoes and then turn them thoroughly in the mixture. Stir in the drained chick peas with 450 ml (¾ pint) stock or water. Bring to the boil, cover and cook gently for about 15 minutes until the potatoes are soft. Add the remaining stock or water with salt and pepper to taste. Serve hot as a chowder or liquidize to make a smooth thick soup. Accompany with crusty bread.

bean and pasta soup

Preparation time 5 minutes	*1 large onion, sliced* *1.2 litres (2 pints) vegetable stock*
Cooking time 25 minutes	*75 g (3 oz) pasta shapes* *2 tablespoons tomato purée*
Serves 4–6	*50 g (2 oz) All-Bran cereal* *1 x 300 g (10 oz) can red kidney beans*
Calories 215–145 per portion	*125 g (4 oz) canned broad beans* *salt and pepper* *1 tablespoon chopped parsley, to garnish* * (optional)*

Simmer the onion in the stock in a large covered saucepan for 10 minutes. Add the pasta and tomato purée and cook for another 10 minutes. Add the salt and pepper, cereal, kidney beans and broad beans and cook gently for a further 5 minutes. Pour into soup bowls and sprinkle with parsley, if you like.

■ COOK'S TIP

Buy ready-ground spices and store them in an airtight jar ready for use. Alternatively, coriander seeds can be ground easily using a small pestle and mortar to give the most fragrant results.

■ COOK'S TIP

All-Bran cereal is a versatile storecupboard item – use it to add texture and valuable fibre to plain cake, pastry or bread mixtures. Combine it with unsweetened crumbly mixtures and grated cheese to make a tasty savoury topping for vegetables and pulses. Combine it in nut loaves, vegetable burgers and terrines for added flavour.

3

mulligatawny soup

Preparation time 5 minutes	*1 apple, chopped* *1 large carrot, chopped*
Cooking time 1 hour	*2 tablespoons oil* *25 g (1 oz) plain flour*
Serves 6	*1 tablespoon curry powder* *1.2 litres (2 pints) vegetable stock*
Calories 95 per portion	*1 tablespoon mango chutney* *25 g (1 oz) sultanas*
	pinch of sugar
	2 teaspoons lemon juice or wine or * cider vinegar*
	salt and pepper

Cook the apple and carrot in the hot oil for 2 minutes. Stir in the flour and curry powder to make a paste. Gradually stir in the stock, bring to the boil and cook until thickened. Add the chutney, sultanas, sugar, a little salt and pepper, and the lemon juice, wine or vinegar. Cook very gently for 45 minutes–1 hour or until the vegetables are very soft.

Cool slightly and either press through a sieve or blend until smooth in a food processor or blender. Pour the purée into the rinsed pan. Taste and adjust the seasoning, if necessary. Reheat gently before serving.

4

pea soup

Preparation time 10 minutes, plus soak ing	*250 g (8 oz) dried split peas* *1.2 litres (2 pints) vegetable stock*
Cooking time 1½–1¾ hours	*2 onions, chopped* *1 carrot, chopped*
Serves 4	*1 small turnip, chopped* *1 mint sprig*
Calories 210 per portion	*1 teaspoon sugar* *salt and pepper*

Cover the split peas with water and soak them overnight. Drain well. Place in a large saucepan with the stock, onions, carrot, turnip, a little salt and pepper, and the mint. Bring slowly to the boil, then simmer for 1¼–1½ hours or until the peas are very soft. Cool slightly and either press through a sieve or blend until smooth in a food processor or blender. Pour the purée back into the rinsed pan, add the sugar to taste, then taste and adjust the seasoning. Reheat very gently and serve hot.

■ COOK'S TIP

Try serving a basket of crisp cooked poppadoms with this soup. Look out for these flavoured with chilli, cumin seeds and other spices as well as the plain variety. Instead of frying them, cook them under the grill, keeping them away from the hot element.

■ COOK'S TIP

Swirl a little soured cream, natural yogurt or plain fromage frais into this soup before serving – delicious!

5

chestnut soup

Preparation time 35 minutes	*500 g (1 lb) chestnuts*

Preparation time
35 minutes

Cooking time
35 minutes

Serves 4–6

Calories
360–240 per portion

500 g (1 lb) chestnuts
1 large onion, sliced
40 g (1½ oz) butter
1 potato, chopped
3 celery sticks, chopped
1.5 litres (2½ pints) vegetable stock
15 g (½ oz) plain flour
½ teaspoon light brown sugar
pinch of dried mixed herbs
300 ml (½ pint) milk
1 tablespoon dry sherry
salt and pepper
FOR THE GARNISH
croûtons (optional)
1 tablespoon chopped parsley (optional)

Slit the hard shell of each chestnut. Put the chestnuts into a pan of boiling water and simmer for 20 minutes. Remove the hard shells, rub off the brown skins and roughly chop the chestnuts.

Put the onion and half of the butter into a pan and gently cook until soft. Add the potato, celery, chestnuts, stock, salt and pepper, and bring to the boil. Cover and simmer until the chestnuts are soft. Press through a sieve, or purée in a food processor or blender.

Melt the remaining butter, work in the flour and cook for 2 minutes. Stir in the sugar, herbs and chestnut purée, and heat through gently. Add the milk and reheat, but do not boil. Stir in the sherry and serve, garnished with the croûtons and parsley, if you like.

■ COOK'S TIP

If you have a garden, then try drying some herbs for the winter. For example, sage, thyme and tarragon can be tied in bunches and hung in a cool, dry place.

6

winter warmer

Preparation time
5 minutes

Cooking time
40 minutes

Serves 4

Calories
355 per portion

25 g (1 oz) butter
500 g (1 lb) onions, chopped
750 g (1½ lb) potatoes, chopped
900 ml (1½ pints) vegetable stock
1 x 300 g (10 oz) can creamed sweetcorn
pinch of mace or nutmeg
2 bay leaves
¼ teaspoon celery salt
pepper
1 x 175 g (6 oz) can evaporated milk
*   or single cream*
1 tablespoon chopped fennel, to garnish
*   (optional)*

Heat the butter in a large saucepan, add the onions and cook over a moderate heat for about 8 minutes until golden. Add the potatoes, stock, sweetcorn, mace or nutmeg, bay leaves, celery salt and pepper. Bring to the boil, stirring, cover and simmer for 30 minutes or until the potatoes are very soft. Remove the bay leaves. Stir in the evaporated milk or cream, then taste for seasoning; heat through gently and serve in warmed individual bowls. Garnish with fennel, if using.

■ COOK'S TIP

A delicious accompaniment for soup: clean potato peelings, dipped in a thin batter and deep fried until crisp and golden.

7

carrot soup

Preparation time 15 minutes	*500 g (1 lb) carrots, diced* *900 ml (1½ pints) vegetable stock*
Cooking time 35 minutes	*25 g (1 oz) All-Bran cereal* *175 g (6 oz) onions, chopped*
Serves 4	*125 g (4 oz) potatoes, diced* *1 celery stick, chopped*
Calories 145 per portion	*1 tablespoon chopped parsley* *½ teaspoon caraway seeds* *salt and pepper* *150 ml (¼ pint) single cream (optional)*

Put all the ingredients, except the cream, into a large pan and bring gently to the boil. Cover and simmer for 30 minutes, or until the vegetables are soft. Allow the soup to cool slightly and then purée in a food processor or blender until smooth and thick. Alternatively press the soup through a sieve.

Return the soup to the pan and reheat when required, stirring in the cream just before serving. Serve with rolls.

8

tomato and carrot soup

Preparation time 25 minutes	*125 g (4 oz) carrots, sliced* *1 small onion, chopped*
Cooking time 42 minutes	*1 garlic clove, chopped* *2 tablespoons oil*
Serves 6	*500 g (1 lb) tomatoes, skinned and* *chopped*
Calories 160 per portion	*600 ml (1 pint) vegetable stock* *a little grated nutmeg* *25 g (1 oz) tomato purée* *300 ml (½ pint) single cream* *salt and pepper* *1 tablespoon chopped parsley, plus extra* *to garnish*

Cook the carrots, onions and garlic in the oil over a gentle heat for about 10 minutes, without browning. Stir in the tomatoes and stock. Season well with salt and pepper and nutmeg, then stir in the tomato purée. Bring to the boil, reduce the heat and simmer for 30 minutes.

Purée the soup in a food processor or blender, return to the pan and stir in the cream and parsley. Heat gently, without boiling, then serve garnished with a sprinkling of fresh chopped parsley.

■ COOK'S TIP

If you have a food processor, then simply roughly chop all the vegetables using the knife attachment. Take care not to over-process the ingredients so that they become too fine.

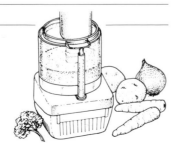

■ COOK'S TIP

Flavour this soup with the grated rind and juice of 1 orange if you like. Add to the soup with the tomatoes and stock.

creamy onion soup

Preparation time 10 minutes	*50 g (2 oz) butter*
	3 large onions, chopped
Cooking time 55 minutes	*1.2 litres (2 pints) vegetable stock*
	500 g (1 lb) potatoes, chopped
Serves 4	*2 teaspoons paprika*
Calories 325 per portion	*½–1 tablespoon tomato purée*
	150 ml (¼ pint) single cream
	salt and pepper
	fried onion rings, to garnish

Melt the butter in a pan and fry the onions until soft. Add the stock, potatoes, paprika, tomato purée and salt and pepper.

Simmer for about 45 minutes. Sieve or blend the soup and reheat. Stir the cream into the hot soup and heat through very gently. Garnish with fried onion rings and serve.

creamy leek and cheese soup

Preparation time 15 minutes	*25 g (1 oz) butter*
	2 leeks, thinly sliced
Cooking time 40–45 minutes	*375 g (12 oz) potatoes, thinly sliced*
	750 ml (1¼ pints) vegetable stock
Serves 4	*¼ teaspoon ground nutmeg*
Calories 220 per portion	*2–4 tablespoons milk or water (optional)*
	75–125 g (3–4 oz) Danish blue cheese
	salt and pepper
	chopped chives, to garnish (optional)

Melt the butter in a large pan and add the leeks. Cover and cook gently, stirring occasionally, for 8–10 minutes, until soft. Reserve a few rings for garnish. Add the potatoes to the pan with the stock, salt and pepper and nutmeg. Bring to the boil, cover and simmer for 25–30 minutes, until the potatoes are soft.

Cool slightly then rub the soup through a sieve, or purée in a food processor or blender until smooth. Return to the pan and reheat, adding the milk or water if the soup is too thick. Just before serving, crumble in the blue cheese and stir until melted. Garnish with the reserved leek rings and chopped chives, if using.

■ COOK'S TIP

Serve this soup cold as a smooth summer starter. Chill the sieved soup and add the cream just before serving. Omit the fried onion rings and float a spring onion curl on the top of each portion instead.

■ COOK'S TIP

To make vegetable stock, fry 2 chopped onions, 2 diced potatoes and 2 celery sticks. Stir in 1 sliced parsnip and 1 sliced turnip, add 1.2 litres (2 pints) water. Pop in a bouquet garni bring to the boil, lower heat and simmer for 1 hour.

11

cream of mushroom soup

Preparation time 10 minutes	*1 tablespoon sunflower oil*
	1 onion, chopped
Cooking time 25–30 minutes	*500 g (1 lb) mushrooms, finely chopped*
	600 ml (1 pint) vegetable stock
Serves 4	*1 tablespoon chopped parsley*
	2 teaspoons cornflour
Calories 135 per portion	*150 ml (¼ pint) single cream*
	salt and white pepper
	croûtons, to garnish

Heat the oil and cook the onion gently for about 5 minutes until soft. Add the mushrooms and cook, stirring, for 3–4 minutes. Stir in the stock, parsley and salt and pepper; bring to the boil, cover and simmer gently for 15 minutes. Blend the cornflour with a little cold water and stir into the soup, cooking for a further 2–3 minutes until thickened. Stir in the cream and serve at once with croûtons.

12

country mushroom soup

Preparation time 15 minutes	*2 tablespoons oil*
	1 onion, finely chopped
Cooking time 20 minutes	*1 garlic clove, crushed*
	2 teaspoons ground coriander
Serves 6	*250 g (8 oz) flat mushrooms, finely chopped*
Calories 105 per portion	*1.2 litres (2 pints) vegetable stock*
	grated rind of 1 lemon
	3 tablespoons chopped parsley
	125 g (4 oz) fresh wholewheat breadcrumbs
	salt and pepper
	FOR THE GARNISH
	2 tablespoons soured cream
	1 tablespoon chopped parsley

Heat the oil and cook the onion gently until just soft, about 5 minutes. Stir in the garlic and coriander and cook for a minute to bring out the flavours. Add the mushrooms and cook for a further 3–4 minutes. Stir in the stock, lemon rind and parsley. Bring to the boil, cover and simmer for 10 minutes. stir in the breadcrumbs and salt and pepper to taste and cook for 1 minute longer. Remove from the heat and swirl through the soured cream. Sprinkle with the parsley and serve at once.

■ COOK'S TIP

Cultivated mushrooms contain essential minerals, potassium, iron, sulphur, magnesium and phosphorus. Low in calories, they are a source of B vitamins and vegetable protein.

■ COOK'S TIP

Make a large batch of vegetable stock (see Cook's Tip, recipe 10) leave it to cool and freeze it for future use. Fill plastic bags, supporting them in a basin, freeze, then remove the basin when hard.

13

chickpea, pasta and spinach soup

Preparation time
10 minutes

Cooking time
45 minutes

Serves 6

Calories
153 per portion

2 x 425 g (14 oz) cans of chickpeas
75 g (3oz) small pasta shapes
125 g (4 oz) fresh spinach leaves,
*   shredded*
1.2 litres (2 pints) vegetable stock
2 tablespoons extra virgin olive oil
2 garlic cloves crushed
1 onion crushed
1 tablespoon chopped fresh rosemary
salt and pepper
FOR THE GARNISH
freshly grated nutmeg
croûtons (see Cook's Tip)
freshly grated vegetarian Parmesan
*   cheese*

Heat the oil in a large saucepan and fry the garlic, onion and rosemary over a low heat for 5 minutes until softened but not golden. Add the chickpeas with their liquid and the vegetable stock, bring to the boil, cover and simmer for 30 minutes.

Add the pasta, return to the boil and simmer for 6–8 minutes.

Stir in the spinach and continue cooking for a further 5 minutes until both the pasta and spinach are tender. Season to taste and serve at once, sprinkled with nutmeg, croûtons and grated Parmesan.

14

pea and celery soup

Preparation time
10 minutes, plus
soaking

Cooking time
2½–3½ hours

Serves 4–6

Calories
198–132 per portion

Suitable for
vegetarians

1 tablespoon oil
1 onion, chopped
1 garlic clove, crushed
2 celery sticks, chopped
250 g (8 oz) dried marrowfat peas, soaked
*   overnight*
1.5 litres (2½ pints) water
1 bouquet garni
salt and pepper
mint sprigs, to garnish

Heat the oil in a large pan, add the onion and cook until softened. Add the garlic and celery and cook for 5 minutes, stirring occasionally.

Drain the peas and add to the pan with the water, bouquet garni and salt and pepper to taste. Cover and boil rapidly for 10 minutes, then simmer gently for 2–3 hours, until the peas are soft. Remove the bouquet garni.

Cool slightly, then place half the soup in a food processor or blender and work to a smooth purée. Repeat with the remaining soup. Return to the pan. Reheat the soup gently, adding a little more water if it is too thick. Pour into a warmed tureen and garnish with mint sprigs.

▩ COOK'S TIP

To make croûtons, remove the crusts from 4 thick slices of one day old bread. Cut all of the bread into cubes. Heat 4 tablespoons of olive oil in a frying pan. When the oil is hot, add the bread and stir-fry for 2–3 minutes until the bread cubes are golden and crisp on all sides and all the way through. Remove the croûtons from the frying pan with a slotted spoon, and drain thoroughly on kitchen paper.

▩ COOK'S TIP

Swirl a little soured cream, natural yogurt, crème frâiche or plain fromage frais into this soup before serving – delicious!

15

16

chinese leaf and pepper soup

Preparation time
25 minutes

Cooking time
45 minutes

Serves 4

Calories
339 per portion

2 tablespoons vegetable oil
50 g (2 oz) butter
250 g (8 oz) green peppers, cored, seeded and diced
2 onions, chopped
½ head of Chinese leaves, shredded
40 g (1½ oz) plain flour
450 ml (¾ pint) vegetable stock
450 ml (¾ pint) milk
salt and pepper
3 tablespoons single cream, to garnish

Heat the oil in a saucepan, then add the butter. When melted, add the peppers, onions and Chinese leaves and cook gently for 5 minutes. Blend in the flour and cook for 1 minute. Gradually stir in the vegetable stock and bring to the boil. Add salt and pepper to taste and simmer, covered, for 30 minutes or until the vegetables are tender.

Purée the soup in a food processor or blender or work through a sieve. Return to the pan, stir in the milk and heat through. Taste and adjust the seasoning and, just before serving, swirl in the cream.

mushroom and walnut soup

Preparation time
10 minutes, plus chilling

Cooking time
25 minutes

Serves 4

Calories
188 per portion

25 g (1 oz) walnut pieces
25 g (1 oz) butter
1 onion, chopped
125 g (4 oz) button mushrooms, roughly chopped
900 ml (1½ pints) vegetable stock
large pinch of grated nutmeg
6 tablespoons double cream
salt and pepper
FOR THE GARNISH
snipped chives (see Cook's Tip)
chopped walnuts

Cover the walnuts with boiling water and leave for 1 minute. Drain on kitchen paper. Melt the butter in a medium pan, add the onion and fry until softened. Add the mushrooms and cook for 1 minute. Stir in the stock, nutmeg, salt and pepper and bring to the boil. Cover and simmer for 15 minutes.

Chop the walnuts in a food processor or blender. Add the cooked vegetables and liquid and blend until the mushrooms are finely chopped. Taste and adjust the seasoning. Chill well.

To serve, stir the cream into the soup and sprinkle with the chives and walnuts.

■ COOK'S TIP

Peppers are a rich source of vitamin C. They also contain vitamins A, B1, B2 and E, and small amounts of potassium and folic acid. Peppers are also an excellent source of fibre.

■ COOK'S TIP

To chop fresh chives, hold the washed bunch firmly and use a pair of scissors to snip them into a small bowl. Instead of cream, stir in some Greek yogurt.

17

spinach soup

Preparation time 20 minutes	*750 g (1½ lb) fresh spinach, washed thoroughly and stalks removed*
Cooking time 20 minutes	*25 g (1 oz) butter 1 small onion, finely chopped*
Serves 4	*25 g (1 oz) plain flour*
Calories 272 per portion	*600 ml (1 pint) vegetable stock about 300 ml (½ pint) milk freshly grated nutmeg salt and pepper* FOR THE GARNISH *about 2 tablespoons natural yogurt 4 lemon slices (optional)*

Cook the spinach without water in a covered pan for 6–8 minutes, then turn into a bowl. (Heat frozen spinach until just thawed, see Cook's Tip.)

Rinse out the pan and melt the butter in it. Add the chopped onion, fry gently without browning for 5 minutes then add the flour. Cook for 3 minutes, then pour in the stock. Stir well, bring to the boil and simmer for 3–4 minutes.

Cool slightly, then pour into a food processor or blender, add the cooked spinach and blend until smooth. Pour back into the pan and stir in sufficient milk to give a pouring consistency. Add salt, pepper and nutmeg to taste. Reheat the soup gently and serve, garnishing each bowl with a swirl of yogurt and a slice of lemon, if liked.

The soup can be frozen for up to 6 weeks. Thaw overnight at room temperature and reheat gently.

■ COOK'S TIP

If fresh spinach is not available use a 275 g (10 oz) pack of frozen spinach instead. Spinach should be cooked for the shortest possible time to retain its colour and nutritional value, so for this soup it is cooked separately. No water is necessary, as spinach contains a high proportion of water.

18

light vegetable soup

Preparation time 30 minutes	*25 g (1 oz) butter 1 small onion, finely chopped*
Cooking time 30 minutes	*175 g (6 oz) carrots, cut into narrow matchstick strips*
Serves 4	*3 celery sticks, trimmed and sliced*
Calories 114 per portion	*1 teaspoon cornflour 900 ml (1½ pints) vegetable stock 1 teaspoon tomato purée 2 tablespoons chopped parsley celery leaves* FOR THE OMELETTE GARNISH *2 medium eggs salt and pepper 15 g (½ oz) butter*

Melt the butter in a large pan and fry the onion gently without browning for about 5 minutes. Add the carrots and celery, cover the pan and cook gently for a few minutes until the butter is absorbed. Stir in the cornflour, then add the stock and tomato purée. Bring to the boil, half cover the pan and simmer for about 20 minutes until the vegetables are tender.

Meanwhile, make the omelette. Beat the eggs with the salt and pepper. Melt the butter in a small frying pan, add the eggs and fry until set and pale brown on the underside. Turn and brown the other side. Cut into 1 cm (½ inch) dice.

Taste the soup and season with pepper and a little salt if needed. Stir in the chopped parsley. Serve in bowls garnished with a few pieces of the omelette and a celery leaf.

■ COOK'S TIP

This vegetable soup can be frozen in a plastic container for up to 6 weeks, but only make the omelette garnish just before serving.

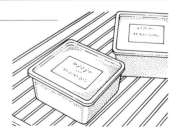

artichoke soup

Preparation time	25 g (1 oz) butter
15 minutes	1 small onion, thinly sliced
Cooking time	500 g (1 lb) Jerusalem artichokes,
30 minutes	scrubbed and sliced
Serves 4	600 ml (1 pint) milk
Calories	300 ml (½ pint) vegetable stock
293 per portion	salt and pepper
	FOR THE GARNISH
	snipped chives (optional)
	Sesame croûtons (see Cook's Tip)

Melt the butter in a large pan and fry the onion gently without browning for about 5 minutes. Add the artichokes, cover and cook for a further 5 minutes so that the artichokes completely absorb the butter.

Add salt and pepper then pour in the milk and stock. Bring to the boil and simmer gently, half covered, for about 20 minutes until the artichokes are tender.

Purée in a food processor or blender until smooth. Return the soup to the pan and reheat gently. Taste and adjust the seasoning.

Serve piping hot sprinkled with chives, if liked, and sesame croûtons (see Cook's Tip).

vegetable soup with nori

Preparation time	2 tablespoons olive oil
20 minutes	2 onions, chopped
Cooking time	4 celery sticks, diced
25 minutes	250 g (8 oz) carrots, diced
Serves 4	375 g (12 oz) courgettes, trimmed and
Calories	diced
107 per portion	250 g (8 oz) Chinese leaves or cabbage,
Suitable for vegans	shredded
	4 garlic cloves, crushed
	900 ml (1½) pints vegetable stock
	salt and pepper
	2–4 sheets of nori (see Cook's Tip)

Heat the olive oil in a large saucepan and add the onions, celery and carrots. Fry gently for 5 minutes, without letting the vegetables brown, then add the courgettes, cabbage and garlic. Stir and fry gently for a further 5 minutes. Add the stock, bring to the boil, then let the soup simmer for about 15 minutes, until the vegetables are just tender. You can serve the soup as it is, but you may liquidize two cupfuls, then stir this back into the soup. This has the effect of slightly thickening the soup. Season to taste with salt and pepper. Serve the soup in bowls and sprinkle with the nori, or serve the nori separately in a small bowl for people to sprinkle over their soup if they like.

■ COOK'S TIP

To make the sesame croûtons, cut the crusts from 4 slices of brown bread. Dip each slice into seasoned beaten egg then into sesame seeds. Cut the dipped slices into squares, then cut each square into 2 triangles. Fry in shallow hot oil for about 30 seconds then drain on kitchen paper.

■ COOK'S TIP

Nori is a seaweed usually sold in dried form. Simply take 2–4 sheets, crisp over a gas flame or under the grill for several seconds, then crumble over the soup.

21

leek and potato soup

Preparation time 15 minutes	*25 g (1 oz) butter or margarine*
	375 g (12 oz) trimmed leeks, washed and
Cooking time 25–30 minutes	*sliced (see Cook's Tip, recipe 23)*
	750 g (1½ lb) potatoes, diced
Serves 6	*salt and pepper*
Calories 155 per portion	*900 ml (1½ pints) vegetable stock*

Melt the butter or margarine in a large saucepan, add the leeks and potatoes and fry these gently with a lid on the pan, for 10 minutes, stirring often. Sprinkle a little salt and pepper over the potatoes and leeks, stir, then continue to cook gently, still covered, for a further 10 minutes, stirring often. It doesn't matter if the vegetables brown slightly, but don't let them get too brown.

Add the vegetable stock, stir, then simmer for 5–10 minutes, until the vegetables are cooked. Taste for seasoning, then serve with hot garlic bread (see Cook's Tip).

22

roasted hazelnut soup with red pepper cream

Preparation time 30 minutes	*125 g (4 oz) hazelnuts, roasted and skins*
	removed (see Cook's Tip)
Cooking time About 30 minutes	*1 onion, chopped*
	25 g (1 oz) butter
Serves 4	*500 g (1 lb) diced potatoes*
Calories 46 per portion	*1 garlic clove, crushed*
	900 ml (1½ pints) vegetable stock
	1 tablespoon lemon juice
	1 small red pepper
	150 ml (¼ pint) whipping cream
	salt and pepper

Grate the hazelnuts finely in a food processor or nut mill. Fry the onion in the butter for 5 minutes, then add the potatoes, garlic and a little salt and pepper, and cook gently, with a lid on the pan, for a further 5–10 minutes. Pour in the stock, bring to the boil, then simmer for 10–15 minutes, until the potatoes and onions are cooked. Liquidize the soup and stir in the hazelnuts, lemon juice and salt and pepper to taste.

To make the red pepper cream, put the red pepper under a hot grill until the outer skin is charred all over. Rinse under the cold tap and remove the stalk, seeds and outer skin. Mash the red pepper finely. Whip the cream until just forming peaks, then whisk in enough red pepper to colour the cream pink. Season and serve in individual bowls, with a spoonful of red pepper cream on top.

■ COOK'S TIP

To make garlic bread: crush 2–3 garlic cloves and mix into 50 g (2 oz) butter. Spread between slices cut across a French stick and bake 15–20 minutes at 180°C (350°F), gas 4.

■ COOK'S TIP

To dry roast nuts, spread them on the bottom of a pan, place over a high flame and shake quickly to keep the contents moving. They are done when slightly brown.

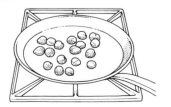

23

carrot and coriander soup

Preparation time
15 minutes

Cooking time
30 minutes

Serves 6

Calories
105 per portion

15 g (½ oz) butter or margarine
500 g (1 lb) carrots, scraped and sliced
375 g (12 oz) leeks, washed and sliced
    (see Cook's Tip)
1 tablespoon coriander seeds, lightly
    crushed
rind of ½ lemon
900 ml (1½) pints vegetable stock
1 tablespoon lemon juice
salt and pepper
FOR THE GARNISH
150 ml (¼ pint) single cream
parsley sprigs

Melt the butter or margarine in a large saucepan, add the carrots and leeks and fry gently, covered, for 15 minutes, until the vegetables are almost soft. Stir in the coriander seeds and lemon rind and fry for a further 2–3 minutes. Add the vegetable stock, bring to the boil, and simmer for about 10 minutes. Add the lemon juice, cream and salt and pepper, then purée in a food processor or blender. Reheat and serve garnished with a swirl of cream and a sprig of parsley.

24

chilled cucumber soup with dill and radishes

Preparation time
5 minutes, plus chilling

Serves 4

Calories
195 per portion

1 cucumber, peeled and cut into
    rough chunks
475 ml (16 fl oz) thick natural yogurt
2 tablespoons double cream
8 mint sprigs
2–3 teaspoons white wine vinegar
salt and pepper
FOR THE GARNISH
8 thin slices of radish
4 feathery dill leaves or mint leaves

Put the cucumber into a food processor with the yogurt, cream and mint and blend until smooth. Add enough wine vinegar to sharpen the flavour, and salt and pepper to taste. Chill. Serve in chilled bowls garnished with the radish slices and fresh dill or mint leaves.

■ COOK'S TIP

To clean leeks, make a lengthways cut halfway down to the white part of the trimmed leek and hold the leaves open under running water.

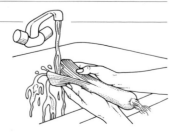

■ COOK'S TIP

Use natural or plain Greek yogurt for this recipe. Greek yogurt has a creamier taste, is thicker and has a higher fat content than ordinary natural yogurt.

starters

When selecting a starter for a main meal, consider the menu as a whole and pick and choose from the recipe ideas in this chapter. A juice or a fruity starter like Melon and Grapefruit Cocktail with a fresh mint garnish will sharpen the appetite, and the unusual Crunchy Brie, served with the colourful and contrastingly flavoured cherry sauce will create enthusiastic anticipation of things to come.

melon and grapefruit cocktail

Preparation time	
10 minutes, plus 1 hour to chill	1 ripe honeydew melon, halved and deseeded
	2 grapefruit, peeled
Serves 4	3–4 tablespoons clear honey
Calories	4 mint sprigs
104 per portion	

Scoop out the melon flesh, using a melon baller, and place in a bowl.

Cut between the segments of the grapefruit, removing the pith and pips, and catch any juice from the fruit by working over a plate. Mix the grapefruit segments and juice with the melon, and trickle over the honey. Add the sprigs of mint to the fruit and chill thoroughly.

Serve the cocktail in glasses, carefully removing the mint to use as a garnish.

■ COOK'S TIP

For special occasions, frost the tops of the glasses by dipping the rims lightly in beaten egg white, then in sugar.

grapefruit and avocado salad

Preparation time	
20 minutes	2 avocados, halved, peeled and stoned
	2 grapefruit
Serves 6	2 oranges
Calories	½ teaspoon sugar
165 per portion	2 tablespoons olive oil
	1 teaspoon chopped mint
	6–10 lettuce leaves, washed and torn into bite-sized pieces, or 2 heads of chicory, washed
	salt and pepper

Cut the avocado flesh into thin slices. Spread the slices out in a shallow bowl.

Holding a grapefruit over the bowl (so that the juice will go over the avocado slices), peel it with a sharp knife. Using a sawing action, cut round the fruit down to the flesh and remove all the white pith. Cut each segment of fruit away from the inner white skin. When all the segments have been removed from the grapefruit, squeeze the remaining juice from the skin over the avocado slices. Repeat this with the other grapefruit and the oranges, putting the segments on a plate.

Turn the avocado slices in the juice. Drain off any excess juice into a small bowl and add the sugar, oil, mint and salt and pepper to make a dressing.

To assemble the dish, cover individual plates with lettuce or chicory leaves, then arrange segments of grapefruit, orange and avocado on top, dividing them between the plates. Spoon a little dressing over each salad.

■ COOK'S TIP

Sprinkling the avocado slices with the citrus fruit juices prevents them from discolouring. The watercress sprigs and sprinkling of herbs shown in the photograph give additional colour to the salad.

27

grapefruit sorbet

Preparation time	25 g (1 oz) clear honey
10 minutes, plus	300 ml (½ pint) water
freezing	2 x 540 g (1 lb 3 oz) cans grapefruit
Cooking time	segments in natural juice
7–8 minutes	150 ml (¼ pint) lemon juice
Serves 6	grated rind of 2 lemons
Calories	2 medium egg whites
50 per portion	mint sprigs, to garnish

Bring the honey and water gently to the boil and simmer for 5 minutes. Cool slightly. Use one can of grapefruit to make the sorbet; reserve the second can for serving. Drain the grapefruit juice from the segments in one can and add to the honey liquid with the lemon juice and rind. Cool and freeze until half frozen.

Whisk the egg whites until stiff and fold into the mixture. Freeze again until firm. Serve the sorbet on a bed of grapefruit segments, reserving a few for decoration. Top with mint sprigs.

28

pears with mustard cream mayonnaise

Preparation time	2 ripe eating pears
30 minutes, plus	1 tablespoon lemon juice
chiling	4 tablespoons mayonnaise
Serves 4	1 tablespoons Dijon mustard
Calories	2 tablespoons double cream, whipped
175 per portion	FOR THE GARNISH
	flaked almonds
	lettuce leaves

Peel the pears, keeping them in good shape. Using a teaspoon, scoop out the seeds and core. Brush each pear with some lemon juice to prevent it discolouring.

Whisk the mayonnaise with the mustard and whipped double cream, adding 1 teaspoon of boiling water if the consistency is too thick to coat the pears smoothly. Split the almonds and toast under the grill until golden brown. Cool.

To serve, place a few lettuce leaves on four small plates. Place a pear half, cut side down, on each plate and coat with mustard mayonnaise. Sprinkle with the toasted almonds. Chill before seving.

■ COOK'S TIP

Crystallized mint leaves make an attractive decoration for sorbets. Dip clean leaves in egg white, then in caster sugar. Dry on a wire rack.

■ COOK'S TIP

Watch the almonds closely. It only takes a few seconds for beautifully golden nuts to become burnt offerings.

29

citrus refresher with mint sorbet

Preparation time 20 minutes, plus freezing	*2 large grapefruits* *2 large oranges* *a little clear honey*
Serves 4	*mint sprigs, to garnish*
Calories 99 per portion	FOR THE MINT SORBET *2 tablespoons clear honey* *150 ml (¼ pint) water* *2 tablespoons finely chopped mint*

First, make the sorbet. Mix together the honey, water and mint, then pour into a shallow container and freeze until the mixture is half solid. Break up the mixture with a fork, then freeze until firm.

With a small serrated knife, and holding the fruit over a bowl, cut all the skin and pith from the grapefruits and oranges. Cut the segments from between the pieces of skin. Sweeten with honey to taste, then divide the fruit between four bowls. Put a spoonful of sorbet on each, decorate with mint, and serve immediately.

30

blue cheese pears

Preparation time 10 minutes	*125 g (4 oz) vegetarian Stilton* *250 g (8 oz) cottage cheese or curd cheese*
Serves 4	*2 celery sticks, chopped*
Calories 308 per portion	*50 g (2 oz) hazelnuts, skinned and chopped* *6 large pears* *2 tablespoons lemon juice* *salad burnet leaves, to garnish*

Mash together the Stilton, soft cheese and celery.

Place the chopped nuts in an ungreased heavy-based frying pan over a low heat and stir for 2–3 minutes until slightly browned. Place in a bowl.

Peel and halve the pears and scoop out the cores with a teaspoon. Brush immediately with the lemon juice. Fill the centres of the pears with about half the cheese mixture. Place 3 halves, cut side down, on 4 plates.

Using a teaspoon, shape the remaining cheese mixture into 12 balls the size of marbles. Roll each one in the bowl of nuts. Place 3 on each plate. Garnish each plate with a sprig of salad burnet and serve.

■ COOK'S TIP

This makes a great starter to get the taste buds going for the main course. It's also low in fat and high in vitamin C. Try it for breakfast as an ideal wake-me-up.

■ COOK'S TIP

Vegetarian Stilton, made from vegetarian rennet, is now widely available. Choose curd cheese instead of `light' soft cheese which may contain gelatine.

31

savoury pear mousse

Preparation time
20 minutes, plus setting

Cooking time
15 minutes

Serves 8

Calories
95 per portion

2 pears, peeled and chopped
1 small onion, chopped
125 ml (4 fl oz) water
pinch of chilli powder
pinch of turmeric
4 juniper berries, crushed
175 g (6 oz) low-fat soft cheese
4 tablespoons double cream
125 g (4 oz) button mushrooms, finely chopped
2 teaspoons agar-agar or 3 teaspoons powdered gelatine
salt and pepper
FOR THE GARNISH
cress
capers
TO SERVE
Melba toast
2 hard-boiled eggs, sliced
2 tomatoes, cut into wedges

Place the pears and onion in a small pan with 2 tablespoons of the water, the chilli, turmeric, juniper berries and salt and pepper. Cover and cook gently for about 15 minutes, or until tender.

When the pears are soft, drain, blend in a food processor or press through a sieve. Add the soft cheese, cream and mushrooms and blend until smooth. Dissolve the agar-agar in the remaining cold water in a small saucepan, then bring to the boil, stirring constantly. Stir into the mousse. Pour into individual dishes and chill to set. Garnish with cress and capers and serve.

■ COOK'S TIP

To make Melba toast, toast medium-thick bread slices, cut off the crusts and slice through to give very thin pieces – work quickly before the toast cools. Lightly toast the second side.

32

tomato coupe

Preparation time
10 minutes, plus setting

Cooking time
15 minutes

Serves 6

Calories
95 per portion

1 x 400 g (13 oz) can tomatoes
grated rind of ½ lemon
1 bay leaf
1 garlic clove, crushed
3 tablespoons white wine
2 teaspoons agar-agar or 3 tablespoons powdered gelatine
150 ml (¼ pint) cold water
½ teaspoon sugar
125 g (4 oz) Cheddar cheese, grated
6 spring onions, thinly sliced
salt and pepper
brown bread and butter, to serve

Pour the tomatoes and their juices into a saucepan, add the lemon rind, bay leaf and garlic. Chop the tomatoes roughly, bring to the boil, cover and simmer for 10 minutes. Press the tomato mixture through a sieve into a measuring jug and add the wine. Dissolve the agar-agar in the cold water in a small saucepan, bring to the boil, stirring constantly, then add to the tomato and wine mixture. Add more boiling water if necessary to make 600 ml (1 pint). Stir in salt, pepper and sugar to taste. Cool. Pour into 6 individual ramekins or coupe glasses and refrigerate until set.

Mix together the Cheddar cheese and spring onions and top each coupe with some of the mixture. Serve chilled with brown bread and butter.

■ COOK'S TIP

If you like, set the tomato mixture in one large mould, then turn it out before serving. Offer the cheese and spring onions in a separate dish.

33

greek mushroom salad

Preparation time
10 minutes, plus chilling

Cooking time
15 minutes

Serves 6

Calories
30 per portion,
180 per piece of pitta bread

2 garlic cloves, crushed
3 tablespoons tomato purée
3 tablespoons lemon juice
150 ml (¼ pint) water
1 teaspoon oregano
½ teaspoon basil
250 g (8 oz) button mushrooms
500 g (1 lb) cauliflower florets
12 black olives, roughly chopped
salt and pepper
pitta bread, to serve

Place the garlic, tomato purée, lemon juice and water in a large saucepan and mix well. Stir in the herbs, mushrooms and cauliflower. Cover and bring to the boil, then reduce the heat and simmer gently for 10 minutes, stirring frequently. Stir in the olives and season to taste with salt and pepper. Transfer to a serving bowl and chill until cold.

This salad is best served chilled, accompanied by warm pitta bread cut into fingers.

34

savoury
stuffed tomatoes

Preparation time
10 minutes

Serves 4

Calories
50 per portion

4 large firm tomatoes
75 g (3 oz) cream cheese, softened
½ teaspoon finely chopped chives or onion
1 tablespoon mayonnaise
125 g (4 oz) frozen peas, cooked
salt and pepper
parsley or watercress sprigs, to garnish

Slice the tops off the tomatoes and scoop out the pulp with a teaspoon. Beat the cream cheese with the chives or onion and mayonnaise and season well with salt and pepper. Stir in the peas and fill the tomatoes with the mixture, replacing the top of each. Garnish with sprigs of parsley or watercress.

■ COOK'S TIP

If you prefer, mix tomatoes with the mushrooms in this salad instead of the cauliflower. Cook the mushrooms as above, then add 6 peeled and quartered tomatoes at the end of the cooking time.

■ COOK'S TIP

For best results, when you have scooped out the tomatoes, leave them to drain on double-thick absorbent kitchen paper.

35

mushrooms indienne

Preparation time
10 minutes, plus chilling

Serves 4

Calories
100 per portion

150 ml (¼ pint) soured cream or natural yogurt
1–2 teaspoons curry paste
1 tablespoon sieved mango chutney
1 dessert apple, peeled, cored and chopped
175 g (6 oz) button mushrooms
Chinese leaves, shredded
salt and pepper
4 lemon slices, to garnish

Mix together the cream and curry paste according to taste. Add the chutney, apple, mushrooms and salt and pepper to taste and mix well. Chill for at least 30 minutes before serving.

Pile each portion on to a bed of shredded Chinese leaves and garnish with a twist of lemon.

36

peanut dip with crudités

Preparation time
15–20 minutes

Cooking time
5 minutes

Serves 6

Calories
190 per portion

2 tablespoons sunflower oil
1 onion, finely chopped
2 garlic cloves, crushed
½ teaspoon chilli powder
1 teaspoon ground cumin
1 teaspoon ground coriander
6 tablespoons crunchy peanut butter
6 tablespoons water
1 teaspoon shoyu
1 teaspoon lemon juice
FOR THE CRUDITES
1 small cauliflower
1 bunch of radishes
1 red pepper, deseeded
6 celery sticks
6 carrots

Heat the oil in a small saucepan, add the onion and fry for a few minutes until softened. Add the garlic and spices, stir and cook for 1 minute. Mix in the peanut butter, then gradually blend in the water, stirring until thickened. Add the shoyu and lemon juice, stir well and leave to cool.

Break the cauliflower into florets and halve the radishes if large. Cut the remaining vegetables into long thin pieces.

Turn the dip into a small dish, place on a large plate and surround with the crudités.

■ COOK'S TIP

Instead of the curry paste, you can use curry powder but halve the quantity. Cook the powder in a little butter in a small pan for 3 minutes before adding to the cream.

■ COOK'S TIP

Wholemeal grissini – Italian breadsticks – make excellent dippers, much favoured by children. If serving the dip for a child's party, eliminate the spices.

37

mushroom and avocado starter

Preparation time	250 g (8 oz) button mushrooms, sliced
15 minutes, plus chilling	3 tablespoons lemon juice
	4 spring onions, chopped
Serves 4	1 tablespoon sunflower seeds, toasted
Calories	1 ripe avocado
100 per portion	salt and pepper

Put the mushrooms in a mixing bowl with 2 tablespoons of the lemon juice, the spring onions, sunflower seeds and salt and pepper. Mix well and chill for at least 30 minutes.

Just before serving, remove the stone and peel from the avocado, slice the flesh and sprinkle with the remaining lemon juice. Arrange the avocado slices on individual serving plates with the mushroom salad at the side.

38

cheese croustades

Preparation time	25 g (1 oz) butter, melted
15 minutes	12 slices, medium-sliced bread
Cooking time	FOR THE FILLING
24 minutes	250 g (8 oz) small button mushrooms
Oven temperature	25 g (1 oz) butter
200°C (400°F) gas 6	125 g (4 oz) Danish Bania cheese, plain
Makes 12	½ teaspoon cornflour
Calories	2 tablespoons chopped parsley
11 per croustade	salt and pepper
	FOR THE GARNISH
	paprika
	parsley sprigs

Brush a 12-hole bun tin with a little of the melted butter. Cut the crusts off the bread and flatten each slice with a rolling pin. Cut out an 8.5 cm (3½ in) circle from each piece of bread, then press into the tins. Brush with the remaining melted butter and bake in a preheated oven for 15 minutes.

To make the filling, wipe and quarter the mushrooms. Melt the butter and cook the mushrooms, covered, for 5 minutes. Remove the rind, then add the cheese to the mushrooms, stirring until melted.

Mix the cornflour to a smooth paste with a little water, stir into the mushroom mixture and bring just to boiling point to thicken, still stirring. Lower the heat, add half the parsley and salt and pepper and cook for 30 seconds.

Divide the mushroom mixture between the warm croustades and sprinkle with paprika. Add the sprig of parsley to each and serve immediately.

■ COOK'S TIP

To remove the stone easily from a halved avocado, pierce it with the point of a knife, then pull it out.

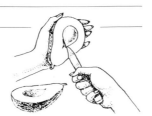

■ COOK'S TIP

Croustades lend themselves perfectly to lots of different fillings. Try ratatouille, sautéed vegetables or leeks au gratin, adding the filling of your choice just before serving to prevent the croustades becoming soggy.

39

mushroom puffs with spicy sauce

Preparation time
15 minutes

Cooking time
20–30 minutes

Serves 4

Calories
230 per portion

250 g (8 oz) mushrooms
oil, for deep-frying
FOR THE SAUCE
1 tablespoon oil
1 small onion, finely chopped
½ garlic clove, crushed
1 teaspoon dark soft brown sugar
2 teaspoons lemon juice
1 tablespoon tomato purée
1 x 250 g (8 oz) can tomatoes
1 tablespoon mushroom ketchup
salt and pepper
parsley sprigs, to garnish
FOR THE BATTER
50 g (2 oz) plain flour
4 tablespoons lukewarm water
1 medium egg white, stiffly beaten
salt and pepper

First make the sauce. Heat the oil in a pan, add the onion and garlic and cook until tender. Add the remaining ingredients and boil, season and keep warm. To make the batter, place the flour in a bowl with salt and pepper, then beat in the water and fold in the stiffly beaten egg white. Heat the oil for deep frying to 190°C (375°F). Dip the mushrooms in the batter, then deep fry until golden. Drain on absorbent kitchen paper, garnish with parsley sprigs and serve with the sauce.

40

mushroom pâté

Preparation time
15 minutes plus
chilling

Cooking time
20 minutes

Serves 4

Calories
190 per portion

75 g (3 oz) butter
2 shallots or small onions, finely sliced
1 garlic clove, crushed (optional)
250 g (8 oz) flat mushrooms, sliced
25 g (1 oz) fresh wholewheat
  breadcrumbs
125 g (4 oz) cottage cheese
pinch of grated nutmeg
pinch of ground mace
salt and pepper
FOR THE GARNISH
1 tablespoon chopped parsley
lemon wedges

Melt 25 g (1 oz) of the butter in a saucepan and cook the shallots or onions and garlic gently for 3 minutes. Add the mushrooms, cover and cook for 15 minutes. Remove the lid, turn up the heat and reduce the liquid until the mushrooms are just moist. Add a further 25 g (1 oz) butter.

Cool slightly, then put the mushrooms, breadcrumbs, cheese, nutmeg, mace, salt and pepper and the remaining butter in a or food processor or blender and blend until smooth.

Taste and adjust the seasoning, and spoon the pâté into a small dish. Cover and chill for 1–2 hours. Just before serving sprinkle the top with parsley and garnish with lemon wedges.

■ COOK'S TIP

When deep frying, make sure that the food absorbs the minimum of fat: have the oil hot before cooking, then drain the food on absorbent kitchen paper.

■ COOK'S TIP

A useful vegetarian spread. Tasty with chopped watercress as a sandwich filling, or served with warm granary bread and butter.

41

cheese balls

Preparation time
30 minutes plus
chilling

Serves 6

Calories
280 per portion

250 g (8 oz) low-fat hard cheese, finely
grated
75 g (3 oz) butter
1 tablespoon milk
cayenne pepper
2 teaspoons sherry
125 g (4 oz) walnuts, finely chopped
salt and pepper

Mix all the ingredients together, except the walnuts, adding a little cayenne to taste. Take small spoonfuls of the cheese mixture
and roll them into balls. Coat each with chopped walnuts. Chill
for at least an hour before serving.

42

crunchy brie

Preparation time
15 minutes, plus
chilling

Cooking time
5–6 minutes

Serves 4

Calories
385 per portion

150 g (5 oz) Blue Brie cheese
150 g (5 oz) plain flour
1 medium egg, beaten
40 g (1½ oz) fresh white breadcrumbs
oil, for deep-frying
dill sprigs, to garnish (optional)
FOR THE SAUCE
1 x 225 g (7½ oz) can pitted black
cherries
1½ teaspoons arrowroot
2 teaspoons caster sugar

Cut the cheese into four equal wedges. Dip each into the flour
and shake off the excess. Dip in the egg, allow the excess to run
off, then coat completely in the breadcrumbs. Re-coat in egg and
breadcrumbs. Place on a plate, cover and refrigerate for at least
30 minutes.

Meanwhile, make the sauce. Drain the juice from the cherries
and reserve the fruit. In a small saucepan blend the arrowroot to
a smooth paste with a little of the juice. Add the remaining juice
and bring to the boil, stirring all the time, until thickened.
Sweeten to taste, add the cherries and heat through gently. Pour
into a sauceboat.

Heat the oil in a deep pan to 180°C (350°F), or until a day-
old bread cube browns in 60 seconds. Lower the cheese portions
in the hot oil, two at a time, and fry for 30–60 seconds, until the
coating is golden. remove from the pan and drain on absorbent
kitchen paper. Cook the remaining cheese portions, garnish with
dill, if liked, and serve immediately with the cherry sauce.

■ COOK'S TIP

Serve these tasty cheese balls as a
cocktail snack with drinks, instead of
serving a starter. Alternatively, arrange
a few balls on a little shredded lettuce
on individual plates and garnish with
chopped tomato for a first course.

■ COOK'S TIP

This unusual dish can be served
as a savoury at the end of a meal
or even at a cheese and wine
party for a change. Prepare the
cheese earlier in the day, ready to
be cooked just before serving.

43

glamorgan sausages

Preparation time 20 minutes	*1 onion, finely chopped* *175 g (6 oz) Cheddar cheese, grated*
Cooking time 5–7 minutes	*300 g (10 oz) fresh breadcrumbs* *pinch of dried sage*
Serves 4	*pinch of mustard powder* *2 eggs, separated*
Calories 520 per portion	*salt and pepper* *fresh breadcrumbs, for coating* *oil, for frying*

Mix together the onion, cheese, breadcrumbs, sage, mustard, egg yolks, and salt and pepper. Divide the mixture in 12 pieces and roll each portion into a small sausage shape.

Lightly beat the egg whites in a shallow bowl. Place the breadcrumbs on a large plate. Coat each sausage shape with egg white and then press on a coating of crumbs.

Heat about 2.5 cm (1 inch) of oil in a large saucepan. Fry the sausages for 5–7 minutes or until golden, turning once. Drain on absorbent kitchen paper. Serve hot.

44

avocado and cheese mousse

Preparation time 15 minutes, plus chilling	*1 large ripe avocado* *75 g (3 oz) cream cheese*
Serves 4	*1 garlic clove, crushed* *juice of 1 lemon*
Calories 180 per portion	*2 tablespoons single cream* *salt and pepper* *watercress sprigs, to garnish* *Melba toast (see Cook's Tip, recipe 56),* *to serve*

Halve the avocado, remove the stone and scoop out the flesh into a bowl. Mash and mix with the cream cheese, garlic and lemon juice. Season well with salt and pepper and stir in the cream. Spoon the mixture into individual glasses and chill for up to 2 hours. Serve garnished with watercress and accompany with melba toast.

■ COOK'S TIP

Try using other types of cheese in these delicious savouries: Edam or Cheddar with chives, Sage Derby, or blue Stilton for a rich flavour.

■ COOK'S TIP

Do not prepare this mousse more than about 2 hours in advance as it tends to discolour.

45

garnished artichoke hearts

Preparation time
10 minutes, plus chilling

Serves 4

Calories
245 per portion

2 x 90 g (3½ oz) packets soft cream cheese
1 garlic clove, crushed
1 medium egg yolk
6 tablespoons double cream, lightly whipped
pinch of paprika
2 tablespoons chopped herbs (e.g. sage, parsley, thyme)
1 x 400 g (13 oz) can artichoke hearts in brine, drained
salt and pepper
FOR THE GARNISH
shredded lettuce
red pepper

Beat the cream cheese with the crushed garlic, egg yolk, cream, paprika, herbs and salt and pepper to taste. Spoon into the piping bag fitted with a star-shaped nozzle and pipe swirls of the mixture on to the artichoke hearts.

Chill the artichoke hearts lightly before placing on a bed of lettuce on a serving plate. Garnish with red pepper slices.

46

vegetable pâté

Preparation time
15 minutes, plus chilling

Cooking time
1 hour 25 minutes

Oven temperature
160°C (325°F) gas 3

Serves 6

Calories
210 per portion

2 tablespoons olive oil
1 onion, thinly sliced
375 g (12 oz) courgettes, sliced
250 g (8 oz) curd cheese
50 g (2 oz) fresh white breadcrumbs
2 tablespoons chopped basil
2 teaspoons chopped marjoram (optional)
1 egg, beaten
2 tablespoons melted butter
375 g (12 oz) spinach, cooked and chopped
½ teaspoon freshly grated nutmeg
salt and pepper
blanched courgette slices, to garnish

Heat the oil in a frying pan and cook the onion and courgettes until softened. Drain and purée, then dry out in a saucepan over a low heat (2–3 minutes). Beat in the curd cheese, breadcrumbs, basil, marjoram, if using, egg and salt and pepper.

Spoon half the courgette mixture into a lined and well-buttered, 500 g (1 lb) loaf tin. Season the spinach, add the nutmeg and spread in an even layer over the courgettes. Cover with the remaining courgette mixture and press down firmly. Cover with buttered foil, place in a bain-marie and cook in a preheated oven for 1¼ hours. Cool and chill overnight. Turn out and serve garnished with courgette slices.

■ COOK'S TIP

Garnished Artichoke Hearts make a delicious party snack, or hors d'oeuvre. Serve with garlic bread and a light dry red wine.

■ COOK'S TIP

A bain-marie is a roasting tin (or other suitable vessel) filled with hot water. Containers of food that need gentle cooking are placed in the water to ensure that the outside does not overheat during cooking.

47

classic greek salad

Preparation time
15 minutes, plus
standing

Serves 4

Calories
125 per portion

1 onion, sliced and separated into rings
1 tablespoon olive oil
1 tablespoon wine vinegar
4 tomatoes, thinly sliced
½ cucumber, peeled and diced
10–12 black olives (optional)
125 g (4 oz) feta cheese or other white,
    crumbly cheese, diced
salt and pepper

Put the onion into a bowl with the oil, vinegar and a little salt and pepper. Mix well, then leave to stand for 30–60 minutes to allow the onion to soften slightly. Stir occasionally.

Add the tomatoes, cucumber, olives and feta cheese, mixing gently to distribute all the ingredients. Serve at once.

48

smoked cheese and nut salad

Preparation time
15 minutes

Serves 6

Calories
270 per portion

50 g (2 oz) hazelnuts, coarsely chopped
6 tablespoons vegetable oil
2 tablespoons wine vinegar
pinch of cayenne pepper
½ teaspoon prepared English mustard
½ teaspoon sugar
1 crisp lettuce, shredded
1 head of radicchio, separated into leaves
2 dessert apples
1 tablespoon lemon juice
150 g (5 oz) German smoked cheese, cut
    into 1 cm (½ inch) cubes
salt and pepper
watercress, to garnish

To make the dressing, toast the chopped hazelnuts under a medium grill until evenly browned. Cool. Put the oil, vinegar, salt and pepper, cayenne, mustard and sugar into a screwtop jar, add the hazelnuts and shake for 1 minute until well mixed.

Arrange the lettuce and radicchio on 6 individual plates. Cut the apples into 1 cm (½ inch) cubes, toss in the lemon juice and arrange with the cubes of cheese on top of the salad. Spoon the dressing over the cheese and apple just before serving and garnish with sprigs of watercress.

▧ COOK'S TIP

Feta cheese has a distinctive salty flavour which perfectly complements the other ingredients in this salad. Alternatively, you can use another mild, crumbly cheese such as Cheshire. For a creamy texture, try mozzarella.

▧ COOK'S TIP

An unusually colourful starter using radicchio. The same quantities will serve 2–3 as a main meal salad.

49

speedy party dip

Preparation time
5 minutes, plus chilling

Serves 4–6

Calories
1075 (270–180 per portion)

250 g (8 oz) full-fat soft cheese with garlic
150 ml (¼ pint) natural yogurt
½ small green pepper, deseeded and finely shredded

Beat the cheese to soften, add the yogurt and beat until smooth. Stir in the green pepper and mix well. Turn into a serving dish and chill.

Serve with a selection of small pieces of raw carrot, courgette, celery, green and red pepper, broccoli and cauliflower, and crisp savoury biscuits.

50

blue cheese dip

Preparation time
10 minutes, plus chilling

Serves 4–6

Calories
1100 (275–185 per portion)

125 g (4 oz) Danish Blue cheese
2 tablespoons mayonnaise
150 ml (¼ pint) whipping cream
black pepper
FOR THE GARNISH
cucumber slices
parsley sprigs

Mash the blue cheese with a fork or use a food processor. Beat in the mayonnaise until smooth. Lightly whip the cream and fold it into the cheese mixture. Add pepper to taste and turn into a serving bowl to chill. Garnish with cucumber and parsley to serve.

Offer cucumber sticks, olives, breadsticks, tomato wedges and other savoury snacks as dippers.

■ COOK'S TIP

This dip also makes a delicious topping for baked potatoes.

■ COOK'S TIP

Blue cheese is easier to mash when at room temperature. For a variation to the dip, dry adding half a green pepper, deseeded and finely chopped, or 25–50 g (1–2 oz) finely chopped walnuts.

51

aubergine dip

Preparation time 10 minutes	*2 large aubergines, about 500 g (1 lb) total weight*
Cooking time about 20 minutes	*1 small onion, roughly chopped* *2 garlic cloves, roughly chopped*
Serves 4	*4 tablespoons olive oil*
Calories 155 per portion	*2 tablespoons lemon juice* *salt and pepper*
Suitable for vegans	TO SERVE
	1–2 tablespoons chopped flat-leaf parsley
	black or green olives
	radishes
	warm pitta bread

Thread the aubergines on to a skewer. Place them on the greased grill of a preheated grill or barbecue and cook for 10 minutes, then turn over and cook for a further 10 minutes.

Leave the aubergines until they are cool enough to handle, then peel and chop.

Put the aubergine flesh into a food processor or blender with all the remaining ingredients and blend until smooth.

Transfer the purée to a bowl. Sprinkle with the chopped parsley. Serve with olives, radishes and pitta bread.

52

globe artichokes with minty yogurt dressing

Preparation time 40 minutes, plus cooling	*4 large globe artichokes (see Cook's Tip)* *3–4 tablespoons lemon juice*
Cooking time 45 minutes	*1 tablespoon vegetable oil* *salt*
Serves 4	*mint sprigs, to garnish*
Calories 213 per portion	FOR THE DRESSING
	300 ml (½ pint) Greek yogurt
	½ teaspoon lemon rind
	1 tablespoon lemon juice
	1 tablespoon olive oil
	10 cm (4 inch) piece cucumber, peeled, deseeded and grated
	2 tablespoons chopped mint
	2 hard-boiled eggs, finely chopped
	2 spring onions, finely chopped

Cook the artichokes in a pan of boiling, salted water with 1 tablespoon lemon juice added, for 35–45 minutes. When they are tender you will easily be able to pull away the outer leaves. Open out the centre of each artichoke, pull out the tight inner ring of pale leaves and, using a teaspoon, scrape out the prickly centre or choke. Wash and drain the artichokes and leave them to cool for about 1 hour before serving.

Mix all the ingredients for the dressing. Pour into a bowl, garnish with sprigs of mint and serve with the artichokes.

■ COOK'S TIP

Instead of grilling the aubergines on a barbecue, place on a baking tray in a preheated oven 190°C (375°F), gas 5, for 20–30 minutes until softened. Leave to cool.

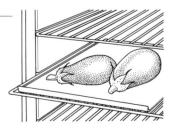

■ COOK'S TIP

To prepare the artichokes brush all the cut surfaces with lemon juice as you prepare them, and drop them into acidulated water. Trim the artichoke stems level with the base of the leaves and cut off the 2 outside layers of leaves. Cut off the top third of the leaves.

53
raw winter vegetables with skordalia

Preparation time
45 minutes

Serves 4

Calories
170 per portion

300 ml (½ pint) low-calorie mayonnaise
25 g (1 oz) fresh wholemeal breadcrumbs
25 g (1 oz) ground almonds
2 garlic cloves, crushed (or more
  if you like)
squeeze of lemon juice
2 tablespoons sesame seeds, toasted
3 tablespoons chopped fresh parsley
2–4 tablespoons natural yogurt (optional)
vegetables (see Cook's Tip)
salt and pepper
toasted sesame seeds, to garnish

To make the skordalia, put the mayonnaise into a bowl and stir in the breadcrumbs and almonds. Add the garlic, salt, pepper and lemon juice. Stir in the sesame seeds and parsley. If the mixture seems a little stiff, add natural yogurt to give a softer consistency.

Taste and adjust the seasoning. Cover and set aside while you prepare the vegetables. Grate the celeriac and carrot, shred the white and red cabbage and thinly slice the broccoli, cauliflower, Brussels sprouts and onions.

Serve clusters of the vegetables on a large platter or in small separate dishes, with the dip in the centre. Garnish with the extra sesame seeds. The dip can be made up to 2 hours in advance, covered and kept at room temperature.

54
asparagus with butter and lemon

Preparation time
5 minutes

Cooking time
10–15 minutes

Serves 2

Calories
190 per portion

½ bunch asparagus – about 12 spears
25–50 g (1–2 oz) butter
1 tablespoon fresh lemon juice
salt and pepper
lemon wedges, to serve

Wash and trim the asparagus, removing the tough stalk ends. Cook in 1 cm (½ inch) boiling water or in a steamer saucepan for 10–15 minutes or until the spears feel tender when pierced with the point of a knife. Drain the asparagus then heat the butter and lemon juice in a small saucepan and season with salt and pepper. Serve the asparagus spears immediately with the butter and lemon wedges.

■ COOK'S TIP

Use about 175 g (6 oz) each of: celeriac, carrot, white cabbage, red cabbage, broccoli, cauliflower, Brussels sprouts, peeled onions.

■ COOK'S TIP

Asparagus should only be lightly cooked. Never buy asparagus that looks woody, wrinkled or dry. Choose a bunch with even-sized spears.

55

chickpea purée
with vegetable sticks

Preparation time
10 minutes

Cooking time
about 1 hour

Serves 4

Calories
195 per portion

175 g (6 oz) chickpeas, soaked overnight
1 bay leaf
1 small bunch of mint
1 teaspoon salt
4 tablespoons lemon juice
2 large garlic cloves, crushed
1 tablespoon olive oil
4 tablespoons natural yogurt
pinch of paprika
2–3 tablespoons warm water
salt and pepper
a selection of fresh vegetable sticks
(see Cook's Tip)

Drain the chickpeas and put them into a pan with the bay leaf and mint, add sufficient water to cover and simmer for 1 hour until tender, adding salt during the last 10 minutes of cooking. Drain and remove bay leaf and mint.

Put the chickpeas into a food processor or blender with the lemon juice and garlic. Blend until smooth, gradually adding the olive oil and yogurt. Add pepper to taste, the paprika, and a little warm water to adjust consistency.

Serve with a selection of prepared vegetables.

56

mushroom and red wine
pâté with melba toast

Preparation time
10 minutes, plus chilling

Cooking time
5 minutes

Serves 6

Calories
145 per portion

50 g (2 oz) butter or margarine
750 g (1½ lb) small firm button
mushrooms, wiped and thinly sliced
3 tablespoons double cream
1 tablespoon dry red wine
salt and pepper
6–8 slices wholewheat bread for Melba
toast (see Cook's Tip)

Heat the butter or margarine in a large saucepan and add the mushrooms. Keeping the heat up high, fry the mushrooms quickly for 3–4 minutes, until just tender and lightly browned. If they begin to make liquid, the butter is not hot enough; the mushrooms should be dry. Remove 6 perfect mushroom slices and reserve for garnish. Work the rest in a food processor or blender with the cream, red wine and salt and pepper to taste. Spoon the mixture into 6 individual ramekins or pâté dishes, level the tops, then press one of the reserved mushroom slices into the top of each. Cool, then chill the pâtés.

■ COOK'S TIP

Choose fresh vegetables such as red and green peppers, celery, cucumber, carrots, French beans, spring onions, radishes and broccoli or cauliflower florets.

■ COOK'S TIP

To make the Melba toast, first toast the bread on both sides as usual, then with a sharp knife cut through the bread to split each piece in half. Toast the uncooked sides until crisp and brown – the edges will curl up. Allow the toast to curl.

57

fried mushrooms kiev

Preparation time
about 1 hour, plus chilling

Cooking time
about 20 minutes

Serves 4

Calories
400 per portion

24 cup mushrooms
125 g (4 oz) unsalted butter, softened
2–3 garlic cloves, crushed
2 tablespoons finely chopped parsley
2 medium eggs, beaten
75 g (3 oz) dried breadcrumbs
salt and pepper
vegetable oil, for deep-frying
FOR THE GARNISH
chicory leaves
parsley sprigs

Wipe the mushrooms clean with a damp cloth. Carefully pull out the stalks, keeping the caps whole. Chop the stalks finely. Put the softened butter in a bowl with the chopped mushroom stalks, garlic, parsley and salt and pepper to taste. Beat together well. Spoon into the mushroom cavities, then sandwich the mushrooms together in pairs. Use wooden cocktail sticks to secure them.

Dip the mushroom pairs one at a time into the beaten egg, then roll in the breadcrumbs. Repeat once more. Chill for 1 hour.

Heat the oil in a deep-fryer to 190°C (375°F), or until a stale bread cube turns golden in 40–50 seconds. Fry the mushrooms a few at a time for about 5 minutes, turning them frequently with a slotted spoon until golden brown and crisp on all sides. Drain and keep hot while frying the remainder.

Remove the cocktail sticks and serve immediately, garnished with chicory leaves and parsley sprigs.

■ COOK'S TIP

Mushrooms Kiev are ideal as a starter served with a garlic mayonnaise or yogurt dip (see recipe 49). Alternatively, serve as a main course with a salad and yogurt dressing.

58

tzatziki

Preparation time
10 minutes

Serves 4

Calories
117 per portion

1 cucumber, about 500 g (1 lb), peeled
300 ml (½ pint) thick Greek yogurt
2 tablespoons lemon juice
2 tablespoons chopped spring onions or chives
2 tablespoons chopped parsley
1 tablespoon chopped mint
1–2 garlic cloves, crushed, or 1 shallot, finely chopped
black pepper
large pinch of salt

Chop the cucumber finely. Mix all the other ingredients together and combine with the cucumber in a serving bowl.

Serve the Tzatziki with warmed wholemeal pitta bread, cut into fingers, and maybe some vegetable crudités (see recipe 55).

■ COOK'S TIP

This salad is served as a first course in Greece. Instead of cucumber you can also use grated carrot, fennel, celery mixed with apple, Cos lettuce or mushrooms.

59

vegetables
à la grecque

Preparation time
20 minutes, plus chilling

Cooking time
about 10 minutes

Serves 6

Calories
78 per portion

Suitable for vegans

2 tablespoons olive oil
1 large onion, chopped
3 garlic cloves, crushed
1 small–medium cauliflower, trimmed
    and broken into florets
375 g (12 oz) French beans, trimmed and
    cut into 2.5 cm (1 inch) pieces
175 g (6 oz) button mushrooms, wiped
    and cut into even-sized pieces
1 tablespoon coriander seeds, crushed
6 tablespoons lemon juice
salt and pepper
chopped parsley or a few black olives, to
    garnish

Heat the oil in a large saucepan, then fry the onion for 5 minutes, without letting it brown. Add the garlic, cauliflower and beans and stir-fry for a further 2–3 minutes, then add the mushrooms and coriander seeds and continue to fry for about 2 minutes, until the mushrooms are beginning to soften. Remove from the heat, add the lemon juice, salt and pepper to taste. Cool, then chill. Serve on individual plates, sprinkled with chopped parsley and garnished with black olives. Serve with warm rolls or a French stick.

60

hot stuffed avocados

Preparation time
15 minutes

Cooking time
15–20 minutes

Oven temperature
200°C (400°F)
Gas Mark 6

Serves 8

Calories
462 per portion

4 large ripe avocado pears
rind and juice of 1 well-scrubbed lemon
1 bunch of spring onions, trimmed and
    chopped
200 g (7 oz) skinned hazelnuts
175 g (6 oz) vegetarian Cheddar cheese,
    grated
4 tablespoons chopped parsley
4 tablespoons dry white wine
salt and pepper

Cut the avocado pears in half and remove the stones. Put the avocado halves, cavity side up, in a shallow casserole dish then brush the cut surfaces with a little of the lemon juice.

Mix together the onions, hazelnuts, cheese, parsley and wine. Add 2 teaspoons lemon juice and the lemon rind. Season to taste with salt and pepper. Divide this mixture between the avocado halves, and bake in a preheated oven for 15–20 minutes, until golden brown.

■ COOK'S TIP

This delicious, lightly spiced mixture can be made with other vegetables in season. Try replacing the cauliflower with baby Brussels sprouts, quartered, and the French beans with sliced leeks. Carrots would also make a colourful addition.

■ COOK'S TIP

On a ripe avocado, the flesh should yield slightly. If very soft, the avocado is over-ripe. If hard, wrap in paper and leave in a warm place for 2–3 days.

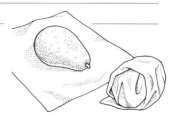

61

cèpes with herb sauce

Preparation time 20 minutes	*40 g (1½ oz) butter* *1 garlic clove, peeled and halved*
Cooking time about 40 minutes	*750 g (1½ lb) cèpes or other wild* * mushrooms, washed, trimmed and cut*
Serves 6	* into bite-sized pieces* *1 tablespoon chopped parsley*
Calories 93 per portion	*1 tablespoon chopped chervil* *1 tablespoon chopped basil* *1 tablespoon plain flour* *4 tablespoons dry white wine* *150 ml (¼ pint) double or soured cream* *salt and pepper*

Melt the butter in a pan. Add the garlic and fry until golden brown. Remove and discard the garlic. Add the cèpes or other mushrooms to the pan and cook over a low heat for about 20 minutes, or until softened.

Add half of the chopped herbs to the pan and mix well. Stir in the flour and cook for 2–3 minutes, stirring well. Gradually add the wine, blending well after each addition to make a smooth sauce. Simmer over a low heat for about 3 minutes. Fold in the double or soured cream and season with salt and pepper to taste. Transfer to a serving dish, sprinkle with the remaining herbs and serve immediately. Serve with French bread and a light, dry white wine.

62

nut-stuffed tomatoes

Preparation time 20 minutes	*2 large Mediterranean tomatoes* *2 tablespoons vegetable oil*
Cooking time 20 minutes	*75 g (3 oz) button mushrooms, finely* * chopped*
Oven temperature 180°C (350°F) gas 4	*65 g (2½ oz) brown rice, cooked* *25 g (1 oz) Brazil nuts, coarsely chopped* *25 g (1 oz) currants*
Serves 2	*1 tablespoon chopped basil* *salt and pepper*
Calories 312 per portion	FOR THE GARNISH *4 teaspoons soured cream* *watercress sprigs*

Cut the tomatoes in half and scoop out the pulp. Sprinkle the shells with salt and place in a baking dish. To prepare the stuffing, heat the oil in a small pan and gently fry the mushrooms for 5 minutes. Stir in the cooked rice, nuts, currants and basil. Add a little salt and plenty of pepper. Spoon the stuffing into the tomato halves.

Cover the dish with foil to keep the stuffing moist and bake for 20 minutes in a preheated oven. Remove from the oven, top each stuffed tomato with a spoonful of soured cream and garnish with watercress. Serve piping hot.

The tomatoes can be prepared up to 8 hours in advance, covered and kept in the refrigerator until needed.

■ COOK'S TIP

Many unusual varieties of mushrooms are now widely available. Common varieties are Chinese and Japanese mushrooms which are usually sold dried and must be reconstituted in water. Other European varieties include oyster mushrooms and the brown sponge-like morel (both available dried).

■ COOK'S TIP

As a starter, these are delicious served hot, but they are equally good uncooked for a picnic or cold buffet; serve with salad and French bread to make a light lunch.

63

mushrooms in herbed vinaigrette

Preparation time
5 minutes, plus chilling

Cooking time
about 15 minutes

Serves 4

Calories
140 per portion

Suitable for vegans

2 tablespoons walnut oil
2 tablespoons tarragon vinegar
4 tablespoons dry white wine
1 garlic clove, crushed
½ teaspoon grated orange rind
1 tablespoon chopped tarragon
1 tablespoon chopped parsley
250 g (8 oz) button mushrooms
salt and pepper
2 wholemeal pitta breads, cut into fingers

Put the walnut oil, vinegar, wine and garlic into a shallow pan and add salt and pepper to taste; simmer for 3 minutes. Add the orange rind, tarragon, parsley and mushrooms; cover and simmer for 8 minutes.

Pour the mushrooms and their juices into a shallow dish and allow to cool. Cover and chill for 4 hours. Serve with fingers of warm pitta bread.

64

estouffade de boletus

Preparation time
20 minutes, plus standing

Cooking time
about 2 hours

Serves 6

Calories
111 per portion

Suitable for vegans

500 g (1 lb) aubergines (see Cook's Tip)
2 tablespoons sunflower oil
375 g (12 oz) onions, sliced
3 large garlic cloves, quartered
750 g (1½ lb) large flat mushrooms, preferably field mushrooms
2 x 400 g (13 oz) cans tomatoes
2½ tablespoons tomato purée
1 tablespoon red wine vinegar
1 tablespoon brown sugar
1 tablespoon soy sauce
2 bay leaves
salt and pepper

Heat the oil in a large heavy-based pan and soften the onion and garlic. Slice the mushrooms into strips about 1 cm (½ inch) wide.

Rinse the aubergines then squeeze to extract as much liquid as possible. Add the aubergines to the pan. Stir over a medium heat for 1 minute, then add the mushrooms, stir and cover.

Push the tomatoes through a vegetable mill or sieve to remove the seeds and add to the pan. Bring to simmering point, cover and cook for 1 hour, stirring occasionally. Add the remaining ingredients. Stir thoroughly, then continue to simmer uncovered for approximately 45 minutes.

Remove from the heat, cover and leave to stand for 24 hours. Remove the bay leaves. Serve cold, or very slightly warmed, with small wholemeal rolls.

■ COOK'S TIP

Mushrooms are great for vegetarians as they are not only very versatile, they have a 'meaty' taste and texture. Mushrooms are best eaten within a day or two of purchase as they dehydrate very quickly. Store them in a cool place, preferably in a paper bag tucked inside a polythene one.

■ COOK'S TIP

To prepare the aubergines, slice into pieces approximately the size of French fries. Transfer to a colander, sprinkle with salt, and set aside to drain.

beans and pulses

In a vegetarian diet, versatile dried peas and beans provide valuable sources of protein and fibre. Many people will be familiar with delicious dhals – made from lentils, chickpeas and mung beans, among others – but may not have experimented at home to make the most of the huge variety of pulses available.

65

vegetable salad with tarragon mayonnaise

Preparation time
45 minutes

Cooking time
8–10 minutes

Serves 6

Calories
444 per portion

4 carrots, cut into thin strips
250 g (8 oz) French beans, trimmed
2 leeks, cleaned and cut into rounds
6 tablespoons unsweetened orange juice
3 tablespoons olive oil
1 garlic clove, crushed
1 x 425 g (14 oz) can black-eyed beans, drained and rinsed
175 g (6 oz) Brussels sprouts, trimmed, and finely shredded
10–12 good-shaped spinach leaves
salt and pepper
tarragon sprigs, to garnish
Tarragon mayonnaise (see Cook's Tip), to serve

Steam the carrots, beans and leek rounds until just tender – the vegetables should still have a bite to them. Allow to cool.

Mix the orange juice with the olive oil, garlic and salt and pepper to taste; toss the black-eyed beans and the Brussels sprouts in the orange dressing.

Arrange a bed of spinach leaves on each serving plate; spoon the black-eyed beans and shredded sprouts on top.

Arrange the carrots, leeks and beans a round the salad. Garnish with sprigs of tarragon and serve as a complete light meal, accompanied by the tarragon mayonnaise.

66

falafel

Preparation time
10 minutes, plus soaking and resting

Cooking time
about 20 minutes

Serves 6

Calories
180 per portion

250 g (8 oz) chickpeas, soaked overnight
4 spring onions
2 garlic cloves, chopped
3 tablespoons water
4 large parsley sprigs
½ teaspoon ground cumin
1 teaspoon ground coriander
salt and pepper
vegetable oil, for deep-frying
coriander sprig, to garnish
Tomato yogurt dip (see Cook's Tip), to serve

Drain the chickpeas and place in a food processor or blender with the spring onions, garlic, water and parsley. Work to a purée, scraping down the sides when necessary. Stir in the cumin and coriander, with salt and pepper to taste, then turn into a bowl and leave for 1–2 hours to dry out slightly.

Form the mixture into walnut-sized balls and flatten slightly. Heat the oil in a deep-fryer, add the falafel, a few at a time, and fry for about 4 minutes, until golden. Drain on kitchen paper.

Serve hot with tomato yogurt dip (see Cook's Tip) and garnish with a sprig of coriander.

■ COOK'S TIP

To make the Tarragon mayonnaise, beat 2 egg yolks with 1 tablespoon lemon juice; gradually whisk in 150 ml (¼ pint) olive oil. Blend in 1 crushed garlic clove, ½ teaspoon French mustard, 1½ tablespoons chopped tarragon and 4 tablespoons natural yogurt. Season to taste.

■ COOK'S TIP

To make the Tomato yogurt dip, mix together 150 g (5 oz) natural yogurt, 1 teaspoon tomato purée, 1 teaspoon ground coriander and 1 teaspoon clear honey.

67

cracked wheat salad

Preparation time
5 minutes, plus
soaking

Serves 4

Calories
147 per portion

Suitable for vegans

125 g (4 oz) bulgur wheat
300 ml (½ pint) boiling water
2 tablespoons lemon juice
1 tablespoon olive oil
4 tablespoons chopped parsley
4 tablespoons chopped spring onions
2 tablespoons chopped mint
2 tomatoes, skinned and finely chopped
salt and pepper
4 lettuce leaves
FOR THE DRESSING
lemon slices
tomato slices

Put the wheat into a bowl and cover with the boiling water. Leave for 10–15 minutes until the wheat has absorbed all the water and puffed up. Add the lemon juice, oil, chopped parsley, spring onions, mint and tomatoes. Mix well and season to taste. Put 2 lettuce leaves on 2 serving plates, or in one large bowl, then spoon the salad mixture on top. Garnish with the lemon and tomato slices.

68

bean-stuffed tomatoes

Preparation time
20–25 minutes

Cooking time
15–20 minutes

Oven temperature
180°C (350°F)
gas 4

Serves 4

Calories
270 per portion

Suitable for vegans

1 x 425 g (14 oz) can red kidney beans,
  drained
1 small onion, finely chopped
2 tablespoons finely chopped blanched
  almonds (see Cook's Tip)
1 teaspoon chopped sage
1 garlic clove, finely chopped
2 tablespoons wholemeal breadcrumbs
1 small parsnip, peeled and grated
4 large Mediterranean or 8 medium
  tomatoes
1 tablespoon olive oil
salt and pepper

Mix the beans with the onion, almonds, sage, garlic, breadcrumbs, grated parsnip and salt and pepper.

Cut the tops off the tomatoes and carefully hollow them out. Fill each with some of the bean mixture. Stand the stuffed tomatoes upright in a lightly greased ovenproof dish. Brush with a little olive oil.

Bake in a preheated oven for 15–20 minutes. Serve with brown rice (see Rice and Pasta chapter for recipes) and a fresh leafy green salad.

■ COOK'S TIP

This is a traditional Lebanese salad that is quick and easy to prepare. It is based on wheat which has been cracked and steamed. This wheat, called bulgur or burghul, is widely available at supermarkets and only needs soaking. The salad should contain almost as much greenery as wheat.

■ COOK'S TIP

To blanch almonds, drop them into boiling water, bring back to the boil then drain. Squeeze the nuts while warm to slip them out of their skins. Blot dry.

69

crisp lentil patties

Preparation time
20 minutes

Cooking time
about 1 hour

Serves 4–5

Calories
367–244 per portion

250 g (8 oz) green or brown (Continental) lentils, washed
450 ml (¾ pint) vegetable stock
1 tablespoon oil
1 onion, finely sliced
1 green pepper, cored, deseeded and finely chopped
1 teaspoon ground cumin
1 teaspoon ground coriander
¼ teaspoon chilli powder
125 g (4 oz) jumbo or porridge oats
1 medium egg, beaten
salt and pepper
oil, for frying

Place the lentils in a pan with the stock. Bring to the boil and simmer gently until all the stock is absorbed and the lentils are tender, about 40 minutes.

Meanwhile, heat the oil in a pan and fry the onion slowly until cooked but not brown, about 20 minutes. Stir in the green pepper and cook for a further 4 minutes then stir in the cumin, coriander, chilli powder and salt and pepper. Add the lentils, mix well and leave to cool. Shape into 8–10 round flat cakes.

Mix the oats with the salt on one plate and pour the beaten egg on to another. Dip each patty first into the egg then into the oats to coat completely. Shallow fry the patties in oil for about 6 minutes, turning once until brown and crisp. Drain.

■ COOK'S TIP

Serve the patties with a rich tomato sauce (see recipe 88) and a ribbon pasta, such as tagliatelle or a crunchy salad.

70

sunset stripe salad

Preparation time
25 minutes, plus soaking

Cooking time
1¼ hours

Serves 4

Calories
276 per portion

Suitable for vegans

175 g (6 oz) dried red kidney beans, soaked overnight and drained
small bunch of parsley
1 small onion, halved
175 g (6 oz) red cabbage, shredded
2 small heads fennel, very thinly sliced into rings
2 oranges, segmented
tomato roses (see Cook's Tip)
FOR THE DRESSING
4 tablespoons vegetable oil
½ teaspoon grated orange rind
4 tablespoons orange juice
½ teaspoon fennel seeds, crushed
1 garlic clove, halved
large pinch of mustard powder
salt and pepper

Cook the beans in fast-boiling unsalted water for 15–20 minutes. Add half the parsley and onion and slow boil for about 1 hour, or until just tender. Drain, discard the parsley and onion, run hot water through the beans and drain again.

Meanwhile, mix the dressing ingredients and set aside for about 1 hour. Strain the dressing. Toss the beans in the dressing while they are still hot. Set aside to cool.

In a glass dish, make a layer of the red cabbage, then the fennel, then the orange segments, and cover them with the beans. Cover and set aside for at least 1 hour. Make a pad of parsley sprigs on the salad and place tomato roses on top.

■ COOK'S TIP

To make a tomato rose, choose a firm, slightly under-ripe tomato. Starting at the top and using a sharp knife, peel off a continuous spiral of skin about 1 cm (½ inch) wide. With the skin outside, curl the strip into a tight spiral. Arranged on a 'pad' of parsley sprigs, it will look mighty like a rose!

71

three bean curry

Preparation time	*125 g (4 oz) butter or soya margarine*
25 minutes	*2 onions, finely chopped*
Cooking time	*3 garlic cloves, crushed*
30–35 minutes	*1 tablespoon ground coriander*
Serves 4	*1 teaspoon garam masala*
Calories	*1 teaspoon chilli powder*
485 per portion	*1 x 400 g (13 oz) can chopped tomatoes*
Suitable for vegans	*1 teaspoon sugar*
using soya margarine	*1 x 425 g (14 oz) can butter beans,*
	drained

1 x 425 g (14 oz) can red kidney beans,
drained
1 x 425 g (14 oz) can cannellini beans,
drained
salt and pepper
coriander sprigs, to garnish

Heat the butter or margarine in a saucepan, add the onions and fry for 10 minutes until golden brown.

Add the garlic and fry for a few seconds only, then add the coriander, garam masala and chilli powder and stir-fry for a few seconds. Stir in the tomatoes, salt and pepper and sugar. Reduce the heat and cook for 10 minutes.

Add the drained beans, stir thoroughly then cover and cook gently until heated through.

Garnish with the coriander sprigs and serve with poppadums (see Cook's Tip) and a spicy vegetable dish.

72

bean and cabbage hotpot

Preparation time	*175 g (6 oz) aduki beans, soaked*
30 minutes, plus	*overnight in cold water*
soaking	*1 tablespoon vegetable oil*
Cooking time	*3 onions, chopped*
1¾ hours	*175 g (6 oz) carrots, sliced into rings*
Oven temperature	*375 g (12 oz) white cabbage, shredded*
220°C (425°F)	*½ teaspoon celery seed*
Gas Mark 7	*900 ml (1½ pints) hot vegetable stock*
Serves 4	*750 g (1½ lb) potatoes, cooked whole in*
Calories	*their skins, then sliced*
379 per portion	*salt and pepper*
Suitable for vegans	*15 g (½ oz) butter or soya margarine*
using soya margarine	*paprika, to garnish*

Drain the aduki beans then rinse under cold running water. Put them in a pan, cover with cold water and bring to the boil. Boil fast for 10 minutes then lower the heat. Half cover the pan and simmer for 35–45 minutes until tender. Drain and rinse.

Heat the oil in a large pan with a lid and cook the onions, carrots and cabbage, covered, for about 5 minutes. Add the celery seed, hot stock and salt and pepper to taste. Cover the pan and simmer gently for 15 minutes then stir in the cooked beans.

Spoon the mixture into a large, shallow casserole dish and arrange the slices of potatoes to cover the top. Brush with melted butter or soya margarine and bake near the top of a preheated oven for about 30 minutes until the potatoes are browned and crisp. Sprinkle with paprika before serving.

■ COOK'S TIP

Crisp, golden poppadums make the perfect accompaniment to curries. They can be prepared under the grill, by shallow frying or deep frying.

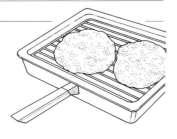

■ COOK'S TIP

The sweet-flavoured aduki bean is peanut-shaped, small and reddish brown with a creamy coloured seam. Aduki beans are low in fat, rich in fibre, cholesterol-free and an excellent source of protein. Available from health food shops their nutty flavour blends well with this hotpot.

73

bean and
mushroom salad

Preparation time
15 minutes, plus
soaking

Cooking time
45 minutes

Serves 6

Calories
150 per portion

Suitable for vegans

175 g (6 oz) black-eyed beans,
soaked overnight
125 g (4 oz) button mushrooms, sliced
4 tablespoons French dressing
(see Cook's Tip)
1 small red pepper, cored, deseeded and
sliced
2 tablespoons chopped parsley
salt

Drain the beans, place in a pan and cover with cold water. Bring to the boil, cover and simmer for 40–45 minutes until tender, adding a little salt towards the end of the cooking.

Drain the beans thoroughly and place in a bowl with the mushrooms. Pour over the dressing and toss well while still warm. Leave to cool.

Add the red pepper and parsley, toss thoroughly and transfer to a salad bowl.

74

curried butter
bean salad

Preparation time
12 minutes, plus
soaking

Cooking time
1 hour 10 minutes

Serves 4

Calories
286 per portion

375 g (12 oz) butter beans, soaked
overnight
2 teaspoons vegetable oil
2 onions, finely chopped
2 teaspoons curry powder
150 ml (¼ pint) natural yogurt
1 tablespoon lemon juice
½ lettuce, washed (optional)
salt and pepper
1 rosemary sprig, to garnish

Drain the butter beans from their soaking water, put in a large pan, cover with fresh water and bring to the boil. Cover and simmer for 1 hour, or until tender but not broken. Drain.

Heat the oil in a heavy-based pan, add the onions and cook gently for 8 minutes, covering the pan. Add the curry powder and cook for a further 2 minutes.

Meanwhile, mix the yogurt with the lemon juice and salt and pepper. Add this to the onion mixture, then stir in the butter beans.

To serve, arrange a bed of lettuce on a serving plate, spoon the butter beans on top and garnish with a sprig of rosemary.

■ COOK'S TIP

For the French dressing,
place in a screw-topped jar:
5 tablespoons olive oil,
2 tablespoons wine vinegar,
1 teaspoon Dijon mustard,

1 crushed garlic clove,
½ teaspoon honey and salt and
pepper to taste. Shake well
before serving.

■ COOK'S TIP

One of Britain's most popular
dried beans, the butter bean is a
member of the kidney bean
family, though it is much more
subtle in taste.

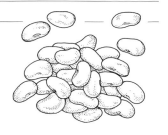

75

lentil and tomato salad

Preparation time 15 minutes	*300 g (10 oz) green or Continental* *lentils, washed (see Cook's Tip)*
Cooking time 10–15 minutes	*175 g (6 oz) long-grain rice* *6 large tomatoes, skinned, deseeded and*
Serves 6	*chopped*
Calories 190 per portion	*1 tablespoon olive oil* *2 garlic cloves, finely chopped*
Suitable for vegans	*1 teaspoon cumin seeds* *1 teaspoon black mustard seeds* *1 tablespoon vinegar* *2 teaspoons lemon juice* *salt and pepper*

Place the lentils in a large saucepan with plenty of cold water. Do not add salt. Bring to the boil, cover and simmer gently for about 10–12 minutes. When tender, strain and set aside.

Bring a pan of water to the boil and add the rice, simmer for 10–12 minutes then drain and set aside.

Combine the lentils, rice and tomatoes in a serving bowl. Heat the oil in a frying pan and fry the garlic, cumin and mustard seeds until the garlic is almost burnt. Tip over the lentil mixture at once.

Sprinkle over the vinegar and lemon juice, season with salt and pepper and mix thoroughly.

76

chickpea and red pepper salad

Preparation time 15 minutes, plus soaking	*175 g (6 oz) chickpeas, soaked overnight* *and drained* *2 red peppers*
Cooking time about 2 hours	*12 black olives* *2 tablespoons chopped coriander or*
Serves 4	*parsley*
Calories 248 per portion	*parsley sprigs, to garnish* FOR THE DRESSING
Suitable for vegans	*3 tablespoons vegetable oil* *½ teaspoon orange rind* *2 tablespoons orange juice* *1 garlic clove, crushed* *salt and pepper*

Cook the chickpeas in boiling unsalted water for 2 hours, or until they are tender (see Cook's Tip). Drain the chickpeas, rinse with hot water and drain them again.

Place the red peppers on a grill rack and cook under a moderate heat for about 20 minutes, turning frequently until the skins are black and blistered. Hold the peppers under cold water then, using a small, sharp knife, peel off the skins. Halve the peppers, remove the core and seeds and thinly slice.

Mix together the dressing ingredients. Toss the chick peas in the dressing while still hot. Set aside to cool. Stir in the peppers, olives and half the coriander or parsley. Turn the salad into a serving dish and sprinkle with the remaining coriander or parsley and garnish with parsley sprigs.

■ COOK'S TIP

Like red lentils, green or Continental lentils do not need pre-soaking. They hold their shape well when cooked, so are ideal for salads.

■ COOK'S TIP

Chickpeas that have been kept for a long time will take longer to cook. Buy chickpeas in small quantities and store in an airtight jar in a cool, dry place.

77

greek bean salad

Preparation time 15 minutes, plus soaking	*275 g (9 oz) dried black-eyed or white haricot beans, soaked overnight in cold water*
Cooking time 1¼ hours	*1 litre (1¼ pints) water* *4 tomatoes, diced*
Serves 4	*2 large onions, chopped* *125 g (4 oz) vegetarian feta cheese, cubed*
Calories 437 per portion	*salt and cayenne pepper* FOR THE DRESSING *2 garlic cloves, crushed with salt* *2 tablespoons wine vinegar* *4 tablespoons olive oil* *1 teaspoon chopped fresh oregano*

Drain the beans and place in a pan with the water. Bring slowly to the boil, then lower the heat and cook gently for about 1 hour. Season to taste with salt and cayenne pepper and cook for a further 10–20 minutes, until just tender. Drain in a sieve and leave to cool.

Place the beans in a large serving bowl and mix with the tomatoes, onion and cheese.

To make the dressing, beat the garlic with the vinegar, olive oil and oregano. Pour over the salad and toss to mix. Leave to stand for 10–15 minutes to allow the flavours to develop. Toss again before serving.

78

lentil and mushroom gratin

Preparation time 30 minutes	*2 tablespoons oil* *1 onion, chopped*
Cooking time about 1½ hours	*1 carrot, chopped* *2 celery sticks, chopped*
Oven temperature 190°C (375°F) gas 5	*1 garlic clove, crushed* *250 g (8 oz) red lentils* *600 ml (1 pint) water*
Serves 4	*2 tablespoons soy sauce* *salt and pepper*
Calories 397 per portion	FOR THE MUSHROOM FILLING *25 g (1 oz) margarine* *250 g (8 oz) flat mushrooms, sliced* *2 garlic cloves, crushed* *3 tablespoons chopped parsley* *75 g (3 oz) vegetarian Cheddar, grated*

Heat the oil in a pan, add the onion, carrot and celery and fry gently for 10 minutes, until softened. Add the remaining ingredients, with salt and pepper to taste. Cover and simmer for 50–60 minutes, stirring occasionally, until tender.

For the filling, melt the margarine in a frying pan, add the mushrooms and fry for 2 minutes, stirring. Add the garlic, parsley and salt and pepper to taste and mix well.

Place half the lentil mixture in an oiled ovenproof dish. Spread the mushrooms over the top, then cover with the remaining lentil mixture. Top with the cheese and bake in a preheated oven for 20–25 minutes until golden.

■ COOK'S TIP

This salad can be served as part of a cold buffet for parties or picnics, or with a wholemeal roll for lunch. If fresh oregano isn't available, use parsley.

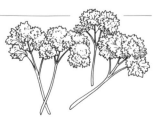

■ COOK'S TIP

Red lentils are ideal for soups and stews as they are quick cooking and do not require pre-soaking. As they lose their shape when cooked, do not use in salads.

79

provençale bean stew

Preparation time
15 minutes, plus soaking

Cooking time
2–2¼ hours

Serves 4

Calories
344 per portion

Suitable for vegans

375 g (12 oz) haricot beans or pinto
    beans, soaked overnight
2 tablespoons olive oil
2 onions, sliced
1 red pepper, cored, deseeded and sliced
1 green pepper, cored, deseeded and sliced
2 garlic cloves, crushed
1 x 400 g (13 oz) can chopped tomatoes
2 tablespoons tomato purée
1 bouquet garni
50 g (2 oz) black olives, halved and
    stoned
2 tablespoons chopped parsley
salt and pepper

Drain the beans, place in a pan and cover with cold water. Bring to the boil, boil for 10 minutes, then cover and simmer for 1–1¼ hours, until almost tender, adding a pinch of salt towards the end of cooking. Drain, reserving 300 ml (½ pint) of the liquid.

Heat the oil in a pan, add the onions and fry until softened. Add the peppers and garlic and fry gently for 10 minutes. Add the tomatoes with their juice, tomato purée, beans, reserved liquid, bouquet garni and salt and pepper to taste. Cover and simmer for 45 minutes, adding the olives and parsley 5 minutes before the end of the cooking time. Remove the bouquet garni.

Serve with garlic bread and salad.

■ COOK'S TIP

Never add salt to dried beans during the early stages of cooking – it will make the skins tough and prevent the beans becoming tender. Add salt (not too much) during the last 10 minutes of the calculated cooking time.

80

multi-coloured bean salad

Preparation time
15 minutes, plus marinating

Serves 6

Calories
325 per portion

Suitable for vegans

1 x 250 g (8 oz) can chickpeas, drained
1 x 250 g (8 oz) can red kidney beans,
    drained
1 x 250 g (8 oz) can white kidney beans,
    drained
250 g (8 oz) cooked French beans,
    chopped into 2.5 cm (1 inch) lengths
1 red pepper, cored, deseeded and finely
    sliced
1 bunch of spring onions, chopped
2 garlic cloves
½ teaspoon salt
2 tablespoons tahini
1 tablespoon lemon juice
1 tablespoon soy sauce
2 tablespoons water
1 tablespoon chopped parsley or
    coriander, to garnish

Rinse all the canned beans under cold running water and drain well. Combine with the French beans, red pepper and spring onions in a deep serving bowl.

Crush the garlic with the salt and combine with the tahini, lemon juice, soy sauce and water. If the dressing is too thick, add a little more water. Stir the dressing into the beans and sprinkle the parsley or coriander over.

Leave to marinate for 2 hours before serving as part of a picnic, buffet, or light lunch snack.

■ COOK'S TIP

Tahini (sesame seed paste), combined with the beans, means a complete protein is obtained. Red pepper also increases the vitamin C content.

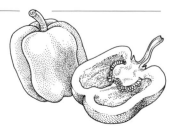

81

vegetarian hotpot

Preparation time 15 minutes, plus soaking	*25 g (1 oz) dried chickpeas* *25 g (1 oz) dried haricot beans*
Cooking time 2–2¼ hours	*25 g (1 oz) dried black-eyed beans* *25 g (1 oz) dried red kidney beans* *15 g (½ oz) butter*
Serves 2	*1 small onion, chopped* *1 carrot, sliced*
Calories 420 per portion	*1 celery stick, chopped* *1 garlic clove, crushed* *1 x 250 g (8 oz) can tomatoes* *½ teaspoon dried mixed herbs* *75 g (3 oz) vegetarian Cheddar, grated* *salt and pepper*

Place the chickpeas, haricot beans and black-eyed beans in a bowl and cover with cold water. Place the kidney beans in a separate bowl and cover with water. Soak overnight.

Drain and place the chickpeas, haricot beans and black-eyed beans in a saucepan; put the kidney beans in a separate pan (to avoid tinting the others pink). Cover the pulses with fresh cold water. Bring to the boil, boil for 10 minutes, then cover and simmer for 40 minutes or until tender. Drain, rinse under cold water, then drain thoroughly.

Melt the butter in a saucepan, add the onion, carrot and celery and fry until soft. Stir in the garlic, pulses, tomatoes with their juice, herbs, and salt and pepper to taste.

Bring to the boil, cover and simmer for 1–1¼ hours, adding a little water if the mixture becomes too dry. Sprinkle with the cheese. Serve with rice (see Cook's Tip).

82

banana muesli

Preparation time 15 minutes, plus soaking	*125 g (4 oz) rolled oats* *50 g (2 oz) sunflower seeds*
Serves 4	*300 ml (½ pint) water* *2 tablespoons clear honey*
Calories 285 per portion	*2 large bananas, sliced* *250 g (8 oz) black grapes, halved and* *deseeded* *grated rind of 1 large well-scrubbed* *orange and 1 large, well-scrubbed* *lemon* *50 g (2 oz) flaked almonds, toasted*

Put the rolled oats and sunflower seeds into a bowl with the water; leave to soak overnight if possible (see Cook's Tip). Mix well until creamy, and add the honey, bananas, grapes and orange and lemon rind. Spoon into a large serving dish or four small ones and sprinkle with toasted almond flakes.

■ COOK'S TIP

To cook long-grain rice, place the rice in a pan with double its volume in water. Bring to the boil, cover and simmer for 20 minutes. By the end of the cooking time the rice grains will have absorbed all the water and be dry and separate. Simply fluff with a fork and serve.

■ COOK'S TIP

Soaking the oats overnight in water gives the muesli extra creaminess. If you also soak the sunflower seeds, they will begin to germinate, adding extra health-giving enzymes.

83

two-bean vegetable goulash

Preparation time
30 minutes, plus soaking

Cooking time
about 1¾ hours

Serves 4

Calories
352 per portion

Suitable for vegans if soured cream omitted

125 g (4 oz) each black-eyed and
    cannellini beans, soaked overnight
    (see Cook's Tip)
1 tablespoon vegetable oil
125 g (4 oz) very small onions, or
    shallots, peeled but left whole
4 celery sticks, sliced into chunks
4 small courgettes, cut in chunks
3 small carrots, cut in chunks
1 x 400 g (13 oz) can tomatoes
300 ml (½ pint) vegetable stock
1 tablespoon paprika
½ teaspoon caraway seeds
1 tablespoon cornflour
2 tablespoons water
salt and pepper
soured cream, to serve (optional)

Heat the oil in a large pan and fry the onions, celery, courgettes and carrots quickly over a high heat until lightly browned. Pour in the tomatoes with their juice and the stock. Stir in the paprika, caraway seeds, salt and pepper. Cover and simmer for 20 minutes until the vegetables are tender.

Stir both lots of cooked beans into the vegetables. Blend the cornflour with the water and add to the pan. Bring to the boil, stirring, until the sauce thickens a little. Cover the pan and simmer again for about 10 minutes. Spoon the goulash into a warmed dish and serve with soured cream, if liked.

■ COOK'S TIP

Drain the beans and rinse under cold running water. Put them in two separate pans, cover with water and bring to the boil. Boil fast for 10 minutes then lower the heat, half cover the pans and simmer for about 1 hour until tender. Drain, rinse and set aside.

84

blackberry and apple muesli

Preparation time
10 minutes

Serves 4

Calories
340 per portion

Suitable for vegans using soya milk

8 tablespoons porridge oats
2 tablespoons jumbo oats
1 tablespoon bran
1 tablespoon sunflower seeds
4 tablespoons mixed chopped nuts
4 tablespoons sultanas
2 dessert apples, cored and thinly sliced
1 tablespoon lemon juice
250 g (8 oz) blackberries
natural yogurt, soya milk or buttermilk,
    to serve

Mix together the porridge oats, jumbo oats, bran, sunflower seeds, nuts and sultanas. Toss the sliced apple in the lemon juice.

Spoon the muesli mixture into 4 cereal bowls, arrange the apple slices in a ring around the outside and pile the blackberries in the centre. Serve with natural yogurt or buttermilk for breakfast or a family supper.

■ COOK'S TIP

You can make the muesli mix of the cereals, seeds, nuts and dried fruits in larger quantities and store in an airtight container in a cool, dry place.

85

black-eyed bean bake

Preparation time
15 minutes, plus soaking

Cooking time
2 hours 10 minutes

Oven temperature
180°C (350°F)
gas 4

Serves 4

Calories
491 per portion

Suitable for vegans without the Cheddar

250 g (8 oz) dried black-eyed beans, soaked for at least 1 hour
3 tablespoons olive oil
1 large onion, chopped
2 potatoes, sliced
2 large carrots, sliced
2 turnips, diced
2 parsnips, diced
2 celery sticks, sliced
1 tablespoon chopped parsley
1 tablespoon. dried thyme
1 teaspoon dried oregano
2 bay leaves
1 teaspoon black treacle
2 tablespoons tomato purée
50 g (2 oz) vegetarian Cheddar, grated
salt and pepper

Cook the beans (see Cook's Tip). Meanwhile, heat the oil in a flameproof casserole, add the onion and fry until softened. Stir in the vegetables. Cover and cook over a gentle heat for 10 minutes.

Drain the beans, reserving their cooking liquid. Stir the beans into the casserole with the herbs and salt and pepper. Pour over 600 ml (1 pint) of the cooking liquid, to cover the vegetables. Stir in the black treacle and tomato purée. Cover tightly and transfer to a preheated oven for 1½ hours.

Uncover the casserole and discard the bay leaves. Sprinkle over the cheese. Cook without a lid for a further 10 minutes.

86

broad bean salad

Preparation time
15 minutes

Cooking time
10–12 minutes

Serves 4

Calories
86 per portion

500 g (1 lb) fresh or frozen broad beans (shelled weight)
1 tablespoon chopped summer savory, dill or tarragon
4 spring onions, trimmed and finely chopped
1 tablespoon horseradish sauce
150 ml (¼ pint) natural yogurt
salt and pepper
summer savory, dill or tarragon sprig, to garnish

If using fresh beans, plunge them into 1 cm (½ inch) boiling water in a saucepan. Bring back to the boil, cover and simmer for 10–12 minutes. If using frozen beans, cook according to the instructions on the packet. Drain well.

Mix together all the other ingredients for the salad in a serving dish.

Toss the warm beans in the dressing. Taste, and add a little more horseradish or salt if necessary. Serve immediately, garnished with a sprig of summer savory, dill or tarragon.

■ COOK'S TIP

Put the beans and their soaking water in a large saucepan. Bring to the boil and fast boil for 10 minutes, then cover and simmer gently for 20 minutes.

■ COOK'S TIP

If you are able to buy fresh horseradish, use ½–1 teaspoon of finely grated horseradish instead of the horseradish sauce.

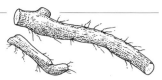

87

mexican refried beans

Preparation time
5 minutes, plus soaking

Cooking time
about 2½ hours

Serves 8

Calories
267 per portion

Suitable for vegans

500 g (1 lb) dried black-eyed, pinto or red kidney beans, soaked overnight and drained
1 onion, diced
1 garlic clove, crushed
1.2 litres (2 pints) water
125 g (4 oz) white vegetable fat
pinch of chilli powder
salt
mint sprigs, to garnish

Put the beans in a large pan with the onion, garlic and water. Bring to the boil and fast boil for 10 minutes, then lower the heat and simmer until the beans are tender – about 2 hours. adding more water if necessary.

Drain, reserving some of the liquid. Lightly mash the beans with a fork – do not purée.

Heat the fat in a wide, heavy frying pan and add the chilli powder and mashed beans. Cook, stirring and turning until the beans are thickened and the fat is absorbed. Season with salt to taste. Add a little of the reserved bean liquid if the beans look dry. Serve garnished with sprigs of mint.

■ **COOK'S TIP**

Refried beans are ideal with taco shells. Simply heat the shells in the oven, fill with the beans and top with salad, salsa sauce, soured cream and cheese.

88

lentil and watercress patties

Preparation time
30 minutes

Cooking time
50 minutes

Serves 6

Calories
423 per portion

Suitable for vegans

3 tablespoons vegetable oil
1 large onion, finely chopped
1 garlic clove, crushed
250 g (8 oz) split red lentils
600 ml (1 pint) vegetable stock
few parsley stalks
2 tablespoons tomato purée
125 g (4 oz) blanched almonds, chopped
1 bunch of watercress, finely chopped
1 tablespoon chopped mint
2 tablespoons plain flour
oil, for frying
salt and pepper

Heat the oil in a medium pan and fry the onion and garlic over a moderate heat for 2 minutes, stirring once or twice. Add the lentils and stir to coat them with oil. Pour on the stock, add the parsley stalks and bring to the boil. Lower the heat, cover the pan and simmer for 40 minutes. The lentils should be soft and the stock absorbed – increase the heat to evaporate any stock remaining. Discard the parsley and remove the pan from the heat.

Beat the lentils with a wooden spoon and stir in the tomato purée, almonds, watercress and mint. Season with salt and pepper. Divide the mixture into 12 and mould into 'burger' shapes. Toss in the flour to coat them thoroughly. Fry the patties in hot oil over a moderate heat for about 5 minutes on each side, or until they are crisp. Serve with Tomato sauce (see Cook's Tip) and a green salad.

■ **COOK'S TIP**

For the Tomato sauce, heat 2 tablespoons olive oil in a pan, add a chopped onion and sauté, for 5 minutes. Stir in a 400 g (13 oz) can chopped tomatoes, 150 ml (¼ pint) vegetable stock, 2 teaspoons tomato purée and salt and pepper to taste. Simmer for 30 minutes.

93

walnut and lentil loaf

Preparation time
10 minutes

Cooking time
1½ hours

Oven temperature
190°C (375°F)
gas 5

Serves 6

Calories
245 per portion

1 tablespoon oil
1 onion, chopped
1 garlic clove, crushed
2 celery sticks, sliced
175 g (6 oz) green lentils
450 ml (¾ pint) water
125 g (4 oz) walnuts, ground
50 g (2 oz) wholewheat breadcrumbs
2 tablespoons chopped parsley
1 tablespoon shoyu
1 medium egg, beaten
salt and pepper
thyme sprigs, to garnish

Heat the oil in a saucepan, add the onion and fry for a few minutes until softened. Add the garlic, celery, lentils and water and bring to the boil. Cover and simmer for 30–40 minutes, until the lentils are tender, stirring occasionally and removing the lid for the last 10 minutes to allow the moisture to evaporate.

Stir in the walnuts, breadcrumbs, parsley, shoyu, egg and salt and pepper to taste, and mix thoroughly.

Line a 500 g (1 lb) loaf tin with foil to cover the bottom and long sides. Brush with oil. Spoon the mixture into the tin, cover with foil and bake in a moderately hot oven for 45–50 minutes.

Leave in the tin for 2 minutes, then loosen with a knife and turn out on to a warmed serving dish. Garnish with thyme. Serve with a tomato sauce (see recipe 88) or tomato mayonnaise.

94

lentil croquettes

Preparation time
15–20 minutes, plus chilling

Cooking time
30–35 minutes

Serves 4–6

Calories
567–375 per portion

250 g (8 oz) red lentils, rinsed
600 ml (1 pint) water
1 tablespoon oil
175 g (6 oz) low-fat hard cheese, grated
50 g (2 oz) peanut butter
50 g (2 oz) fresh wholemeal breadcrumbs
2 tablespoons chopped parsley
juice of 1 lemon
1–2 teaspoons yeast extract
salt and pepper
FOR THE COATING
1 medium egg, beaten
50–75 g (2–3 oz) wholemeal breadcrumbs
2–3 tablespoons oil, for cooking

Place the lentils in a pan with the water and simmer, covered, for 30 minutes, until the water is absorbed and the lentils form a purée. Add the oil, cheese, peanut butter, breadcrumbs, parsley, lemon juice, yeast extract and salt and pepper to taste. Mix well. Cool, then chill lightly.

Shape large spoonfuls of the mixture into croquettes. Coat each with egg and breadcrumbs. Chill again. Fry the croquettes in the oil, turning once until golden all over. Drain on absorbent kitchen paper and serve with a salad.

■ COOK'S TIP

If you do not have a food processor or blender, then you will find a rotary grater useful for grinding nuts.

■ COOK'S TIP

Dry, uncooked breadcrumbs are best for coating food before frying. Make the fresh crumbs, then dry them in a very cool oven until crisp. For a fine texture put them through the food processor once more. If thoroughly dried they store well in an airtight container in a cool place.

95

lentil patties

Preparation time
15 minutes, plus cooling

Cooking time
1 hour 20 minutes

Serves 4

Calories
320 per portion

175 g (6 oz) lentils, rinsed
450 ml (¾ pint) cold water
1 large onion, finely chopped
4 tablespoons wholemeal flour
2 tablespoons chopped mixed herbs
grated nutmeg
oil, for shallow-frying
salt and pepper
FOR THE GARNISH
watercress sprigs
tomato wedges

Place the lentils and water in a saucepan and bring to the boil. Reduce the heat, cover the pan and simmer gently for 30–40 minutes until all the water has been absorbed. Remove from the heat and allow to cool.

Mix the onion into the lentils, and stir in the flour, herbs, nutmeg and salt and pepper. Shape the mixture into eight patties, about 10 cm (4 inches) in diameter, on a floured board.

Shallow fry the patties slowly in oil until golden brown, then turn them over and brown the second side. Drain, then serve, garnished with watercress sprigs and tomato wedges.

■ COOK'S TIP

These patties are delicious served with mayonnaise or soured cream, accompanied by baked potatoes and a green salad.

96

spiced lentil dhal

Preparation time
5 minutes

Cooking time
35 minutes

Serves 4–6

Calories
110–70 per portion

125 g (4 oz) red lentils
2 small onions, chopped
450 ml (¾ pint) boiling vegetable stock
3 garlic cloves, crushed
½ teaspoon ground turmeric
1 teaspoon paprika
1 teaspoon ground coriander
1 teaspoon ground cumin

Place all the ingredients in a large saucepan, bring to the boil, then reduce the heat and simmer for about 30 minutes or until cooked. The dhal should be thick and the lentils should be soft and still retain their shape. Serve the dhal as an accompaniment to an Indian main dish.

■ COOK'S TIP

Cook the dhal, pack into a rigid container, label and freeze. Use within 3 months. Reheat from frozen in a moderately hot oven, 200°C (400°F) gas 6, for about 20 minutes or cook on high in the microwave for 10–15 minutes.

101

sesame butter beans

Preparation time 20 minutes **Cooking time** 25–30 minutes **Serves 4** **Calories** 575 per portion	*125 ml (4 fl oz) oil* *1 teaspoon cumin seeds* *1 large onion, chopped* *125 g (4 oz) sesame seeds, finely ground* *1 tablespoon ground coriander* *1 x 400 g (13 oz) can chopped tomatoes* *2 teaspoons sugar* *1 teaspoon chilli powder* *1 teaspoon ground turmeric* *2 x 425 g (14 oz) cans butter beans, drained* *salt* *1 tablespoon chopped coriander, to garnish*

Heat the oil in a pan, add the cumin seeds and fry until they begin to crackle. Add the onion and fry until soft and transparent.

Add the ground sesame seeds and fry for 3–5 minutes, then add the ground coriander and fry for a further minute. Stir in the tomatoes, salt to taste, the sugar, chilli powder and turmeric. Mix well and cook the sauce for 3–5 minutes.

Add the drained beans and stir carefully until well coated with the sauce. Simmer until the beans are thoroughly hot. Sprinkle with chopped coriander.

■ COOK'S TIP

For textural contrast and a good protein mix, combine this curry with a nutty, crunchy salad, such as Fruit Coleslaw (see recipe 276) or Crunchy Cabbage Salad (see recipe 277).

102

bean curry

Preparation time 10 minutes, plus soaking **Cooking time** 1 hour 10 minutes **Serves 4** **Calories** 345 per portion	*375 g (12 oz) red kidney beans, soaked overnight* *2 tablespoons oil* *1 garlic clove, crushed* *2.5 cm (1 inch) piece fresh root ginger, grated or finely chopped* *1 onion, chopped* *2 carrots, diced* *2 celery sticks, sliced* *125 g (4 oz) mushrooms, sliced* *¼ teaspoon chilli powder* *2 x 400 g (13 oz) cans tomatoes* *450 ml (¾ pint) water* *salt* *2 tablespoons chopped coriander leaves, to garnish*

Drain the beans and bring them to the boil with enough water to cover them by at least 2.5 cm (1 inch). Boil vigorously for 10 minutes, then reduce the heat, cover and simmer for about 1 hour or until tender. Check that the water level is maintained throughout cooking.

Meanwhile, heat the oil and cook the garlic, ginger and onion for 3 minutes. Add the carrots, celery and mushrooms and cook for 3 minutes. Stir in the chilli powder, drained cooked beans, tomatoes and the juice, water and a little salt. Cook for 15 minutes until the carrots are tender and the mixture fairly thick. Taste for seasoning and sprinkle with chopped coriander leaves. Serve with natural yogurt.

■ COOK'S TIP

Fresh root ginger keeps well in the salad drawer of the refrigerator. Look out for smooth, plump ginger with a fine skin that shows it is young and tender.

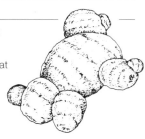

103

chilli bean tacos

Preparation time
15 minutes

Cooking time
35 minutes

Oven temperature
200°C (400°F),
gas 6

Serves 2–3

Calories
505–335 per portion

125 g (4 oz) frozen Mexican mix, or an equivalent weight of fresh vegetables including diced red and green peppers, sweetcorn and chopped onion
1 x 425 g (14 oz) can red kidney beans, juice reserved
½ teaspoon Tabasco sauce
2 garlic cloves, crushed
2 tablespoons tomato purée
6 Mexican taco shells
1 small lettuce, shredded
1 small onion, chopped
50 g (2 oz) Cheddar cheese, grated

Place the Mexican mix or fresh vegetables in a medium saucepan with a small amount of boiling water. Bring back to the boil, reduce the heat and cook for 10 minutes. Stir the kidney beans, Tabasco, crushed garlic, and tomato purée into the vegetables, then add enough of the reserved juice to make a thick sauce. Cook for another 10 minutes. Place the tacos on a baking tray and heat in a moderately hot oven for 10 minutes until hot.

Let guests fill their own tacos. First spoon a few tablespoons of the bean and vegetable mixture into the taco shells then top with the lettuce, onion and cheese.

104

green pea and potato curry

Preparation time
30 minutes

Cooking time
20–30 minutes

Serves 4

Calories
190 per portion

50 g (2 oz) butter or margarine
250 g (8 oz) fresh or frozen peas
250 g (8 oz) potatoes, diced
250 g (8 oz) onions, diced
1 tablespoon garam masala
1 teaspoon ground turmeric
1 teaspoon chilli powder

Heat the butter or margarine in a pan, add all the ingredients and stir-fry for a few minutes to mix well. Cover and cook over a low heat for about 25–30 minutes or until the vegetables are tender. Stir occasionally during the cooking time to prevent sticking.

■ COOK'S TIP

The tacos need to be eaten with the fingers so have plenty of paper napkins available.

■ COOK'S TIP

When cooking with spices, it is a good idea to use a plastic cooking spoon instead of a wooden spoon which discolours and picks up flavours easily.

Alternatively, if you prepare spicy food frequently, then set aside a special wooden spoon for the purpose.

109

kidney bean coleslaw

Preparation time
30 minutes

Serves 4–6

Calories
210–140 per portion

250 g (8 oz) white cabbage, shredded
175 g (6 oz) carrots, grated
½ small onion, chopped
1 dessert apple, cored and grated
1 x 425 g (14 oz) can red kidney beans,
  drained
4 spring onions, chopped
2 tablespoons chopped parsley
50 g (2 oz) low-fat soft cheese
1 tablespoon lemon juice
2 tablespoons sunflower oil
2 tablespoons natural yogurt
salt and pepper
watercress sprigs, to garnish (optional)

Mix the cabbage, carrots, onion and apple. Add the beans, spring onions and parsley then season to taste with salt and pepper.

Mix the low-fat cheese with the lemon juice, oil and yogurt. Toss this dressing with the salad before serving.

A watercress garnish may be added, if liked.

110

colourful bean salad

Preparation time
15–20 minutes

Cooking time
15 minutes

Serves 4–6

Calories
275–185 per portion

500 g (1 lb) green beans, topped and
  tailed
pinch of grated nutmeg
3–4 tomatoes, quartered
625 g (1¼ lb) new potatoes, scrubbed and
  cooked
1 onion, chopped
1 small bunch of herbs, (e.g. chives,
  parsley, thyme) chopped
2 tablespoons mayonnaise
6 tablespoons double or soured cream
salt and pepper

Bring a large saucepan of water to the boil, add the beans with a little salt and the nutmeg. Bring back to the boil, then reduce the heat and cook gently for 10–12 minutes until tender. Drain, rinse under cold water, drain again and place in a serving bowl. Add the tomatoes and potatoes and toss well. Scatter the onion and herbs on top.

To make the dressing, blend the mayonnaise with the cream and salt and pepper to taste. Pour over the bean salad and toss well to mix.

■ COOK'S TIP

Sunflower oil is a polyunsaturated fat – a good choice for the health-conscious eater. Avoid blended oils, which may contain coconut or palm oil, both high in saturated fatty acids.

■ COOK'S TIP

Counting calories? Use low-fat yogurt in place of the double cream – you may need slightly less than the 6 tablespoons suggested above.

111

kidney bean and stilton salad

Preparation time 10 minutes	*1 x 425 g (14 oz) can red kidney beans* *250 g (8 oz) French beans, finely sliced or*
Serves 4	*250 g (8 oz) mangetout*
Calories 192 per portion	*juice of ½ lemon* *125 g (4 oz) cottage cheese* *75 g (3 oz) blue Stilton, broken into* *small pieces* *chopped parsley, to garnish (optional)*

Drain the kidney beans. Mix with the French beans or mangetout and the lemon juice. Spoon the cottage cheese on top and sprinkle over the crumbled Stilton. Garnish with parsley, if liked. Serve with hot garlic bread.

112

rice and bean salad

Preparation time 10 minutes	*1 bunch of watercress* *375 g (12 oz) cooked rice*
Serves 4	*1 x 425 g (14 oz) can black-eyed beans,*
Calories 285 per portion	*drained* *6 radishes, sliced* *12 olives, pitted* *1 tablespoon mayonnaise* *½ teaspoon salt*

Reserve a sprig of watercress for the garnish. Trim and separate the rest into small sprigs.

Mix together the rice, beans, radishes, olives, watercress, mayonnaise and salt. Serve immediately, garnished with the watercress sprig.

■ COOK'S TIP

To make garlic bread, beat a crushed garlic clove into butter and spread on slices of French bread, leaving them attached at the base. Wrap in foil and heat through in the oven.

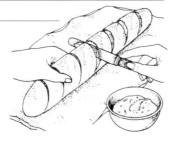

■ COOK'S TIP

To produce 375 g (12 oz) cooked rice, prepare 125 g (4 oz) raw rice. Instead of white or brown rice you may like to try wild rice – dark, long thin grains which require a little extra cooking.

113

felafel in pitta pockets

Preparation time 20 minutes	*2 x 425 g (14 oz) cans chickpeas* *1 onion, grated*
Cooking time 20 minutes	*1 garlic clove, crushed* *1 teaspoon ground cumin*
Oven temperature 110°C (255°F), gas ¼	*1 teaspoon ground coriander* *¼ teaspoon ground chilli* *½ teaspoon caraway seeds*
Serves 4	*3 tablespoons chopped parsley* *1 medium egg, beaten*
Calories 520 per portion	*75 g (3 oz) wholemeal flour* *vegetable oil, for shallow-frying* *salt and pepper*
	TO SERVE
	4 wholemeal pitta breads *mixed salad*

Drain the chick peas and reduce to a coarse paste in a food
processor. Mix with the next eight ingredients.

Form the mixture into small balls then pat them into small
flat cakes about 4 cm (1½ inches) across. Dip into the beaten egg,
then into the flour. Shallow fry in oil in batches for about 5 minutes until crisp and brown. Drain on absorbent kitchen paper.

Warm pitta breads for 5 minutes, split along one side and fill
the pockets with salad and the hot felafel. Serve immediately.

114

bean pâté

Preparation time 10 minutes	*1 onion, chopped* *2 garlic cloves, crushed*
Cooking time 5 minutes	*1 tablespoon oil* *1 tablespoon peanut butter, smooth or*
Serves 4	*crunchy, or tahini* *juice of 1 lemon*
Calories 145 per portion	*2 tablespoons chopped parsley* *1 x 425 g (14 oz) can butter beans* *dill sprigs, to garnish (optional)*

Cook the onion and garlic in the oil until softened, about 5 minutes. Mix together the onion mixture, peanut butter or tahini,
lemon juice and parsley. Mash with a fork or blend briefly in a
food processor. Press into an oiled dish, cover and chill. Garnish
with dill sprigs, if using.

■ COOK'S TIP

For convenience, the uncooked
felafel can be prepared up to
8 hours in advance and kept tightly
covered with cling film to prevent
the flavours permeating the other
foods in the refrigerator.

■ COOK'S TIP

This pâté looks good served in
individual ramekin dishes. Place
each on a saucer and garnish
with wedges of lemon and
parsley sprigs.

115

spanish chickpeas

Preparation time
20 minutes, plus soaking

Cooking time
1½–2 hours

Serves 4

Calories
320 per portion

175 g (6 oz) dried chickpeas
900 ml (1½ pints) cold water
1 tablespoon oil
1 teaspoon salt
25 g (1 oz) butter
1 onion, chopped
1 garlic clove, crushed
1 green pepper, cored, deseeded and
    chopped
1 x 400 g (13 oz) can chopped tomatoes
1 x 375 g (12 oz) can sweetcorn, drained
2 green chillies, deseeded and chopped
¼ teaspoons oregano
generous pinch of ground cumin

Soak the chickpeas overnight in water to cover. Drain, discarding peas that have not absorbed any water. Place in a saucepan, add the measured cold water and the oil and bring to the boil. Reduce the heat, cover the pan and simmer for 1–1½ hours, until the chickpeas are tender, adding the salt towards the end of cooking. Drain and return the chickpeas to the saucepan.

Melt the butter in a heavy-based frying pan and sauté the onion, garlic and green pepper until the onion is soft. Stir in the tomatoes, sweetcorn, chillies, oregano and cumin.

Add the sautéed onion mixture to the chickpeas. Cover and cook gently, stirring frequently, for 20 minutes. Serve hot.

116

creamed lentils

Preparation time
10 minutes

Cooking time
30–35 minutes

Serves 4

Calories
470 per portion

25 g (1 oz) butter
1 small onion, chopped
1 garlic clove, crushed
1 leek, sliced and washed
2 carrots, chopped
375 g (12 oz) green lentils
1 litre (1¼ pints) water
2 cloves
1 bay leaf
3 white peppercorns
3 tablespoons snipped chives
300 ml (½ pint) soured cream
salt and pepper

Melt the butter in a saucepan and cook the onion, garlic, leek and carrots for 3 minutes, stirring frequently. Add the lentils and cook for 1 minute, stirring. Add the water, cloves, bay leaf and peppercorns, bring to the boil, cover and cook very gently for 25–30 minutes or until the lentils are tender but still have some bite. Check that the mixture doesn't become too dry. Remove the cloves and bay leaf. Turn into a warmed serving dish. Stir half the chives into half the soured cream and swirl through the lentils.

Swirl over the remaining soured cream and sprinkle with the remaining chives. Serve with wholewheat pasta or brown rice.

■ COOK'S TIP

Canned chickpeas can be used instead of the dried variety. They should be drained and mixed with the sautéed mixture, then cooked as above.

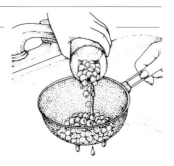

■ COOK'S TIP

Dried flower buds of the Asian clove tree, cloves have a wonderful spicy fragrance. They are used in sweet and savoury dishes but extracted before serving to avoid the rather over powering effect of biting on them.

main courses

These superb nutritionally balanced dishes are packed with flavour, colour and goodness. Perfect for the family, and for special occasions, choose from the substantial Winter Stew or the lighter Courgette Flan. There are lots of ideas for delicious accompaniments, and variations to give every meal time a different twist.

117
spinach pancakes

Preparation time
25 minutes, plus standing

Cooking time
about 25 minutes

Oven temperature
190°C (375°F) gas 5

Serves 4

Calories
472 per portion

125 g (4 oz) wholemeal flour
1 medium egg, beaten
300 ml (½ pint) milk
FOR THE FILLING
350 g (12 oz) frozen chopped spinach
175 g (6 oz) ricotta cheese
2 tablespoons grated Parmesan cheese
1 medium egg
grated nutmeg
Cheese Sauce (see Cook's Tip)
1 tablespoon grated Parmesan cheese
1 tablespoon wholemeal breadcrumbs
salt and pepper

Make and cook the pancakes as for Pancakes with Celery and Peanuts (see recipe 118).

To make the filling, place the spinach in a pan and heat gently until completely thawed. Cook for 2 minutes, then pour off any liquid. Beat in the cheeses, egg, nutmeg and salt and pepper to taste. Divide the filling between the pancakes, roll up and place in an oiled, shallow ovenproof dish.

Make the cheese sauce.

Spoon the sauce over the pancakes, then sprinkle with the Parmesan cheese and breadcrumbs. Cook in a preheated moderately hot oven for 15–20 minutes, until golden.

118
pancakes with celery and peanuts

Preparation time
25 minutes, plus standing

Cooking time
about 25 minutes

Serves 4

Calories
203 per portion

50 g (2 oz) wholemeal flour
pinch of salt
1 egg
150 ml (¼ pint) skimmed milk and water mixed
1 tablespoon chopped parsley
FOR THE FILLING
1 tablespoon olive oil, plus extra for cooking the pancakes
6 celery sticks, roughly chopped
125 g (4 oz) button mushrooms, chopped
50 g (2 oz) unsalted, skinned peanuts, roughly chopped
½ teaspoon dried oregano
pepper
2 tablespoons chopped parsley

Mix the flour and salt in a bowl; make a well in the centre, and add the egg and the milk plus water. Beat until smooth and stir in the parsley. Cover and leave for 20 minutes.

Heat 1 tablespoon of oil in a frying pan and fry the celery for 3–4 minutes. Add the mushrooms, peanuts, oregano and pepper and cook for 4–5 minutes. Stir in the parsley.

Brush the base of a small frying pan with oil. When hot add sufficient batter to thinly cover the base; cook until golden on both sides. Cook 7 more pancakes.

Divide the filling between the pancakes, roll them up and serve, garnished with parsley, if liked.

■ COOK'S TIP

Cheese sauce: heat 2 tablespoons oil, stir in 2 tablespoons wholemeal flour, off the heat. Blend in 300 ml (½ pint) milk and bring to the boil, stirring, until thickened. Take off the heat and stir in 50 g (2 oz) grated vegetarian Cheddar cheese.

■ COOK'S TIP

Don't worry if the pancake batter has lumps. Simply push it through a sieve into a clean bowl for smooth results.

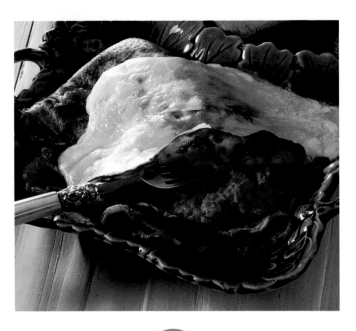

119

pancakes with red pepper and tomato filling

Preparation time 30 minutes, plus standing	*750 g (1½ lb) red peppers* *2 tablespoons olive oil* *1 onion, chopped.*
Cooking time 1 hour 10 minutes	*1½ kg (3 lb) tomatoes, skinned, deseeded* * and chopped*
Oven temperature 190°C (375°F) gas 5	*8 pancakes (see recipe 118)* *300 ml (½ pint) soured cream or thick* * Greek yogurt*
Serves 4	*paprika*
Calories 442 per portion	*salt and pepper*

First make the filling. Heat the red peppers under a hot grill until they are browned all over, and the outer skins will come off easily. Put the peppers into cold water and peel off the skins. Remove the stalk ends and seeds and cut the flesh into small pieces. Heat the oil in a large saucepan and fry the onion for 10 minutes, then put in the peppers and tomatoes and cook, uncovered, for about 30 minutes, until the mixture is fairly thick and dry. Stir frequently to prevent burning. Season to taste with salt and pepper.

Make and cook the pancakes.

To assemble the dish, put a spoonful of the pepper and tomato mixture on each pancake and roll up neatly. Place the pancakes in a shallow ovenproof dish. Give the cream a quick stir, then spoon over the pancakes. Sprinkle with paprika and cover with foil. Place in a preheated oven and bake for about 20 minutes, until heated through. Serve at once.

■ COOK'S TIP

Pancakes can be made in advance and deep-frozen. To freeze the pancakes, stack them up on top of each other with a layer of greaseproof paper between each one. Allow to cool, then pack in a polythene bag. Defrost and bake the pancakes for about 10–15 minutes until hot through.

120

tomato-stuffed pancakes

Preparation time 45 minutes	*8 pancakes (see recipe 118)* FOR THE FILLING
Cooking time 1½ hours	*25 g (1 oz) butter* *½ onion, finely chopped*
Oven temperature 190°C (375°F) gas 5	*4 tomatoes, skinned and chopped* *125 g (4 oz) mushrooms, chopped* *1 teaspoon mixed herbs*
Serves 4	*25 g (1 oz) fresh white breadcrumbs* *salt and pepper*
Calories 500 per portion	FOR THE TOPPING *40 g (1½ oz) butter* *40 g (1½ oz) plain flour* *300 ml (½ pint) milk* *75 g (3 oz) vegetarian Cheddar, grated*

Make the pancakes. To make the filling, melt the butter in a medium pan and fry the onion, tomatoes and mushrooms until reduced to a pulp. Stir in the herbs and breadcrumbs and season well with salt and pepper. Divide the filling between the pancakes and roll them up. Arrange side by side in an ovenproof dish.

To make the topping, melt the butter in a heavy pan, remove from the heat and stir in the flour. Gradually beat in the milk, then return to the heat and bring to the boil, stirring constantly. Simmer for 3–4 minutes, stirring. Stir 50 g (2 oz) of the cheese into the white sauce, season with salt and pepper and pour over the pancakes. Sprinkle over the remaining cheese. Bake in a preheated oven for 30 minutes until golden brown.

■ COOK'S TIP

Instead of the fresh tomatoes, use a 200 g (7 oz) can of chopped tomatoes. Add 1 tablespoon of freshly chopped basil instead of the mixed herbs, if liked.

121

winter stew

Preparation time 30 minutes	*2–3 tablespoons vegetable oil*
	1 large onion, chopped
Cooking time 1½ hours	*5–6 root vegetables (carrots, parsnips etc),* *in bite-sized pieces*
Oven temperature 200°C (400°F) gas 6	*2 leeks, halved, washed and sliced*
	3 potatoes, cut into chunks
	1 tablespoon plain white flour
Serves 4	*1.2 litres (2 pints) hot vegetable stock*
Calories 392 per portion	*1 tablespoon tomato purée*
	¼ teaspoon celery seeds
Suitable for vegans using soya margarine	*dumplings (see Cook's Tip)*
	salt and pepper
	1 tablespoon chopped parsley, to garnish

Heat a little of the oil in a pan, and fry the onion quickly until golden brown. Transfer to an ovenproof casserole. Adding a little more oil as necessary, brown the vegetables in batches then transfer to the casserole. Add a little more oil to the pan, stir in the flour, and cook over a steady heat, stirring, until the flour is browned. Pour in the stock and bring to the boil, stirring, until the stock has thickened. Add the tomato purée, celery seeds, salt and pepper, then pour over the vegetables. Cover the casserole and cook in a preheated oven for 50 minutes. Meanwhile, make the dumplings.

When the casserole has cooked 50 minutes, remove the lid and add the dumplings. Replace the lid and put back into the oven for a further 20–30 minutes. The dumplings will rise to the top and swell to double their size. Serve the stew hot, garnished with parsley.

■ COOK'S TIP

For the dumplings, rub 25 g (1 oz) vegetable or soya margarine into 175 g (6 oz) wholemeal self-raising flour. Add 1 teaspoon dried mixed herbs and salt and pepper.

Mix to a soft dough with 1 tablespoon vegetable oil and 8 tablespoons water. Shape into 8 balls.

122

walnut-stuffed aubergines

Preparation time 30 minutes	*2 large aubergines*
	2 tablespoons olive oil
Cooking time 40 minutes	*1 onion, chopped*
	2 garlic cloves, crushed
Oven temperature 190°C (375°F) gas 5	*3 celery sticks, chopped*
	175 g (6 oz) mushrooms, chopped
	6 tablespoons brown rice, cooked *according to packet instructions*
Serves 4	*50 g (2 oz) walnuts, ground*
Calories 248 per portion	*1 tablespoon tomato purée*
	2 tablespoons chopped parsley
	75 g (3 oz) vegetarian Cheddar cheese, *grated*
	salt and pepper
	watercress sprig, to garnish

Prick the aubergines all over, cut in half lengthways and place cut side down on a greased baking sheet. Bake in a preheated oven for 30 minutes.

Meanwhile, heat the oil in a pan, add the onion and fry until softened. Add the garlic and celery and fry for 5 minutes. Add the mushrooms and cook, stirring, for 3 minutes. Stir in the rice, walnuts, tomato purée, parsley and salt and pepper. Turn off the heat.

Scoop the flesh from the aubergines, without breaking the skins, chop finely and mix with the fried mixture. Pile into the aubergine skins, sprinkle with the cheese and heat under a hot grill until bubbling. Garnish with watercress and serve with a crisp, mixed salad.

■ COOK'S TIP

To scoop out the flesh of an aubergine, halve it lengthways and make criss-cross cuts through each half with a sharp knife without penetrating the skin. Carefully cut out the flesh.

123

hot boston beans

Preparation time
20 minutes, plus
soaking

Cooking time
2¾ hours

Oven temperature
150°C (300°F)
gas 2

Serves 4

Calories
303 per portion

*250 g (8 oz) haricot beans, soaked
    overnight in cold water*
1 tablespoon vegetable oil
2 onions, chopped
4 tablespoons clear honey
3 tablespoons soy sauce
½ teaspoon Tabasco sauce
3 tablespoons wine vinegar
1 teaspoon English mustard powder
½–1 teaspoon ground chilli
1 teaspoon paprika
4 tablespoons tomato purée
450 ml (¾ pint) hot vegetable stock
4 tablespoons orange juice
2 teaspoons plain wholemeal flour
2 tablespoons water
2 red peppers, cored, deseeded and sliced

Rinse the beans and put in a pan with water to cover. Bring to the boil and simmer for 30 minutes. Drain. Tip into a casserole.

Heat the oil in a large pan and gently fry the onions until golden. Stir in the honey, soy sauce, Tabasco sauce, vinegar, mustard, chilli, paprika and tomato purée.

Pour in the hot stock and orange juice and bring to the boil. Pour over the beans, cover the casserole and cook in the centre of a preheated oven for 1½ hours.

Blend the flour with the water and stir into the beans. Add the red peppers. Cover and return to the oven for 1 hour until the sauce is rich and thick and the beans tender.

■ COOK'S TIP

The dish can be prepared up to 24 hours in advance and kept covered and chilled. Reheat in the oven for about 1 hour. Serve it with lots of hot garlic bread.

124

stuffed vegetables

Preparation time
40 minutes

Cooking time
20–25 minutes

Oven temperature
200°C (400°F)
gas 6

Serves 4

Calories
483 per portion

Suitable for vegans

2 aubergines
2 large courgettes
2 large Mediterranean tomatoes
4 large flat field mushrooms
vegetable oil, for brushing
1 tablespoon vegetable oil
1 garlic clove, crushed
1 large onion, chopped
125 g (4 oz) mushrooms, chopped
200 g (7 oz) wholemeal breadcrumbs
2 tablespoons chopped basil
½ teaspoon yeast extract

Trim the aubergines and courgettes and halve lengthways. Hollow out the centres and cut the flesh into small pieces. Blanch the shells in boiling water for 2 minutes, then drain and set aside. Cut the tomatoes in half and scoop the flesh and seeds into a bowl. Trim the stalks from the mushrooms and reserve. Brush all the vegetable cases with oil, inside and out, and arrange in 2 roasting tins.

Heat the oil in a pan and fry the garlic and onion until golden brown. Chop the reserved mushroom stalks and add them together with the mushrooms, breadcrumbs, basil, yeast extract, aubergine and courgette pieces and the tomato flesh. Mix the stuffing, season and spoon into the prepared vegetable cases. Pour 2–3 tablespoons of water into each roasting tin and bake in a preheated oven for about 20 minutes.

Lift the vegetables carefully on to a warm serving dish and sprinkle over the garnish (see Cook's Tip).

■ COOK'S TIP

For the garnish, heat 2 teaspoons vegetable oil in a small pan, then add 2 tablespoons pumpkin seeds. Cook for 1–2 minutes until browned. Drain on absorbent kitchen paper, cool and mix with 1 tablespoon chopped fresh parsley.

125

savoury nut roast

Preparation time 30 minutes	*50 g (2 oz) butter or soya margarine* *2 large onions, finely chopped*
Cooking time 50 minutes	*125 g (4 oz) cashew nuts, grated, or* *125 g (4 oz) peanuts, grated*
Oven temperature 180°C (350°F) gas 4	*125 g (4 oz) hazelnuts or almonds, grated* *125 g (4 oz) soft wholewheat* *breadcrumbs*
Serves 4	*1 tablespoon chopped mixed herbs*
Calories 618 per portion	*1–2 teaspoons yeast extract* *salt and pepper*
Suitable for vegans using soya margarine	*parsley sprigs, to garnish*

Grease a 20 cm (8 inch) square tin or shallow casserole dish. Melt the fat in a large saucepan and fry the onions gently for 10 minutes, until tender. Add the nuts, breadcrumbs, herbs, yeast extract and salt and pepper to taste. Press into the prepared tin or casserole dish and smooth the top. Bake in a preheated oven for 35–40 minutes. Ease the nut roast out of the tin or casserole; cut it into wedges and serve these on individual plates or arrange them on a warmed serving dish with vegetables and garnished with sprigs of parsley if wished. Serve with vegetarian sherry gravy (see Cook's Tip) and vegetables.

126

couscous with spiced vegetable stew

Preparation time 25 minutes	*375 g (12 oz) couscous* *½ teaspoon salt dissolved in 600 ml* *(1 pint) warm water*
Cooking time 45 minutes	*4 tablespoons olive oil* *2 onions, chopped*
Serves 4	*500 g (1 lb) carrots, sliced*

Calories
725 per portion
	2 teaspoons each cinnamon, ground
	    cumin and ground coriander
	125 g (4 oz) raisins
	2 x 425 g (14 oz) cans chickpeas, drained,
	    or 500 g (1 lb) frozen beans, peas or
	    sweetcorn
	900 ml (1½ pints) water
	4 tablespoons tomato purée
	2 tablespoons chopped parsley
	salt and pepper
	lemon wedges, to garnish

Place the couscous in a bowl. Add the water and set aside. Heat half the oil in the saucepan part of a steamer. Add the onions and carrots and fry gently for 10 minutes. Add the spices and cook for 2–3 minutes, stirring. Put in the raisins and the chosen pulse, water and tomato purée. Bring to the boil then reduce the heat so the stew just simmers. Now put the couscous into the top part of the steamer, over the stew. Cover and steam 25–30 minutes. Season to taste with salt and pepper. Stir the remaining oil and the parsley into the couscous. Garnish with lemon wedges.

■ COOK'S TIP

For the gravy, put 300 ml (1 pint) vegetable stock, 1½ teaspoons soy sauce and 1 tablespoon redcurrant jelly into a pan and bring to the boil.

Blend 1½ teaspoons cornflour with 1½ tablespoons sherry. Stir in a little hot liquid, tip into pan, stir and simmer until thickened.

■ COOK'S TIP

Couscous is a pre-cooked grain, so it only needs to be soaked in water, which it will absorb, as described in the recipe, then heated through.

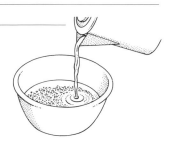

127

vegetable layer

Preparation time
20 minutes
 	
Cooking time
45 minutes
 	
Oven temperature
200°C (400°F)
gas 6
 	
Serves 4
 	
Calories
315 per portion
	1 kg (2 lb) fresh spinach, washed and
	   stalks removed
	1 small cauliflower, cut into florets
	125 g (4 oz) low-fat vegetarian Cheddar,
	   grated
	250 g (8 oz) tomatoes, skinned and sliced
	2 tablespoons chopped parsley
	125 g (4 oz) button mushrooms, sliced
	600 ml (1 pint) natural yogurt
	3 medium eggs
	pinch of grated nutmeg
	25 g (1 oz) jumbo oats
	salt and pepper

Cook the spinach, without added water, over moderate heat for about 10 minutes, stirring frequently until the leaves have wilted. Turn into a colander and press it to extract the moisture. Cook the cauliflower in boiling, salted water for about 10 minutes until the florets are beginning to soften.

Place the spinach in a shallow, greased baking dish. Sprinkle with 25 g (1 oz) of the cheese. Cover with the tomatoes, season with pepper, sprinkle on 1 tablespoon of the parsley, then cover with the mushrooms and the cauliflower.

In a bowl, beat the yogurt and beat in the eggs. Season with salt, pepper and nutmeg and stir in 50 g (2 oz) of the cheese. Pour the sauce over the vegetables. Mix the remaining cheese and parsley with the oats and sprinkle on top.

Place the dish on a baking sheet and cook in a preheated oven for 30 minutes or until the topping is brown.

■ COOK'S TIP

Parsley is especially rich in vitamins A and C, and also iron, iodine and calcium. It is said that chewing a sprig freshens the breath, especially after eating garlic.

128

ratatouille au gratin

Preparation time
30 minutes
 	
Cooking time
50 minutes
 	
Oven temperature
190°C (375°F)
gas 5
 	
Serves 4
 	
Calories
486 per portion
	6 tablespoons olive oil
	1 small aubergine, sliced
	2 garlic cloves, crushed
	375 g (12 oz) courgettes, sliced
	1 red pepper, cored, deseeded and sliced
	375 g (12 oz) tomatoes, skinned and
	   sliced
	1 tablespoon chopped basil
	500 g (1 lb) potatoes, boiled and sliced
	250 g (8 oz) vegetarian Mozzarella
	   cheese, thinly sliced
	salt and pepper

Heat half the oil in a frying pan, add the aubergine and fry on both sides until just beginning to brown, adding more oil if necessary. Remove from the pan and drain on kitchen paper.

Add the remaining oil to the pan and fry the garlic, courgettes and red pepper for 8–10 minutes, until softened, stirring occasionally. Add the tomatoes, basil, aubergine and salt and pepper to taste and simmer for 10 minutes.

Place the potatoes in a shallow ovenproof dish and cover with the ratatouille. Spread evenly to the edges and arrange the cheese slices over the top. Bake in a preheated oven for 15–20 minutes, until the cheese begins to melt. Serve immediately.

■ COOK'S TIP

For a lower fat version, steam the sliced aubergines gently over simmering water for about 3 minutes instead of frying them.

129

savoury sandwich pudding

Preparation time
20 minutes

Cooking time
45 minutes

Oven temperature
180°C (350°F)
gas 4

Serves 4

Calories
297 per portion

25 g (1 oz) butter
6 slices brown bread from a small loaf,
  crusts removed
125 g (4 oz) vegetarian Cheddar cheese,
  grated
3 tomatoes, skinned and sliced
2 eggs
½ teaspoon prepared English mustard
pinch of cayenne pepper
300 ml (½ pint) milk
salt and pepper

Lightly oil a 900 ml (1½ pint) pie dish.

Butter the bread and make 3 sandwiches using 75 g (3 oz) of the cheese and the tomatoes. Cut each one into 4 triangles and arrange in the dish.

Whisk together the eggs, mustard, cayenne pepper, milk and salt and pepper and gently pour over the sandwiches.

Sprinkle the remaining cheese on top and place near the top of the oven for about 45 minutes until puffed and golden.

130

nut-stuffed marrow

Preparation time
20 minutes

Cooking time
45 minutes–1 hour

Oven temperate
180°C (350°F)
gas 4

Serves 4

Calories
270 per portion

1 medium marrow
1 large onion, finely chopped
1 garlic clove, crushed
2 tablespoons olive oil
250 g (8 oz) fresh spinach, cooked and
  drained
125 g (4 oz) button mushrooms, finely
  chopped
50 g (2 oz) chopped pine nuts
25 g (1 oz) chopped toasted almonds
2 medium hard-boiled eggs, chopped
salt and pepper
flat leaf parsley, to garnish

Cut a slice from each end of the marrow, about 1 cm (½ inch) thick. Slice the marrow in half horizontally and scoop out and discard all the centre seeds.

Fry the onion and garlic gently in the olive oil for 4–5 minutes then mix with the remaining ingredients, to make a firm stuffing.

Pack the stuffing tightly into the marrow halves and wrap each half securely in foil. Bake in a preheated oven for about 45 minutes–1 hour until the marrow is tender.

Serve hot, cut into thick slices, accompanied by new potatoes with fennel and mint (see recipe 194) and garnished with parsley.

■ COOK'S TIP

Accompanied by a crisp green salad and followed by fresh fruit, this would make a satisfying and calcium-rich meal. Serve on its own for a light lunch.

■ COOK'S TIP

Instead of using marrow, try using peppers. Select a variety of colours and blanch in boiling water for a few minutes. Drain, plunge into cold water and drain again. Cut a slice from the stalk end of each pepper (for 'lids'), remove core and seeds, fill with stuffing, replace 'lids' and bake as above.

131

gougère with ratatouille

Preparation time 50 minutes	*50 g (2 oz) hard vegetable margarine*
	150 ml (¼ pint) water
Cooking time about 40 minutes	*65 g (2½ oz) plain wholemeal flour*
	2 medium eggs, beaten
Oven temperature 220°C (425°F) gas 7	*½ teaspoon prepared English mustard*
	50 g (2 oz) mature vegetarian Cheddar cheese, grated
Serves 4	*Ratatouille filling (see Cook's Tip)*
Calories 262 per portion	*salt and pepper*
	1 tablespoon chopped parsley, to garnish

First make the choux pastry. Put the margarine, water and ¼ teaspoon salt in a large pan. Have the flour ready on a small plate nearby. Bring the margarine and water to a fast boil, draw the pan off the heat and tip in the flour all at once. Beat briskly with a wooden spoon until the mixture forms a ball that rolls cleanly around the pan. Leave to cool for 5 minutes.

Slowly add the beaten egg, a little at a time, beating well between each addition. When all the egg is incorporated, beat in plenty of black pepper, the mustard and the grated cheese. Place adjoining heaped teaspoons of the mixture in a 25 cm (10 inch) circle on a greased baking tray, leaving rough peaks. Bake in a preheated oven for about 40 minutes, or until the choux pastry is puffy and brown. Transfer to a heated platter and spoon in the ratatouille filling. Serve garnished with parsley.

■ COOK'S TIP

A basic ratatouille includes onion, aubergine, courgettes, green and red peppers and tomatoes, all coarsely chopped or diced and cooked to a thick stew with 1–2 tablespoons oil, tomato purée and salt and pepper to taste, and chopped fresh basil.

132

vegetable gratin

Preparation time 20 minutes	*750 g (1½ lb) parsnips, sliced*
	1 large onion, sliced
Cooking time 40 minutes	*250 g (8 oz) carrots, scraped and sliced*
	250 g (8 oz) courgettes, sliced
Oven temperature 200°C (400°F) gas 6	*175 g (6 oz) cauliflower florets*
	250 g (8 oz) grated vegetarian Cheddar cheese
Serves 4	*salt and pepper*
Calories 311 per portion	*parsley sprigs, to garnish*

Boil the parsnips and onion in 2.5 cm (1 inch) water for 5–7 minutes, until nearly tender. In a separate saucepan boil or steam the carrots, courgettes and cauliflower for about 5 minutes, until nearly tender. Drain both lots of vegetables (keeping the cooking water for soup or stock).

Grease a large shallow ovenproof dish. Put half the onion mixture in a layer in the base, sprinkle with a third of the cheese, then the carrots, courgettes and cauliflower. Sprinkle with another third of the cheese and a little salt and pepper. Cover with the remaining onion mixture and the remaining cheese. Bake in a preheated oven for 30 minutes. Garnish with parsley sprigs and serve immediately.

■ COOK'S TIP

Use a fully matured Cheddar to give this dish plenty of flavour. Try using other vegetables such as broccoli, potato, French green beans, swede or turnip.

133

roulade with mushroom filling

Preparation time 30 minutes	*Mushroom filling (see Cook's Tip)* *5 medium eggs, separated*
Cooking time 20 minutes	*½ teaspoon prepared English mustard* *1 teaspoon vinegar*
Oven temperature 200°C (400°F) gas 6	*125 g (4 oz) grated mature vegetarian* * Cheddar cheese* *1 tablespoon grated Parmesan cheese*
Serves 4	*1 bunch of watercress, chopped*
Calories 278 per portion	*salt and pepper*

Line a 23 x 33 cm (9 x 13 inch) Swiss roll tin with greased grease-proof paper. Make the filling.

To make the roulade, whisk the egg yolks, mustard and vinegar with salt and pepper in a small bowl until light and thick. Fold in the Cheddar. In a large bowl, whisk the egg whites until stiff. Take 2 tablespoons of the whisked whites and fold them into the cheese and yolk mixture to loosen it, then spoon it into the remaining whites and gently fold together. Pour the mixture into the prepared tin and smooth the surface. Bake near the top of a preheated oven for 10–12 minutes until risen and golden brown. Remove from the oven but leave the oven on.

Sprinkle a sheet of greaseproof paper with Parmesan cheese and turn the roulade on to it. Peel off the greaseproof lining.

Gently reheat the filling, but do not let it boil, and spoon it over the roulade. Sprinkle with watercress, then roll the roulade up. Return to the oven for about 4 minutes.

■ COOK'S TIP

Mushroom filling: fry 1 chopped shallot in a little oil. Add 250 g (8 oz) chopped mushrooms. Cook 2–3 minutes. Add 65 ml (2½ fl oz) each white wine, vegetable stock, and salt and pepper. Cook gently for 5 minutes, then boil rapidly to reduce the liquid to 2 tablespoons. Stir in 3 tablespoons double cream.

134

creamy onion flan

Preparation time 20 minutes	*125 g (4 oz) self-raising wholewheat flour* *½ teaspoon salt*
Cooking time 1 hour 20 minutes	*65 g (2½ oz) butter or margarine* *1 tablespoon cold water*
Oven temperature 200°C (400°F) gas 6 then 180°C (350°F) gas 4)	FOR THE FILLING *500 g (1 lb) onions, sliced* *15 g (½ oz) butter or margarine* *150 ml (¼ pint) single cream* *2 medium egg yolks* *grated nutmeg*
Serves 4	*salt and pepper*
Calories 295 per portion	*chopped parsley, to garnish*

Sift the flour and salt into a bowl, then add 50 g (2 oz) of the fat and rub it into the flour until the mixture resembles breadcrumbs Add the water, then press the mixture together to make dough. Roll out on a lightly floured board, then use to line 20 cm (8 inch) flan tin. Lightly prick the base of the flan.

Bake in a preheated oven at the higher setting for 15–20 minutes, until the pastry is firm and golden brown. Just before you take the flan out of the oven, put the remaining 15 g (½ oz) fat into a small saucepan and melt. When the flan case is cooked, use the hot fat to brush the inside surface. Turn the oven down to the lower setting.

Fry the onions in the butter or margarine for 15–20 minutes, until very soft. Take off the heat and add the cream, egg yolks, nutmeg and salt and pepper. Pour into the flan case, and bake for 30–35 minutes until just set. Serve the flan sprinkled with parsley.

■ COOK'S TIP

While making the pastry, place a baking tray in the oven to heat. If you place the flan tin on the baking tray while cooking the pastry, the flan will have a crisper base.

 135

courgette flan

Preparation time 35 minutes	*175 g (6 oz) plain wholemeal flour*
Cooking time 35 minutes	*75 g (3 oz) hard vegetable margarine*
Oven temperature 200°C (400°F) gas 6	*3 tablespoons water*
	1 tablespoon vegetable oil
	salt and pepper
Serves 4	FOR THE FILLING
Calories 373 per portion	*1 tablespoon vegetable oil*
	3 courgettes, about 125 g (4 oz), sliced
	2 bunches of watercress, stalks removed
	2 medium eggs
	150 ml (¼ pint) soured cream
	5 tablespoons milk

To make the pastry, put the flour and ¼ teaspoon salt in a bowl and rub in the margarine until the texture resembles fine breadcrumbs. Mix to a firm dough with the water and oil. Roll out on a floured surface and use to line a 20 cm (8 inch) fluted flan ring. Place the flan on a baking sheet and bake in a preheated oven for 15 minutes to set the pastry without browning.

Meanwhile, prepare the filling. Heat the oil in a pan and fry the courgettes quickly on both sides until brown. Drain. Fry the watercress for 30 seconds until soft, and chop coarsely. Spread the courgettes and watercress over the base of the flan.

Put the eggs, soured cream, milk and salt and pepper into a bowl and whisk together. Pull the centre shelf of the preheated oven out slightly and place the flan case on it, then pour the egg and cream mixture over the courgettes and slide the shelf gently into place. Bake for 25 minutes until the flan is set and lightly browned on top.

■ COOK'S TIP

The flan can be made up to 24 hours in advance and kept covered in the refrigerator. Warm through gently in a moderate oven before serving.

136

spinach roulade

Preparation time 30 minutes	*1 kg (2 lb) fresh spinach*
Cooking time 35 minutes	*15 g (½ oz) butter or margarine*
	4 medium eggs, separated (see Cook's Tip)
Oven temperature 200°C (400°F) gas 6	*a little grated Parmesan cheese*
	salt and pepper
Serves 4	FOR THE FILLING
Calories 376 per portion	*15 g (½ oz) butter or margarine*
	175 g (6 oz) button mushrooms, wiped and sliced
	300 ml (½ pint) soured cream
	grated nutmeg

Cook the spinach in a saucepan without water for about 10 minutes, until the spinach is tender. Drain thoroughly and chop. Add the butter or margarine, egg yolks and salt and pepper.

Line a shallow 18 x 28 cm (7 x 11 inch) Swiss roll tin with greased greaseproof paper to cover the base of the tin and extend 5 cm (2 inches) up each side. Sprinkle with Parmesan cheese. Whisk the egg whites until stiff and fold them into the spinach mixture. Pour into the tin and bake in a preheated oven for 10–15 minutes, until risen and springy to touch.

To make the filling, heat the fat in a saucepan and fry the mushrooms over a high heat for 2–3 minutes. Add the soured cream, a little salt, pepper and nutmeg and heat gently.

Turn out the cooked roulade on to greaseproof paper dusted with Parmesan; strip off the first greaseproof paper. Spread the filling over the roulade and roll it up. Slide on to an ovenproof dish, return to the oven and heat through for 5 minutes. Serve garnished with watercress if liked.

■ COOK'S TIP

To separate the egg white from the yolk, crack the shell in two over a bowl. Catch the yolk in one half of the shell and let the white fall into the bowl.

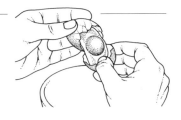

asparagus loaf

Preparation time 20 minutes	*1 small onion, grated*
Cooking time 1 hour	*125 g (4 oz) Parmesan cheese, grated*
Oven temperature 190°C (375°F) gas 5	*125 g (4 oz) ground almonds* *2 medium eggs* *150 ml (¼ pint) single cream* *grated nutmeg*
Serves 4	*500 g (1 lb) cooked, trimmed green asparagus (make sure that all the tough part has been removed)*
Calories 333 per portion	*salt and pepper* *parsley or watercress sprigs, to garnish*

Grease a 500 g (1 lb) loaf tin and line with a long strip of grease-proof paper to cover the base and the short sides. Mix together the onion, cheese, almonds, eggs and cream. Season with salt, pepper and grated nutmeg. Put a layer of this mixture in the bottom of the loaf tin, then arrange a layer of asparagus spears on top. Continue in layers like this until all the ingredients are used up, ending with the nut mixture. Bake in a preheated oven for 45–60 minutes, until risen and firm in the centre. Cool in the tin, then slip a knife round the sides and carefully turn out on to a plate. Strip off the greaseproof paper. Cut into slices, then cut in half again. Arrange the slices on a plate and garnish with parsley or watercress sprigs.

138

swede and apple casserole

Preparation time 15 minutes	*750 g (1½ lb) swede, cubed* *1 large cooking apple, peeled, cored and sliced*
Cooking time 50 minutes	*50 g (2 oz) light soft brown sugar*
Oven temperature 180°C (350°F) gas 4	*25 g (1 oz) butter* *3–4 tablespoons medium sherry (optional)*
Serves 4	*salt and pepper*
Calories 180 per portion	

Cook the swede in boiling, salted water for 20–30 minutes until tender. Drain well.

Put half the swede in a greased casserole and cover with half the apple slices. Sprinkle over half the brown sugar and salt and pepper to taste. Dot with half the butter. Repeat the layers. Sprinkle over the sherry, if using.

Cover and cook in a preheated oven for 30 minutes. Serve with baked potatoes or crusty French bread.

■ COOK'S TIP

It's well worth taking the time to arrange the asparagus neatly into the loaf tin. Season carefully as Parmesan tends to be salty. This loaf also makes a lovely summer dinner party

dish, served with mayonnaise, mangetout peas and some crisp lettuce.

■ COOK'S TIP

If preparing the apple in advance, remember to sprinkle over some lemon juice to prevent it going brown. Bramley apples are ideal for this dish.

139

sweetcorn and tomato bake

Preparation time 20 minutes	*3 tablespoons oil* *1 garlic clove, peeled* *275 g (9 oz) tomatoes, cut into wedges*
Cooking time about 50 minutes	*1 green pepper, cored, deseeded and* *chopped*
Oven temperature 220°C (425°F) Gas Mark 7	*1 x 325 g (11 oz) can sweetcorn* *pinch of grated nutmeg* *2 tablespoons unsalted peanuts, chopped*
Serves 4	*4–5 tablespoons double cream* *1 medium egg yolk*
Calories 284 per portion	*2 medium egg whites* *salt and pepper*

Heat the oil in a pan, add the garlic and fry until golden brown. Remove with a slotted spoon and discard. Add the tomatoes and green pepper and cook for 5 minutes. Add the sweetcorn with the can juice, nutmeg and salt and pepper to taste. Cook over a low heat for about 8 minutes. Transfer to a medium ovenproof dish or a 1.2 litre (2 pint) soufflé dish and stir in the peanuts.

Mix the cream with the egg yolk and stir into the vegetable mixture, blending well. Whisk the egg whites until they stand in stiff peaks, then fold into the vegetable mixture with a metal spoon. Cook in a preheated hot oven for 25–30 minutes.

140

spanish vegetable omelette

Preparation time 30 minutes	*8 tablespoons olive oil* *4 large potatoes, cubed* *2 onions, chopped*
Cooking time 30 minutes	*1 red pepper, cored, deseeded and* *chopped or cut into strips*
Serves 4–6	*1 green pepper, cored, deseeded and* *chopped or cut into strips*
Calories 446–298 per portion	*2 courgettes, cut into julienne strips* *2 small aubergines, finely chopped* *2–3 garlic cloves, crushed or finely* *chopped* *375 g (12 oz) tomatoes, finely chopped* *4 medium eggs* *salt and pepper*

Heat 5 tablespoons of the oil in a pan, add the potatoes and fry, over a low heat, turning frequently for about 15 minutes.

Meanwhile, heat the remaining oil in a large nonstick frying pan. Add the onions, peppers, courgettes and aubergines and fry over a low heat for about 8–10 minutes. Just before the vegetables are cooked, add the garlic, tomatoes and the cooked potatoes.

Beat the eggs with a little salt and black pepper. Pour the mixture evenly over the vegetables and cook over a low heat until the egg has just set.

Turn the omelette out on to a large plate and serve cut into wedges with a crisp salad.

■ COOK'S TIP

This savoury bake is delicious and very filling. It can be served as a meal in itself with French bread or Mangetout in Garlic Butter (see recipe 247).

■ COOK'S TIP

A Spanish omelette offers many possibilities for variation. The potato, onion, garlic and peppers are a must (the peppers especially, as these make the omelette juicy and moist), but the remaining vegetables can be replaced with others of your choice. It provides an ideal opportunity to use leftovers.

141

soufflé cheese potatoes

Preparation time
25 minutes

Cooking time
About 1½ hours

Oven temperature
190°C (375°F)
gas 5

Serves 4

Calories
291 per portion

4 medium potatoes, washed
20 g (¾ oz) butter
125 g (4 oz) vegetarian curd cheese
2 tablespoons grated Parmesan cheese
2 teaspoons French or wholegrain
*   mustard*
2 medium eggs, separated
salt and pepper

Place the potatoes on a baking sheet and bake in a preheated oven for about 1¼ hours, until tender. Cut a lengthways slice from the top of each potato; carefully scoop most of the centre potato into a bowl, leaving a shell.

Mix the scooped-out potato with the butter, salt and pepper to taste, curd cheese, 1 tablespoon of Parmesan, the mustard and egg yolks.

Whisk the egg whites until stiff but not dry; fold lightly into the potato mixture. Spoon into the potato shells then sprinkle with the remaining cheese.

Return the potatoes to the oven for a further 15–20 minutes, until well risen, golden and puffed. Serve immediately with a crisp salad.

142

broccoli soufflé

Preparation time
15–20 minutes

Cooking time
45–50 minutes

Oven temperature
190°C (375°F)
gas 5

Serves 4

Calories
355 per portion

500 g (1 lb) broccoli
2 tablespoons butter
2 tablespoons plain flour
150 ml (¼ pint) slimmed milk
3 tablespoons dry white wine
4 medium eggs, separated
3 tablespoons grated Parmesan cheese
2 tablespoons wholemeal breadcrumbs
salt and pepper

Cook the broccoli in boiling salted water until quite tender. Drain very thoroughly and liquidize.

Heat the butter in a pan, stir in the flour and cook for 1 minute. Gradually stir in the milk and wine; bring to the boil, stirring until the sauce has thickened.

Stir in the broccoli purée, egg yolks, 2 tablespoons of the Parmesan cheese and salt and pepper to taste.

Grease a 1.5 litre (2½ pint) soufflé dish and sprinkle with the breadcrumbs. Whisk the egg whites until stiff but not dry then fold lightly into the broccoli mixture. Transfer to the prepared soufflé dish and sprinkle with the remaining cheese.

Bake in a preheated oven for 25–30 minutes, until risen and golden. The soufflé will not rise as high as a standard soufflé. Serve immediately.

■ COOK'S TIP

Try different cheeses to vary the flavour. Choose a soft cheese with garlic and herbs, instead of curd cheese; vegetarian Stilton or Gouda instead of the Parmesan.

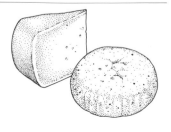

■ COOK'S TIP

Broccoli is a good source of vitamins A, B2 and C. It also supplies a good amount of iron. Choose broccoli heads which are a good colour and look fresh.

143

vegetable-cheese soufflé

Preparation time
30 minutes

Cooking time
40 minutes

Oven temperature
220°C (425°F)
gas 7

Serves 4

Calories
319 per portion

250 g (8 oz) potatoes
250 g (8 oz) prepared cauliflower, carrots,
    swede, parsnips, or Brussels sprouts
    (or a mixture)
4 tablespoons single cream
3 medium eggs, separated
125 g (4 oz) vegetarian Cheddar cheese,
    grated
salt and pepper

Cook the potatoes in boiling salted water until tender. At the same time, cook the cauliflower or other vegetables in boiling salted water. Drain well.

Mash the potatoes with the other vegetables until quite smooth, then beat in the cream, egg yolks, grated cheese, and salt and pepper to taste.

Whisk the egg whites until stiff, then fold into the vegetable mixture. Spoon into a greased 18 cm (7 inch) soufflé dish.

Bake in a preheated oven for 20 minutes until well risen and lightly coloured on top. Serve immediately with a mixed salad.

144

curried vegeburgers

Preparation time
30 minutes

Cooking time
15 minutes

Serves 4

Calories
175 per portion

2 tablespoons oil
2 onions, chopped
1 garlic clove, crushed
2 carrots, chopped
2 celery sticks, chopped
2 teaspoons curry powder
2 tablespoons chopped parsley
500 g (1 lb) potatoes, boiled and mashed
fresh wholemeal breadcrumbs
oil, for shallow-frying
salt and pepper

Heat the oil in a pan, add the onions and fry until softened. Add the garlic, carrots and celery and fry for 5 minutes, stirring. Mix in the curry powder and cook for 1 minute.

Add the fried vegetables and parsley to the potato and season with salt and pepper to taste. Divide the mixture into 8 pieces, shape into rounds, and coat with breadcrumbs. Press to flatten slightly and fry for 2 minutes on each side until golden. Serve with a tomato sauce (see recipe 88).

■ COOK'S TIP

Instead of Cheddar cheese, try using something different. Vegetarian Stilton, Edam, Gruyère or Red Leicester are all good alternatives which add an individual flavour.

■ COOK'S TIP

For a filling snack, place a vegeburger in a wholemeal bun with some salad, a slice of vegetarian Cheddar, and some tomato relish.

145

lettuce parcels

Preparation time
45 minutes, plus chilling

Serves 4

Calories
435 per portion

8 tablespoons cooked brown rice
3 spring onions, finely chopped
3 hard-boiled eggs, finely chopped
175 g (6 oz) vegetarian cottage cheese, sieved
1 tablespoon chopped tarragon
2 tablespoons low calorie mayonnaise
16 leaves from a round lettuce
salt and pepper
Avocado sauce (see Cook's Tip)
FOR THE GARNISH
12 mangetout, blanched
1 small red pepper, cored, deseeded and cut into matchstick strips

Mix the cooked rice with the spring onions, hard-boiled eggs, cottage cheese, tarragon, mayonnaise and salt and pepper.

Trim the excess stalk from the lettuce leaves. Cup one lettuce leaf in your hand; place an eighth of the rice mixture in the centre, and fold the lettuce leaf over and around it. Wrap another lettuce leaf over the top, and place 'seam-side' down in a shallow serving dish or a platter with a rim.

Repeat with the remaining lettuce leaves and rice filling, so that you have 8 parcels in all.

Spoon the prepared sauce over the lettuce parcels – if the sauce seems too thick, thin it with extra vegetable stock. Chill for 1 hour.

Garnish with mangetout and strips of red pepper.

■ COOK'S TIP

For the sauce, peel, halve and stone an avocado; chop the flesh and put it in a food processor with 1 garlic clove, 1 drained canned pimento, 1 tablespoon lemon juice and the rind from ½ lemon, 150 ml (¼ pint) vegetable stock and salt and pepper to taste. Blend until smooth; chill for 2 hours.

146

spinach soufflé

Preparation time
15 minutes

Cooking time
1–1¼ hours

Oven temperature
180°C (350°F) gas 4

Serves 4

Calories
300 per portion

165 g (5½ oz) frozen or fresh leaf spinach, chopped
50 g (2 oz) butter
½ onion, finely chopped
25 g (l oz) plain flour
150 ml (¼ pint) milk
3 medium eggs, separated
½ teaspoon dried thyme
25 g (1 oz) vegetarian Cheddar cheese, finely grated
salt and pepper

Grease a 15 cm (6 inch) soufflé dish.

Heat the frozen or fresh spinach over a low heat and add 15 g (½ oz) of the butter. Stir in the onion and season well with salt and pepper. Leave to cook gently.

Melt the remaining butter in another pan and stir in the flour. Cook for a few minutes. Allow to cool slightly then gradually stir in the milk. Bring to the boil, stirring, and simmer until thickened. Cook for a further 3 minutes. Allow to cool, then add the egg yolks, beating in well. Stir in the thyme and cheese.

Stir the sauce into the spinach mixture. Whisk the egg whites until just holding their shape and fold into the spinach mixture using a metal spoon. Spoon into the soufflé dish.

Bake in a preheated oven for 45–50 minutes until risen and golden brown. Serve immediately.

■ COOK'S TIP

Spinach has a very high vitamin A content and is rich in iron and vitamin C. It will keep for a short time in the refrigerator, but it is best eaten as soon as possible.

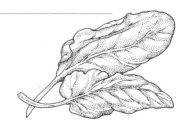

147

leek and egg puffs

Preparation time
30 minutes (or 45 minutes if making pastry)

Cooking time
30 minutes

Oven temperature
220°C (425°F)
Gas Mark 7

Serves 4

Calories
351 per portion

1 leek, about 200 g (7 oz), washed and sliced
1 tablespoon vegetable oil
1 small onion, thinly sliced
½ teaspoon coriander seeds, crushed
50 g (2 oz) mature vegetarian Cheddar cheese, cut into small cubes
250 g (8 oz) frozen and thawed puff pastry
2 hard-boiled eggs, halved lengthways
salt and pepper
beaten egg, for glazing

Cook the sliced leek in boiling salted water for 6 minutes, then strain and set aside.

Heat the oil in a small pan and fry the onion until golden brown. Add salt, pepper and coriander then stir in the cooked leek. Allow the mixture to cool slightly and stir in the cheese. Roll out the pastry thinly and trim to a 30 cm (12 inch) square. Cut it into four 10 cm (4 inch) squares. Cut the trimmings into leaf shapes to decorate the puffs.

Brush the edges of each pastry square with beaten egg. Divide the filling between the squares, placing it just off centre, and top with half a boiled egg. Fold the pastry over to make a triangle. Seal the edges firmly and brush the tops with beaten egg. Arrange the pastry leaves on top and brush with beaten egg. Bake in a preheated oven for 15–20 minutes until puffed up and golden brown. Serve hot.

148

potato and pea curry

Preparation time
20 minutes

Cooking time
20 minutes

Serves 4

Calories
301 per portion, with Turmeric rice;
177 per portion, without rice

Suitable for vegans using soya margarine

2 tablespoons butter or soya margarine
1 onion, chopped
2 teaspoons each turmeric, ground cumin and ground coriander
¼ teaspoon chilli powder
2 bay leaves
1 x 250 g (8 oz) can tomatoes
500 g (1 lb) potatoes, peeled and quartered
300 ml (1.2 pints) water
300 g (10 oz) frozen peas
salt and pepper

Melt the butter or soya margarine in a large saucepan and fry the onion until soft. Stir in the spices and bay leaves. Add the tomatoes, potatoes, peas and salt and pepper to taste. Bring to the boil, then cover and simmer for 15 minutes. Serve with Turmeric rice (see Cook's Tip).

■ COOK'S TIP

The pastry is good eaten cold, making the puffs a good picnic or packed lunch dish.

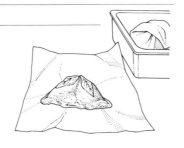

■ COOK'S TIP

For Turmeric rice, heat 1½ tablespoons oil in a pan, add 250 g (8 oz) uncooked brown rice and fry for 3–4 minutes. Stir in ¾ teaspoon turmeric, 3 cloves and a bay leaf. Cook for a few seconds, then stir in 600 ml (1 pint) water and salt and pepper to taste. Bring to boil, then simmer for 40–45 minutes until tender.

149

courgette moussaka

150

cheese crust pie

Preparation time
20 minutes

Cooking time
50 minutes

Oven temperature
200°C (400°F)
gas 6

Serves 4

Calories
576 per portion

750 g (1½ lb) courgettes, thinly sliced
120 m1 (4 fl oz) olive oil
1 large onion, thinly sliced
2 green peppers, cored, deseeded and diced
1 garlic clove, crushed
500 g (1 lb) tomatoes, skinned and sliced
1 tablespoon tomato purée
1 tablespoon chopped mint
125 g (4 oz) Gruyère cheese, thinly sliced
2 tablespoons plain flour
300 ml (½ pint) natural yogurt
2 medium egg yolks
75 g (3 oz) vegetarian Cheddar, grated
salt and pepper

Fry the courgette slices a few at a time in the oil over a moderate heat. Turn them to brown evenly. Set aside.

Fry the onion, peppers and garlic in the pan for about 4 minutes, stirring once or twice. Add a little more oil if necessary. Stir in the tomatoes, tomato purée, mint, and salt and pepper to taste. Cook for a further 2 minutes.

Arrange a layer of courgettes in a greased, shallow baking dish. Cover with half the tomato mixture, then with the sliced cheese. Make a layer of the remaining tomato mixture, and cover with the remaining courgette slices.

Mix together the flour, yogurt, egg yolks, grated cheese, and salt and pepper to taste. Pour over the courgettes. Cook in a preheated oven for 25 minutes, until the top is golden brown.

Preparation time
1 hour

Cooking time
45 minutes

Oven temperature
200°C (400°F)
Gas Mark 6 then
180°C (350°F)
gas 4

Serves 4

Calories
622 per portion

FOR THE CHEESE PASTRY
175 g (6 oz) plain flour
pinch of salt
125 g (4 oz) butter, cubed
75 g (3 oz) vegetarian Cheddar cheese,
    finely grated
2–3 tablespoons cold water, to mix
1 medium egg, beaten, to glaze
FOR THE FILLING
50 g (2 oz) butter
1 onion, sliced
3 carrots, sliced
1 x 200 g (7 oz) can sweetcorn kernels
50 g (2 oz) mushrooms, sliced
2 celery sticks, chopped
1 x 50 g (2 oz) packet leek soup

To make the pastry, sift the flour and salt into a mixing bowl. Rub in the butter and stir in the cheese. Bind with water. Wrap and chill until needed.

To make the filling, melt the butter in a pan and fry the vegetables for a few minutes. Drain. Make up the packet of leek soup as directed, but using 600 ml (1 pint) water only. Stir in the vegetables and pour into a 750 ml (1½ pint) pie dish.

Roll out the pastry to top the pie, trim and flute the edges. Use the pastry trimmings to make leaves for the top. Brush the pastry with egg and bake in a preheated oven for 15 minutes; reduce the heat and bake for a further 20 minutes. Serve hot.

■ COOK'S TIP

Courgettes are baby marrows which are also known as zucchini in the USA. Choose smooth, brightly coloured and firm courgettes. Keep them in a cool place.

■ COOK'S TIP

For pastry packed with protein, add 50 g (2 oz) ground walnuts or hazelnuts instead of 50 g (2 oz) of the flour. It will add a delicious rich, nutty flavour to the pie.

individual asparagus flans

Preparation time
20 minutes

Cooking time
35 minutes

Oven temperature
200°C (400°F)
gas 6 then
190°C (375°F)
gas 5

Serves 6

Calories
560 per portion

FOR THE PASTRY
375 g (12 oz) plain wholemeal flour
½ teaspoon salt
200 g (7 oz) butter or margarine
4–5 tablespoons cold water
FOR THE FILLING
1 bunch asparagus, trimmed and cooked
(see Cook's Tip)
300 ml (½ pint) single cream
2 medium egg yolks
freshly grated nutmeg
salt and pepper

Sift the flour and salt into a bowl, add 175 g (6 oz) of the butter or margarine, then rub it into the flour with your fingertips. Add the water, and bind to a dough. Roll the dough out on a lightly floured board, then use to line six 10 cm (4 inch) flan tins. Prick the flan bases and place in a preheated oven on a baking tray. Bake for 15–20 minutes, until golden brown. Melt the remaining butter in a pan. Remove the flan cases from the oven and brush with the butter. Turn the oven down.

Trim the asparagus spears and divide between the flans. Whisk the cream and egg yolks together; season with nutmeg and salt and pepper. Pour a little of this mixture into each flan, on top of the asparagus. Return the flans to the oven and bake for about 15 minutes, until the filling has set. They should be just firm to the touch and no more.

■ COOK'S TIP

These flans make a superb summer starter. To cook asparagus, drop into a pan of boiling salted water and cook until just tender – about 3–4 minutes.

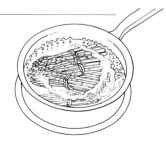

family vegetable pie

Preparation time
45 minutes, plus chilling

Cooking time
35 minutes

Oven temperature
200°C (400°F)
gas 6

Serves 4

Calories
572 per portion

Extra light pastry (see Cook's Tip)
300 ml (½ pint) salted water
125 g (4 oz) carrots, sliced
125 g (4 oz) leeks, sliced
125 g (4 oz) celery, sliced
125 g (4 oz) cauliflower, cut into florets
about 300 ml (½ pint) milk
25 g (1 oz) butter
25 g (1 oz) plain flour
2 tablespoons chopped parsley
1 x 250 g (8 oz) can red kidney beans
beaten egg, for brushing
salt and pepper

Make the pastry. To make the filling, boil the water in a pan. Put in the carrots, simmer 5 minutes, then add the remaining vegetables and cook 10 minutes.

Strain the vegetables, reserving the liquid. Make up to a generous 600 ml (l pint) with milk. Melt the butter in the pan, add the flour and cook, stirring, for 3 minutes. Pour in the milk mixture and bring to the boil, stirring, and simmer 1 minute. Add salt and pepper then the vegetables, parsley and drained beans. Pour into a 1.2 litre (2 pint) pie dish with a pie funnel.

Roll out the pastry 2.5 cm (1 inch) larger than the pie dish. Cut a strip off to cover the rim of the dish, brush with egg and place the lid in position. Trim and flute the edges. Cut any leftover pastry into decorations. Brush with beaten egg, arrange the decorations on the pie and brush again with egg. Bake in a preheated oven for 25 minutes until the pastry is golden brown.

■ COOK'S TIP

To make the pastry: mix 175 g (6 oz) wholemeal self-raising flour, salt and 1 teaspoon dried mixed herbs in a bowl. Mix in 125 g (4 oz) grated hard vegetable margarine. Mix gently to a dough with 3 tablespoons water and 1 tablespoon oil. Chill until required.

153

little leek quiches

154

quick pizza

Preparation time
45 minutes, plus chilling

Cooking time
50 minutes

Oven temperature
180°C (350°F)
gas 4

Makes 8

Calories
735 per quiche

FOR THE PASTRY
500 g (1 lb) plain flour
pinch of salt
375 g (12 oz) butter, cubed
2 medium egg yolks
3 tablespoons water
FOR THE FILLING
50 g (2 oz) butter
5 large leeks, sliced
1 teaspoon dried oregano
5 medium eggs
300 ml (½ pint) single cream
1 tablespoon chopped parsley
salt and pepper

To make the pastry, sift the flour and salt into a mixing bowl. Rub in the butter. Bind with the egg yolks and water, then wrap and chill for 20 minutes.

Roll out the pastry dough and use to line eight 11.5 cm (4½ inch) flan rings placed on baking sheets. Line the pastry cases with greaseproof paper and weigh down with baking beans. Bake in a preheated oven for 15 minutes, then remove the paper and beans and bake for a further 5 minutes.

To make the filling, melt the butter in a frying pan, add the leeks and fry gently until softened. Remove from the heat and allow to cool. Sprinkle over the oregano and divide between the pastry shells. Beat together the eggs, cream and salt and pepper to taste and pour over the leeks. Sprinkle with the chopped parsley. Bake in a preheated oven for 20 minutes.

Preparation time
30 minutes

Cooking time
30 minutes

Oven temperature
220°C (425°F)
gas 7

Serves 4

Calories
475 per portion

250 g (8 oz) self-raising wholemeal flour
2 teaspoons baking powder
½ teaspoon salt
50 g (2 oz) butter or margarine
8–9 tablespoons water
FOR THE TOPPING
2 onions, chopped
2 tablespoons oil
2 tablespoons tomato purée
1–2 teaspoons dried oregano
salt, sugar and pepper
125 g (4 oz) button mushrooms, sliced
small green pepper, deseeded, chopped and fried
75 g (3 oz) grated vegetarian Gouda cheese

Brush a 30 cm (12 inch) round pizza plate with oil. Sift the flour and baking powder into a bowl, tipping in the residue of bran. Add the salt, rub the fat into the flour, then pour in the water and mix to a pliable dough. Roll out to fit the pizza plate. Put the dough on the plate and prick all over. Bake in a preheated oven for 10 minutes.

Meanwhile, prepare the topping. Fry the onion in the oil for 10 minutes, then remove from the heat and add the tomato purée, oregano, salt, sugar and pepper to taste. Spread the mixture on the pizza base, top with the mushrooms, and green pepper and sprinkle with the cheese. Bake for 15–20 minutes.

■ COOK'S TIP

The leek is a member of the onion family. If young, leeks can be chopped finely and used raw in salads. The tougher green tops are best used in long-cook hotpots.

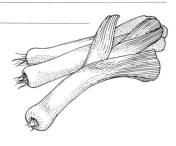

■ COOK'S TIP

There are many different vegetables that can be used as a topping. Try broccoli, asparagus, sweetcorn, peas, or red pepper. Try mozzarella cheese instead of Gouda.

Radish slices and parsley sprigs make a pretty garnish.

155

spinach filo pie

Preparation time
30–35 minutes

Cooking time
50–55 minutes

Oven temperature
190°C (375°F)
gas 5

Serves 6

Calories
664 per portion

1 large onion, thinly sliced
8 spring onions, chopped or thinly sliced
6 tablespoons olive oil
125 g (4 oz) butter, melted
1.25 kg (2½ lb) fresh spinach, washed
*   and shredded*
6 tablespoons chopped parsley
4 teaspoons dried dill or oregano
3 medium eggs, beaten
500 g (1 lb) filo pastry, thawed if frozen
salt and pepper

Fry the onion and spring onions in 4 tablespoons of the oil and 25 g (l oz) of the butter until softened. Stir in the spinach, cover and cook gently for 3–4 minutes. Drain any excess moisture from the spinach. Season, mix in the parsley, herb and eggs.

Mix the remaining oil and butter together and use a little to grease a rectangular tin, 35 x 25 x 7.5 cm (14 x 10 x 3 inches) deep. Brush a sheet of pastry with the butter and oil, and press it into the tin. Add 6 more sheets, each brushed with butter and oil. Spread the spinach filling evenly over the layers of pastry. Lay another 7 layers of oiled pastry on top. Do not press the layers down.

Brush the top layer well with butter and oil. Using a sharp knife mark squares or diamond shapes. Cut through only the top layers of pastry and not through to the spinach filling. Bake in a preheated oven for 40 minutes until golden.

■ COOK'S TIP

Filo pastry is available either chilled or frozen. Defrost thoroughly before use and keep the pile of pastry sheets covered with a damp tea towel while using.

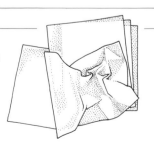

156

mushroom and onion quiche

Preparation time
15 minutes

Cooking time
about 25 minutes

Oven temperature
200°C (400°F)
gas 6

Serves 4

Calories
408 per portion

FOR THE PASTRY
250 g (8 oz) plain flour
pinch of salt
125 g (4 oz) butter
2–3 tablespoons cold water
FOR THE FILLING
15 g (½ oz) butter
1 large onion, thinly sliced
150 ml (¼ pint) milk or single cream
2 eggs
125 g (4 oz) button mushrooms
50 g (2 oz) vegetarian Cheddar, grated
salt and pepper

Sift the flour and salt into a bowl, then rub in the butter until it resembles fine breadcrumbs. Add enough water to make a firm dough and gently knead together. Roll out the pastry and line a 20 cm (8 inch) flan ring on a baking sheet or a flan dish.

To make the filling, melt the butter in a frying pan, add the onion and cook gently until soft but not brown. Cool slightly and place in the pastry case.

Lightly beat together the milk, eggs and salt and pepper to taste. Reserve 3 mushrooms and finely chop the rest. Add to the egg mixture and pour into the pastry case. Thinly slice the reserved mushrooms and scatter on top. Sprinkle with the cheese. Bake in a preheated oven for 25 minutes until the pastry is cooked and the filling set.

■ COOK'S TIP

Instead of using mushrooms, try a variety of other vegetables. Small broccoli florets, thinly sliced courgettes or fresh peas would work well.

157

filo pie
with seaweed filing

Preparation time
25 minutes, plus
making gravy and
steaming vegetables

Cooking time
45 minutes

Oven temperature
190°C (375°F),
gas 5

Serves 4

Calories
200 per portion

4 tablespoons extra virgin olive oil
1 onion, finely chopped
1 garlic clove, crushed
2 teaspoons grated fresh root ginger
175 g (6 oz) button mushrooms
175 g (6 oz) dried dulse seaweed
1 tablespoon dark soy sauce
1 tablespoon lemon juice
2 tablespoons chopped coriander
50 g (2 oz) fresh white breadcrumbs
50 g (2oz) pine nuts
2 tablespoons sesame seeds
12 sheets filo pastry, thawed if frozen
pepper

Heat the oil and fry the onion, garlic and ginger gently for 5 minutes. Add the mushrooms and fry for 5 minutes, stirring. Cut the seaweed into small pieces. Add to the pan with the soy sauce, lemon juice and coriander. Stir over a low heat until the seaweed is soft. In another pan, heat the remaining oil and stir-fry the breadcrumbs, pine nuts and sesame seeds for 4–5 minutes. Take 1 sheet of the filo pastry and trim to fit an oiled 20 x 30 cm (8 x 12 inch) roasting tin. Press into the base and brush with oil. Scatter on 2 teaspoons of the breadcrumb mixture. Repeat with 5 more sheets of pastry and half the breadcrumb mixture. Spread over the seaweed mixture then repeat the layers, ending with a layer of pastry. Brush liberally with oil, mark into 6 portions and bake in a preheated oven for 30 minutes until crisp and golden.

■ COOK'S TIP

There are several varieties of edible seaweed; most are rich sources of useful minerals. Dulse seaweed is sold dried and is similar to Japanese nori, which could be used instead.

158

spinach roulade

Preparation time
30 minutes, plus
chilling

Cooking time
15–20 minutes

Oven temperature
190°C (375°F),
gas 5

Serves 4

Calories
310 per portion

50 g (2 oz) butter, softened
375 g (12 oz) spinach, cooked
3 eggs, separated
salt and pepper
FOR THE FILLING
375 g (12 oz) cream cheese
1 bunch of spring onions, chopped
175 g (6 oz) broccoli, trimmed, blanched
    and drained
4 tomatoes, skinned

Line a 23 x 30 cm (9 x 12 inch) Swiss roll tin with greaseproof paper and brush lightly with melted butter. Squeeze all the liquid from the spinach; chop finely or purée. Beat in the remaining butter, the egg yolks and salt and pepper to taste. Whisk the egg whites until just stiff and fold into the spinach. Turn into the prepared tin and cook in a moderately hot oven for 10–15 minutes.

Beat the cheese and spring onions together. Finely chop the broccoli. Halve the tomatoes, discard the seeds and chop the flesh. Mix the broccoli and tomatoes into the cream cheese and season well.

Turn the cooked roulade out on to clean greaseproof paper. Carefully peel off the lining paper and trim the edges. Spread the filling evenly over three-quarters of the roulade and roll up from the unfilled end. Wrap paper tightly over the roulade and chill for 30 minutes.

■ COOK'S TIP

Serve this splendid roulade as a dinner party starter with a simple garnish or frilled endive and radishes.

159

cottage pancakes

Preparation time
10 minutes

Cooking time
30–35 minutes

Oven temperature
190°C (375°F),
gas 5

Serves 4

Calories
385 per portion

50 g (2 oz) wholemeal flour
50 g (2 oz) plain flour
1 egg
1 egg yolk
300 ml (½ pint) water
salt and pepper
oil, for frying
FOR THE FILLING
25 g (1 oz) butter
1 small onion, finely chopped
250 g (8 oz) cottage cheese
50 g (2 oz) salted peanuts, chopped
1 teaspoon dried rosemary, crushed

Mix together the flours, egg and egg yolk, stir in about a third of the water and beat to make a smooth batter. Stir in the salt and pepper and remaining water.

Heat a little oil in a 15 cm (6 inch) frying pan. Pour in a little batter, so it just covers the base, and cook until the underside is golden. Turn and cook the second side. Remove and keep warm. Repeat with the remaining batter.

To make the filling, heat the butter in a saucepan and fry the onion until softened, about 5 minutes. Stir in the cottage cheese, peanuts and rosemary.

Divide the filling between the pancakes and roll up. Place close together in one layer in an ovenproof dish. Cover with foil and heat through in the oven for 15–20 minutes. Serve hot.

160

provençal pancakes

Preparation time
25 minutes

Cooking time
50 minutes

Serves 4

Calories
345 per portion

50 g (2 oz) buckwheat flour
50 g (2 oz) plain flour
1 egg, beaten
300 ml (½ pint) milk
1 tablespoon vegetable oil
oil, for cooking
2 tablespoons olive oil
1 onion, chopped
2 garlic cloves, crushed
1 green or red pepper, deseeded and chopped
1 small aubergine, chopped
4 large tomatoes, skinned and chopped
1 tablespoon tomato purée
25 g (1 oz) margarine, melted
2 tablespoons grated Parmesan cheese
salt and pepper

Place the flours in a bowl, add salt and make a well in the centre. Add the egg, then gradually stir in half of the milk and the vegetable oil. Beat until smooth then add the remaining milk. Use to make 12 small pancakes.

Heat the olive oil in a pan and cook the onion until softened. Add the garlic, pepper and aubergine and fry for 10 minutes, stirring occasionally. Add the tomatoes and tomato purée, cover and cook for 15 minutes. Season to taste. Fill the pancakes, roll up and place in an ovenproof dish. Top with the margarine and cheese; grill to brown.

■ COOK'S TIP

Cottage cheese is made from skimmed milk curds which have been washed and rinsed. It is low in fat and therefore a good choice for slimmers.

■ COOK'S TIP

Pancakes can be made in advance. Place the stack of pancakes in a plastic bag and store in the refrigerator for 2–3 days.

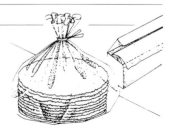

161

cheese mille feuilles

Preparation time
30 minutes

Cooking time
10–15 minutes

Oven temperature
220–230°C
(425–450°F),
gas 7–8

Serves 6

Calories
500 per portion

250 g (8 oz) frozen puff pastry, defrosted
cocktail gherkins, to garnish
FOR THE FILLING
250 g (8 oz) blue Stilton cheese
75 g (3 oz) butter
2–3 tablespoons double cream, lightly
whipped
1–2 tablespoons milk
125 g (4 oz) Lancashire cheese, grated
pinch of cayenne pepper
pinch of mustard powder
1 tablespoon chutney, chopped
salt and pepper

Roll out the pastry to about 25 x 35 cm (10 x 14 inches). Prick all over and bake in a hot oven for 10–15 minutes. Cool slightly, then cut lengthways into three even strips; crush the trimmings and reserve.

Remove the rind from the Stilton. Cream the cheese with the butter and season well with salt and pepper, adding a little cream.

Beat the milk into the Lancashire cheese, season and add the cayenne, mustard and chutney. If necessary, add a little cream to soften. Spread half the Stilton mixture over one pastry strip. Place the second strip on top and spread with the Lancashire cheese. Top with the last strip of pastry, press down gently then spread with the remaining Stilton mixture. Mark with a knife and garnish, adding the crushed pastry as shown.

162

courgette soufflé

Preparation time
20 minutes

Cooking time
1 hour

Oven temperature
180°C (350°F),
gas 4

Serves 6

Calories
145 per portion

375 g (12 oz) courgettes, diced
375 g (12 oz) low-fat soft cheese
4 eggs, separated
½ teaspoons tarragon
pinch of cayenne pepper
salt and pepper

Cook the courgettes in boiling salted water until tender – about 5 minutes. Drain well, then sieve or blend in a food processor until smooth. Beat the soft cheese and egg yolks together. Stir in the courgettes, tarragon and cayenne. Whisk the egg whites until stiff and fold into the courgette mixture.

Pour carefully into a 1.2 litre (2 pint) soufflé dish and bake in a preheated oven for about 45–55 minutes, without opening the oven, until well risen and golden brown on top. Serve immediately with a green salad.

■ COOK'S TIP

Gherkin fans make an attractive garnish. Drain the gherkins and place them on a board, then, with a sharp knife, slice them lengthways, almost to the end. Ease the slices apart to make the fans.

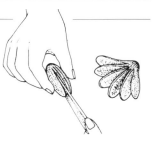

■ COOK'S TIP

It is the air incorporated into the egg whites during beating that makes a soufflé rise. Adding a pinch of salt will help to stabilize the mixture. Never beat eggs so stiffly that they look dry – if this happens then they will soon collapse.

163

blue cheese soufflé

Preparation time
15 minutes

Cooking time
30–35 minutes

Oven temperature
200°C (400°F),
gas 6

Serves 4

Calories
310 per portion

40 g (1½ oz) butter
25 g (1 oz) plain flour
300 ml (½ pint) milk
pinch of grated nutmeg
4 egg yolks
125 g (4 oz) Danish blue cheese,
*   crumbled*
3 egg whites
salt and pepper

Melt the butter in a pan and use a little to brush the inside of a
1.5 litre (2½ pint) souffle dish. Stir the flour into the remaining
butter and cook for 1 minute. Gradually stir in the milk, bring to
the boil and cook for 2 minutes, stirring constantly. Add the nutmeg and allow to cool slightly. Beat in the egg yolks and cheese.
Whisk the egg whites until stiff, lightly fold into the sauce and
season to taste with salt and pepper.

Turn into the prepared soufflé dish and cook in a preheated
moderately hot oven for 25–30 minutes until well risen and gold-
en brown. Serve at once with green vegetables or a salad.

164

surprise soufflé

Preparation time
20 minutes

Cooking time
1 hour

Oven temperature
190°C (375°F),
gas 5

Serves 4

Calories
475 per portion

4 large carrots, thickly sliced
3 large potatoes, cut into
*   1 cm (½ inch) dice*
1 small turnip, cut into 1 cm (½ inch) dice
1 large onion, chopped
8 tomatoes, skinned and deseeded
25 g (1 oz) butter
25 g (1 oz) plain flour
½ teaspoon mustard powder
300 ml (½ pint) milk
3 eggs, separated
125 g (4 oz) Cheddar cheese, grated
salt and pepper
1 tablespoon chopped parsley, to garnish
*   (optional)*

Cook the carrots, potatoes, turnip and onion in a pan of boiling
salted water for 15 minutes. Drain, season to taste with salt and
pepper then place in a 1.8 litre (3 pint) ovenproof souffle dish.
Purée the tomatoes with a little salt and pepper and pour over the
vegetables.

Melt the butter in a pan over a low heat, then add the flour
and mustard powder. Cook for 2 minutes, stirring. Gradually add
the milk and bring the sauce to the boil, stirring constantly.
Simmer gently for 2–3 minutes. Allow it to cool slightly, then beat
in the egg yolks and cheese. Whisk the egg whites until stiff and
fold into the sauce. Pour the sauce over the vegetables in the
soufflé dish. Bake in a preheated oven for about 40 minutes until
well risen and golden. Garnish with parsley, if using.

■ COOK'S TIP

When serving a soufflé, use a
large serving spoon to reach
down to the lightly cooked
mixture at the bottom of the
dish. Each portion should also
include some of the crust.

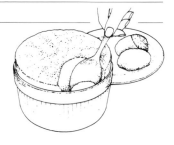

■ COOK'S TIP

The surprise in this soufflé is the
vegetable mixture at the bottom
of the dish, which makes the
soufflé sufficiently substantial
to serve on its own.

 165

cheese fondue

Preparation time 15 minutes	1 garlic clove, halved 300 ml (½ pint) dry white wine
Cooking time 10 minutes	1 teaspoon lemon juice 250 g (8 oz) Danish Samsoe or Danbo
Serves 4	Cheese, grated 250 g (8 oz) Havarti cheese, grated
Calories 435 per portion	2 tablespoons cornflour pinch of grated nutmeg 1 tablespoon Kirsch or milk black pepper TO SERVE French bread raw vegetables

Thoroughly rub the inside of a fondue pot or flameproof casserole with the garlic, then discard. Pour the wine and lemon juice into the pot and warm over a gentle heat. Add the cheese gradually and continue to heat gently, stirring until the cheese has melted. Blend the cornflour, pepper and nutmeg to a smooth paste with the Kirsch or milk and add to the melted cheese. Stir over the heat for a further 2–3 minutes. Place in the centre of the table. Serve at once with cubes of French bread and pieces of vegetables as dippers. Each guest is given a long fork with which to dip his bread and vegetables into the fondue pot. Keep the fondue warm over a spirit lamp or on a plate warmer.

■ COOK'S TIP

To make a change from bread, accompany the fondue with a selection of vegetables to dip. Try carrots, cauliflower, celery, courgettes and different coloured peppers, all prepared and cut into bite-sized pieces.

166

fruit and vegetable kebabs

Preparation time 20 minutes, plus marinating	8 button onions, peeled and left whole 1 small green pepper, cored, deseeded and cut into 8 pieces
Cooking time 11–14 minutes	1 small red pepper, cored, deseeded and cut into 8 pieces
Serves 4	16 button mushrooms 2 large bananas, cut into
Calories 195 per portion	8 chunks 1 x 375 g (12 oz) can pineapple cubes, drained FOR THE MARINADE 6 tablespoons vegetable oil 1 tablespoon lemon juice 1 teaspoon grated orange rind 1 tablespoon finely chopped walnuts salt and pepper

Blanch the onions and peppers in boiling water for 3 minutes so that they cook in the same time as the other ingredients. Drain and pat dry with kitchen paper. Thread all the ingredients on to eight kebab skewers. Place the kebabs in a shallow dish while making the marinade. In a small bowl, stir together the oil, lemon juice, orange rind, walnuts, salt and pepper. Spoon the marinade over the kebabs and leave for about 1 hour. Grill the kebabs for 8–10 minutes until evenly browned, brushing them frequently with the marinade.

■ COOK'S TIP

In the summer, cook these colourful kebabs over a barbecue.

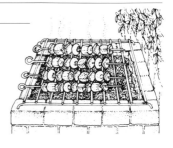

167
danish blue cheesecake

Preparation time
35 minutes, plus chilling

Serves 8

Calories
375 per portion

FOR THE BASE
75 g (3 oz) butter
175 g (6 oz) wholemeal bran biscuits, crushed
FOR THE TOPPING
125 g (4 oz) Danish Blue cheese
125 g (4 oz) cream cheese
2 large eggs, separated
1 teaspoon French mustard
150 ml (¼ pint) double cream
2 teaspoons agar-agar or 3 teaspoons powdered gelatine
6 tablespoons water
garlic salt and pepper
FOR THE GARNISH
cucumber slices
black grapes

Melt the butter and stir in the biscuit crumbs. Press firmly into the base of a greased 20 cm (8 inch) loose-bottomed cake tin and chill. Soften both cheeses and beat together until creamy. Beat in the egg yolks, mustard, cream, garlic salt and pepper. Dissolve the agar-agar in the cold water in a small saucepan then bring to the boil, stirring constantly. Beat into the cheese mixture and set aside. When on the point of setting, whisk the egg whites until stiff but not dry and gently fold in. Pour over the biscuit base and smooth the surface. Refrigerate for 3–4 hours. Garnish and serve.

168
spinach and flageolet layer

Preparation time
25 minutes

Cooking time
1 hour 10 minutes

Oven temperature
180°C (350°F), gas 4

Serves 4

Calories
135 per portion

500 g (1 lb) fresh spinach
1 egg, beaten
1 x 425 g (14 oz) can flageolet beans
1 teaspoon French mustard
1 teaspoon curry powder
175 g (6 oz) raspberries, puréed

Steam the spinach for 10 minutes. Set about a quarter of the leaves aside and chop the rest very finely or purée in a food processor or blender. Mix in the beaten egg. Oil a 500 g (1 lb) loaf tin and line with some of the reserved spinach leaves.

Drain and mash the flageolet beans. Mix with the mustard and curry powder, place in the spinach-lined tin and top with the spinach mixture. Arrange the remaining spinach leaves on top. Cover with foil. Place in a baking tin containing 2.5 cm (1 inch) of water and cook in a preheated oven for 1 hour.

Leave to cool in the tin, turn out and serve with a sauce of puréed raspberries. Accompany with hot garlic bread.

■ COOK'S TIP

As an alternative garnish, make spring onion curls. Cut the bulb from each onion to leave about 2.5 cm (1 inch) of white stalk then make parallel cuts down the green part. When the onions are placed in iced water they will curl.

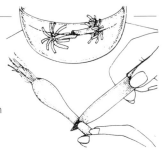

■ COOK'S TIP

To make the sauce or coulis, simply purée fresh raspberries and press them through a sieve to remove the seeds. A little lemon juice or gin may be added to sharpen the flavour.

169

kohlrabi with walnuts

Preparation time 15 minutes	*1 kg (2 lb) young, tender kohlrabi* *1 tablespoon vegetable oil*
Cooking time 18–20 minutes	*2 shallots, finely chopped* *grated nutmeg*
Serves 4	*125 ml (4 fl oz) double cream*
Calories 345 per portion	*2 tablespoons chopped basil or marjoram* *125 g (4 oz) walnuts, coarsely chopped* *salt and pepper*

Trim the kohlrabi, cutting off the feathery leaves and reserving them for garnish. Peel the kohlrabi, cut out any tough parts, wash and halve. Cut the halves first into 1 cm (½ inch) slices and then into sticks.

Heat the oil in a frying pan and fry the shallots over a moderate heat until transparent, stirring continuously. Add the kohlrabi and stir until completely coated in oil.

Season with nutmeg and salt and pepper to taste. Add the cream, reduce the heat, cover and cook over low heat for 5–8 minutes until the kohlrabi is tender but still firm to the bite.

Rinse the kohlrabi leaves, pat dry and finely chop. Stir the basil into the kohlrabi mixture and transfer to a warmed serving dish. Sprinkle with the kohlrabi leaves and walnuts. Accompany with jacket-boiled new potatoes or brown rice.

170

walnut-filled fennel

Preparation time 15–20 minutes	*4 large fennel bulbs* *50 g (2 oz) fresh breadcrumbs*
Cooking time 1½ hours	*75 g (3 oz) walnuts, chopped* *2 tablespoons clear honey*
Oven temperature 180°C (350°F), gas 4	*1 tablespoon snipped chives* *1 tablespoon milk* *50 g (2 oz) butter*
Serves 2–4	*salt and pepper*
Calories 630–315 per portion	FOR THE GARNISH *tomato wedges* *parsley sprigs*

Cut out the hard core of the fennel bulbs and discard. Remove and chop up a little more fennel, ensuring there is a reasonably large cavity to fill with stuffing.

Mix the chopped fennel, breadcrumbs, walnuts, honey, chives and milk, and season well with salt and pepper. Press this stuffing into the fennel cavities and place in an ovenproof dish.

Dot the surface with butter, cover tightly with foil and bake in a moderate oven for about 1½ hours, until the fennel is tender. Garnish with tomato and parsley.

■ COOK'S TIP

Kohlrabi looks like a large green turnip but is actually a member of the cabbage family. It is high in vitamins and low in calories.

■ COOK'S TIP

Serve this dish as an interesting main course. Alternatively, it can be offered as an accompaniment or an appetising starter.

171

baked gnocchi

Preparation time 15 minutes	450 ml (¾ pint) milk
	450 ml (¾ pint) water
Cooking time 40 minutes	¼ teaspoon salt
	250 g (8 oz) semolina
Oven temperature 200°C (400°F), gas 6	125 g (4 oz) grated Parmesan cheese
	2 egg yolks
	250 g (8 oz) mushrooms, sliced
Serves 4	500 g (1 lb) tomatoes, skinned and sliced
Calories 520 per portion	2 tablespoons chopped parsley
	1 teaspoon oregano
	50 g (2 oz) pitted black olives, chopped
	3 tablespoons melted butter

Bring the milk, water and salt nearly to the boil. Sprinkle in the semolina and cook, stirring, until it thickens to a purée consistency. Reduce the heat as low as possible and cook for 4 minutes. Remove the pan from the heat and stir in about two-thirds of the cheese and egg yolks.

Moisten a large roasting tin. Press the gnocchi mixture into an even-sided oblong shape. Cut neatly into squares. Place the mushrooms in a buttered ovenproof dish, cover with the tomatoes and sprinkle over the parsley, oregano and olives. Cover with the gnocchi squares, spoon over the melted butter and sprinkle with the remaining cheese. Bake for 25–30 minutes until the topping is just beginning to brown.

172

spinach bake

Preparation time 20 minutes	2 tablespoons raisins
	4 tablespoons apple juice
Cooking time 35 minutes	1 kg (2 lb) fresh spinach, or 500 g (1 lb) frozen spinach
Oven temperature 200°C (400°F), gas 6	1 small onion, finely chopped
	50 g (2 oz) butter
	¼ teaspoon grated nutmeg
Serves 4	1 kg (2 lb) potatoes, cooked and puréed with milk, butter and salt and pepper
Calories 365 per portion	150 ml (¼ pint) soured cream
	4 tablespoons fresh breadcrumbs
	2 tablespoons grated Parmesan cheese
	salt and pepper

Soak the raisins in the apple juice. Wash the spinach several times in lukewarm water then cook it gently in just the water that clings to the leaves, until wilted. Drain in a sieve and press out the excess water. Cook the onion in the butter for 3 minutes until softened, add the spinach, raisins and apple juice, nutmeg and salt and pepper to taste. Cook for 5 minutes over very gentle heat.

Meanwhile, pipe the creamed potato round the edge of an ovenproof dish. Turn the spinach mixture into the centre, spoon over the cream, sprinkle with the breadcrumbs and cheese and cook for 20–25 minutes until crisp and golden on top.

■ COOK'S TIP

A simple salad, such as Orange and Watercress (see recipe 283) would be an excellent accompaniment to this dish.

■ COOK'S TIP

Soaking the raisins in apple juice plumps them up and adds flavour. Pear juice may be used instead, if preferred.

173

melanzane parmigiana

Preparation time
10 minutes

Cooking time
50 minutes

Serves 4

Oven temperature
200°C (400°F)
gas 6

Calories
415–315 per portion

6 aubergines
2 tablespoons extra virgin olive oil
1 quantity Tomato sauce (see recipe 88)
250g (8 oz) vegetarian Cheddar cheese, grated
50 g (2 oz) vegetarian Parmesan cheese, grated
salt

Trim the aubergines and cut them lengthways into thick slices. Sprinkle with salt and leave to drain in a colander for 30 minutes. Wash well, drain and pat dry on kitchen paper.

Brush the aubergine slices with oil and place on 2 large baking sheets. Roast the aubergines at the top of a preheated oven for 20 minutes, turning once, until golden and tender. Meanwhile, heat the tomato sauce and keep warm. Spoon a little of the tomato sauce into a lasagne dish and top with a layer of aubergines and some of the Cheddar. Continue with the layer, finishing with the Cheddar. Sprinkle over the Parmesan cheese and bake for 30 minutes in a preheated oven until the cheese is bubbling and golden.

■ COOK'S TIP

This layered bake of aubergines and cheese is a classic Italian dish. The original version uses layers of mozzarella, but Cheddar gives a better texture and richer flavour.

174

gougère

Preparation time
30 minutes

Cooking time
1 hour

Oven temperature
200°C (400°F),
gas 6

Serves 4

Calories
425 per portion

50 g (2 oz) margarine
150 ml (¼ pint) water
65 g (2½ oz) wholemeal flour
2 eggs
50 g (2 oz) Cheddar cheese, grated
FOR THE FILLING
2 tablespoons oil
1 onion, chopped
250 g (8 oz) mushrooms, sliced
2 garlic cloves, crushed
1 tablespoon wholemeal flour
150 ml (¼ pint) vegetable stock
75 g (3 oz) walnuts, chopped
2 tablespoons chopped parsley
salt and pepper

Melt the margarine in a large pan, add the water and bring to the boil. Add the flour all at once and beat until the mixture leaves the sides of the pan. Cool slightly, then add the eggs, one at a time, beating vigorously until glossy. Beat in the cheese. Spoon the pastry around the edge of a greased 1.2 litre (2 pint) ovenproof dish.

To make the filling, heat the oil and cook the onion until softened. Add the mushrooms and garlic and fry for 2 minutes. Stir in the flour, then add the stock and bring to the boil, stirring. Cook for 3 minutes until thickened. Reserve 2 tablespoons of the walnuts and stir the remainder into the mushroom mixture, with the parsley and salt and pepper. Pour the filling into the centre of the dish and sprinkle with the reserved walnuts. Bake in a preheated oven for 40–45 minutes.

■ COOK'S TIP

To avoid choux pastry collapsing, do not open the oven door to check the pastry until three-quarters of the cooking time is completed.

175

broccoli flan

Preparation time
35 minutes, plus chilling

Cooking time
50–55 minutes

Oven temperature
200°C (400°F), gas 6 then 190°C (375°F), gas 5

Serves 4

Calories
530 per portion

1 quantity shortcrust pastry (see recipe 156)
FOR THE FILLING
250 g (8 oz) frozen broccoli, defrosted
125 g (4 oz) Danish Blue cheese
3 eggs, beaten
150 ml (¼ pint) single cream
¼ teaspoon ground nutmeg
salt and pepper

Make the shortcrust pastry. Roll out on a lightly floured surface and line a 20 cm (8 inch) flan dish or tin and chill for 30 minutes. Bake blind (see Cook's Tip, recipe 177) in a moderately hot oven for 15 minutes. Remove the beans and foil and reduce the oven setting to the lower temperature.

Thoroughly drain the defrosted broccoli on kitchen paper and cut into 2.5 cm (1 inch) pieces, breaking up any large florets. Arrange over the base of the flan. Beat the cheese to soften it slightly. Add the eggs and beat until smooth. Mix in the cream, nutmeg and salt and pepper and pour over the broccoli. Cook for 35–40 minutes until the filling has set.

Serve with baked jacket potatoes and tomato salad.

176

mushroom flan

Preparation time
35 minutes, plus setting

Cooking time
55–60 minutes

Oven temperature
200°C (400°F), gas 6 then 180°C (350°F), gas 4

Serves 6

Calories
425 per portion

1 quantity shortcrust pastry (see recipe 156)
1 tablespoon horseradish mustard
250 g (8 oz) flat mushrooms
4 tablespoons oil
375 g (12 oz) cottage cheese
2 eggs, beaten
1 tablespoon chopped parsley
1½ teaspoons agar-agar or 2 teaspoons powdered gelatine
200 ml (7 fl oz) very hot clear vegetable stock
salt and pepper

Roll out the pastry to line a 23 cm (9 inch) flan tin. Bake blind (see Cook's Tip, recipe 177) in a preheated oven for 15 minutes. Reduce the oven temperature. Spread the flan case with the mustard. Reserve one large mushroom and slice the remainder.

Heat the oil and cook all the mushrooms in two batches until softened. Drain well on kitchen paper and scatter half over the mustard. Beat the cheese, eggs, parsley and together with salt and pepper to taste, then turn into the flan case. Cook in a preheated oven for 30 minutes. Place the cooked whole mushroom in the centre of the flan and surround with the reserved mushroom slices. Dissolve the agar-agar or gelatine in the hot stock and use to glaze the flan when half set.

■ COOK'S TIP

Danish blue cheese is white with blue veins. The texture should be creamy and slightly crumbly. Avoid any cheeses that have a dull bloom or show signs of sweating.

■ COOK'S TIP

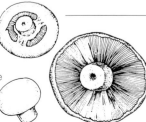

The fully mature open or flat mushrooms are the richest in flavour. When a mushroom is small and firm it is called a button; if a little larger but still closed underneath, it is called a cup mushroom.

177

watercress and brie quiche

Preparation time	FOR THE PASTRY
25 minutes	*125 g (4 oz) plain flour*
Cooking time	*125 g (4 oz) wholemeal flour*
45 minutes	*½ teaspoon salt*
Oven temperature	*50 g (2 oz) butter, softened*
200°C (400°F),	*25 g (1 oz) lard*
gas 6 then	*about 3 tablespoons water*
180°C (350°F),	FOR THE FILLING
gas 4	*300 g (10 oz) ripe Brie cheese*
Serves 6	*300 ml (½ pint) milk*
Calories	*125 g (4 oz) watercress, trimmed*
445 per portion	*3 eggs, beaten*
	1 teaspoon mustard powder
	pepper

Sift the flours and salt into a bowl or food processor, adding the bran remaining in the sieve to the bowl. Rub in the fats or process until the mixture resembles breadcrumbs. Add just enough water to mix to a firm dough. Roll out on a lightly floured surface and use to line a 23 cm (9 inch) loose-bottomed flan tin. Bake blind in a moderately hot oven for 10 minutes (see Cook's Tip).

Meanwhile, remove the rind from the Brie. Dice the cheese, place in a saucepan with the milk and stir over a low heat until blended. Remove from the heat, stir in the watercress, beaten eggs, mustard and salt and pepper. Pour into the flan case and cook in a preheated oven for 35 minutes. Cool slightly before removing from the tin.

■ COOK'S TIP

To bake blind, line the pie shell with greaseproof paper and fill with baking beans. Bake in a moderately hot oven for 10 minutes, then remove paper and beans. Proceed as in the recipe above. If, however, the pie shell is to have a cold (or separately cooked) filling, bake for 15 minutes with the beans, and a further 5 minutes after the beans and paper have been removed.

178

rainbow quiche

Preparation time	FOR THE PASTRY
25 minutes	*125 g (4 oz) wholemeal flour*
Cooking time	*50 g (2 oz) plain flour*
35–40 minutes	*pinch of salt*
Oven temperature	*50 g (2 oz) butter, softened*
220°C (424°F),	*2 tablespoons poppy seeds*
gas 7 then	*2–3 tablespoons water*
190°C (375°F),	FOR THE FILLING
gas 5	*15 g (½ oz) butter*
Serves 4	*1 red onion, sliced*
Calories	*175 g (6 oz) red, green or yellow pepper,*
555 per portion	*cored, deseeded and sliced*
	1 courgette, sliced
	1 tablespoon chopped basil
	125 g (4 oz) Cheddar cheese, grated
	1 tomato, sliced
	3 eggs
	150 ml (¼ pint) single cream
	pepper
	basil leaves, to garnish

Mix the flours and salt in a large bowl and rub in the butter. Stir in the poppy seeds and enough water to mix to a firm dough. Roll out and line a 19 cm (7½ inch) flan tin. Melt the butter for the filling in a large pan and fry the onion, pepper and courgette until softened. Place in the flan case with the basil, Cheddar, tomato and black pepper. Beat the eggs and cream and pour over.

Cook in a preheated oven for 15 minutes, then reduce the temperature and cook for a further 15 minutes, until set. Garnish with basil.

■ COOK'S TIP

If possible, use a red or purple onion, and red, yellow or green peppers, or even a combination, to make this quiche live up to its name.

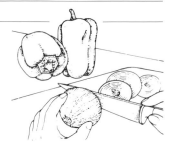

179

leek flans

Preparation time
25 minutes

Cooking time
45 minutes

Oven temperature
200°C (400°F),
gas 6 then
190°C (375°F),
gas 5

Serves 4

Calories
540 per portion

FOR THE SHORTCRUST PASTRY
175 g (6 oz) wholemeal or plain flour
75 g (3 oz) butter
2–3 tablespoons cold water
FOR THE FILLING
2 leeks, halved
1 celery stick
25 g (1 oz) butter
135 g (4½ oz) Danish Bolina cheese
2 eggs, beaten
150 ml (¼ pint) milk
¼ teaspoon grated nutmeg
15 g (½ oz) flaked almonds (optional)
salt and pepper

Place the flour in a bowl and rub in the butter until the mixture resembles fine breadcrumbs. Add enough water to make a stiff dough. roll out on a lightly floured board and use to line 4 individual flan tins. Bake blind (see Cook's Tip, recipe 177) in a preheated oven for 10 minutes, removing the baking beans and greaseproof paper after 7 minutes . Reduce the oven temperature.

Slice the leeks and celery. Melt the butter and cook the vegetables, covered, for 5–7 minutes until softened. Crumble the cheese into a bowl, beat to soften, then work in the eggs, a little at a time, to make a smooth mixture. Stir in the milk, nutmeg and salt and pepper.

Divide the vegetables between the flan cases, pour the cheese mixture over the top, scatter with the almonds, if using, and bake for 20–25 minutes.

■ COOK'S TIP

The flans make a superb summer starter; alternatively, make them a feature of a summer picnic basket – much more impressive than a pile of sandwiches!

180

carrot and cumin quiche

Preparation time
20 minutes

Cooking time
40 minutes

Oven temperature
200°C (400°F),
gas 6

Serves 4

Calories
510 per portion

175 g (6 oz) plain flour
pinch of salt
75 g (3 oz) margarine
2 tablespoons cold water
FOR THE FILLING
175 g (6 oz) cooked carrots
1 x 425 g (14 oz) can butter beans,
drained
¾ teaspoon ground cumin
3 eggs
125 g (4 oz) Cheddar cheese, grated

Sift the flour and salt into a bowl. Cut the margarine into small pieces and rub into the flour until the mixture resembles fine breadcrumbs. Add enough water to mix to a dough. Roll out on a lightly floured board to line a 20 cm (8 inch) flan dish or ring placed on a baking sheet.

To make the filling, blend the carrots, beans, cumin and eggs in a food processor. Pour half the mixture into the flan case, sprinkle with half the Cheddar cheese, cover with the remaining mixture then top with remaining cheese. Bake in a preheated oven for 40 minutes. Serve hot or cold.

If liked, follow the attractive serving suggestion in the photograph by bordering the quiche on a serving plate with mixed salad leaves, for example, curly endive and radicchio.

■ COOK'S TIP

When buying carrots, look for firm bright orange ones without splits. From the point of view of nutrition, they are best eaten raw, but if cooked whole, and scrubbed rather than peeled, you will still be rewarded with plenty of vitamin A.

181

vegetable pie

Preparation time
45 minutes

Cooking time
55–65 minutes

Oven temperature
190°C (375°F),
gas 5

Serves 4

Calories
650 per portion

1 turnip, diced and cooked
1 parsnip, diced and cooked
4 carrots, diced and cooked
125 g (4 oz) cooked yellow split peas
1 leek, washed, sliced and cooked
2 courgettes, diced and cooked
FOR THE SAUCE
40 g (1½ oz) butter
2 tablespoons plain flour
4 tablespoon natural yogurt
250 ml (8 fl oz) milk
1 teaspoon mixed herbs
1 teaspoon paprika
salt and pepper
FOR THE CHEESE PASTRY
125 g (4 oz) plain flour
125 g (4 oz) wholemeal flour
125 g (4 oz) margarine
125 g (4 oz) low-fat hard cheese, grated
2–3 tablespoons cold water
1 egg, beaten, to glaze

Put the vegetables into a pie dish. Whisk all the sauce ingredients in a pan over a low heat until smooth and thickened. Pour over the vegetables. Mix the flours in a bowl, then rub in the fat and stir in the cheese. Mix in enough water to bind the pastry. Roll out to a shape slightly larger than the top of the pie dish. Cover the pie, sealing the edges well. Use the trimmings for decoration. Brush with beaten egg. Bake the pie in a preheated moderately hot oven for 40–50 minutes.

■ COOK'S TIP

Pastry trimmings bring out the artist in every cook. Shape leaves or flowers, make letters that spell out a guest's name or use pastry cutters to add decorative shapes like Christmas trees or hearts.

182

leek pie

Preparation time
25 minutes

Cooking time
45 minutes

Oven temperature
200°C (400°F),
gas mark 6

Serves 4

Calories
455 per portion

FOR THE SHORTCRUST PASTRY
250 g (8 oz) plain flour
pinch of salt
125 g (4 oz) margarine
3 tablespoons cold water
FOR THE FILLING
6 large leeks, sliced
25 g (1 oz) butter
300 ml (½ pint) creamy milk
2 eggs
25 g (1 oz) Cheddar cheese, grated
salt and pepper

Sift the flour and salt into a bowl. Cut the margarine into small pieces and rub into the flour until the mixture resembles fine breadcrumbs. Add enough water to mix to a dough. Roll out half the pastry on a lightly floured board and line an 18 cm (7 inch) sandwich cake tin.

To make the filling, cook the leeks with the butter in a large saucepan until softened, about 5 minutes. Cool and place in the pie case. Beat the milk and eggs together and season well with salt and pepper. Pour over the leeks and sprinkle with the cheese. Roll out the remaining pastry and use to cover the filling. Seal the edges with water. Brush the dough with a little extra milk and bake in a preheated oven for 40 minutes or until golden. Serve hot.

■ COOK'S TIP

A piecrust may be decorated before it is placed on the pie. Roll out the pastry to a round 2.5 cm (1 inch) larger than the top of the pie, cut out a simple design, then flip the pastry over a rolling pin to transfer to the pie.

183

pumpkin pie

Preparation time
30 minutes, plus
chilling

Cooking time
1 hour

Oven temperature
220°C (425°F),
gas 7 then
190°C (375°F),
gas 5

Serves 6–8

Calories
455–340 per portion

500 g (1 lb) pumpkin
50 g (2 oz) butter
1 large onion, sliced
250 g (8 oz) potatoes
125 g (4 oz) cooked peas
125 g (4 oz) Cheshire cheese, crumbled
1 x 400 g (13 oz) packet frozen puff
  pastry, defrosted
beaten egg, to glaze
salt and pepper

Peel the pumpkin and cut the flesh into cubes, discarding the seeds. Cook the cubes in simmering salted water for 15 minutes. Drain very thoroughly. Melt the butter in a pan and gently cook the onion until browned. Mix with the pumpkin. Dice and cook the potatoes; add to the pumpkin with the peas, cheese and season with salt and pepper.

Roll out the pastry thinly and cut out two circles – one 25 cm (10 inches) in diameter, the other 30 cm (12 inches) in diameter. Place the smaller circle on a greased baking tray. Pile the filling on the pastry, leaving a 1 cm (½ inch) border. Brush the border with beaten egg, then top with the second pastry circle. Seal the edges and decorate with pastry trimmings. Glaze and bake in a preheated hot oven for 15 minutes, then reduce the oven temperature to moderately hot and bake for a further 15 minutes.

■ COOK'S TIP

Pumpkins shouldn't be reserved just for Hallowe'en lanterns. A nutritious vegetable, high in vitamin A, it is delicious roasted in the oven or boiled and mashed with a little butter and lots of black pepper and nutmeg.

184

corn fritters

Preparation time
10 minutes

Cooking time
15 minutes

Serves 4

Calories
235 per portion

40 g (1½ oz) wholemeal flour
250 g (8 oz) canned sweetcorn, drained
2 tablespoons snipped chives
2 eggs, beaten
3 tablespoons water
25 g (1 oz) butter
250 g (8 oz) mushrooms, sliced
250 g (8 oz) tomatoes, skinned and
  chopped
1 tablespoon chopped parsley
vegetable oil, for cooking
salt and pepper

Put the flour in a bowl, stir in the sweetcorn and chives, reserving a small quantity for garnish, and beat in the eggs. Add enough water to make a thick batter and transfer to a jug.

Heat the butter in a saucepan and cook the mushrooms for 3 minutes. Stir in the tomatoes, parsley and salt and pepper and set aside.

Heat a little vegetable oil in a heavy-based frying pan or griddle until hot. Pour spoonfuls of the batter on to the pan and cook quickly until golden underneath and just set on top. Turn over and quickly cook the other side. Drain on absorbent kitchen paper and keep warm while cooking the remaining batter.

Towards the end of cooking, return the mushroom mixture to the heat and warm through gently. Serve the fritters topped with the mushroom mixture and garnished with the reserved chives.

■ COOK'S TIP

Only a little oil is needed for cooking the fritters, so either brush it on with a bristle brush or use a pad of absorbent kitchen paper to rub it on, taking care not to burn your fingers!

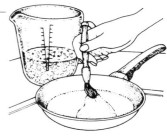

185

mushroom vol-au-vents

Preparation time 20 minutes **Cooking time** 35 minutes **Oven temperature** 220°C (425°F), gas 7 **Makes 12** **Calories** 130 per vol-au-vent	*12 frozen puff pastry vol-au-vent cases* *beaten egg, to glaze* FOR THE FILLING *1 tablespoon oil* *1 onion, finely chopped* *125 g (4 oz) carrot, diced* *250 g (8 oz) mushrooms, sliced* *2 tablespoons plain flour* *200 ml (7 fl oz) skimmed milk* *¼ teaspoon dried sage* *salt and pepper* *75 g (3 oz) Sage Derby cheese, cubed* *salad ingredients, to garnish*

Place the vol-au-vent cases on a dampened baking tray. Brush with beaten egg and bake in a preheated oven for 15–20 minutes, or as directed on the packet.

Heat the oil and cook the onion and carrot slowly in a covered pan for 5 minutes. Add the mushrooms and cook for a further 3 minutes. Stir in the flour and cook for 1 minute. Gradually add the milk and bring to the boil, stirring. Add the sage, seasoning and cheese. Spoon into the cooked vol-au-vent cases and serve at once, garnished with salad.

186

feta parcels

Preparation time 30 minutes **Cooking time** 35 minutes **Oven temperature** 180°C (350°F), gas 4 **Serves 6** **Calories** 570 per parcel	*150 g (5 oz) butter* *1 large onion, chopped* *750 g (1½ lb) frozen chopped spinach,* * defrosted and drained* *250 g (8 oz) feta cheese* *2 bunches of spring onions, chopped* *25 g (1 oz) chopped parsley* *1 tablespoon dill* *2 eggs, beaten* *10 sheets filo pastry* *salt and pepper*

Melt 25 g (1 oz) of the butter and cook the onion for 5 minutes until softened. Place the spinach in a bowl, crumble the cheese over it, then stir in the spring onions, parsley, dill, eggs and salt and pepper to taste and mix well.

Melt the remaining butter. Unwrap the filo pastry sheets. Place one on the work surface and brush with some of the butter, cover with a second sheet and brush with butter. Continue until 5 sheets have been brushed with butter. Brush the top sheet. (Cover any pastry not being used with a cloth). Cut the layered pastry into three, widthways. Divide half of the spinach mixture between the strips leaving a 2.5 cm (1 inch) border down the long edges. Fold in the long edges, brush with butter and fold up the short edges to make parcels 13 x 9 cm (5 x 3½ inches).

Place the parcels on a baking sheet, mark the tops and brush with butter. Repeat with the remaining filo pastry sheets and spinach mixture. Bake for 25–30 minutes until golden.

■ COOK'S TIP

Don't save vol-au-vents for parties and weddings. With interesting fillings, they make tasty suppers or quick starters for unexpected guests. Children enjoy them too, particularly if they can choose their own fillings.

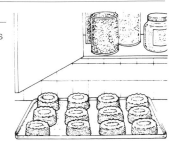

■ COOK'S TIP

Filo pastry is available in continental delicatessens and large supermarkets. If it's not to hand, the parcels may be made with puff pastry instead. Use 1 x 400 g (13 oz) packet, defrosted. Cut in half and roll each piece to a rectangle 30 x 37.5 cm (12 x 15 inches). The parcels will be slightly smaller.

187

quick pasties

Preparation time
15 minutes

Cooking time
20–25 minutes

Oven temperature
220°C (425°F),
gas 7

Serves 4

Calories
540 per portion

*250 g (8 oz) shortcrust pastry (see
recipe 156)*
4 vegeburgers
125 g (4 oz) cream cheese
½ teaspoon oregano or marjoram
1 garlic clove, crushed
*4 large mushrooms, stalks removed and
chopped*
beaten egg or milk, to glaze

Roll out the pastry on a lightly floured board and cut out
8 rounds slightly larger than the vegeburgers. Place a vegeburger
on four of the circles. Mix together the cream cheese, herb, garlic and chopped mushroom stalks and spread equal amounts on
each burger. Top with a mushroom. Cover each with a circle of
pastry and seal the edges with water. Flute the edges and brush
with beaten egg or milk. Decorate with pastry leaves, if liked.
Bake in a preheated oven for 20–25 minutes or until crisp and
golden. Serve hot or cold.

188

blue cheese parcels

Preparation time
35 minutes

Cooking time
35–40 minutes

Oven temperature
200°C (400°F),
gas 4 then
180°C (350°F),
gas 4

Serves 4

Calories
655 per parcel

250 g (8 oz) wholemeal fl our
125 g (4 oz) plain flour
125 g (4 oz) butter
125 g (4 oz) Danish Blue cheese, grated
about 4 tablespoons water
FOR THE FILLING
175 g (6 oz) carrots, coarsely grated
250 g (8 oz) potatoes, diced
175 g (6 oz) onions, finely chopped
25 g (1 oz) Danish Blue cheese, grated
1½ teaspoons dried mixed herbs
3 tablespoons vegetable stock
salt and pepper

Place the flours in a bowl and rub in the butter. Stir in the grated
cheese and add enough water to give a soft but not sticky dough.
Knead lightly and divide the dough into four equal pieces. Roll
out each one on a lightly floured surface and cut to an 18 cm
(7 inch) circle, using a tea plate as a guide.

Mix together the ingredients for the filling and season to taste
with salt and pepper. Divide the mixture evenly between the pastry rounds, then lightly dampen the edges and draw together to
meet in the centre, pressing well to seal. Place on a baking tray
and cook in a preheated moderately hot oven for 20 minutes,
then reduce the heat to moderate for a further 15–20 minutes.
Serve hot or cold.

■ COOK'S TIP

It's worth pointing out that
home-made Vegetable Burgers
(see recipe 227) are delicious
when cooked in this way.

■ COOK'S TIP

Save time by grating the butter
into the flour mixture. Grate the
cheese first, then the firm butter.
Run the grater under hot water
and it will be very easy to clean.

189

cheese and onion flans

Preparation time 30 minutes, plus chilling	*175 g (6 oz) self-raising wholemeal flour*
	75 g (3 oz) margarine
	2 tablespoons crunchy peanut butter
Cooking time 30–35 minutes	*1–2 tablespoons water*
Oven temperature 200°C (400°F), gas 6, then 180°C (350°F), gas 4	FOR THE FILLING
	1 tablespoon groundnut oil
	2 onions, thinly sliced
	1 egg
Serves 4	*150 ml (¼ pint) milk*
	75 g (3 oz) Edam cheese, grated
Calories 515 per flan	*25 g (1 oz) salted peanuts, chopped*
	salt and pepper

Place the flour in a bowl, add the margarine and rub in until the mixture resembles fine breadcrumbs. Stir in the peanut butter and sufficient water to form a firm dough. Knead lightly then chill for 20 minutes. Roll out on a floured surface to line four 10 cm (4 inch) flan dishes.

Heat the oil in a pan, add the onions and cook gently until very soft, about 5 minutes. Cool slightly. Beat together the egg and milk and season with salt and pepper. Divide the onion between the flan cases and pour the egg mixture over the top. Sprinkle with the cheese and peanuts. Bake in a preheated moderately hot oven for 15 minutes, then reduce to moderate for a further 10–15 minutes until the filling is set and golden brown. Serve warm or cold.

190

tomato triangles

Preparation time 20 minutes	*250 g (8 oz) frozen wholemeal puff pastry, defrosted*
	beaten egg, to glaze
Cooking time 20 minutes	FOR THE FILLING
	275 (9 oz) ripe tomatoes
Oven temperature 220°C (425°F), gas 7	*250 g (8 oz) feta cheese, mashed*
	1 garlic clove, finely chopped
Makes 4	*2 tablespoons chopped parsley*
	2 tablespoons fresh wholewheat breadcrumbs
Calories 405 per triangle	

To make the filling, blanch the tomatoes in boiling water for 30 seconds. Rinse in cold water and skin. Dice the tomatoes, removing the core and the seeds. Mix the tomatoes with the cheese, garlic, parsley and breadcrumbs.

Roll out the pastry into a square just larger than 25 x 25 cm (10 x 10 inches). Cut out four 13 cm (5 inch) squares. Divide the filling between the pastry squares and dampen the edges. Fold the pieces of pastry in half diagonally and press the edges with a fork to seal in the filling. Glaze with beaten egg. Bake in a preheated hot oven for 20 minutes until puffed and golden.

■ **COOK'S TIP**

To make a large flan, roll out the pastry to line a 20 cm (8 inch) flan dish. Fill and bake in a moderately hot oven for 15 minutes, as above, then reduce the heat to moderate for a further 20–25 minutes.

■ **COOK'S TIP**

These triangles make perfect picnic fare. When cooked, pack them in rigid plastic boxes, using crumpled greaseproof paper to fill up any gaps and prevent them moving (and possibly disintegrating) en route.

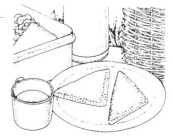

191

mushroom puffs

Preparation time 20 minutes	*250 g (8 oz) frozen wholemeal puff pastry, defrosted*
Cooking time 3 minutes	*18 button mushrooms*
Makes 18	*oil, for deep-frying*
Calories 55 per puff before frying	FOR THE DRESSING *125 g (4 oz) Stilton cheese, finely crumbled or grated*
Total for dressing 540	*150 ml (¼ pint) natural yogurt* *2 tablespoons chopped coriander leaves or snipped chives*

Roll out the pastry to a 30 cm (12 inch) square. Cut the square into six 10 x 15 cm (4 x 6 inch) strips. Cut each of these strips into 5 cm (2 inch) squares (total 36).

Clean the mushrooms, remove the stalks and use for another recipe, and place each mushroom on a square of pastry. Dampen the edges with water and place a pastry square on top. Press the edges together to seal. Heat the oil in a deep-fryer or saucepan to 180°C (350°F) and deep-fry the pastry squares a few at a time for 2–3 minutes or until puffed and golden. Drain on absorbent kitchen paper and keep warm while cooking the remainder.

To make the dressing, mash the Stilton with the yogurt until creamy. Stir in the coriander or chives. Serve the puffs hot or warm with the dressing.

■ COOK'S TIP

Do not add too may pastry-coated mushrooms to the oil at a time or the temperature will drop and the pastry will fail to puff up properly.

192

cheese and apple pie

Preparation time 10 minutes	*250 g (8 oz) frozen puff pastry, defrosted*
Cooking time 30 minutes	*50 g (2 oz) butter* *1 large onion, finely chopped*
Oven temperature 200°C (400°F), gas 6	*500 g (1 lb) cooking apples, peeled, cored and sliced*
Serves 4	*75 g (3 oz) walnuts, chopped* *250 g (8 oz) Sage Derby cheese, sliced*
Calories 700 per portion	*salt and pepper* *a little beaten egg or milk, to glaze*

Roll out the pastry on a lightly floured surface until slightly larger than the top of a 1.2 litre (2 pint) pie dish. Cut a strip from the edge and use to line the dampened rim of the dish.

Melt the butter in a frying pan, add the onion and apple and cook for 5 minutes until slightly softened. Layer the onion and apple mixture with the walnuts and cheese in the pie dish, seasoning each layer with salt and pepper.

Dampen the pastry strip and cover with the pastry lid. Trim and flute the edges. If liked, use the pastry trimmings to decorate. Brush with beaten egg or milk and bake for 20–25 minutes until crisp and golden.

■ COOK'S TIP

The combination of onion, apple, walnuts and cheese would be just as good in a double crust pie and in that form would be ideal for a picnic. Serve it with a simple salad (transported separately).

vegetable dishes

Packed with vitamins, minerals and fibre, fresh vegetables are a delight to cook with, and are often more efficient in conserving nutritional content. Vegetables form a colourful accompaniment to a main course, contributing subtle or distinctive flavours. Some of the recipes in this chapter make a complete main course.

193

button mushrooms with green peppercorns

Preparation time 10 minutes	500 g (1 lb) small white button mushrooms
Cooking time 15 minutes	1 tablespoon olive oil 4 tablespoons water
Serves 4	salt
Calories 217 per portion	4 slices brown bread 2 tablespoons vegetable oil 25 g (1 oz) butter 3 teaspoons green peppercorns, crushed 2 tablespoons double or whipping cream coriander leaves, to garnish

Wash the mushrooms and pat them dry on kitchen paper. If they are all small leave them whole, but halve any larger ones.

Heat the oil in a large frying pan and fry the mushrooms quickly for about 5 minutes until just beginning to brown. Add the water and a little salt, cover and simmer for 10 minutes, by which time there will be a fair amount of liquid in the pan.

While the mushrooms are cooking, make the croûtons. Cut the crusts off the bread and cut the slices into 1 cm (½ inch) dice. Heat the oil and butter in a frying pan until sizzling and add the bread cubes. Fry quickly until golden brown then drain on kitchen paper.

Stir the peppercorns and cream into the mushrooms and reheat gently without boiling. Tip into a warm serving dish and scatter with the croûtons. Garnish with the coriander leaves.

194

new potatoes with fennel and mint

Preparation time 10 minutes	1 kg (2 lb) tiny new potatoes 15 g (½ oz) butter or soya margarine
Cooking time 15–20 minutes	1 small fennel bulb, trimmed and finely chopped
Serves 4	salt and pepper
Calories 213 per portion	2 tablespoons chopped fresh mint, plus mint sprigs, to garnish
Suitable for vegans using soya margarine	

Bring a pan of salted water to the boil and add the potatoes. Simmer for about 15 minutes until tender and drain.

Put the butter or soya margarine into the warm pan and heat gently. Add the fennel and fry for about 5 minutes until just beginning to brown then season well with pepper.

Tip the cooked potatoes into the pan, add the mint and toss the potatoes so that they are coated with butter or soya margarine, mint and fennel. Serve hot, garnished with sprigs of mint.

■ COOK'S TIP

This is a simple but unusual way to serve button mushrooms which also makes a delicious starter. Green peppercorns are sold either in jars or small cans in most delicatessens or large stores. They are quite soft, and so can be crushed easily.

■ COOK'S TIP

Jersey or English new potatoes are the best for this dish. When out of season or for a quick cooking dish, use canned new potatoes. Cook as instructed on the can.

195

pan-braised peppers with tomato

Preparation time 25 minutes	*1 tablespoon vegetable oil* *2 onions, roughly chopped*
Cooking time 30 minutes	*3 large peppers, red, green and yellow,* *total weight about 500 g (l lb),*
Serves 4	*deseeded and cut into strips*
Calories 68 per portion	*500 g (1 lb) tomatoes, skinned and* *chopped*
Suitable for vegans	*1 teaspoon coriander seed* *1 teaspoon black peppercorns* *½ teaspoon salt* *½ teaspoon ground chilli*

Heat the oil in a large frying pan and fry the onions for about 5 minutes until golden. Add the peppers and cook gently for 2–3 minutes, then stir in the tomatoes.

Crush the coriander seeds and peppercorns. Use a pestle and mortar if you have one; otherwise put the seeds and peppercorns between double sheets of kitchen paper and crush with a rolling pin. Add the salt and chilli to the crushed seeds and sprinkle the mixture over the peppers and tomatoes. Mix together lightly, cover the pan and cook gently for 20 minutes. This dish can be prepared up to 24 hours in advance and kept covered in the refrigerator.

196

fennel with walnuts

Preparation time 10 minutes	*2 small fennel bulbs with leaves* FOR THE DRESSING
Cooking time 1 minute	*4 tablespoons olive oil* *1 garlic clove, crushed (optional)*
Serves 4	*125 g (4 oz) walnuts, chopped*
Calories 293 per portion	*salt and pepper*
Suitable for vegans	

Slice the fennel into thin, short strips, reserving the feathery leaves. Divide between 4 individual dishes.

Heat the olive oil in a small pan and add the garlic, if using, and walnuts. Fry quickly until the walnuts just begin to brown. Add salt and pepper then spoon the hot dressing over the cold fennel strips.

Garnish the dish with the reserved fennel leaves and serve immediately.

■ COOK'S TIP

A vegetable recipe full of flavour and colour. It is not essential to use different coloured peppers, but it does look attractive. This dish is wonderful hot and almost as good served cold with a salad selection.

■ COOK'S TIP

This dish of crisp aniseed-flavoured fennel smothered in hot walnut dressing is quick to prepare and delicious. You could also use celery instead of fennel.

197

stuffed spinach leaves

Preparation time 15 minutes **Cooking time** 55 minutes **Oven temperature** 190°C (375°F) gas 5 **Serves 4** **Calories** 111 per portion	*12 large spinach leaves, stalks removed* *1 tablespoon oil* *1 onion, chopped* *2 garlic cloves, crushed* *250 g (8 oz) mushrooms, chopped* *75 g (3 oz) wholemeal breadcrumbs* *1 tablespoon chopped mixed herbs,* * e.g. parsley, thyme and marjoram* *1 medium egg, beaten* *salt and pepper*

Put the spinach into a large pan with 300 ml (¼ pint) salted water and boil for 2 minutes. Drain, reserving the liquid. Rinse the spinach and pat dry.

Heat the oil in a pan, add the onion and fry until softened. Add the garlic and mushrooms and cook for 5 minutes. Stir in the breadcrumbs, herbs, egg, and salt and pepper.

Place 1 tablespoon of the mixture in the centre of each spinach leaf, fold in both sides and roll up. Place the spinach rolls in a shallow ovenproof dish and pour over 150 ml (¼ pint) of the reserved liquid. Cover with foil and bake in a preheated oven for 45 minutes. Lift out with a slotted spoon and reserve the juices. Serve with Lemon sauce (see Cook's Tip).

198

vegetable curry

Preparation time 30 minutes **Cooking time** 30 minutes **Serves 4** **Calories** 145 per portion	*2 tablespoons oil* *1 onion, sliced* *2 teaspoons ground coriander* *2 teaspoons ground cumin* *2 garlic cloves, crushed* *5 cm (2 inch) piece of fresh root ginger,* * chopped* *1 x 400 g (13 oz) can chopped tomatoes* *1 green chilli, finely chopped* *2 potatoes, diced* *2 carrots, sliced* *175 g (6 oz) okra, chopped* *250 g (8 oz) cauliflower, broken into* * florets* *2 tablespoons chopped coriander* *salt and pepper*

Heat the oil in a large pan, add the onion and fry until softened. Add the ground coriander, cumin, garlic and ginger and fry for 1 minute, stirring constantly. Add the tomatoes, 150 ml (¼ pint) water, chilli, potatoes, carrots, okra, cauliflower and salt and pepper to taste. Mix to coat the vegetables with the sauce. Cover and cook gently for 20 minutes, until tender. Stir in the chopped coriander.

Serve the Vegetable curry on a bed of brown rice and with such typical curry accompaniments as Cucumber raita (see Cook's Tip).

■ COOK'S TIP

For Lemon sauce, whisk 2 medium egg yolks with 1 tablespoon lemon juice over a pan of simmering water. Add the reserved vegetable juices and stir for about 5 minutes until thickened. Season with salt and pepper and pour over the rolls.

■ COOK'S TIP

For Cucumber raita, grate ¼ cucumber and drain off any juices. Mix with 150 g (5 oz) natural yogurt and salt to taste. Sprinkle with paprika before serving.

199

popovers

Preparation time 25 minutes	*1 tablespoon vegetable oil* *1 large onion, thinly sliced*
Cooking time 25 minutes	*500 g (1 lb) ripe tomatoes, skinned and* *chopped*
Oven temperature 220°C (425°F) gas 8	*1 teaspoon soy sauce* *2 teaspoons tomato purée* *salt and pepper*
Serves 4–6	FOR THE BATTER *50 g (2 oz) plain wholemeal flour*
Calories 246–164 per portion	*50 g (2 oz) plain white flour* *pinch of cayenne pepper*
	1 teaspoon dried mixed herbs *2 eggs, beaten* *1 tablespoon vegetable oil, plus extra* *150 ml (5 fl oz) milk* *150 ml (5 fl oz) water*

Heat the oil in a pan and fry the onion for 10 minutes until brown. Add the tomatoes, soy sauce, tomato purée, salt and plenty of pepper. Bring to simmering point, stirring, then cover the pan and cook gently for 10 minutes.

To make the batter, put the flours, ½ teaspoon salt, pepper, cayenne and herbs into a bowl. Add the eggs, oil and half the milk and mix to a smooth paste. Gradually whisk in the remaining milk and the water. Pour the batter into a jug.

Oil 2 trays of 12 tart tins and put them in a preheated oven until smoking hot. Remove from the oven, pour the batter into the tins, almost filling them, and bake for about 12 minutes until puffed up and golden. Serve with the hot sauce.

■ COOK'S TIP

The sauce can be prepared up to 24 hours in advance and kept tightly covered with clingfilm in the refrigerator. Reheat when the popovers are ready to come out of the oven.

The batter can be made up to 8 hours in advance and kept in the refrigerator.

200

curried sweetcorn and potato fritters

Preparation time 25 minutes	*50 g (2 oz) plain wholemeal flour* *1 medium egg, lightly beaten*
Cooking time 25 minutes	*4 tablespoons milk* *1 teaspoon hot curry paste*
Oven temperature 110°C (250°F) gas ¼	*500 g (1 lb) potatoes, unpeeled, washed* *and coarsely grated*
Serves 4	*1 onion, grated*
Calories 288 per portion	*1 x 200 g (7 oz) can sweetcorn, drained* *4–6 tablespoons vegetable oil, for frying* *salt and pepper*

Put the flour, egg, milk, curry paste and salt and pepper to taste into a large bowl and mix to a smooth, thick batter.

Put the grated potato into a clean cloth and twist both ends towards the middle to squeeze out any surplus, starchy liquid. Pat the potato dry with kitchen paper and add to the batter with the onion and sweetcorn.

Heat 1 tablespoon of the oil in a large frying pan and drop the mixture in 1 tablespoon at a time, gently nudging each fritter into a round flat shape with a fish slice. Cook about 4 fritters at a time.

Fry the fritters for 3–4 minutes on each side, then drain on kitchen paper and keep hot while frying the next batch.

Arrange the fritters on a warm dish and serve with a bowl of Yogurt and watercress dressing (see Cook's Tip).

■ COOK'S TIP

For Yogurt and watercress dressing, mix 150 ml (5 fl oz) natural yogurt and 1 bunch of finely chopped watercress with salt and pepper to taste. Let the dressing stand at room temperature for 1 hour.

201

eggs in the nest

Preparation time 15 minutes	*375 g (12 oz) potatoes*
	250 g (8 oz) parsnips, sliced
Cooking time 40 minutes	*25 g (1 oz) soft margarine*
	5 medium eggs
Oven temperature 190°C (375°F) gas 5	*pinch of grated nutmeg*
	2 tablespoons chopped parsley
	75 g (3 oz) low-fat vegetarian Cheddar
Serves 4	*cheese, grated*
Calories 185 per portion	*salt and pepper*
	parsley sprigs, to garnish

Cook the potatoes and parsnips in boiling salted water for 15–20 minutes until they are tender. Drain and mash. Beat in the margarine and 1 of the eggs and season with salt, pepper and nutmeg. Stir in the chopped parsley and 40 g (1½ oz) of the cheese.

Spoon the potato mixture into four 10 cm (4 inch) greased individual baking rings standing on a baking sheet, or muffin tins, and shape it to make nests. Make a ridge round the top with a fork. Break 1 egg into each nest and sprinkle the remaining cheese on top.

Bake in a preheated oven for 15–20 minutes until the eggs are set. Garnish with the parsley and serve at once.

202

stuffed vine leaves

Preparation time 45 minutes, plus cooling	*250 g (8 oz) preserved vine leaves, drained (see Cook's Tip)*
	175 g (6 oz) brown rice
Cooking time 1½ hours	*1 small onion, finely chopped*
	2 tablespoons chopped parsley
Serves 4	*2 tablespoons chopped mint*
	generous pinch of ground cinnamon
Calories 240 per portion	*generous pinch of mixed spice*
	2 garlic cloves, crushed
Suitable for vegans	*50 g (2 oz) pine nuts, chopped*
	50 g (2 oz) currants
	finely grated rind of ½ lemon
	250 ml (8 fl oz) water
	salt and pepper

Soak the brown rice in boiling water for 2–3 minutes, then rinse under cold water, drain and mix with the onion, parsley, mint, spices, garlic, pine nuts, currants, lemon rind and salt and pepper to taste.

Use a few damaged or misshapen vine leaves to line the base and sides of a large frying pan; reserve 4–6 perfect leaves for serving. Divide the rice mixture among the remaining leaves; fold in the edges and roll up the leaves, so that the filling is completely enclosed. Pack the stuffed leaves closely together in the lined pan. Pour over the water. Cover the pan tightly, and simmer very gently for 1½ hours; top up with more water if the liquid evaporates too much during cooking.

Allow to cool in the pan. Place a perfect vine leaf on each serving plate, and arrange 5–6 stuffed leaves on top.

■ COOK'S TIP

Eggs are an important source of protein and iron, but are also high in saturated fat. Two or three a week is the nutritional recommendation.

■ COOK'S TIP

Put the vine leaves into a bowl and cover with boiling water. Stir the leaves so that they separate. Drain the leaves separately on absorbent kitchen paper.

203

colcannon

Preparation time
15 minutes

Cooking time
40 minutes

Oven temperature
200°C (400°F)
gas 6

Serves 4

Calories
142 per portion

250 g (8 oz) shredded white cabbage
625 g (1¼ lb) potatoes, cooked and
*   mashed without milk or butter*
25 g (1 oz) butter
1 onion, chopped
2 teaspoons poppy seeds
salt and pepper

Cook the cabbage in a little boiling, salted water for about 6 minutes until crisply tender. Drain and put into a bowl with the mashed potato.

Meanwhile, melt half the butter in a small pan and gently fry the onion until golden. Stir into the cabbage and potato and add a little salt and plenty of black pepper.

Use the remaining 15 g (½ oz) butter to grease a 500 g (1 lb) loaf tin, and scatter the poppy seeds over the base and sides of the tin to coat.

Spoon the cabbage and potato mixture into the tin, smooth the top and cover with foil. Bake in a preheated oven for 40 minutes, then turn out on to a hot dish and serve immediately.

204

stuffed avocado salad

Preparation time
20 minutes

Serves 2

Calories
341 per portion

1 large ripe avocado, halved and stoned
1 tablespoon lemon juice
2 tomatoes, skinned and chopped
2 spring onions, chopped
½ small green pepper, deseeded and finely
*   chopped*
50 g (2 oz) vegetarian Cheddar cheese,
*   grated*
salt and pepper
4 lettuce leaves
few sprigs of watercress
1 carrot, scraped and cut into matchsticks

Using a teaspoon, scoop out the avocado flesh, being careful not to damage the skin which will be needed for serving the salad. Dice the flesh and place in a bowl with the lemon juice, tomatoes, spring onions, green pepper and cheese. Season to taste with salt and pepper. Spoon the mixture into the avocado skins. Arrange the stuffed avocados on the lettuce leaves and garnish with watercress and carrot sticks.

■ COOK'S TIP

This dish, which can be served with Two-bean vegetable goulash (see recipe 83), Tomato sauce (see Cook's Tip, recipe 88) or just on its own, is an excellent way of using the insides of the potatoes left from the Potato jackets (see recipe 377).

■ COOK'S TIP

Cover the avocado with the lemon juice as soon as possible after cutting to prevent discoloration. If the salad has to stand for a while, cover the dishes with clingfilm.

205

summer vegetables with yogurt and mint

Preparation time 25 minutes	*250 g (8 oz) broad beans (shelled weight)*
Cooking time 15 minutes	*250 g (8 oz) runner beans, strings removed and sliced*
Serves 4	*250 g (8 oz) peas (shelled weight)*
Calories 101 per portion	*150 ml (¼ pint) natural yogurt*
	salt and pepper
	1 tablespoon chopped mint

Cook the broad beans for 8 minutes in a little boiling salted water then drain.

Cook the runner beans and peas together for 5 minutes and drain thoroughly.

Heat the yogurt gently in one of the vegetable pans, add the vegetables and toss to coat thoroughly. Gently stir in pepper and the mint and serve.

206

cauliflower with peanut sauce

Preparation time 25 minutes	*1 cauliflower, about 500 g (1 lb)*
Cooking time 15 minutes	*2 tablespoons chopped salted peanuts, to garnish*
Serves 4	FOR THE SAUCE
Calories 220 per portion	*15 g (½ oz) butter*
	15 g (½ oz) plain flour
	150 ml (¼ pint) milk
	150 ml (¼ pint) vegetable stock
	4 tablespoons crunchy peanut butter
	½ teaspoon yeast extract
	salt and pepper

Cut the cauliflower into florets, leaving some of the contrasting green leaves on. Cook the cauliflower in boiling salted water for about 6–8 minutes; it should be slightly crisp. Drain and keep warm in a serving dish.

While the cauliflower is cooking, make the sauce. Melt the butter in a small pan, add the flour and cook for 3 minutes. stirring all the time. Pour in the milk and vegetable stock and bring to the boil, still stirring. Simmer for 2–3 minutes then stir in the peanut butter, a spoonful at a time. The peanut butter will thicken the sauce. Add the yeast extract, a little salt if necessary and black pepper.

Pour the sauce over the cauliflower and sprinkle with the chopped peanuts. Serve hot.

■ COOK'S TIP

Frozen vegetables can be used instead of fresh ones, but cook for slightly less time than indicated on the packs. Use Greek yogurt for a creamier taste.

■ COOK'S TIP

If you have a grinder, try making your own peanut butter. Grind 125 g (4 oz) roasted peanuts finely and mash them to a paste in a bowl, adding a little vegetable oil, if necessary. Try using hazelnuts, cashews or walnuts to vary the taste.

207
noodles with mung beans

Preparation time
20 minutes

Cooking time
55–60 minutes

Serves 4

Calories
345 per portion

50 g (2 oz) dried mung beans, soaked
  overnight
6 tablespoons sunflower oil
1 garlic clove, crushed
1 teaspoon grated ginger root
2 tablespoons light soy sauce
1 tablespoon lime juice
pinch of cayenne pepper
50 g (2 oz) dried thread egg noodles
125 g (4 oz) carrots, sliced thinly
1 small red pepper, cored, deseeded and
  sliced thinly
125 g (4 oz) asparagus tips
15 g (½ oz) basil leaves

Drain the beans then cover with fresh water and boil rapidly for 10 minutes. Lower the heat and simmer gently for 35–40 minutes until tender. Whisk together 4 tablespoons of the oil, the garlic, soy sauce, lime juice and cayenne. Drain the cooked beans and toss with half the dressing. Set aside to cool.

Cook the noodles according to the packet instructions. Drain, and toss with the remaining dressing. Heat half the remaining oil in a frying pan and stir-fry the vegetables for 2–3 minutes until just tender, then transfer to a large bowl. Add the remaining oil to the pan and fry the basil leaves for 1–2 minutes. Arrange the noodles on serving plates. Toss the mung beans with the vegetables and spoon on to noodles. Top with the crispy basil leaves.

208
creamed swede duchesse

Preparation time
25 minutes

Cooking time
45 minutes

Oven temperature
200°C (400°F)
gas 6

Serves 4

Calories
245 per portion

750 g (1½ lb) potatoes, cubed
375 (12 oz) swedes, cubed
75 g (3 oz) low-fat soft cheese
25 g (1 oz) butter
50 g (2 oz) low-fat hard cheese, grated
salt and pepper
watercress sprigs, to garnish

Cook the potatoes and swede in boiling salted water until tender – about 20 minutes. Mash with salt and pepper, the soft cheese and butter. When cool enough to handle, pipe large vegetable rosettes on to a greased baking sheet. Bake for 20 minutes, until lightly browned. Sprinkle with the grated cheese and cook for a further 5–10 minutes until well browned. Serve at once, garnished with watercress.

■ COOK'S TIP

Noodles work equally well cold or hot, but when they are served cold they do need plenty of dressing or they can become rather dry.

■ COOK'S TIP

For piping savoury foods such as potato you will need a large star nozzle, sometimes referred to as a potato pipe. Make sure you have a large piping bag to hold plenty of the creamed vegetable.

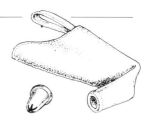

209

mediterranean potatoes

Preparation time 5 minutes	*750 g (1½ lb) potatoes* *1 teaspoon oil*
Cooking time 35 minutes	*50 g (2 oz) butter* *1 garlic clove, crushed*
Serves 4	*1 onion, sliced*
Calories 335 per portion	*125 g (4 oz) mushrooms, sliced* *1 small green pepper, cored, deseeded and* * sliced* *1 x 400 g (13 oz) can tomatoes* *2 teaspoons brown sugar* *1 teaspoon mixed herbs* *50 g (2 oz) fresh breadcrumbs* *grated Parmesan cheese (optional)* *salt and pepper*

Cut the potatoes into even-sized pieces and cook in enough boiling water to just cover for 10–15 minutes or until just done.

Meanwhile, heat the oil and half the butter in a frying pan. Add the garlic, onion, mushrooms and green pepper and cook for 5 minutes or until softened. Add the tomatoes and can juices, sugar, herbs and salt and pepper. Break up the tomatoes and cook for 10 minutes or until the onion is tender and the sauce not too runny. Melt the remaining butter in a small pan, add the breadcrumbs and fry until brown and crisp.

Place the drained potatoes in a warm dish, pour over the sauce and sprinkle with the breadcrumbs. Serve hot with Parmesan cheese handed separately, if liked.

210

almond potatoes

Preparation time 10 minutes	*375 g (12 oz) potatoes, cooked and* * mashed with milk and butter*
Cooking time 12–18 minutes	*plain flour, seasoned with salt and pepper* *1 egg, beaten*
Serves 4	*125 g (4 oz) almonds, finely chopped*
Calories 320 per portion	*25 g (1 oz) butter* *1 tablespoon oil* *parsley sprigs, to garnish*

Divide the mashed potato into 12 pieces. Place the seasoned flour on a plate and form each potato piece into a medallion shape coating it with flour as you do so. Coat each medallion in the beaten egg and then the almonds.

Heat the butter and oil in a large frying pan and cook the medallions, a few at a time, for about 6 minutes, turning once, until golden. Drain on absorbent kitchen paper. Serve hot, garnished with parsley.

■ COOK'S TIP

If you are fond of Parmesan, for example with pasta, then a cheese mill is useful. This is a cylindrical enclosed grater. The cheese is stored in it and the lid is turned to grate it straight on to the food. From cookshops only.

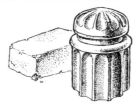

■ COOK'S TIP

These crunchy cakes can be frozen. Open freeze on trays lined with clingfilm, then pack in bags for storage. Cook from frozen, allowing time to heat through. They are also good dotted with butter and baked.

211

stir-fried potatoes

Preparation time 15 minutes	*500 g (1 lb) potatoes, grated and rinsed to* * extract starch*
Cooking time 20 minutes	*3 tablespoons oil* *375 g (12 oz) vegetables, finely chopped*
Serves 4	*1 teaspoon soy sauce*
Calories 225 per portion	*1 teaspoon ground ginger* *salt and pepper*

Use a cloth to squeeze the excess moisture from the grated potato. Heat the oil in a large nonstick pan or wok. Fry the grated potato for 5–10 minutes or until nearly cooked, stirring frequently. Add the chosen vegetables, soy sauce, ginger and salt and pepper and fry briskly for a further 5–10 minutes to cook the vegetables yet keep them crisp. Serve hot.

212

potatoes madras

Preparation time 15 minutes	*3 tablespoons oil or ghee* *750 g (1½ lb) potatoes, cut into large dice*
Cooking time 30 minutes	*250 g (8 oz) cauliflower, cut into florets* *1 large onion, sliced*
Serves 4–6	*2 garlic cloves, crushed (optional)*
Calories 380–255 per portion	*1 tablespoon curry powder* *½ teaspoon ground ginger* *125 g (4 oz) red lentils* *1 x 400 g (13 oz) can chopped tomatoes* *300 ml (½ pint) vegetable stock* *2 tablespoons malt vinegar* *1 tablespoon mango chutney* *salt and pepper* *chopped parsley or coriander leaves, to* * garnish*

Heat the oil in a large frying pan and quickly fry the potatoes, cauliflower, onion and garlic until just beginning to brown.

Stir in the curry powder and ginger. Continue to fry for a few minutes. Stir in all the remaining ingredients except the parsley. Cover and simmer for about 20 minutes, stirring occasionally until the vegetables and lentils are tender. Garnish and serve.

■ COOK'S TIP

Use a combination of the following: onion, cauliflower, peppers, runner beans, sweetcorn, broccoli, celery, courgettes, mushrooms, cabbage, leeks, parsnip. Add chopped cashew nuts too if you like.

■ COOK'S TIP

This makes a colourful main dish for a dinner party. Serve with a selection of accompaniments such as poppadoms, slices of banana, chutney, yogurt and desiccated coconut.

213

potato cake with cheese topping

Preparation time	750 g (1½ lb) potatoes, scrubbed but
15 minutes, plus cooling	*unpeeled*
	75 g (3 oz) butter
Cooking time	1 onion, chopped
35 minutes	125 g (4 oz) Danish Danbo or Havarti
Serves 4	*cheese, grated*
Calories	salt and pepper
375 per portion	sliced tomato, to garnish

Boil the potatoes for 10 minutes. Drain and cool slightly, then peel and leave for 20 minutes to cool completely. Coarsely grate the potatoes into a large bowl. Melt 25 g (1 oz) of the butter in a large frying pan and gently fry the onion for 5 minutes until softened. Remove the onion with a slotted spoon and gently stir into the potato.

Melt the remaining butter in the pan, add the potato mixture, sprinkle with salt and pepper and form into a cake. Cook gently for 5–7 minutes until golden on the underside. Invert a plate over the pan and turn the cake on to it, slide the cake back into the pan and fry for a further 7–10 minutes until golden.

Towards the end of the cooking time, heat a grill to moderate. Sprinkle the cake with the cheese and grill until bubbling. Garnish with tomato slices and serve with a mixed salad.

214

egg tatties

Preparation time	2 large potatoes
15 minutes	3 medium eggs
Cooking time	1 tablespoon milk
1 hour 25 minutes	15 g (½ oz) butter
Oven temperature	2 tablespoons finely chopped chives
200°C (400°F)	2 tablespoons thick Greek yogurt
gas 6	salt and pepper
Serves 2	watercress sprigs, to garnish
Calories	
395 per portion	

Clean the skins of the potatoes and prick at regular intervals with a fork. Bake in a moderately hot oven for about 1¼ hours, until tender. Just before the potatoes are ready, beat the eggs with the milk and salt and pepper to taste. Melt the butter and stir in the egg mixture; scramble lightly over a gentle heat, until the egg forms soft creamy flakes. Halve each potato lengthways and scoop out the cooked centre. Mix gently with the scrambled egg, half the chives and the yogurt then spoon back into the potato shells. Cover loosely with foil and return to the oven for a further 4–5 minutes. To serve, sprinkle with the remaining chives and garnish with watercress.

■ COOK'S TIP

If you like, add extra topping before the cheese – sliced tomatoes, chopped walnuts and mushrooms, cooked leeks, sweetcorn and pepper or any mixed, braised vegetables can be used.

■ COOK'S TIP

For a simple variation, why not add some diced mozzarella cheese and chopped spring onions to the egg mixture? The filled potatoes can be topped with chopped cashew nuts or walnuts and a little extra diced mozzarella.

215

mushrooms montebello

Preparation time
10 minutes, plus
marinating

Serves 4

Calories
130 per portion

250 g (8 oz) button mushrooms
4 tablespoons sunflower oil
1 garlic clove, crushed
pinch of dill
½ teaspoon oregano
2 tablespoons red wine vinegar
1 teaspoon lemon juice
salt and pepper

Combine all the ingredients in a bowl. Cover with clingfilm and leave to marinate in the refrigerator overnight. Serve to accompany rice or pasta dishes, as part of salad buffet or as a starter.

216

stilton-stuffed mushrooms

Preparation time
10 minutes

Cooking time
6–8 minutes

Serves 4

Calories
310 per portion

50 g (2 oz) butter
8 medium flat mushrooms, stalks
*   removed, wiped*
4 small tomatoes, thinly sliced
175 g (6 oz) blue Stilton cheese, sliced
celery leaves, to garnish (optional)

Melt the butter in a sauté pan and cook the mushrooms open side uppermost for 3–4 minutes, until tender. Place in a flameproof dish, top each one with slices of tomato and cheese, then brown under a hot grill until the cheese is melted and bubbling. Serve at once, garnished with celery leaves if you like.

■ COOK'S TIP

These flavoursome marinated mushrooms make an excellent filling for a plain omelette. Add the well–drained mushrooms to the omelette when the egg is half set, cook until firm, then fold over and serve at once.

■ COOK'S TIP

Serve the mushrooms with ratatouille and baked potatoes for a tasty meal. For a starter or supper dish, serve them on neat rounds of wholemeal toast.

217

creamed chicory and mushrooms

Preparation time 15 minutes	*50 g (2 oz) onion, chopped*
	40 g (1½ oz) butter
Cooking time 10 minutes	*300 g (10 oz) chicory, sliced in half*
	125 g (4 oz) button mushrooms, sliced
Serves 4	*125 ml (4 fl oz) vegetable stock*
Calories 200 per portion	*125 ml (4 fl oz) double cream*
	salt and pepper
	chopped parsley, to garnish

Soften the onion in the butter over a gentle heat, without browning. Add the chicory and mushrooms and cook for a few minutes. Pour in the stock and simmer, covered, for 5 minutes. Remove from the heat, add the cream, season well with salt and pepper and reheat for a few minutes without boiling. Transfer to a warmed dish and sprinkle with chopped parsley.

218

mushroom fondue

Preparation time 15 minutes	*½ garlic clove*
	150 ml (¼ pint) medium dry cider
Cooking time 10–15 minutes	*1 teaspoon lemon juice*
	400 g (13 oz) Gouda cheese, grated
Serves 4	*1 tablespoon cornflour*
Calories 665 per portion	*1½ tablespoons gin*
	125 g (4 oz) button mushrooms, chopped
	pepper
	pinch of grated nutmeg
	TO SERVE
	1 French stick, cut into cubes
	125 g (4 oz) button mushrooms

Rub the inside of a fondue pot or flameproof casserole with the cut garlic, and place a little finely chopped garlic in the pot. Pour in the cider and lemon juice and heat slowly until nearly boiling. Gradually add the grated cheese, at little at a time, stirring continuously with a fork until all the cheese has melted. When the mixture is bubbling, blend the cornflour with the gin until smooth and add to the fondue, stirring well. Ad the chopped mushrooms, pepper and nutmeg.

Serve the cheese fondue in the cooking pot at the table. There should be a fondue fork for each person, and the cubes of French bread and whole button mushrooms are speared with the fork and dipped into the fondue. This is delicious accompanied by an orange and cucumber salad.

■ COOK'S TIP

Frozen double cream is a useful item to keep in the freezer. Packed in neat sticks, just remove the number required for the dish and defrost at room temperature.

■ COOK'S TIP

If gin is not to your taste, substitute an equivalent amount of any of the following: kirsch, whisky, brandy or dry sherry.

219
celery with mushrooms

Preparation time 15 minutes	*1 head of celery, trimmed*
	50 g (2 oz) butter
Cooking time 30 minutes	*1 onion, finely chopped*
	125 g (4 oz) mushrooms, thinly sliced
Serves 4	*coarsely grated rind of 1 lemon*
Calories 175 per portion	*75–100 g (3–4 oz) mozzarella cheese, cut into thin slivers*
	salt and pepper

Cut the celery diagonally into 4 cm (1½ inch) lengths. Blanch in a pan of boiling salted water for 5 minutes.

Melt the butter in a pan and fry the onion until soft. Add the celery and cook gently for 5–10 minutes until tender but still crisp. Add the mushrooms and stir-fry for 5 minutes. Stir in the lemon rind and season to taste with salt and pepper.

Transfer the mixture to a flameproof dish. Arrange the cheese slices over the vegetables and grill until golden.

220
continental-style pancakes

Preparation time 15 minutes	*1 x 300 g (10 oz) packet frozen Continental stir-fry vegetables*
Cooking time 15 minutes	*50 g (2 oz) Cheddar cheese, grated*
	1 tablespoon finely chopped parsley
Serves 4	*oil, for frying*
Calories 245 per portion	FOR THE PANCAKE BATTER
	50 g (2 oz) plain flour
	pinch of salt
	1 egg
	150 ml (¼ pint) milk
	2 teaspoons melted butter
	pinch of dried mixed herbs

First make the pancakes. Sift the flour and salt. Beat to a smooth batter with the egg, half the milk and the melted butter. Stir in the remaining milk with a pinch of mixed herbs. Heat a little oil in a small frying pan and cook a quarter of the batter each time, to make 4 pancakes. Keep warm.

Cook the stir-fry vegetables according to the packet instructions. Divide between the pancakes and fold each one in half carefully. Put them in a flameproof dish and sprinkle with the cheese. Place under a hot grill and cook until golden brown and bubbling. Sprinkle with chopped parsley and serve at once.

■ COOK'S TIP

Mozzarella has a delicate flavour, and is ideal for cooking as it does not become stringy when heated. Store in a bowl of water in the refrigerator, but use as soon as possible after purchase.

■ COOK'S TIP

Do not worry if the batter contains a few lumps. Simply press it through a fine sieve into a clean bowl.

221

carrot and mushroom loaf

Preparation time
10 minutes

Cooking time
about 1 hour

Oven temperature
200°C (400°C)
gas 6

Serves 4

Calories
200 per portion

500 g (1 lb) carrots, diced
40 g (1½ oz) butter
2 teaspoons soft brown sugar
30 ml (½ pint) vegetable stock
125 g (4 oz) button mushrooms, sliced
1 small onion, finely chopped
1 tablespoon chopped parsley
2 teaspoons chopped dill
3 eggs
25 g (1 oz) Cheddar cheese, grated
salt and pepper
parsley sprig, to garnish

Cook the carrots in 25 g (1 oz) of the butter until lightly browned, about 8 minutes. Sprinkle over the sugar and salt and pepper, then stir in the stock. Cook gently until the carrot is tender and the liquid has evaporated. Transfer the carrot mixture to a bowl.

Heat the remaining butter and cook the mushrooms and onion until softened, about 5 minutes. Stir in the parsley and dill. Beat the eggs and stir into the carrot mixture. Stir in the mushroom mixture and the cheese. Spoon into a 500 g (1 lb) loaf tin.

Place the tin in a larger tin with enough warm water to come halfway up the sides and cook in a preheated oven for 30–40 minutes or until firm to the touch. Carefully turn out the loaf and garnish with parsley.

222

spiced potatoes

Preparation time
30 minutes

Cooking time
30–35 minutes

Serves 4

Calories
355 per portion

1 large onion, chopped
2 garlic cloves, crushed
2 tablespoons oil
1 kg (2 lb) potatoes, cubed
2 teaspoons ground coriander
½ teaspoon turmeric
2 teaspoons ground cumin
1 bay leaf
1 x 400 g (13 oz) can chopped tomatoes
150 ml (¼ pint) water
125 g (4 oz) frozen peas
2 dessert pears or apples, peeled, cored and cubed
grated rind of ½ lemon
salt and pepper
bay leaves, to garnish (optional)

Cook the onion and garlic in the oil until soft but not browned. Add the potatoes and stir in the spices. Add the bay leaf, tomatoes and water with salt and pepper to taste. Bring to the boil, cover and simmer for 15 minutes.

Add the remaining ingredients and cover again. Simmer for a further 5–10 minutes or until the potatoes are tender. Serve with brown or basmati rice. Garnish with bay leaves, if you like.

■ COOK'S TIP

Try other vegetables in this loaf to replace the carrots; cauliflower broken into tiny florets, parsnips, celeriac and swede. It can also be made with a selection of different vegetables.

■ COOK'S TIP

Keep the potato cubes fairly large – dice them and they are liable to disintegrate, which spoils the appearance of this tasty dish.

vegetable terrine

Preparation time
25 minutes

Cooking time
1 hour

Oven temperature
180°C (350°F)
gas 4

Serves 4

Calories
305 per portion

500 g (1 lb) carrots (peeled weight)
250 g (8 oz) broccoli
375 g (12 oz) cauliflower florets
2 eggs
75 g (3 oz) Danish Havarti cheese, grated
1 teaspoon mild mustard
125 g (4 oz) fresh white breadcrumbs
75 g (3 oz) Danish Buko soft cheese with
  garlic
¼ teaspoon ground coriander
salt and pepper
sage leaves, to garnish

Line and butter a 1 kg (2 lb) loaf tin. Cook the vegetables separately in boiling salted water until just tender. Drain, rinse in cold water and cool separately.

Purée the cauliflower in a food processor until smooth. Add 1 egg, the Havarti cheese, mustard, 50 g (2 oz) of the breadcrumbs and salt and pepper. Turn into the prepared tin and smooth the surface. Arrange the broccoli in small florets on top.

Purée the carrots until smooth. Add the remaining egg, the garlic-flavoured cheese, coriander, the remaining breadcrumbs and salt and pepper. Mix thoroughly. Spoon carefully over the broccoli and smooth the surface. Cover with buttered greaseproof paper and aluminium foil. Bake in a preheated oven for 45–50 minutes or until firm. Remove from the oven and leave to stand for 10 minutes. Turn out carefully, garnish and serve with a tomato sauce (see below).

stuffed aubergines

Preparation time
10 minutes

Cooking time
45–60 minutes

Oven temperature
200°C (400°F), gas 6

Serves 4

Calories
305 per portion

2 tablespoons oil
2 onions, chopped
2 garlic cloves, crushed
250 g (8 oz) cooked haricot beans (or use
  canned beans)
2 tomatoes, chopped
1 teaspoon basil
1 teaspoon thyme
2 teaspoons tomato purée
2 aubergines
1 x 400 g (13 oz) can chopped tomatoes
250 g (8 oz) low-fat hard cheese, grated
salt and pepper
watercress sprigs, to garnish

Heat the oil in a saucepan. Add the onions and garlic and cook until soft but not browned. Stir in beans, tomatoes, herbs and tomato purée. Season well with salt and pepper.

Cut the aubergines in half lengthways. Scoop out the flesh, chop this and add it to the beans; cook gently for 10 minutes. Meanwhile, parboil the aubergine shells for 5 minutes, drain well and fill with the bean mixture. Pour the tomatoes into a baking dish and arrange the aubergines on top. Sprinkle with cheese, cover with foil and bake in a preheated oven for 20 minutes. Remove the foil and cook for 15 minutes more. Garnish with watercress and serve with brown rice or potatoes.

■ COOK'S TIP

To make a Tomato sauce, place 2 x 400 g (13 oz) cans tomatoes with their juices in a pan. Add 50 g (2 oz) butter, 2–3 teaspoons sugar, a few drops of Tabasco and salt and pepper and mash the tomatoes as the mixture comes to the boil. Cook for 8–10 minutes until blended and thickened. Press through a sieve to remove seeds. Reheat as required.

■ COOK'S TIP

A quick way of scooping out and chopping aubergines: cut in half and cut the middle criss-cross with a sharp knife. Carefully cut out the flesh or scoop out with a spoon.

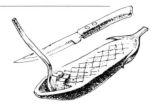

225
stuffed marrow rings

Preparation time	*1 marrow*
15 minutes	*1 onion, chopped*
Cooking time	*1 celery stick, sliced*
50 minutes	*25 g (1 oz) butter*
Oven temperature	*125 g (4 oz) mushrooms, sliced*
180°C (350°F)	*1 tablespoon tomato purée*
gas 4	*125 g (4 oz) mixed nuts, chopped*
Serves 4	*½ teaspoon ground cinnamon*
Calories	*½ teaspoon rosemary*
325 per portion	*50 g (2 oz) Danish Blue cheese, crumbled*
	75 g (3 oz) fresh breadcrumbs
	1 egg, beaten
	salt and pepper
	rosemary sprigs, to garnish

Peel the marrow and cut it into four. Scoop out the seeds. Cook in boiling water for 4–5 minutes until just starting to soften. Drain and place the rings in a lightly buttered ovenproof dish. Gently fry the onion and celery in the butter for 5 minutes until softened. Add the mushrooms, cover and cook for a further 2 minutes. Add the tomato purée, nuts, cinnamon, rosemary, cheese, breadcrumbs, egg and salt and pepper and mix well.

Fill the rings with the stuffing, placing any extra in a small ovenproof dish. Cover the stuffed marrow and bake for 40 minutes or until the marrow is tender. Cover the extra stuffing and bake at the same time (although it probably won't need quite as long). Garnish with sprigs of rosemary and serve with jacket potatoes.

226
cheese courgettes

Preparation time	*4 large courgettes*
10 minutes	*125 g (4 oz) butter*
Cooking time	*1 large onion, finely chopped*
40 minutes	*1 tablespoon chopped parsley*
Oven temperature	*50 g (2 oz) Cheddar cheese, grated*
180°C (350°F)	*salt and pepper*
gas 4	
Serves 2	
Calories	
545 per portion	

Trim the courgettes and cook whole in a saucepan of boiling salted water for 15 minutes or until just cooked. Drain. Cut the courgettes in half lengthways and carefully scoop out the flesh leaving a thin 'wall' all round. Chop the scooped-out flesh.

Heat the butter in a saucepan and fry the onion for 5 minutes until soft. Add the chopped courgette flesh and cook over high heat until pulpy. Stir in the parsley and half the cheese. Add salt and pepper to taste. Spoon the mixture into the courgette halves, place in an ovenproof dish, sprinkle with the remaining cheese and bake in a preheated oven for 20 minutes. Serve hot accompanied by a side salad.

■ COOK'S TIP

Try using peppers: select 4 dumpy ones about 125–150 g (4–5 oz); blanch in boiling water for 4 minutes, drain and cool in water. Cut a slice from the stalk end of each pepper. discard the core and reserve the lids. Deseed and remove the white pith from peppers, taking care not to puncture the skin. Fill with the stuffing, replace the lids and bake as above.

■ COOK'S TIP

A parsley chopper is useful for chopping a variety of fresh herbs. It is a small metal roller, with several round blades. Trim, wash and dry the herbs, place in a small mound on a board and roll away.

227

vegetable burgers

Preparation time 25 minutes, plus standing	250 g (8 oz) leeks
	375 g (12 oz) celeriac, peeled and finely grated
Cooking time 20 minutes	250 g (8 oz) carrots, finely grated
Serves 4	250 g (8 oz) potatoes, grated
	1 onion, finely chopped
Calories 355 per burger	2 garlic cloves, finely chopped
	1 bunch of parsley, finely chopped
	2 eggs
	125 g (4 oz) wholemeal breadcrumbs
	salt and pepper
	about 6 tablespoons vegetable oil

Trim the leeks, cut a cross down through the green leaves to the white part and wash. cut across the leeks into thin slices including about two-thirds of the green leaves. Place the leeks, celeriac, carrots and potatoes in a tea towel and squeeze well.

Place all the prepared vegetables and the parsley in a bowl and mix with the eggs and breadcrumbs to make a firm, smooth and malleable mixture. Season to taste with salt and pepper, cover and leave to stand for 10 minutes.

With moist hands, shape the mixture into flat cakes or burgers. Heat about half the oil in a frying pan. Fry the vegetable burgers, in two batches, over a high to moderate heat for about 10 minutes, turning once. Add a little more oil to the side of the pan, if necessary.

Serve hot, with a mixed salad.

■ COOK'S TIP

Make the burgers half the usual size and use with salad as a filler for pitta pockets, instead of the traditional felafel.

228

vegetable parcels

Preparation time 20 minutes	2 large cabbage leaves
	1 garlic clove, crushed
Cooking time 1 hour	1 onion, chopped
	75 g (3 oz) long-grain brown rice, cooked
Oven temperature 180°C (350°F) gas 4	2 walnut halves, finely chopped
	50 g (2 oz) yellow pepper, cored, deseeded and finely chopped
Serves 2	1 celery stick, chopped
Calories 105 per portion	300 ml (½ pint) dry white wine or vegetable stock
	2 tablespoons plain flour
	3 tablespoons water
	150 ml (¼ pint) single cream
	salt and pepper

Blanch the cabbage leaves in boiling water for 1 minute, drain and pat dry. Mix together the garlic, onion, rice, walnuts, yellow pepper and celery and season to taste with salt and pepper. Divide this mixture between the cabbage leaves and roll up into parcels. Place in an ovenproof dish and pour in the white wine or stock. Season with black pepper, cover, and bake in a preheated moderate oven for 1 hour.

Transfer the parcels to a warmed serving dish and keep hot. Blend the flour to a smooth paste with the water, add the cooking juices from parcels and pour into a saucepan. Bring to the boil, stirring, then remove from the heat and add the cream. Heat gently without boiling, season to taste and pour over the parcels to serve.

■ COOK'S TIP

Instead of cabbage leaves you may like to stuff vine leaves. Use packet or canned leaves, allowing about 4–6 vine leaves instead of the larger cabbage leaves. They will still serve 2 as a main course or 4 as a starter.

229
savoury bake

Preparation time
20 minutes

Cooking time
45–50 minutes

Oven temperature
180°C (350°F)
gas 4

Serves 4

Calories
370 per portion

1 large onion, sliced
50 g (2 oz) butter
250 g (8 oz) courgettes, thinly sliced
250 g (8 oz) tomatoes, skinned and sliced
1 teaspoon dried mixed herbs
40 g (1½ oz) plain flour
450 ml (¾ pint) milk
125 g (4 oz) Cheddar cheese, grated
50 g (2 oz) fresh breadcrumbs
salt and pepper
FOR THE GARNISH
tomato wedges
parsley sprigs

Cook the onion in 15 g (½ oz) butter until just soft. Place half the courgettes in a 1.8 litre (3 pint) ovenproof dish and cover with half the onion and the tomatoes. Sprinkle with the mixed herbs and season with salt and pepper, then top with the remaining onion and courgettes.

Meanwhile, make the sauce. Melt the remaining butter in a pan, stir in the flour and gradually add the milk, stirring continuously until the sauce thickens and boils. Season and add 75 g (3 oz) of the cheese. Pour the sauce over the vegetables. Mix together the remaining cheese and the breadcrumbs and sprinkle over the sauce. Cook in a preheated oven for 35–40 minutes until golden brown. Garnish with tomato wedges and parsley sprigs.

230
aubergine layer

Preparation time
20 minutes

Cooking time
1 hour 12 minutes

Oven temperature
180°C (350°F)
gas 4

Serves 4

Calories
295 per portion

2 aubergines, trimmed and sliced
4 tablespoons vegetable oil
2 onions, sliced
4 tomatoes, skinned and sliced
50 g (2 oz) walnuts, chopped
300 ml (½ pint) tomato juice
½ teaspoon dried basil
salt and pepper
FOR THE TOPPING
15 g (½ oz) margarine or butter
¼ small onion, finely chopped
50 g (2 oz) fresh wholemeal breadcrumbs
1 tablespoon grated Parmesan cheese
¼ teaspoon mustard powder

Place the aubergine slices in a colander set over a plate, sprinkle with salt and leave to drain for 30 minutes. Rinse and pat dry.

Heat 3 tablespoons of the oil in a large frying pan, add the aubergines and fry until lightly coloured on both sides. Add the remaining oil and fry the onions until softened.

Layer all the vegetables and the walnuts in an ovenproof dish. Season the tomato juice, add the basil and pour over. Cover and cook in a preheated moderate oven for 45 minutes.

Melt the margarine in a saucepan, add the onion and cook for 2–3 minutes. Stir in the remaining ingredients, use to top the vegetables and cook, uncovered, for 15 minutes. Serve at once.

▪ COOK'S TIP

When selecting courgettes, look for smooth-skinned, unblemished specimens. These miniature marrows should be used as soon as possible after picking, so cook them on the day of purchase to enjoy them at their best.

▪ COOK'S TIP

The reason for salting aubergines before cooking is to extract bitter juices which can spoil the flavour of the finished dish. In some recipes this is not an essential process. Make sure you rinse and dry the vegetables before using them or the dish will be very salt.

231

aubergine fans georgia

Preparation time 20 minutes	2 aubergines 175 g (6 oz) mozzarella cheese, thinly sliced
Cooking time 25–30 minutes	4 tomatoes, sliced
Oven temperature 200°C (400°F), gas 6	50 g (2 oz) salted peanuts 1 tablespoon groundnut oil
Serves 4	1 garlic clove, crushed
Calories 260 per portion	1 tablespoon chopped parsley 1 teaspoon oregano salt and pepper

Cut the aubergines in half lengthways. Place each half cut side down on a board and make slits at 1 cm (½ inch) intervals from the stalk end down to the base, taking care not to cut right through. Fan out the aubergines and arrange them in a greased baking tin or individual dishes. Place cheese and tomato slices alternately in the cuts and sprinkle over the peanuts.

Mix the oil with the garlic, herbs and salt and pepper and brush evenly over the aubergines. Cover the tin or dishes with foil and bake in a preheated moderately hot oven for 25–30 minutes, until the aubergines are tender. Serve hot.

232

macaroni and aubergine layer

Preparation time 40 minutes	375 g (12 oz) aubergines, sliced 175 g (6 oz) macaroni
Cooking time 1 hour	3 tablespoons oil 1 onion, sliced
Oven temperature 190°C (375°F), gas 5	1 garlic clove, chopped 150 ml (¼ pint) natural yogurt 150 ml (¼ pint) milk
Serves 4	175 g (6 oz) low-fat hard cheese, grated
Calories 440 per portion	250 g (8 oz) tomatoes, sliced salt and pepper parsley, to garnish

Sprinkle the aubergine slices with salt, place in a colander and leave for 30 minutes. Cook the macaroni in boiling salted water for about 8 minutes, until tender but not soft, then drain.

Rinse and dry the aubergines. Heat the oil in a large frying pan. Quickly toss the aubergine and onion slices in the oil for 2–3 minutes. Add the garlic. Mix the yogurt, milk and two-thirds of the cheese.

Layer the aubergine and onions, macaroni and tomatoes in an ovenproof dish, seasoning the layers with salt and pepper. Pour in the yogurt mixture and top with the remaining grated cheese. Bake in a preheated oven for 45 minutes, until golden. Serve hot, garnished with parsley.

■ COOK'S TIP

Cutting aubergines into fans is a good way of preparing them. For simplicity, sprinkle with spices, dot with butter and grill or bake. Lemon rind and Parmesan cheese made good toppings.

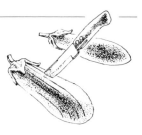

■ COOK'S TIP

To make yogurt, heat milk to 50°C (100°F), then stir in 2–3 tablespoons natural live yogurt. Pour into a vacuum flask and leave overnight, until the yogurt has formed. Remove and chill until required.

233

aubergines bonne femme

Preparation time
20 minutes

Cooking time
30 minutes

Oven temperature
200°C (400°F)
gas 6

Serves 4–6

Calories
295–200 per portion

5 tablespoons olive oil
3 aubergines, cut in quarters
    lengthways, then in 2 cm (¾ inch)
    slices
1 large onion, roughly chopped
2 garlic cloves, halved
275 g (9 oz) tomatoes, roughly chopped
2 teaspoons chopped oregano
1 parsley sprig, chopped
50 g (2 oz) Parmesan cheese, grated
1 tablespoon butter
salt and pepper

Heat the oil in a saucepan, add the aubergines, onion and garlic and fry for 7–8 minutes. Remove and discard the garlic.

Add the tomatoes to the pan and season with salt and pepper to taste. Stir in the oregano and parsley. Cook for a few minutes then transfer the mixture to a shallow ovenproof dish. Sprinkle with the Parmesan cheese and dot with the butter. Cook in a pre-heated moderately hot oven for about 20 minutes. Serve immediately.

234

aubergine and onion gratin

Preparation time
20 minutes, plus preparing the aubergine

Cooking time
50 minutes–1 hour

Oven temperature
200°C (400°F)
gas 6

Serves 4

Calories
350 per portion

4 aubergines
2–3 tablespoons oil
250 g (8 oz) onions, sliced
250 g (8 oz) Cheddar cheese, grated
salt and pepper
chopped parsley, to garnish

Slice the aubergines and layer in a colander, sprinkling each layer with salt. Set aside for 1 hour.

Rinse the aubergine slices under cold running water, then pat dry. Heat the oil in a frying pan and fry the aubergine slices, a few at a time, for 2–3 minutes on each side. Drain on absorbent kitchen paper. Fry the onions in the pan until soft.

Arrange the aubergine and onion slices in layers in a greased ovenproof dish, seasoning each layer with salt and pepper. Sprinkle with the cheese. Cook in a preheated moderately hot oven for 40 minutes. Garnish with parsley and serve.

■ COOK'S TIP

Serve this delicious dish accompanied by salad, French bread and a French red wine.

■ COOK'S TIP

If preferred, courgettes can be used in place of the aubergines in this recipe. Courgettes do not need to be salted prior to cooking but you will need the same weight as the aubergines.

235

sunflower okra
with mushrooms

Preparation time 10 minutes	*2 teaspoons vegetable oil* *2 tablespoons sunflower seeds*
Cooking time 18–20 minutes	*25 g (1 oz) butter* *375 g (12 oz) okra, topped and tailed*
Serves 4	*125 g (4 oz) button mushrooms, halved*
Calories 130 per portion	*salt and pepper*

Heat the oil in a small pan and cook the sunflower seeds for 1–2 minutes until brown. Drain on absorbent kitchen paper and set aside.

It is best to cook the okra whole but, if they are too large, cut them in half lengthways.

Melt the butter in a frying pan or wok and stir-fry the okra quickly for 3–4 minutes. Add the mushrooms and cook for a further 3–4 minutes. Sprinkle with salt and pepper, cover the pan and leave to cook for about 10 minutes until the mushrooms are soft and the okra crisply tender.

Remove the lid and cook quickly for 1–2 minutes to reduce the liquid in the pan. Spoon into a hot dish and sprinkle with the sunflower seeds.

236

leeks au gratin

Preparation time 10 minutes	*1 kg (2 lb) leeks, trimmed and cut into* *2 cm (¾ inch) thick rings*
Cooking time 45 minutes	*15 g (½ oz) butter* *1 garlic clove, halved*
Oven temperature 180°C (350°F) gas 4 then 200°C (400°F) gas 6	*300 ml (½ pint) milk* *pinch of grated nutmeg* *½ teaspoon dried tarragon* *150 ml (¼ pint) double cream*
Serves 6	*125 g (4 oz) Emmental cheese, grated* *salt and pepper*
Calories 280 per portion	

Rinse the leeks and drain thoroughly. Place in a large ovenproof dish.

Heat the butter in a small saucepan and fry the garlic for a few minutes until golden. Remove the pieces of garlic from the pan with a slotted spoon and discard. Pour the butter over the leeks.

Heat the milk with the nutmeg, tarragon and salt and pepper to taste, until almost boiling. Stir in the cream and pour over the leeks. Cover the dish tightly with greased foil and cook in a preheated moderate oven for 20 minutes. Remove the foil and sprinkle with the cheese. Increase the oven temperature to moderately hot and bake for a further 15–20 minutes until the cheese is golden and bubbling. Serve immediately.

■ COOK'S TIP

Make sure the okra you buy are fresh, with no damaged ridges or brown patches.

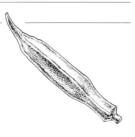

■ COOK'S TIP

This dish can make a filling main course when served with jacket potatoes.

237

cidered hotpot

Preparation time 15 minutes	*250 g (8 oz) swede*
	250 g (8 oz) turnips
Cooking time 1 hour 45 minutes	*75 g (3 oz) butter*
	2 onions, sliced
2 hours 15 minutes	*2 leeks, sliced*
Oven temperature 200°C (400°F) gas 6	*250 g (8 oz) carrots, sliced*
	40 g (1½ oz) plain flour
	450 ml (¾ pint) dry cider
Serves 4	*1 tablespoon tomato purée*
	1 teaspoon yeast extract
Calories 465 per portion	*500 g (1 lb) potatoes, thinly sliced*
	oil, for brushing
	75 g (3 oz) Cheddar cheese, grated
	salt and pepper

Cut the swede and turnips into 2.5 cm (1 inch) cubes. Melt the butter in a large frying pan, add the swede, turnip, onions, leeks and carrots and cook gently for 10 minutes until softened. Transfer the vegetables to a lightly oiled ovenproof dish.

Mix the flour to a paste with a little of the cider in the saucepan, gradually stir in the remaining cider and bring to the boil, whisking all the time. Add the tomato purée, yeast extract and salt and pepper. Pour over the vegetables. Arrange the sliced potatoes on top. Brush the potato slices with oil and sprinkle over the cheese. Cover the dish.

Bake in a preheated oven for 1½–2 hours or until the vegetables are cooked. Uncover the dish for the last 30 minutes to brown the topping. Serve hot.

238

parsnip casserole

Preparation time 10 minutes	*about 750 g (1½ lb) parsnips*
	75 g (3 oz) butter
Cooking time 1 hour	*1 onion, chopped*
	50 g (2 oz) Cheddar cheese, grated
Oven temperature 160°C (325°F) gas 3	*a few drops of Tabasco sauce*
	300 ml (½ pint) vegetable stock
	2 tomatoes, thinly sliced
Serves 4	*50 g (2 oz) fresh breadcrumbs*
	salt and pepper
Calories 290 per portion	

Peel the parsnips and cut them into chunks. Heat 50 g (2 oz) of the butter in a large saucepan and cook the onion until softened, about 5 minutes. Remove the pan from the heat, stir in the parsnips, cheese, Tabasco, stock and salt and pepper. Spoon into a lightly greased ovenproof dish. Arrange the sliced tomatoes on top. Bake in a preheated oven, covered, for 45–50 minutes or until the parsnip is just cooked.

Melt the remaining butter and stir in the breadcrumbs. Sprinkle over the tomatoes and press down. Return to the oven, uncovered, for 10 minutes. Serve hot.

▪ COOK'S TIP

This delicious hotpot makes an excellent family meal. Serve chunks of crusty granary bread as an accompaniment. You can vary the vegetables to suit the season.

▪ COOK'S TIP

Use a matured Cheddar to give the parsnip plenty of flavour. Instead of parsnip you can use courgettes or pumpkin in this dish. Serve with baked potatoes or crunchy roast potatoes if liked.

239

spinach, cauliflower and courgette bhaji

Preparation time 5 minutes	*250 g (8 oz) frozen leaf spinach*
	250 g (8 oz) cauliflower florets
Cooking time 35 minutes	*250 g (8 oz) courgettes, sliced*
	1 small onion, sliced
Serves 4	*2 garlic cloves, crushed*
Calories 50 per portion	*½ teaspoon grated or very finely chopped fresh root ginger*
	¼ teaspoon garam masala
	1–2 teaspoons black mustard seeds
	1–2 tablespoons thick-set natural yogurt

Put all the vegetables in a large saucepan with some water, the garlic and ginger. Bring to the boil, then reduce the heat and cook for about 20 minutes.

Add the garam masala and mustard seeds and cook for a further 10 minutes, or until the vegetables are just tender.

Just before serving, stir the yogurt into the vegetables.

■ COOK'S TIP

Try using frozen broccoli in place of the cauliflower. You could also use frozen mixed sliced peppers instead of the courgettes.

240

broccoli ring

Preparation time 15 minutes	*500 g (1 lb) frozen chopped broccoli, defrosted*
Cooking time 35–40 minutes	*1 onion, finely chopped*
	2 garlic cloves, crushed
Oven temperature 180°C (350°F) gas 4	*50 g (2 oz) butter*
	50 g (2 oz) plain flour
	300 ml (½ pint) milk
Serves 6	*250 g (8 oz) mature Cheddar cheese*
Calories 330 per portion	*4 eggs, well beaten*
	salt and pepper
	FOR THE GARNISH
	tomato wedges
	watercress sprigs

Grease a 1.5 litre (2½ pint) ring mould with oil. Drain the broccoli, squeezing out the excess moisture, and put into a large mixing bowl. Add the onion and garlic to the broccoli. Melt the butter in a saucepan, add the flour and cook together for 1 minute. Gradually add the milk, stirring continuously, and bring to the boil. Simmer gently for a few minutes, then remove from the heat. Grate half the cheese and add to the sauce together with the eggs. Season, beat until smooth. Add to the broccoli and mix together well. Pour into the ring mould.

Place the mould in a roasting tin filled with hot water to a depth of 2.5 cm (1 inch). Bake in a preheated moderate oven for 25–30 minutes until set. Cool in the mould for 5 minutes, then turn out the broccoli ring on to a warm serving platter. Slice the remaining cheese thinly and lay the slices over the top of the broccoli ring. Grill until golden and bubbling. Garnish and serve.

■ COOK'S TIP

Fresh broccoli may be used instead of frozen. Trim stems, cutting into 2.5 cm (1 inch) pieces and florets. Steam for 3 minutes, then proceed as above.

241

chicory in mustard sauce

Preparation time
5 minutes

Cooking time
20 minutes

Serves 4

Calories
85 per portion

8 small heads chicory
150 ml (¼ pint) salted water
juice of 1 lemon
15 g (½ oz) butter
scant 1 tablespoon plain flour
150 ml (¼ pint) vegetable stock
2–3 tablespoons single cream
scant 2 tablespoons prepared mild
    mustard
1 teaspoon sugar
1 tablespoon chopped dill, to garnish

Rinse and drain the chicory and remove the thick stems. Bring the water and lemon juice to the boil. Add the chicory heads, lower the heat and cook for about 10 minutes. Drain and keep hot. Reserve the cooking liquid.

Melt the butter in a small pan, stir in the flour and cook for 2–3 minutes. Gradually add the reserved cooking liquid and stock, stirring constantly.

Add the cream, mustard and sugar and bring to the boil, stirring constantly. Cook for 3 minutes, stirring. Arrange the chicory heads on a warmed serving dish then pour over the sauce. Sprinkle with the chopped dill and serve immediately.

242

spinach with flaked almonds

Preparation time
10 minutes

Cooking time
20 minutes

Serves 4

Calories
200 per portion

1 kg (2 lb) leaf spinach
50 g (2 oz) butter
½ onion, finely chopped
grated nutmeg
4 tablespoons natural yogurt
50 g (2 oz) flaked almonds
salt

Place the spinach in a sieve, rinse and drain thoroughly. Tear the leaves into manageable pieces. Melt half the butter in a large saucepan. Add the spinach, a little at a time, turning it in the butter to coat. Season with salt and nutmeg to taste. Cook over a low heat for 10 minutes until tender, depending upon the thickness of the spinach leaves.

Stir the natural yogurt into the spinach mixture. Remove the spinach from the heat and transfer to a warmed serving bowl. Fry the almonds in the remaining butter, stirring until golden. Fold the almonds into the spinach and serve immediately.

■ COOK'S TIP

Look out for different mustards in delicatessens and health food shops. Try wholegrain varieties, those flavoured with herbs and unusual continental types such as Swedish mustard which can be slightly sweet and very mild.

■ COOK'S TIP

Freshly grated nutmeg gives the best flavour. It is best bought whole, as the ground form soon loses its fragrance.

243

chinese-style stir-fry

Preparation time 15 minutes	*4 tablespoons oil*
	175 g (6 oz) Chinese leaves, shredded
Cooking time 5 minutes	*175 g (6 oz) Brussels sprouts, shredded*
	175 g (6 oz) leeks, shredded
Serves 4	*175 g (6 oz) tiny cauliflower florets*
Calories 155 per portion	*2 tablespoons soy sauce*
	salt and pepper

Heat the oil in a wok or deep frying pan. Add the prepared vegetables and stir-fry for 4–5 minutes over a brisk heat. The vegetables should still be slightly crunchy. Sprinkle with a generous quantity of soy sauce and salt and pepper and to taste. Serve immediately.

244

crispy vegetarian nuggets

Preparation time 25 minutes	*1 tablespoon vegetable oil*
	1 onion, finely chopped
Cooking time 15–20 minutes	*250 g (8 oz) mushrooms, finely chopped*
	175 g (6 oz) long-grain rice, cooked
Serves 4	*1½ teaspoons chopped thyme*
Calories 600 per portion	*175 g (6 oz) Lancashire cheese, grated*
	1 egg, beaten
	2 tablespoons wholemeal flour
	salt and pepper
	FOR THE COATING
	2 tablespoons wholemeal flour
	2 eggs, beaten
	125 g (4 oz) wholemeal breadcrumbs
	2 teaspoons sesame seeds
	oil, for frying

Heat the oil in a sauté pan and fry the onion and mushrooms for 5 minutes, stirring occasionally. Turn into a bowl and mix with all the remaining ingredients then shape into 12 balls.

Coat the balls in flour, then dip them in beaten egg and finally roll them in a mixture of breadcrumbs and sesame seeds. Heat the oil in the sauté pan and fry the nuggets until golden brown. Drain on absorbent kitchen paper and serve with a salad.

■ COOK'S TIP

Stir-frying is an excellent method of cooking vegetables. They are cooked so quickly, and in their own juices, that very little of the nutritional content is lost. Have all the ingredients prepared before starting to cook.

■ COOK'S TIP

Make a tasty soured cream sauce to accompany the nuggets. Mix 1 tablespoon grated onion and 2 tablespoons finely grated cucumber (with excess liquid removed) with 150 ml (¼ pint) soured cream. Season to taste and chill lightly before serving.

245

walnut parsnip croquettes

Preparation time
20 minutes

Cooking time
20–25 minutes

Serves 4–6

Calories
360–240 per portion

250 g (8 oz) parsnips, quartered
250 g (8 oz) potatoes, halved
*   if necessary*
15 g (½ oz) butter
50 g (2 oz) walnuts, coarsely chopped
2 tablespoons plain flour
1 egg, beaten
75 g (3 oz) dried breadcrumbs
oil, for shallow-frying
salt

Cook the parsnips and potatoes in a pan of boiling salted water for about 15 minutes, until tender. Drain well.

Chop the parsnips coarsely and mash the potatoes. Mix together with the butter and walnuts. Shape into neat rounds, or if you prefer, into cylindrical croquettes. Coat each croquette with flour, then in beaten egg and finally in breadcrumbs.

Shallow fry the croquettes in hot oil for 3 minutes on each side until golden brown. Drain on absorbent kitchen paper, sprinkle with salt and serve immediately with a simple salad of tomatoes, onions and chopped parsley.

246

vegetable curry

Preparation time
20 minutes, plus draining the aubergine

Cooking time
1 hour

Serves 4

Calories
380 per portion

1 aubergine, diced
2 tablespoons oil
4 teaspoons mustard seeds
½ teaspoon ground turmeric
1½ teaspoons chilli powder
1 garlic clove, crushed
2.5 cm (1 inch) piece of fresh root ginger, peeled and finely chopped
1 small cauliflower, broken into florets
3 potatoes, diced
4 courgettes, thickly sliced
4 tomatoes, skinned, quartered and deseeded
175 g (6 oz) runner beans or French beans, cut into 2.5 cm (1 inch) lengths
125 g (4 oz) almonds, toasted
salt and pepper

Sprinkle the aubergine with salt, place in a colander and leave to drain for 30 minutes. Rinse and drain thoroughly and pat dry.

Heat the oil in a heavy flameproof casserole or in a large heavy frying pan with a lid. Add the mustard seeds, turmeric and chilli powder and cook, stirring constantly, until the seeds begin to pop. Stir in the garlic and ginger and fry for a few seconds then stir in all the vegetables and season with salt and pepper. Cover and cook very slowly for 40–50 minutes until all the vegetables are tender. Taste for seasoning and stir in the almonds.

■ COOK'S TIP

Chill the croquettes in the refrigerator for 1–2 hours after coating in egg and breadcrumbs and they will hold their shape more satisfactorily when being fried.

■ COOK'S TIP

To toast flaked almonds, distribute them evenly on a baking tray, then bake in a moderate oven (160°C/325°F/gas 3), stirring frequently, until brown.

247

mangetout in garlic butter

Preparation time
15 minutes

Cooking time
10 minutes

Serves 4

Calories
115 per portion

Suitable for vegans
using soya margarine

750 g (1½ lb) mangetout, topped and tailed
pinch of salt
1 tablespoon oil
25 g (l oz) butter or soya margarine
1 garlic clove, chopped
1 tablespoon chopped parsley, to garnish

Place the mangetout in a pan with just enough water to cover. Add the salt and the oil. Bring to the boil, then lower the heat and cook gently for about 5–10 minutes, depending on the ripeness and freshness of the mangetout (very young pods will need only about 2 minutes).

Meanwhile, melt the butter or soya margarine in a pan, add the garlic and fry for 2 minutes. Drain the mangetout thoroughly and place in a warmed serving dish. Pour over the hot garlic butter. Sprinkle with parsley before serving.

248

kartoshki

Preparation time
5 minutes

Cooking time
30 minutes

Serves 2–3

Calories
315–210 per portion

Suitable for vegans
using soya margarine

15 g (½ oz) butter or soya margarine
1 tablespoon oil
500 g (1 lb) small potatoes, unpeeled and fairly thickly sliced
salt and pepper
2 spring onions, chopped, to garnish

Use the largest frying pan you have and heat the butter and oil until sizzling. Add the potatoes and stir until all the slices are coated and glistening. Keep the heat high and fry them quickly until golden brown but not cooked.

Turn the slices and sprinkle generously with salt and black pepper. Cover the frying pan, lower the heat and continue to fry/steam the slices for about 20 minutes until tender, shaking the pan occasionally to prevent them sticking. Take the lid off the pan and turn up the heat again for 1–2 minutes.

Serve immediately sprinkled with the spring onions.

■ COOK'S TIP

Mangetout in garlic butter is a delicious vegetable dish to serve with eggs. Instead of mangetout, try using French beans or sliced courgettes.

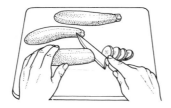

■ COOK'S TIP

This is an economical way of cooking potatoes, and produces an almost roast-like taste without using the oven. It is a traditional Russian recipe.

249

baby parsnips in breadcrumbs

Preparation time
15 minutes

Cooking time
30–35 minutes

Oven temperature
220°C (425°F)
gas 7

Serves 4

Calories
118 per portion

500 g (1 lb) very small parsnips, scrubbed if necessary
1 tablespoon vegetable oil
75 g (3 oz) fresh wholemeal breadcrumbs
2 tablespoons freshly grated Parmesan cheese
salt and pepper
1 tablespoon chopped parsley, to garnish

Cook the parsnips in boiling salted water for 7–10 minutes until just tender. Drain and return to the pan. Toss them in the oil and plenty of black pepper.

Mix the breadcrumbs, Parmesan cheese and ½ teaspoon salt, add to the pan and toss again.

Spoon the parsnips and any crumbs left in the pan into a lightly oiled ovenproof dish and bake near the top of a preheated oven for 15–20 minutes until the breadcrumbs are crisp and lightly browned.

Sprinkle with chopped parsley and serve immediately.

250

broad beans with sesame seeds

Preparation time
5 minutes for frozen beans

15 minutes for fresh beans

Cooking time
10–15 minutes

Serves 4

Calories
216 per portion

Suitable for vegans using soya margarine

500 g (1 lb) broad beans, prepared weight, fresh or frozen
2 tablespoons sesame seeds
25 g (1 oz) butter or soya margarine
1 tablespoon lemon juice
pepper

Cook the beans in boiling salted water until tender, 8–15 minutes depending on whether they are fresh or frozen.

While the beans are cooking, toast the sesame seeds under a moderate grill to brown them evenly.

Drain the beans, and put the butter or soya margarine in the pan. Melt it quickly and, when just beginning to brown, add the lemon juice and pepper. Tip the beans back into the pan and toss well in the butter.

Serve the beans hot, sprinkled with the sesame seeds.

■ COOK'S TIP

If the parsnips are small, cook them whole. For larger ones, cut them in half lengthways first. Do not use really large parsnips for this recipe.

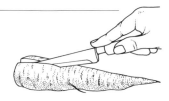

■ COOK'S TIP

Toasted sesame seeds add a special flavour of their own to all types of vegetable dishes and seem to go particularly well with broad beans. They are a good source of calcium, so are particularly valuable to those who do not eat dairy products.

251

corn-on-the-cob with herbs

Preparation time 15 minutes	*4 corn cobs, husks and silky threads* *removed*
Cooking time 35 minutes	*50 g (2 oz) butter or soya margarine* *1 tablespoon chopped mixed herbs*
Oven temperature 200°C (400°F) gas 6	*(parsley, thyme and chives)* *salt and pepper*
Serves 4	
Calories 221 per portion	
Suitable for vegans using soya margarine	

Bring a large pan of unsalted water to the boil, add the corn cobs, cook them for 15 minutes then drain.

Blend together the butter or soya margarine with the herbs and salt and pepper. Spread a little over each corn cob and wrap each one in a piece of foil, crimping the edges securely together.

Place the parcels on a baking sheet in a preheated oven and bake for 20 minutes. Unwrap the foil parcels carefully and serve the corn on hot plates with the herb and butter juices poured over them.

252

red cabbage with apple

Preparation time 15 minutes	*1 kg (2 lb) red cabbage, shredded* *2 tablespoons oil*
Cooking time 1¼–1¾ hours	*1 onion, thinly sliced* *2 cooking apples, peeled, cored and*
Oven temperature 180°C (350°F) gas 4	*chopped* *3 tablespoons wine vinegar* *3 tablespoons water*
Serves 4–6	*1 tablespoon soft brown sugar* *salt and pepper*
Calories 103–69 per portion	*1 tablespoon chopped parsley, to garnish*
Suitable for vegans	

Add the cabbage to a large pan of boiling water and blanch for 2–3 minutes. Drain thoroughly. Heat the oil in a saucepan, add the onion and cook until softened, about 5 minutes. Add the apple, cover and cook for a further 5 minutes, stirring occasionally. Add the cabbage, vinegar, water, sugar, and salt and pepper to taste, blending well.

Transfer to a casserole dish. Cover and cook in a preheated moderate oven for 1–1½ hours until tender. Stir occasionally and add a little more water if necessary. Turn into a warmed serving dish and sprinkle with parsley to serve.

■ COOK'S TIP

Use frozen corn-on-the-cob when fresh corn is out of season, but it will require 10 minutes extra boiling. It is important not to salt the cooking water for this vegetable as it tends to make the corn kernels tough.

■ COOK'S TIP

To shred cabbage finely, choose a long-bladed, sharp knife. Quarter the cabbage and secure each piece with your fingers, moving them back as you shred.

253

celeriac and
carrot remoulade

Preparation time
20 minutes, plus cooling

Cooking time
10 minutes

Serves 4

Calories
165 per portion

1 celeriac root, about 250 g (8 oz), sliced into matchstick strips
250 g (8 oz) carrots, sliced into matchstick strips
1 tablespoon lemon juice
salt
FOR THE DRESSING
4 tablespoons mayonnaise
150 ml (¼ pint) plain Greek yogurt
1 garlic clove, crushed
1 tablespoon chopped parsley
1 tablespoon finely snipped chives
½ teaspoon mustard powder
pinch of cayenne pepper
1 hard-boiled egg, finely chopped
FOR THE GARNISH
1 hard-boiled egg, separated
snipped fresh chives
carrot curls (see Cook's Tip)

Partly cook the celeriac and carrot strips for 5–8 minutes in boiling salted water with the lemon juice. Drain, dry and cool.

Mix together all the dressing ingredients. Toss the celeriac and carrots in the dressing and spoon the salad on to a serving dish. Sieve the egg yolk and arrange it in the centre of the salad. Chop the white finely and place it on top, then arrange the chives around the edge and garnish with carrot curls.

■ COOK'S TIP

For carrot curls, peel the carrots and, using a potato peeler, pare thin strips from the length of each one. Roll up the strips, secure with cocktail sticks and place in ice-cold water for 1 hour. Drain and remove the sticks. Unroll 3 carrot curls and place them one on top of the other in opposite directions.

254

gingered
brussels sprouts

Preparation time
10 minutes, plus standing

Cooking time
8–10 minutes

Serves 8

Calories
45 per portion

Suitable for vegans

1 kg (2 lb) Brussels sprouts (see Cook's Tip)
2 tablespoons lemon juice
1 teaspoon finely grated fresh ginger or ½ teaspoon ground ginger
3–4 strips lemon rind

Steam the Brussels sprouts for 8 minutes then pour the water out of the pan under the steamer and put the sprouts into the hot pan to dry out slightly.

Sprinkle the lemon juice and ginger over the sprouts, toss well and add the strips of lemon rind.

Cover the pan and leave to stand in a warm place for 5 minutes before serving.

■ COOK'S TIP

Prepare the sprouts by trimming the ends and removing any discoloured outer leaves. Do not cut a cross in the ends if you want them to be slightly crunchy.

255

tofu with bamboo shoots and carrots

Preparation time 15 minutes	*2 tablespoons olive oil* *250 g (8 oz) firm tofu (beancurd), drained*
Cooking time 10 minutes	*and diced* *1 teaspoon grated fresh root ginger*
Serves 4	*250 g (8 oz) grated carrot*
Calories 109 per portion	*250 g (8 oz) can bamboo shoots, drained* *1 tablespoon soy sauce*
Suitable for vegans	*½ teaspoon sugar*

Heat the olive oil in a frying pan, add the tofu and fry, turning the pieces so that they become crisp and golden on all sides. Add all the remaining ingredients and stir-fry for about 2 minutes.

256

brussels sprouts with chesnuts

Preparation time 30 minutes	*375 g (12 oz) chestnuts* *25 g (1 oz) butter or soya margarine*
Cooking time 40 minutes	*150 ml (¼ pint) vegetable stock* *500 g (1 lb) Brussels sprouts, trimmed*
Serves 4	*salt and pepper*
Calories 228 per portion	
Suitable for vegans using soya margarine	

Slit the chestnuts with a sharp knife. Place in a pan of cold water, bring to the boil and simmer for 3 minutes. Remove the chestnuts, one at a time, and peel off their outer and inner skins.

Heat the butter or soya margarine in a small pan, add the chestnuts and cook for 5 minutes, stirring occasionally. Add the vegetable stock to the pan and bring to the boil. Cover and simmer for 20 minutes.

Add the Brussels sprouts, adding more liquid if necessary, to just cover the vegetables. Add salt and pepper to taste and cook for a further 10 minutes until the sprouts are just tender. Drain the sprouts and chestnuts, reserving the stock for a soup.

■ COOK'S TIP

Tofu, or beancurd, is made from soya beans. It is packed with protein, low in fat and simple to use. It is available in plain, marinated or smoked varieties.

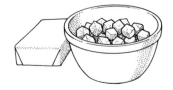

■ COOK'S TIP

Preparing fresh chestnuts can be extremely time consuming. Use pre-cooked chestnuts in jars or cans, or dried ones which simply need soaking. Both types are available from supermarkets and health food shops.

257

skewered peppers

Preparation time 15 minutes	*2 green peppers, cored, deseeded and cut* *into 2.5 cm (1 inch) squares*
Cooking time 7–10 minutes	*2 red peppers, cored, deseeded and cut* *into 2.5 cm (1 inch) squares*
Serves 4	*2 yellow peppers, cored, deseeded and cut* *into 2.5 cm (1 inch) squares*
Calories 299 per portion	*about 125 ml (4 fl oz) olive oil*
Suitable for vegans	*2 garlic cloves, finely chopped*
	1 tablespoon crushed black peppercorns
	3 tablespoons lemon juice
	salt

Thread the peppers on to 8 soaked bamboo skewers. A medium pepper will normally give about 12–16 pieces so there should be about 3–4 pieces of each colour pepper on each skewer. Alternate the colours.

Brush the peppers generously on all sides with the oil and cook under a preheated grill for 7–10 minutes, turning and basting with oil every 1–2 minutes. When they are just beginning to char they are done. Baste again with olive oil.

Put the skewers on to serving plates, then sprinkle each one with a little of the finely chopped garlic. Generously season the skewers with salt and pepper, then pour over some lemon juice. Serve immediately.

258

grilled courgettes with mustard

Preparation time 10 minutes	*500 g (1 lb) courgettes, cut in half* *lengthways*
Cooking time 10 minutes	*25 g (1 oz) butter or soya margarine (see* *Cook's Tip), melted*
Serves 4	*1 tablespoon wholegrain mustard*
Calories 84 per portion	
Suitable for vegans using soya margarine	

Brush the courgettes with the melted butter and place them, cut side down, on a preheated grill pan. Grill under high heat until lightly brown.

Turn the courgettes over and spread with the mustard. Grill until golden. Serve.

■ COOK'S TIP

In summer, cook these kebabs over a barbecue. Other vegetables can be used including mushrooms, chunks of corn-on-the-cob and baby onions.

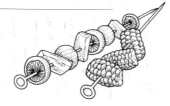

■ COOK'S TIP

Soya margarine can be used instead of butter or vegetable margarine for all dishes. It is suitable for vegans and is very low in saturated fats.

259

spiced okra

Preparation time 20 minutes	2 tablespoons oil 1 onion, chopped
Cooking time 30 minutes	1 garlic clove, crushed 1 teaspoon ground cumin
Serves 4	1 teaspoon ground coriander 2 tomatoes, skinned and chopped
Calories 87 per portion	1 x 250 g (8 oz) can tomatoes 250 g (8 oz) okra, washed and trimmed
Suitable for vegans	4 tablespoons water 1 tablespoon tomato purée sugar salt and pepper

Heat the oil in a sauté pan and fry the onion for 5 minutes without browning, then add the garlic, cumin and coriander. Stir for a couple of minutes, then add the tomatoes and okra. Add the water and tomato purée. Put a lid on the pan and leave to cook for 20 minutes, until the okra is tender, stirring from time to time. Season with salt, a pinch of sugar, and a twist or two of freshly ground black pepper.

260

scalloped potatoes

Preparation time 20 minutes	1 kg (2 lb) potatoes, thinly sliced 1 large onion, thinly sliced
Cooking time About 2 hours	150 ml (¼ pint) vegetable stock 25 g (1 oz) butter, melted
Oven temperature 180°C (350°F) gas 4	salt and pepper
Serves 6	
Calories 162 per portion	

Make layers of the potatoes and onions in a well-buttered oven-proof dish, seasoning the layers with salt and pepper.

Bring the stock to the boil and pour over the potatoes, then brush liberally with the melted butter.

Cover with foil and cook in a preheated oven for 1½ hours. Remove the foil and cook for a further 30 minutes or until the potatoes are cooked through and lightly browned.

Place under a moderate grill until the potatoes are well browned and crispy on top. Serve hot.

■ COOK'S TIP

Avoid tired-looking okra or any over 10 cm (4 inches) long, which are likely to be tough. Keep in the refrigerator and do not store longer than a couple of days.

■ COOK'S TIP

For a richer dish, use full fat milk or single cream instead of the vegetable stock. Sprinkle over 50 g (2 oz) vegetarian Cheddar cheese and grill until melted.

261

parsnip croquettes

Preparation time
45 minutes, plus chilling

Cooking time
about 35 minutes

Serves 4

Calories
421 per portion

500 g (1 lb) parsnips, cut into chunks
2 potatoes, halved
50 g (2 oz) plain flour, plus extra for coating
25 g (1 oz) butter, softened
1 large egg, beaten
75 g (3 oz) dried breadcrumbs
25 g (1 oz) blanched almonds, chopped
vegetable oil, for deep-frying
salt and pepper
parsley sprigs, to garnish

Cook the parsnips and potatoes in boiling salted water for about 20 minutes until tender. Drain thoroughly, then return to the rinsed pan and place over a gentle heat to remove excess moisture. Stir constantly to prevent the vegetables catching on the bottom of the pan.

Transfer the vegetables to a bowl and leave to cool slightly, then mash until smooth. Beat in the flour, butter and salt and pepper to taste until evenly mixed. With well-floured hands, form into 8 croquette shapes. Coat with flour, dip into beaten egg and then coat with the breadcrumbs mixed with the chopped almonds. Chill for at least 1 hour.

Heat the oil in a deep-fryer to 190°C (375°F) or until a stale bread cube turns golden in 40–50 seconds. Lower a few of the croquettes carefully into the hot oil, then deep-fry for about 5 minutes until they are golden brown on all sides. Drain on kitchen paper and keep hot while frying the remainder. Serve immediately, garnished with parsley.

262

lemon-glazed carrots

Preparation time
5 minutes

Cooking time
about 20 minutes

Serves 4

Calories
101 per portion

Suitable for vegans using soya margarine

750 g (1½ lb) new carrots, lightly scraped
juice of ½ lemon
½ teaspoon demerara sugar
25 g (1 oz) butter or soya margarine
carrot tops or chopped parsley, to garnish

Put the carrots in a large saucepan and pour over the lemon juice and just enough boiling water to cover. Add the sugar and half of the butter, cover tightly and simmer for 15 minutes until the carrots are nearly tender.

Remove the lid and allow the liquid to evaporate completely. Turn into a warmed serving dish, top with the remaining butter and garnish with carrot tops or parsley.

■ COOK'S TIP

Add a sprinkling of nutmeg to the croquettes for a spicy, nutty flavour. Keep whole nutmegs in an airtight jar and grate them as required on a miniature, fine grater.

■ COOK'S TIP

Choose bright orange carrots without splits. To obtain all the nutritional benefits, they are best eaten raw but if scrubbed and cooked whole, not peeled, they still contain plenty of Vitamin A.

263

italian tomatoes

Preparation time	4 *large tomatoes, halved*
15 minutes	2 *tablespoons oil*
Cooking time	1 *onion, finely chopped*
15 minutes	2 *garlic cloves, crushed*
Oven temperature	3–4 *tablespoons fresh white breadcrumbs*
200°C (400°F)	1–2 *tablespoons chopped basil or parsley*
gas 6	50 *g (2 oz) Gruyère cheese, grated*
Serves 4	*salt and pepper*
Calories	*chopped parsley, to garnish*
153 per portion	

Scoop a little flesh from the centre of each tomato half.

Heat the oil in a medium pan, add the onion and garlic and cook until soft. Add the breadcrumbs, basil or parsley and salt and pepper to taste. Pile on top of each tomato half and cover with grated cheese. Place in an ovenproof dish.

Bake in a preheated oven for 10–15 minutes until the tomatoes are just cooked and the cheese brown. Garnish with chopped parsley.

264

bean and beansprout stir-fry

Preparation time	15 *g (½ oz) butter or soya margarine*
5 minutes	1 *tablespoon olive oil*
Cooking time	300 *g (10 oz) French beans, or frozen*
about 10 minutes	*whole green beans*
Serves 4	300 *g (10 oz) bean sprouts, washed and*
Calories	*drained*
91 per portion	2 *teaspoons paprika*
Suitable for vegans	*salt and pepper*

Heat the butter or soya margarine and oil in a wok or large frying pan until foamy, then add the beans and stir-fry gently for about 4 minutes.

Push the beans to the side of the wok, turn the heat up a little and add the bean sprouts. Stir-fry for about 2 minutes.

Now mix the beans and bean sprouts together adding the paprika, a little salt and plenty of black pepper. Stir-fry for 1 minute more, then turn into a warm serving dish and serve. Alternatively, serve straight from the wok.

■ COOK'S TIP

Choose any variety of cheese instead of Gruyère – mozzarella has a particular affinity with tomatoes and basil. Vegetarian Cheddar or Red Leicester are good, too.

■ COOK'S TIP

To prepare french beans for cooking, first wash and dry the beans, then top and tail. If the pods are very large, cut them in half or into 4 cm (1½ inch lengths).

salads

Salads offer the perfect opportunity for mingling sweet and sour flavours, for incorporating protein-rich cheese and creating piquant new dressings. Creativity can flourish in salad-making and the following recipes offer plenty of ideas, including salads with herbs, nuts and yogurt, crunchy salads with celery, apple and walnuts and juicy salads with grapes or pineapple that can be served as a meal with cheese and dressings.

265

caerphilly bean salad

Preparation time 20 minutes	*250 g (8 oz) French beans*
Cooking time 8 minutes	*250 g (8 oz) Caerphilly cheese* *1 small red pepper* FOR THE DRESSING
Serves 4	*8 tablespoons salad oil*
Calories 470 per portion	*2 tablespoons red or white wine vinegar* *a little paprika* *1 tablespoon single cream (optional)* *salt and pepper*

Top and tail the French beans and cook in boiling salted water until just tender. Drain, refresh with a little cold water, drain again and allow to cool.

Cut the cheese into neat pieces, either dice or thin strips. Discard the core and seeds from the red pepper and cut the flesh into thin rounds. Prepare the dressing by whisking all the ingredients together. Toss the cheese and beans in sufficient dressing to coat lightly, put in a salad bowl and scatter the rings of pepper over the top.

266

mushroom and leicester salad

Preparation time 15 minutes, plus chilling	*250 g (8 oz) very fresh cup or button mushrooms*
Serves 4	*4–6 tablespoons salad oil* *125 g (4 oz) Red Leicester cheese*
Calories 260 per portion	*1 tablespoon wine vinegar* *1 tablespoon chopped parsley* *2 teaspoons chopped chives (optional)* *salt and pepper*

Trim and carefully wipe the mushrooms. Slice thinly and place in a wide bowl. Add enough oil to coat the mushrooms and season with salt and pepper. Cut the Leicester cheese into strips and add to the mushrooms with the vinegar and herbs. Toss together, turn into a salad bowl, cover and chill briefly before serving.

■ COOK'S TIP

To ring the changes, substitute mangetout for the French beans in this recipe. Like French beans, topping and tailing is the only preparation (apart from rinsing) necessary. Boil briefly in salted water so that they retain a little bite.

■ COOK'S TIP

Red Leicester adds colour to this nutritious salad. Red Windsor, a distinctive marbled cheese flavoured with elderberry wine or annatto berries, could be used instead.

267

spinach cheese salad

Preparation time
15 minutes plus chilling

Serves 4

Calories
385 per portion

1 kg (2 lb) fresh spinach, washed
4 tablespoons olive oil
wine vinegar or lemon juice (optional)
175 g (6 oz) Derby cheese
2 tablespoons mayonnaise
salt and pepper
chopped chives, to garnish (optional)

Blanch the spinach for 1 minute in boiling salted water. Drain and refresh with cold water. Press the spinach between two plates to remove excessive moisture. Place in a wide bowl.

Using two forks to help separate the leaves, dress the spinach with the oil, salt and pepper, adding a little wine vinegar or lemon juice if you like.

Cut the cheese into cubes, mix with the mayonnaise and extra salt and pepper if necessary. Spoon on top of the spinach and serve lightly chilled. Add a garnish of chopped chives, if liked.

268

cheshire salad

Preparation time
10 minutes

Cooking time
5 minutes

Serves 4

Calories
115 per portion

FOR THE DRESSING
4 tablespoons orange juice
1 teaspoon caster sugar
2 tablespoons olive oil
1 tablespoon white wine vinegar
1 tablespoon chopped parsley
1 tablespoon chopped chives
FOR THE SALAD
250 g (8 oz) red cabbage
125 g (4 oz) cooked beetroot
2 red apples
1 tablespoon lemon juice
4–8 lettuce leaves
250 g (8 oz) blue Cheshire cheese
parsley sprigs, to garnish

Whisk the dressing ingredients in a bowl. Shred the cabbage and blanch in boiling water for 2 minutes. Drain and toss into the dressing. Leave to cool, stirring occasionally. Thinly slice the beetroot. Core and chop the apples and toss in the lemon juice. Arrange the lettuce leaves on individual plates and top with the cabbage and apple. Cut the cheese into cubes and scatter over the salad. Garnish with parsley and serve.

■ COOK'S TIP

Spinach has a very high vitamin A content and is rich in iron and vitamin C. As it is low in calories it is an excellent vegetable, especially when served raw as in this flavoursome salad.

■ COOK'S TIP

Although red wine vinegar has an equally good flavour, white wine vinegar is a preferable ingredient in salad dressings as red wine vinegar can turn the dressing an odd pink colour.

269

light cheese and pineapple salad

Preparation time
20 minutes, plus chilling

Serves 4

Calories
220 per portion

175 g (6 oz) low-fat hard cheese, cubed
250 g (8 oz) fresh pineapple, peeled and
    cubed
125 g (4 oz) celery, chopped
125 g (4 oz) apple, chopped
50 g (2 oz) walnut pieces
3–4 tablespoons low-calorie mayonnaise
1 tablespoon chopped parsley
salt and pepper

Mix the cheese, pineapple, celery, apple and walnuts in a bowl. Coat with the mayonnaise and sprinkle with parsley. Season to taste and mix well. Chill for 25–30 minutes before serving.

270

blue cheese and mandarin salad

Preparation time
15 minutes

Serves 6

Calories
135 per portion

1 x 300 g (10 oz) can mandarin orange
    segments in natural juice
75 g (3 oz) blue cheese
150 ml (¼ pint) soured cream or
    mayonnaise
500 g (1 lb) white cabbage, finely
    shredded
salt and pepper
lettuce, to serve

Drain the mandarins. Crumble the blue cheese into the mandarin juice then mix in the soured cream or mayonnaise. Season well with salt and pepper then toss with the cabbage and mandarins. Serve on a bed of lettuce.

■ COOK'S TIP

When selecting a fresh pineapple, check for fragrance and ripeness. Discoloured, drooping leaves indicate that the pineapple is not in peak condition; the fruit itself should be golden orange in colour, never green.

■ COOK'S TIP

Blue cheese and mandarins form a highly successful combination. For an interesting starter, omit the cabbage and use the fruit and cheese mixture to fill well-drained canned pear halves.

271

crunchy bean sprout and cheese salad

Preparation time
10 minutes

Serves 4

Calories
305 per portion

4 tablespoons natural wholenut peanut butter
4 tablespoons lemon juice
1 red pepper, deseeded and cut into thin strips
175 g (6 oz) bean sprouts
175 g (6 oz) Double Gloucester cheese, cubed
½ crisp lettuce, shredded

Stir the peanut butter and lemon juice together until well mixed. Combine the remaining ingredients in a salad bowl then stir in the peanut butter dressing just before serving.

272

two-cheese salad

Preparation time
20 minutes

Serves 4

Calories
485 per portion

1 green pepper, deseeded and cut into thin strips
1 red pepper, deseeded and cut into thin strips
4 tomatoes, sliced
175 g (6 oz) blue cheese, cubed
175 g (6 oz) Edam or Gouda cheese, cubed
12 stuffed green olives
2 tablespoons olive oil
1 tablespoon lemon juice
1 cos lettuce
FOR THE SAUCE
300 ml (½ pint) natural yogurt
1 small avocado
salt and pepper

Place the peppers, tomatoes, cheeses and olives in a bowl. Whisk the oil and lemon juice together until well blended then pour over salad and toss lightly. Separate the lettuce into leaves and arrange it on a serving platter. Pile the cheese salad in the centre.

To make the sauce, mix the yogurt with plenty of salt and pepper. Peel and finely chop the avocado, then fold it lightly into the yogurt. Serve separately.

■ COOK'S TIP

If you have a grinder, making your own peanut butter is easy. Grind 125 g (4 oz) roasted peanuts finely and mash them to a paste in a bowl, adding a little vegetable oil if necessary. Hazelnuts, cashews and walnuts may also be used.

■ COOK'S TIP

Vary the choice of cheese to suit your palate. For example try smoked cheese with Cheshire cheese or Sage Derby cheese with Edam. Strict vegetarians may prefer to make a selection from the rennet-free varieties.

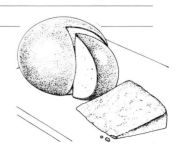

 273

creamy waldorf salad

Preparation time
30 minutes, plus chilling

Serves 6

Calories
170 per portion

2 tablespoons lemon juice
1 teaspoon caster sugar
1 tablespoon mayonnaise
3 green dessert apples
4 celery sticks
50 g (2 oz) walnuts
125 g (4 oz) seedless green grapes
125 g (4 oz) Danish Blue cheese
6 tablespoons natural yogurt
salt and pepper
celery leaves, to garnish

Whisk the lemon juice, sugar and mayonnaise in a large bowl. Core and dice the apples and stir into the lemon mixture. Set aside and turn occasionally while preparing the other ingredients. Thinly slice the celery, chop the walnuts and halve the grapes. Add to the apples and mix to coat thinly in the lemon mixture.

Place the cheese in a bowl and beat to soften. Beat in the yogurt and salt and pepper to make a thick dressing. Alternatively, place the cheese, yogurt and salt and pepper in a food processor and blend until smooth. Pour over the apple mixture and turn gently with a fork until well mixed. Refrigerate for an hour then mix again. Turn into a serving bowl and garnish with celery leaves.

■ COOK'S TIP

If liked, fennel with its aniseed flavour and delicate feathery leaves may be finely chopped and substituted for the celery in this recipe.

274

mushroom slaw

Preparation time
15 minutes, plus chilling

Serves 6

Calories
235 per portion

250 g (8 oz) flat mushrooms, thinly sliced
250 g (8 oz) white cabbage, shredded
50 g (2 oz) sultanas
FOR THE DRESSING
150 ml (¼ pint) mayonnaise
2 tablespoons lemon juice
2 tablespoons Dijon mustard
2 tablespoons single cream
2 tablespoons chopped chives
salt and pepper

In a large bowl, mix the mushrooms with the cabbage and sultanas. In a separate bowl combine all the ingredients for the dressing and season with salt and pepper to taste. Pour the dressing over the salad and mix gently together. Cover and refrigerator for several hours. Toss together well before serving.

■ COOK'S TIP

For an unusual serving idea, make a bowl for the salad from a Savoy cabbage; cut out the centre, wash, dry and reserve the outer leaves. Wash and shred the centre, mix with the other ingredients, dress and place in the cabbage bowl.

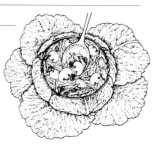

275

pasta slaw

Preparation time 15 minutes, plus cooling	75 g (3 oz) pasta spirals
	1 x 300 g (10 oz) frozen French beans
Cooking time 13–15 minutes	75 g (3 oz) white cabbage, finely chopped
	½ green pepper, cored, deseeded and finely chopped
Serves 4	1 carrot, grated
Calories 225 per portion	4 spring onions, finely chopped
	salt and pepper
	parsley sprigs, to garnish (optional)
	FOR THE DRESSING
	4 tablespoons mayonnaise
	2 tablespoons milk or cream
	1 tablespoon wine vinegar
	2 teaspoons sugar
	salt and pepper

Cook the pasta in a large saucepan of boiling salted water for 10–12 minutes, until just tender. Cook the French beans in boiling salted water for 3–5 minutes. Refresh both under cold water, drain and allow to cool.

Meanwhile, mix together the remaining salad ingredients in a bowl. Combine the ingredients for the dressing and add to the salad bowl with the pasta and chopped French beans. Season to taste, toss and garnish with parsley sprigs to serve.

276

fruit coleslaw

Preparation time 25 minutes	½ white cabbage, finely shredded
	4 celery sticks, cut into matchstick strips
Serves 4	2 red dessert apples, cored and chopped
Calories 280 per portion	50 g (2 oz) raisins
	50 g (2 oz) walnuts, chopped
	125 g (4 oz) seedless grapes, halved
	1 tablespoon chopped chives
	FOR THE DRESSING
	4 tablespoons oil
	1 tablespoon wine vinegar
	pinch of mustard powder
	1 teaspoon sugar
	salt and pepper

To make the dressing, combine all the ingredients in a screw-topped jar and shake well to blend.

Place the cabbage in a large salad bowl and stir in sufficient dressing to just moisten. Add the celery, apples, raisins, walnuts, grapes and chives and toss well.

■ COOK'S TIP

For additional fibre and B vitamins, use wholemeal pasta in this recipe.

■ COOK'S TIP

To shred cabbage finely, choose a long-bladed sharp knife. Secure the cabbage with your fingers, moving them back as you shred.

277

crunchy cabbage salad

Preparation time 15 minutes	*250 g (8 oz) red cabbage, finely shredded*
Serves 4	*125 g (4 oz) white cabbage, finely shredded*
Calories 260 per portion	*1 red pepper, cored, deseeded and chopped*
	50 g (2 oz) sunflower seeds
	125 g (4 oz) salted peanuts
	50 g (2 oz) raisins
	FOR THE DRESSING
	1 tablespoon wine vinegar
	1 teaspoon prepared mustard
	2 tablespoons natural yogurt
	2 tablespoons groundnut oil
	1 tablespoon chopped parsley
	salt and pepper

Place the red and white cabbage in a salad bowl with the pepper, sunflower seeds, peanuts and raisins. Mix well.

Place all the dressing ingredients in a small bowl and whisk with a fork until thickened. Pour over the salad and mix thoroughly. Serve immediately or cover and refrigerate until you are ready to serve.

278

dressed bean and onion salad

Preparation time 15 minutes, plus chilling	*50 g (2 oz) butter or margarine*
	1 garlic clove, finely chopped
Cooking time 5 minutes	*50 g (2 oz) All-Bran cereal, crushed*
	¼ teaspoon salt
Serves 4	*1 x 250 g (8 oz) can red kidney beans, drained*
Calories 445 per portion	*1 x 250 g (8 oz) can black-eyed beans or chickpeas, drained*
	500 g (1 lb) fresh or frozen green beans, cooked and sliced
	onion rings, to garnish
	FOR THE DRESSING
	½ teaspoon salt
	pinch of pepper
	½ teaspoon dried basil
	½ teaspoon mustard powder
	3 tablespoons white wine vinegar
	1 tablespoon clear honey
	5 tablespoons oil

Melt the butter in a pan and sauté the garlic for 2 minutes. Stir in the cereal and salt and fry briskly for 2 minutes more. Leave to cool. Rinse the canned beans and drain well. Mix with the green beans in a salad bowl and chill.

To make the dressing, combine the salt, pepper, basil, mustard, vinegar and honey in a bowl. Gradually beat in the oil. Stir the cereal mixture into the beans and toss with the dressing. Garnish with the onion rings and serve.

■ COOK'S TIP

Sunflower seeds are readily available in health food stores. As well as enhancing all kinds of salads, they provide a healthy nibble, and are good toasted too.

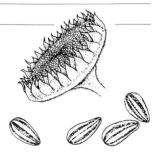

■ COOK'S TIP

Mixing pulse protein with cereal protein in this salad makes it a well-balanced dish which supplies a good combination of amino acids.

279

mushroom and mangetout salad

Preparation time
10 minutes, plus cooling

Cooking time
4–5 minutes

Serves 4

Calories
55 per portion

175 g (6 oz) mangetout
250 g (8 oz) small button mushrooms, sliced
6 spring onions, chopped
150 ml (¼ pint) natural yogurt
salt and pepper
snipped chives, to garnish

Cook the mangetout in boiling salted water for 4–5 minutes until just tender. Drain and cool. Combine the mushrooms, spring onions and yogurt with seasoning to taste.

Arrange the mange tout on a plate and top with the mushrooms. Sprinkle with chives and serve.

280

broad bean salad

Preparation time
15 minutes

Cooking time
10 minutes

Serves 4–6

Calories
420–280 per portion

375 g (12 oz) fresh or frozen broad beans
salt
tarragon or parsley sprigs, to garnish
FOR THE HOLLANDAISE SAUCE
3 egg yolks
2 tablespoons lemon juice
175 g (6 oz) unsalted butter, melted
salt and pepper

Cook the beans in boiling salted water for 5–10 minutes or until tender. Drain the bean, cool and pop the beans out of their outer skins, if liked (with young beans this will not be necessary). Put the beans into a serving bowl.

To make the hollandaise sauce, blend the egg yolks with the lemon juice in a food processor for 30 seconds. Slowly pour in the hot melted butter to make a creamy sauce. Add salt and pepper to taste. Pour over the beans immediately and garnish with the tarragon or parsley. Serve warm or cool.

■ COOK'S TIP

The best way of preparing chives is to hold the washed bunch firmly and use a pair of scissors to snip them into a small basin.

■ COOK'S TIP

If using fresh broad beans, do not remove from the furry lined pods until just before cooking. There is no need to shell young, tender broad beans; top, tail, cut them up, then cook and serve in the pods.

281

mushroom and cucumber side salad

Preparation time 15 minutes	¼ *Webb's lettuce, finely shredded*
	125 *g (4 oz) button mushrooms, wiped*
Serves 4	*and quartered*
	½ *cucumber, diced*
Calories	4 *tablespoons low-calorie mayonnaise*
65 per portion	2 *teaspoons tomato ketchup*
	½ *teaspoon lemon juice*
	paprika, to garnish

Arrange the shredded lettuce in the base of four salad bowls. Mix together the mushrooms and cucumber and place over the lettuce. Combine the mayonnaise with the tomato ketchup and lemon juice and spoon over the salad. Sprinkle with a little paprika and serve at once.

282

mushroom and celeriac salad

Preparation time 25 minutes, plus chilling	250 *g (8 oz) button mushrooms, halved if large*
	½ *large celeriac root, coarsely grated*
Serves 6	250 *g (8 oz) carrots, coarsely grated*
	chopped parsley, to garnish
Calories	FOR THE DRESSING
315 per portion	1 *egg yolk*
	150 *ml (¼ pint) olive oil*
	2 *tablespoons white wine vinegar*
	150 *ml (¼ pint) soured cream*
	salt and pepper

First make the dressing. Place the egg yolk in a small bowl and beat with 2–3 drops of the olive oil. Gradually whisk in the remaining olive oil, drop by drop, until pale and thick. Whisk in the vinegar, soured cream and salt and pepper to taste.

Fold half the dressing into the mushrooms. Fold the rest of the dressing into the celeriac. Turn the celeriac on to a serving dish, top with the carrots and mushrooms, then sprinkle with parsley. Chill before serving.

■ COOK'S TIP

Choose lettuces with care, avoiding any with rust spots, wilted leaves or yellowing tips. Wash the leaves carefully and quickly (do not soak) and dry between sheets of kitchen paper. Store in plastic bags in the refrigerator.

■ COOK'S TIP

For a substantial lunch or supper, serve this salad with a generous slice of quiche or flan.

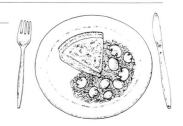

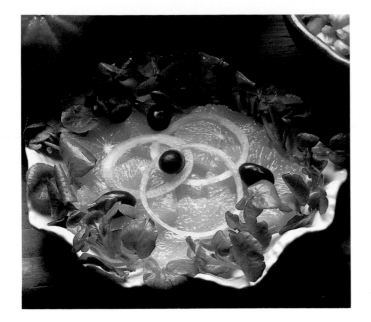

283

orange and watercress salad

Preparation time
15 minutes

Serves 4

Calories
185 per portion

1 large bunch of watercress, trimmed
*3 oranges, peel and pith removed and
    thinly sliced into rounds*
*1 onion, thinly sliced and separated into
    rings*
*1 small green pepper, cored, deseeded,
    and thinly sliced into rings (optional)*
6 tablespoons French dressing
black olives, to garnish

Put the watercress in a salad bowl. Arrange the orange slices on top with the onion and pepper rings, if using. Pour on the dressing and garnish with the olives.

284

brussels sprouts and carrot salad

Preparation time
20 minutes, plus
chilling

Serves 4

Calories
170 per portion

500 g (1 lb) Brussels sprouts
2 carrots, grated
2 tablespoons sultanas
1 tablespoon finely chopped onion
FOR THE DRESSING
4 tablespoons oil
1 tablespoon wine vinegar
1 teaspoon sugar
2 teaspoons Dijon mustard
salt and pepper

Wash the sprouts. Remove and discard a slice from the base of each one. Slice the sprouts thinly. Mix with the carrots, sultanas and onion in a large salad bowl.

Combine the ingredients for the dressing and stir sufficient into the salad to moisten. Chill for at least 1 hour before serving.

■ COOK'S TIP

For an attractive and colourful garnish, shape a tomato water-lily. With a small, sharp knife, make zig-zag cuts around the middle of a tomato, through to the centre. Separate the two halves with care.

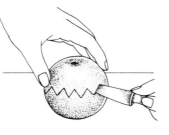

■ COOK'S TIP

Brussels sprouts, although usually served hot, make an excellent base for a winter salad with their delicate colour and flavour. Nor are any of the valuable minerals and vitamins lost through cooking.

285

chicory and sesame salad

Preparation time	3 heads of chicory
15 minutes	2 oranges
Serves 4–6	1 bunch of watercress
Calories	25 g (1 oz) sesame seeds, roasted
205–135 per portion	4 tablespoons olive oil
	1 tablespoon lemon juice
	salt and pepper

Cut the chicory diagonally into 1 cm (½ inch) slices and place in a mixing bowl. Remove the peel and pith from the oranges and cut the flesh into segments, holding the fruit over the bowl so that any juice is retained.

Divide the watercress into sprigs and add to the bowl with the sesame seeds.

Whisk together the oil, lemon juice and salt and pepper to taste, then pour over the salad and toss thoroughly. Transfer to a salad bowl and serve.

286

carrot and apple salad

Preparation time	375 g (12 oz) carrots, coarsely grated
20 minutes	3 Cox's Orange Pippin apples, unpeeled,
Cooking time	cored and sliced
5 minutes	1 tablespoon lemon juice
Serves 4	1 tablespoon sunflower seeds
Calories	3 tablespoons raisins
280 per portion	2 teaspoons vegetable oil
	2 tablespoons cashew nuts
	6 tablespoons French dressing
	lettuce leaves, to serve

Put the grated carrot into a large bowl. Sprinkle the apple slices with lemon juice to prevent discolouration, then add to the bowl. Lightly mix in the sunflower seeds and raisins.

Heat the oil in a small pan and lightly brown the cashew nuts. Lift out and drain on absorbent kitchen paper, then add to the bowl.

Spoon the dressing over the salad and toss lightly. Serve on a bed of lettuce leaves.

■ COOK'S TIP

Sesame seeds have a nutty flavour which is released more fully when they are roasted in a moderate oven (180°C/350°F/gas 4) for about 15 minutes. Stir them frequently to prevent charring.

■ COOK'S TIP

French dressing, without garlic and herbs, keeps well in a screw-topped jar. Store in the refrigerator.

287

celery salad flavia

Preparation time
15 minutes, plus
chilling

Serves 4

Calories
140 per portion

1 garlic clove, halved
1 head of celery, cut into small strips
1 x 200 g (7 oz) can artichoke hearts in
*   brine, drained and halved*
1 tablespoon black olives, pitted
1 tablespoon chopped parsley
3 tablespoons olive oil
1 tablespoon lemon juice
dash of Tabasco sauce
½ teaspoon prepared mustard
pinch of dried oregano
salt
a few celery leaves, to garnish

Using the cut side of the garlic, vigorously rub the inside of a salad bowl, then discard. Add the celery, artichoke hearts, olives and parsley to the bowl.

To make the dressing, beat the olive oil with the lemon juice, Tabasco sauce, mustard, oregano and salt to taste.

Pour the dressing over the salad and toss well. Cover and chill for 30 minutes to allow the flavours to develop well.

Toss the salad again before serving and garnish with the celery leaves.

288

winter radish salad

Preparation time
5 minutes, plus
standing

Serves 4

Calories
90 per portion

1 large winter radish
150 ml (¼ pint) soured cream
salt
1 tablespoon snipped chives, to garnish

Scrub or thinly peel the radish. Grate or cut it into very thin slices. Place in a bowl and sprinkle generously with salt. Leave to stand for 10–12 minutes.

Rinse and dry the radish slices thoroughly and place in a salad bowl. Spoon over the soured cream, toss well and garnish with the chives.

■ COOK'S TIP

To make this salad more filling, garnish with a ring of hard-boiled egg slices and tomato wedges.

■ COOK'S TIP

It is important to rinse the radish slices thoroughly to remove all the salt. Dry thoroughly between sheets of absorbent kitchen paper before mixing with the soured cream.

289

turkish pepper salad

Preparation time
5 minutes, plus 15 minutes to plump raisins

Serves 4

Calories
230 per portion

2 tablespoons seedless raisins
2 green peppers, cored, deseeded and cut into thin strips
2 spring onions, finely chopped
25 g (1 oz) pine nuts
5 tablespoons olive oil
3 tablespoons lemon juice
pinch of paprika
salt and pepper

Soak the raisins in a little warm water for about 15 minutes until plump. Drain well.

Mix together the green peppers, raisins, spring onions and pine nuts and place in a serving bowl.

Mix together the oil, lemon juice, paprika and salt and pepper and pour over the salad. Toss well to mix.

290

radish salad

Preparation time
20–25 minutes, plus chilling

Serves 4–6

Calories
90–60 per portion

3 large bunches of radishes, trimmed and thinly sliced
1 small onion, thinly sliced and separated into rings
2 tomatoes, skinned and chopped
1 tablespoon mint, finely chopped
1 lettuce, shredded
FOR THE DRESSING
2 tablespoons olive oil
2 tablespoons lemon juice
1½ teaspoons salt
¼ teaspoon black pepper

Put the radish slices, onion rings and tomatoes in a bowl and combine with the mint.

Whisk together the oil, lemon juice, salt and pepper. Pour over the salad ingredients and toss well.

Place the salad on a bed of shredded lettuce and chill thoroughly before serving.

■ COOK'S TIP

Seeds of the Mediterranean stone pine, pine nuts are pale and oval and resemble miniature blanched almonds. Look for them in delicatessens and buy in small quantities as they do not keep indefinitely.

■ COOK'S TIP

For an extra zesty taste, make this dish with the large radishes that are often found during the summer months.

291

grapefruit and chicory salad

Preparation time 15 minutes, plus chilling	*2 heads of chicory, trimmed* *2 grapefruit* FOR THE DRESSING
Serves 4	*4 tablespoons olive oil*
Calories 295 per portion	*2 tablespoons white wine vinegar* *Tabasco sauce* *salt and pepper*

Cut the chicory crossways into thin slices, and put in a salad bowl.

Squeeze the juice from half a grapefruit and reserve. Peel and remove the pith from the remaining grapefruit and divide into segments. Cut each segment in half and mix with the chicory slices.

Combine the oil, vinegar and reserved grapefruit juice and season to taste with salt and pepper and a few drops of Tabasco. Pour over the salad, toss well and chill for about 30 minutes before serving.

292

country-style tomato platter

Preparation time 20 minutes	*750 g (1½ lb) beef tomatoes, cut into thick slices*
Serves 4–6	*1 onion, chopped.*
Calories 179–119 per portion	*300 ml (½ pint) soured cream* *1 basil sprig, chopped* *salt and pepper* *basil leaves, to garnish*

Arrange the tomato slices on a flat serving dish and season with salt and pepper to taste. Scatter the onion evenly over the tomatoes. Mix the soured cream with the basil, blending well. Using a teaspoon, place a dot of cream on each tomato slice. Garnish with basil leaves to serve.

■ COOK'S TIP

This slightly sharp salad goes well with a variety of cheeses and French bread to make a tasty and quick supper.

■ COOK'S TIP

Ciabatta makes an ideal accompaniment for this salad. Buy the ready-to-bake version and serve fresh from the oven.

293

green salad with peanut dressing

Preparation time 15 minutes	*selection of salad leaves, e.g. lettuce,*
	endive, radicchio, watercress
Serves 4	*½ cucumber*
Calories	*1 avocado (optional)*
210 per portion	FOR THE DRESSING
	25 g (1 oz) salted peanuts, finely chopped
	1 teaspoon clear honey
	1 tablespoon lemon juice
	3 tablespoons groundnut oil
	salt and pepper

Wash the salad leaves and dry well. Tear into pieces and place in a salad bowl.

To make the dressing, mix together the peanuts, honey and lemon juice. Stir in the oil until well mixed then season with salt and pepper.

Just before serving, slice the cucumber and the avocado, if using, add to the salad and toss well with the dressing.

294

tomato ring salad

Preparation time 15 minutes, plus setting	*750 g (1½ lb) tomatoes, roughly chopped*
	1 onion, chopped
	150 ml (¼ pint) stock or water
Cooking time 25 minutes	*finely grated rind and juice of 1 orange or*
	lemon
Serves 4	*1 small bunch of fresh herbs*
Calories	*1 bay leaf*
125 per portion	*1 garlic clove, crushed (optional)*
	2 teaspoons agar-agar or 3 teaspoons
	powdered gelatine
	125 ml (4 fl oz) water
	1 teaspoon soy sauce
	salt and pepper
	FOR THE GARNISH
	cress
	4 hard-boiled eggs, cut into wedges

Cook the tomatoes and onion with the stock or water, orange or lemon rind and juice, herbs, garlic, if using, and salt and pepper in a covered pan for 20 minutes until pulpy. Rub through a sieve to make a purée.

Dissolve the agar-agar in the cold water in a small saucepan, then bring to the boil, stirring constantly. Stir into the purée, then add the soy sauce and salt and pepper to taste.

Pour into a 600–900 ml (1–1½ pint) ring mould, then chill until set. Unmould before serving and garnish with the cress and egg wedges.

■ COOK'S TIP

In composing a green salad, don't forget about the tiny seedling cress, bought growing in punnets, which will add a welcome piquancy when sprinkled on top.

■ COOK'S TIP

This is a perfect way to use tomatoes that are too soft for an ordinary salad.

295

okra salad

Preparation time 20 minutes	*500 g (1 lb) okra*
	1 onion, chopped
Cooking time 2 minutes	*4 tablespoons sunflower oil*
	2 tablespoons lemon juice
Serves 4	*1 garlic clove, crushed*
	1 teaspoon sugar
Calories 150 per portion	*salt and pepper*

Trim the ends off the okra and cut into short lengths. Select only the best okra for this salad – they must be in perfect condition. Drop the okra into a large pan of boiling water, bring back to the boil, then drain. Place the okra and onion in a bowl. Mix all the remaining ingredients and toss into the okra, then transfer to a dish and serve at once.

296

tabbouleh

Preparation time 15 minutes, plus soaking	*75 g (3 oz) bulgur wheat*
	40 g (1½ oz) chopped parsley
	3 tablespoons chopped mint
Serves 4	*4 spring onions, chopped*
	½ cucumber, finely diced
Calories 150 per portion	*2 tablespoons olive oil*
	juice of 1 lemon
	salt and pepper

Soak the bulgur wheat in cold water for 1 hour. Line a sieve with muslin and tip the wheat into it. Lift out the muslin and squeeze out as much moisture as possible.

Place the wheat in a salad bowl and add all the remaining ingredients and season with salt and pepper to taste. Add more lemon juice if preferred. Toss thoroughly, then transfer to a shallow dish to serve.

■ COOK'S TIP

Cooked okra has a mucilaginous texture that not everyone appreciates. By merely blanching the pods, this problem is largely avoided.

■ COOK'S TIP

Bulgur wheat is available from health food stores and major supermarkets

297

palm heart salad with dill mayonnaise

Preparation time 20 minutes, plus standing	1 x 475 g (15 oz) can palm hearts, drained
Serves 4	2 medium hard-boiled eggs, finely chopped
Calories 127 per portion	FOR THE DRESSING 1 tablespoon mayonnaise 4–5 tablespoons soured cream pinch of cayenne pepper 1–2 teaspoons chopped dill

Cut the palm hearts into 2.5 cm (1 inch) lengths and place in a serving dish. Spread the chopped eggs over the palm hearts.

To make the dressing, beat the mayonnaise with the soured cream, cayenne pepper and dill. Pour the dressing over the palm hearts and toss well to mix. Leave to stand for about 10 minutes to allow the flavours to develop.

298

spring onion and mushroom salad

Preparation time 20 minutes, plus standing	1 bunch of spring onions 1 orange
Serves 4	1 red pepper, cored, deseeded and cut into strips
Calories 95 per portion	125 g (4 oz) button mushrooms, halved FOR THE DRESSING 3 tablespoons dry white wine 1 tablespoon snipped chives 125 ml (4 fl oz) soured cream salt and pepper

Trim the roots from the spring onions and cut both the white and green stems into fine rings. Place the rings in a sieve, rinse and drain thoroughly.

Peel and segment the orange, removing all the pith. Mix the spring onions with the orange segments, pepper strips and mushrooms in a serving bowl.

To make the dressing, beat the white wine with the chives, soured cream and salt and pepper to taste. Pour over the salad and toss well to mix.

Leave the salad to stand for about 30 minutes before serving to allow the flavours to develop.

■ COOK'S TIP

Palm heart salad makes an appetising hors d'oeuvre or vegetable dish. Canned palm hearts are now widely available from supermarkets. They are a luxury because when these tender shoots are cut off the tree, it dies.

■ COOK'S TIP

Serve the salad in individual dishes with buttered toast as an unusual light starter or side salad. Use natural yogurt instead of soured cream for a lower fat version.

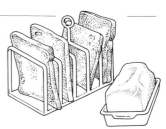

299

radish and cucumber salad

Preparation time	1 daikon radish (see Cook's Tip)
20 minutes	½ cucumber
Serves 4	salt
Calories	FOR THE DRESSING
105 per portion	1 tablespoon white wine vinegar
Suitable for vegans	3 tablespoons sunflower oil
	1 dill sprig, finely chopped

Peel and grate the radish. Peel and thinly slice the cucumber.

Place the radish and cucumber in a bowl and sprinkle with a little salt then mix thoroughly and leave to stand for 10 minutes. Rinse and drain thoroughly. Transfer to a serving bowl.

To make the dressing, beat the wine vinegar with the oil and chopped dill. Pour over the salad and toss well to mix. Serve as a side salad.

300

watercress and egg salad

Preparation time	2 bunches of watercress
30 minutes	FOR THE DRESSING
Serves 4	125 ml (4 fl oz) soured cream
Calories	1 garlic clove, crushed with salt
127 per portion	1 tablespoon chopped parsley
	1 tomato, skinned and chopped
	2 hard-boiled eggs, chopped
	pepper
	FOR THE GARNISH
	1 tomato, cut into wedges
	1 medium hard-boiled egg, sliced

Trim the watercress stems, sort the leaves, place in a sieve, rinse and drain.

To make the dressing, mix the soured cream and garlic together. Fold in the parsley, tomato and chopped egg. Season with pepper to taste.

Arrange the watercress in a serving bowl and top with the egg and tomato dressing. Garnish with the tomato wedges and the sliced egg.

■ COOK'S TIP

The daikon, or Japanese radish, is milder than the red radish, and delicious raw or cooked. Radishes are good sources of calcium, iron and vitamin C.

■ COOK'S TIP

For a special occasion, fill a bowl with watercress marinated in a vinaigrette dressing. Top with halved hard-boiled quail's eggs or hard-boiled eggs in their shells, coloured by soaking in beetroot juice.

301

celeriac and fruit salad

Preparation time 20 minutes	2–3 dessert apples
	2 bananas
Serves 4	1 small celeriac root, peeled and cut into strips
Calories 106 per portion	2 tablespoons chopped walnuts
	FOR THE DRESSING
	2 tablespoons lemon juice
	pinch of salt
	pinch of ground allspice
	2 tablespoons double cream

Peel, core and slice the apples. Peel the bananas and cut into chunks. Mix the apple with the banana, celeriac and walnuts in a serving bowl.

To make the dressing, mix the lemon juice with the salt and allspice and immediately stir into the salad. Add the cream and toss the ingredients well to mix. Serve immediately with buttered wholemeal bread.

302

radicchio and french bean salad

Preparation time 15 minutes	375 g (12 oz) French beans, trimmed
	1 head of radicchio
Cooking time 10 minutes	1 onion, sliced into rings
	2–3 slices white bread, crusts removed
Serves 4–6	salt
Calories 175–116 per portion	FOR THE DRESSING
	2 garlic cloves, crushed
Suitable for vegans	4–5 tablespoons olive oil

Parboil the French beans in boiling salted water for 2 minutes; rinse and drain. Cut into 5 cm (2 inch) lengths.

Separate the radicchio, place the leaves in a sieve, rinse and drain thoroughly. Tear into large pieces and place in a salad bowl with the French beans and onion rings.

To make the dressing, beat the garlic with the olive oil and a pinch of salt. Pour two-thirds of the dressing over the salad and mix thoroughly.

Cut the bread into cubes. Heat the remaining dressing in a frying pan over a high heat, add the bread cubes and fry until golden brown. Drain on kitchen paper. Sprinkle the bread cubes over the salad and serve immediately as a snack or as part of a buffet spread.

■ COOK'S TIP

The uneven surface of celeriac makes it difficult to peel. If the root is first cut into thick slices, it is easier to remove the peel.

■ COOK'S TIP

Raw garlic is used in many salad dressings. It is best known for its power not only to cleanse the blood but to reduce cholesterol. It may also help prevent colds.

303

radicchio rosette

Preparation time	1 head of radicchio
15 minutes	2–3 tablespoons Italian dressing (see
Serves 4	Cook's Tip)
Calories	½ fennel bulb, cut into fine julienne strips
207 per portion	2 teaspoons lemon juice
Suitable for vegans	6–8 black olives, pitted (optional)

Rinse and drain the radicchio without removing the thick stem. Carefully prise the leaves apart with your fingers to form a rosette, being careful not to break the leaves off the stem.

Holding the radicchio firmly by the stem, dip the leaves into the Italian dressing several times to coat. Carefully cut away the stem and place the radicchio rosette in a serving bowl.

Toss the fennel in the lemon juice to prevent discolouration. Fill the middle of the radicchio rosette with the fennel and olives, if using. To serve, sprinkle the remaining fennel on top.

304

iceberg lettuce with hazelnuts

Preparation time	1 small iceberg lettuce
20 minutes, plus	1 carrot, grated
standing	2–3 tablespoons coarsely chopped
Serves 4	hazelnuts (see Cook's Tip)
Calories	avocado slices (sprinkled with lemon
210 per portion	juice) or cucumber slices, to garnish
Suitable for vegans	FOR THE DRESSING
	3 tablespoons olive oil
	2 tablespoons lemon juice
	1 teaspoon prepared English mustard
	salt and pepper

Tear the lettuce into large pieces or strips, place in a sieve, rinse and drain thoroughly. Arrange in a serving bowl. Top with the grated carrot and hazelnuts.

To make the dressing, beat the oil with the lemon juice, mustard and salt and pepper to taste until smooth. Pour the dressing evenly over the salad. Cover and leave to stand in the refrigerator for a few minutes before serving, to allow the flavours to develop.

Garnish the salad with avocado or cucumber slices before serving.

■ COOK'S TIP

To make the Italian dressing, combine 1 tablespoon lemon juice, 1 tablespoon white wine vinegar, 6 tablespoons olive oil, 1 crushed garlic clove, 1 tablespoon chopped basil or oregano, salt and pepper and a pinch of sugar. Stir well.

■ COOK'S TIP

To bring out the nutty flavour of the hazelnuts, toast in a moderate oven for about 10 minutes until golden brown. Cool slightly before chopping.

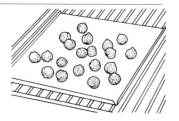

305

californian salad

Preparation time 15 minutes	*1 kg (2 lb) assorted fruit (choose from*
	apricots, fresh cherries, grapefruit,
Serves 4 as a main course	*kiwifruit, melon, nectarines, peaches,*
	raspberries and strawberries)
Calories	*50 g (2 oz) chopped nuts*
394 per portion	*2 bananas*
	1 tablespoon lemon juice
	500 g (1 lb) vegetarian cottage cheese

Prepare all the fruit (except the bananas), peeling, slicing, stoning and hulling as necessary. Combine all the prepared fruit in a large bowl.

Toast the nuts under a preheated medium hot grill for 2 minutes until lightly browned.

Peel the bananas, cut into long diagonal slices and immediately toss in the lemon juice to prevent discolouration. Add the banana slices to the other fruit.

Spoon the cottage cheese into the centre of the fruit in the bowl and sprinkle the chopped nuts over it. Serve immediately.

306

green and white salad

Preparation time 8 minutes	*425 g (14 oz) young turnips, no more*
	than 5 cm (2 inches) across, peeled
Serves 4	*50 g (2 oz) roughly chopped parsley*
Calories	*4 tablespoons cultured buttermilk or*
about 40 per portion	*natural yogurt*
	1 tablespoon lemon juice
	1 tablespoon chopped chives
	pinch of salt (optional)
	black pepper
	paprika, for dusting (optional)

Cut the turnips into paper-thin slices directly into a serving bowl.

Stir in all the remaining ingredients except the paprika. Dust lightly with paprika if liked, just before serving.

■ COOK'S TIP

This healthy and hearty salad is packed with protein, calcium and vitamins, especially vitamin C. It's also low in fat and an excellent source of fibre.

■ COOK'S TIP

Small, young turnips are tender and deliciously sweet. They will keep in a cool, dry place for quite some time. Try grating them for a different texture.

307

apricot and apple salad

Preparation time
15 minutes, plus soaking

Serves 4

Calories
330 per portion

175 g (6 oz) dried apricots
200 ml (7 fl oz) cloudy apple juice
3 dessert apples, cored and thinly sliced
3 tender celery sticks, thinly sliced
3 tablespoons walnut halves
celery leaves, to garnish
FOR THE DRESSING
3 tablespoons olive oil
3 tablespoons cloudy apple juice
2 tablespoons pumpkin seeds
salt and pepper

Soak the dried apricots in the apple juice for about 2 hours. Stir in the sliced apples, celery and walnuts.

Mix together the dressing ingredients. Pour the dressing over the fruit mixture and toss well.

Spoon the salad on to a serving dish and garnish it with the celery leaves.

308

lettuce and fresh herb salad

Preparation time
15 minutes

Serves 4

Calories
110 per portion

Suitable for vegans

1 tablespoon Dijon mustard
½ teaspoon sugar
1 tablespoon red wine vinegar
3 tablespoons olive oil
salt and pepper
½ small cucumber, peeled and thinly sliced
1 small hearty lettuce, shredded
2 tablespoons chopped mixed herbs (see Cook's Tip)

Mix together the mustard, sugar, red wine vinegar and oil. Season with salt and pepper and add the cucumber, lettuce and herbs just before serving.

■ COOK'S TIP

Dried apricots are not only a good source of fibre, they have a high iron content.

■ COOK'S TIP

Use any combination of chopped mixed herbs such as parsley, basil, dill, chervil, oregano, coriander or marjoram.

309
shredded spinach with mushrooms

Preparation time
15 minutes

Serves 4

Calories
124 per portion

Suitable for vegans

1 tablespoon Dijon mustard
1 tablespoon white wine vinegar
1 garlic clove, crushed
½ teaspoon salt
3 tablespoons olive oil
500 g (1 lb) tender spinach leaves,
   washed and finely shredded
125 g (4 oz) button mushrooms, sliced
   (see Cook's Tip)

Put the mustard, vinegar, garlic and salt into a bowl. Gradually stir in the oil to make a thick dressing, then add the spinach and mushrooms and stir gently, until all they are well coated.

310
crisp winter salad

Preparation time
8 minutes

Serves 4

Calories
71 per portion

40 g (1½ oz) flaked almonds
250 g (8 oz) celery, thinly sliced
1 large orange, peeled, segmented and
   roughly chopped
150 ml (¼ pint) natural yogurt
1 teaspoon ground coriander (optional)
½ teaspoon ground cumin or fennel seed
pinch of salt (optional)

Place the almonds in an dry heavy-based frying pan over a low heat for 2–3 minutes, stirring until slightly browned.

Put half the almonds with the prepared celery and orange in a serving bowl and toss lightly.

Mix together the yogurt, coriander, if using, and cumin or fennel seed. Pour the dressing over the salad. Taste and add a little salt if necessary.

Sprinkle the remaining almonds over the salad and serve.

■ COOK'S TIP

It is not necessary to peel mushrooms unless the skin is blemished. Just place in a sieve and rinse under a trickling tap or wipe with a damp cloth.

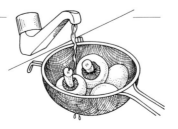

■ COOK'S TIP

A crunchy combination of textures, sweetened with orange and spices, makes this salad a contrast to the rather stodgy or heavy nature of much winter food.

311

waldorf salad

Preparation time 10 minutes	*150 ml (¼ pint) mayonnaise (see Cook's Tip)*
Serves 6–8	*2 tablespoons natural yogurt*
Calories 285–214 per portion	*3 dessert apples, cored and chopped*
	4 celery sticks, chopped
	25 g (1 oz) walnut pieces
	chopped parsley, to garnish

Mix together the mayonnaise and yogurt in a bowl. Add the apples, celery and walnuts and toss well to coat with mayonnaise.

Pile the salad on to a shallow serving dish and sprinkle with the parsley.

312

moroccan salad

Preparation time 10 minutes	*25 g (1 oz) blanched split almonds*
Serves 4	*1 bunch of watercress, coarse stems removed and roughly chopped*
Calories 120 per portion	*2 large oranges, about 300 g (10 oz) flesh, peeled and thinly sliced*
	125 g (4 oz) vegetarian cottage cheese
	50 g (2 oz) fresh or dried dates, stoned and roughly chopped
	1 teaspoon ground coriander (optional)

Grill the blanched split almonds on an ungreased baking sheet for 2–3 minutes, shaking to turn them so that they brown evenly on all sides.

Arrange the prepared watercress and orange slices around the inside edge of a serving dish.

Either stir in the cottage cheese, or place it in a neat mound in the dish. Arrange the dates and toasted almonds on top.

Sprinkle the salad with the coriander, if using, and serve.

■ **COOK'S TIP**

To make your own mayonnaise, beat together 1 medium egg yolk with ¼ teaspoon each salt, pepper and mustard powder Add 150 ml (¼ pint) olive oil drop by drop, beating constantly. As it thickens, add the oil in a steady stream. Add 1 tablespoon white wine vinegar and mix thoroughly.

■ **COOK'S TIP**

Watercress, available all year round, has a spicy rather bitter taste and works well in salads. It has a reasonable iron content as well as vitamins A and C.

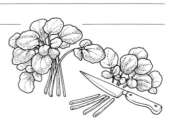

313

californian iceberg lettuce salad

Preparation time
15 minutes

Serves 4

Calories
170 per portion

½ iceberg lettuce
2 hard-boiled eggs, quartered
2 tablespoons salad cress
2 tablespoons mayonnaise (see Cook's Tip, recipe 311)
125 ml (4 fl oz) soured cream
a few stuffed green olives, sliced
1 tablespoon chopped onion
1 teaspoon chilli sauce
salt
tomato wedges, to garnish

Cut the lettuce into wedges or tear the leaves into large strips. Place in a sieve, rinse and drain thoroughly. Arrange in a salad bowl. Mix in the eggs and cress.

To make the dressing, mix the mayonnaise with the soured cream, olives, onion, chilli sauce, and salt to taste. Pour the dressing over the salad and serve immediately, garnished with tomato wedges.

314

cottage coleslaw

Preparation time
15 minutes

Serves 4 as a main course

Calories
260 per portion

250 g (8 oz) white cabbage, finely shredded
250 g (8 oz) carrots, coarsely shredded
3 celery sticks, finely sliced
1 bunch of watercress, base of stems removed, chopped
125 g (4 oz) green-skinned apple, diced
2 teaspoons lemon or orange juice
50 g (2 oz) sultanas
50 g (2 oz) hazelnuts, toasted and chopped (see Cook's Tip, recipe 304)
150 ml (¼ pint) natural yogurt
1 teaspoon white wine vinegar
½ teaspoon dried tarragon or crushed caraway seeds
500 g 1 lb) vegetarian cottage cheese
salt and pepper

Mix all the ingredients except the cottage cheese in a large bowl, making sure the apple is coated in the lemon or orange juice as soon as it is sliced.

Spoon the cottage cheese on to the other ingredients in the bowl and mix well. Serve immediately.

■ COOK'S TIP

Instead of iceberg lettuce, try using cos, or romaine, lettuce. It has a delicious taste and crunchy texture. Top the salad with croûtons if liked.

■ COOK'S TIP

This dish is low in calories and fat. Add some mayonnaise instead of yogurt if you feel like an indulgence!

315

tricolour salad

Preparation time 10 minutes	*125 g (4 oz) leeks, trimmed and sliced into rings*
Serves 4	*125 g (4 oz) red pepper, cored, deseeded and sliced*
Calories about 55 per portion	*2 medium oranges, about 250 g (8 oz) flesh, peeled and cut into quartered slices*
	dill sprig, to garnish
	FOR THE DRESSING
	1 tablespoon chopped dill
	1 tablespoon chopped parsley
	150 ml (¼ pint) natural yogurt
	1 teaspoon clear honey
	pepper

Combine the prepared leeks, red pepper and orange slices in a serving dish or salad bowl.

Blend together the dill, parsley, yogurt, honey and pepper and pour over the salad just before serving. Garnish with dill.

■ COOK'S TIP

Bright colours and contrasting textures make this salad a refreshing antidote to the end of winter. For the best flavour, serve at room temperature.

316

spicy cauliflower, lentil and pepper salad

Preparation time 20 minutes	*125 g (4 oz) Puy lentils, rinsed*
Serves 4	*2 large peppers, cored, deseeded and quartered*
Calories 83 per portion	*3 tablespoons extra virgin olive oil*
	375 g (12 oz) cauliflower florets
	2 teaspoons chilli flakes
	1 garlic clove, crushed
	1 tablespoon grated lemon rind
	50 g (2 oz) pitted black olives, halved
	salt
	FOR THE DRESSING
	4 tablespoons extra virgin olive oil
	2 tablespoons red pesto
	2 tablespoons chopped parsley
	2 teaspoons balsamic vinegar
	salt and pepper

Boil the rinsed lentils rapidly for 10 minutes, then simmer gently for 30 minutes until tender. Meanwhile, brush the peppers with a little of the oil and cook under a hot grill for 6–8 minutes until tender and charred. Once cool, peel off the skin and slice the flesh. Blanch the cauliflower florets in boiling salted water for 1 minute. Dry on kitchen paper. Heat the oil in a pan; add the chilli flakes, garlic and lemon rind and fry gently for 3 minutes. Add the cauliflower florets, and stir-fry for 3 minutes until tender

Blend all the dressing ingredients together. Transfer the cauliflower mixture to a large bowl, stir in the lentils, peppers and the dressing and toss until well coated.

■ COOK'S TIP

Puy lentils are available from health food stores and have a lovely nutty flavour. If unavailable brown lentils are a good alternative.

317

celeriac with lemon-mustard dressing

Preparation time
10 minutes

Serves 4

Calories
58 per portion

½ teaspoon mustard powder
3 tablespoons lemon juice
½ teaspoon clear honey
¼ teaspoon black pepper
150 ml (1¼ pint) natural yogurt
pinch of salt
500 g (1 lb) celeriac, peeled
1 carrot, coarsely shredded
¼ teaspoon paprika

Blend together the mustard, lemon juice, honey, pepper, yogurt and salt and pour into a shallow serving dish.

Shred the celeriac very coarsely directly into the mixture to prevent discolouration. Stir in the carrot.

Sprinkle with the paprika and serve.

318

jacket potato salad

Preparation time
5 minutes

Cooking time
30–45 minutes

Oven temperature
200°C (400°F)
gas 6

Serves 4

Calories
111 per portion

375 g (12 oz) small potatoes, scrubbed
2–3 spring onions, trimmed and finely chopped
150 ml (¼ pint) natural yogurt
2 tablespoons lemon juice
1 teaspoon prepared English mustard
salt and pepper
175 g (6 oz) red peppers, cored, deseeded and roughly sliced

Thread the potatoes on to metal kebab skewers. Bake in a pre-heated oven for about 30 minutes or until tender.

Mix together all the remaining ingredients, except the peppers, in a serving dish.

Allow the potatoes to cool slightly, then cut them roughly into quarters or cubes and add to the dish with the peppers. Toss well and serve.

■ COOK'S TIP

The unattractive knobbly exterior of celeriac hides a distinctive and delicious celery-like flavour, which blends perfectly with lemon and mustard.

■ COOK'S TIP

English mustard adds a sharp flavour to this salad. As an alternative, use Dijon mustard which will give a milder, sweeter flavour.

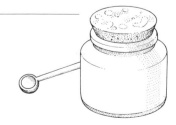

319

carrot, turnip and sesame seed salad

Preparation time 20 minutes	*375 g (12 oz) carrots* *175 g (6 oz) turnip*
Serves 4–6	*50 g (2 oz) seedless raisins*
Calories 408–272 per portion	*2 tablespoons sesame seeds, toasted (see Cook's Tip)* *2 tablespoons snipped chives*

FOR THE DRESSING
150 ml (¼ pint) olive oil
1 tablespoon white wine vinegar
2 tablespoons lemon juice
grated rind of 1 lemon
1 teaspoon French mustard
1 teaspoon clear honey
salt and pepper

Grate the carrot and turnip finely and place in a salad bowl. Add the raisins, sesame seeds and chives and toss well.

Mix together all the dressing ingredients and pour 4 tablespoons over the salad. Store what you do not use in a screw-top jar in the refrigerator for another occasion.

320

beetroot and orange salad

Preparation time 20 minutes	*500 g (1 lb) cooked beetroot, skinned* *150 ml (¼ pint) soured cream*
Serves 4	*1 orange*
Calories 136 per portion	*2 tablespoons snipped chives* *salt and pepper* *snipped chives, to garnish*

Cut the beetroot into dice about 1 cm (½ inch) square and arrange in a shallow serving dish.

Put the soured cream into a mixing bowl. Add the grated rind and juice from half the orange. Cut the peel and pith away from the remaining orange half and cut the flesh into segments. Scatter the orange segments over the beetroot.

Mix the chives and salt and pepper to taste with the soured cream. Pour this dressing over the beetroot and orange, but do not stir. Sprinkle with more chives and serve at once.

■ COOK'S TIP

To toast the sesame seeds, shake them in a heavy-based pan over a moderate heat for a minute or two. You could also put them in a frying pan under a moderate grill, shaking to turn them, until golden brown.

■ COOK'S TIP

Remember always to use a glass or china bowl for salads using beetroot. The juice will stain a wooden bowl. Also, do not use wooden salad servers.

helios salad

Preparation time 10 minutes	*500 g (1 lb) carrots, coarsely shredded*
Serves 4	*25 g (1 oz) walnut pieces*
Calories 96 per portion	*125 ml(4 fl oz) unsweetened apple juice*
	125 ml (4 fl oz) natural yogurt
	½ teaspoon mixed spice
	1 peach, stoned and roughly chopped

Place the shredded carrots in a serving dish.

Blend the walnuts with half the apple juice in a food processor, leaving some walnut pieces intact to give a nutty texture. Transfer to a small bowl.

By hand, stir in the remaining apple juice, yogurt and mixed spice. Stir the apple juice mixture and the chopped peach into the carrots and serve.

322

creamy coleslaw

Preparation time 20 minutes	*500 g (1 lb) white cabbage, finely shredded*
Serves 6	*250 g (8 oz) carrots, coarsely grated*
Calories 140 per portion	*2 onions, finely chopped*
	125 g (4 oz) raisins
	FOR THE DRESSING
	1 teaspoon mustard powder
	150 ml (¼ pint) soured cream
	salt and pepper

Put the cabbage, carrots, onions and raisins into a large bowl.

In a small bowl, blend the mustard with the soured cream, and season to taste with salt and pepper. Add the dressing to the salad, mixing them well together. Check the seasoning before serving the coleslaw.

■ COOK'S TIP

Walnuts tend to turn rancid quickly. Buy in small quantities and store in an airtight container in a cool, dry, dark cupboard or the refrigerator.

■ COOK'S TIP

Try a spicy yogurt dressing. Beat together 150 ml (¼ pint) thick Greek yogurt, 1 teaspoon ground turmeric and 1 crushed garlic clove.

323

red salad

Preparation time
15 minutes

Serves 4

Calories
121 per portion

FOR THE DRESSING
½ teaspoon mustard powder
2 teaspoons clear honey
1 tablespoon red wine vinegar
3 tablespoons olive oil
salt and pepper
FOR THE SALAD
1 bunch of radishes, trimmed and sliced
1 head of radicchio (175–250 g (6–8 oz),
  leaves separated
125–175 g (4–6 oz) red cabbage, shredded
1 red pepper, cored, deseeded and diced

To make the dressing, put the mustard powder, honey, red wine vinegar, oil and a little salt and pepper into a salad bowl and mix well. Add the salad ingredients, and toss to coat the vegetables with the dressing. Serve at once.

324

christmas coleslaw

Preparation time
30 minutes

Serves 4

Calories
432 per portion

125 g (4 oz) red cabbage, finely shredded
125 g (4 oz) white cabbage, finely
  shredded
2 dessert apples, preferably red-skinned,
  cored and thinly sliced
50 g (2 oz) shelled nuts, chopped, e.g.
  walnuts, almonds or hazelnuts
150 ml (¼ pint) mayonnaise
2 tablespoons French dressing
  (see Cook's Tip)
parsley sprigs, to garnish

Mix together the prepared red and white cabbage, apples and chopped nuts in a large bowl.

Mix the mayonnaise with the French dressing. Pour over the cabbage salad and toss until everything is thoroughly coated. Transfer to a serving dish and garnish with the parsley.

■ COOK'S TIP

To garnish this dish, scatter over some thinly sliced red onion rings. They have a sweeter, milder flavour than ordinary onions and an attractive colour.

■ COOK'S TIP

For the French dressing, place in a screw-topped jar 5 tablespoons olive oil, 2 tablespoons white wine vinegar, 1 teaspoon Dijon mustard, 1 crushed garlic clove, ½ teaspoon honey and salt and pepper to taste. Shake well before serving.

325

mushroom and gruyère salad

Preparation time
30 minutes, plus
marinating

Serves 4

Calories
438 per portion

250 g (8 oz) Gruyère cheese, cut into
    small cubes
125 g (4 oz) button mushrooms,
    quartered
8 large lettuce leaves
1 tablespoon chopped parsley
FOR THE DRESSING
6 tablespoons olive oil
2 tablespoons red wine vinegar
1 garlic clove, crushed
½ teaspoon salt
large pinch of black pepper

Put all the dressing ingredients in a screw-topped jar and shake until well mixed.

Place the cheese and mushrooms in a mixing bowl and pour over the dressing. Toss to coat and leave for 20 minutes.

Line a shallow salad bowl with the lettuce leaves. Spoon the cheese mixture on top of the lettuce and sprinkle with the chopped parsley. Serve at once.

326

carrot and apple salad

Preparation time
20 minutes

Serves 4

Calories
351 per portion

Suitable for vegans

375 g (12 oz) carrots, scraped and
    coarsely grated
3 Cox's Orange Pippin apples, cored and
    sliced
1 tablespoon lemon juice
1 tablespoon sunflower seeds
3 tablespoons raisins
2 teaspoons vegetable oil
2 tablespoons cashew nuts
FOR THE FRENCH DRESSING
4 tablespoons olive oil
2½ tablespoons cider vinegar or lemon
    juice
pinch of caster sugar
salt and pepper

Put the grated carrot into a large bowl. Sprinkle the apple slices with lemon juice to prevent them discolouring, then add to the bowl with the sunflower seeds and raisins.

Heat the oil in a small pan and lightly brown the cashew nuts. Lift out with a slotted spoon and drain on kitchen paper, then add to the bowl.

Put all the dressing ingredients into a screw-topped jar and shake well to mix. Spoon over the salad and toss lightly.

■ COOK'S TIP

If you find wine vinegar rather too sharp for your taste, try balsamic vinegar instead. It has a rich, sweet flavour. Raspberry vinegar is another alternative.

■ COOK'S TIP

This salad is also delicious served with Greek or natural yogurt instead of the dressing. Add other nuts for variety. Sprinkle with toasted sesame seeds, if liked.

327

piquant potato salad

Preparation time 5 minutes, plus cooling **Cooking time** 15–20 minutes **Serves 4** **Calories** 206 per portion Suitable for vegans	*750 g (1½ lb) tiny new potatoes* *salt* FOR THE DRESSING *3 tablespoons olive oil* *1 tablespoon white wine vinegar* *½ teaspoon prepared English mustard* *2 teaspoons capers, finely chopped* *1 pickled gherkin, finely chopped* *salt and pepper* *1 tablespoon chopped parsley*

Wash the potatoes and place in a pan of boiling, salted water. Cook for 15–20 minutes until just tender.

While the potatoes are cooking, prepare the dressing. Put the oil and vinegar into a small bowl and stir in the mustard, capers, gherkin and salt and pepper to taste. Add the chopped parsley.

Drain the potatoes well and tip them into a bowl. Pour the dressing over the hot potatoes and stir gently to coat them all thoroughly. Leave to cool, but do not chill. Serve in a shallow dish at room temperature.

328

winter vegetable salad

Preparation time 1 hour **Serves 6** **Calories** 221 per portion Suitable for vegans	*4 waxy potatoes, cooked and diced* *1 large celery stick, finely chopped* *2 carrots, scraped and grated* *1 small onion, finely chopped* *½ small white cabbage, cored and* * shredded* *2 tablespoons chopped pickled gherkins* *8 black olives, pitted and chopped* FOR THE DRESSING *5 tablespoons olive oil* *3–4 tablespoons lemon juice* *1 teaspoon Dijon mustard* *salt and pepper*

Put the potatoes, celery, carrots, onion, cabbage, gherkins and olives into a salad bowl.

Put all the dressing ingredients into a screw-topped jar and shake well. Taste for seasoning then pour the dressing over the vegetables and toss well.

■ COOK'S TIP

This salad could also be served warm. Stir in a chopped hard-boiled egg or some walnuts for extra protein (though eggs are not suitable for vegans).

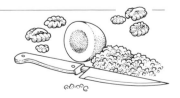

■ COOK'S TIP

Fennel with its aniseed flavour may be chopped finely and substituted for the celery in this dish. Peeled and grated celeriac also tastes good.

rice and pasta

Rice and pasta can be served with an infinite variety of sauces and ingredients and can form the main course of a meal, a tasty supper dish or a light lunch. The pasta recipes in this chapter are mostly based on the excellent packeted shapes, but do have a go at making your own pasta dough.

329

wholemeal pasta salad

Preparation time
5 minutes, plus cooling

Cooking time
12 minutes

Serves 4

Calories
310 per portion

250 g (8 oz) wholewheat pasta twists
3 tablespoons olive oil
1 tablespoon white wine vinegar
¼ teaspoon mustard powder
1 garlic clove, crushed
2 spring onions, chopped
125 g (4 oz) French beans, cooked
4 tomatoes, skinned, quartered and deseeded
50 g (2 oz) black olives, pitted
salt and pepper

Cook the pasta in plenty of boiling salted water for 10–12 minutes or until just tender.

Mix together the oil, vinegar, mustard and garlic with salt and pepper until thickened. Pour over the hot pasta, mix well, cover and leave until cold. Stir in the spring onions, beans and tomatoes and mix well. Turn into a large salad bowl, scatter over the olives and serve.

330

mung bean and fresh herb risotto

Preparation time
15 minutes, plus 6 hours to soak

Cooking time
50 minutes

Serves 4

Calories
835 per portion

375 g (12 oz) mung beans, soaked for 4–6 hours or overnight in cold water
25 g (1 oz) butter
3 tablespoons vegetable oil
1½ large onions, chopped
500 g (1 lb) long-grain brown rice
1.5 litres (2¼ pints) hot vegetable stock
6 tablespoons chopped mixed herbs (parsley, thyme, basil, mint)
salt and pepper
4 tablespoons pumpkin seeds, to garnish

Drain the beans, rinse and drain again. Using a large saucepan with a well-fitting lid, heat the butter and 1 tablespoons of the oil and fry the onions for 3 minutes, then stir in the beans and rice.

Add the hot stock and bring to the boil. Cover and simmer gently for 40 minutes until beans and rice are tender and all the stock has been absorbed. Add the herbs with salt and pepper and gently fork them through the mixture. Spoon the risotto into a serving dish and keep warm.

Fry the pumpkin seeds rapidly in the remaining oil for 30 seconds (take care, as they jump about in the heat) then sprinkle over the risotto. Serve hot.

■ COOK'S TIP

If available, add some chopped basil leaves to the spring onion, bean and tomato mixture.

■ COOK'S TIP

Mung beans will probably be most familiar in their sprouted form, as bean sprouts. In dried form they may be bought whole, split and skinless. These minute olive green beans are known as moong dal in Indian cooking.

331

risotto with spinach and herbs

Preparation time
15 minutes

Cooking time
35 minutes

Serves 4–6

Calories
775–520 per portion

2 tablespoons olive oil
125 g (4 oz) butter
1 onion, finely chopped
125 g (4 oz) mushrooms, sliced
500 g (1 lb) Italian risotto rice
1.5 litres (2½ pints) hot vegetable stock
250 g (8 oz) cooked spinach, chopped
1 teaspoon dried oregano
1 garlic clove, crushed
75 g (3 oz) grated Parmesan or Pecorino cheese
salt and pepper
lemon wedges, to garnish

Heat the oil and half the butter in a large saucepan. Add the onion and mushrooms and cook for a few minutes until the onions are lightly browned. Stir in the rice and cook for 5 minutes. Add the stock, spinach, oregano, garlic and salt and pepper. Stir well and cook for 20–25 minutes or until the rice is tender and has absorbed all the liquid. Stir in the remaining butter and the grated cheese. Serve the risotto garnished with lemon wedges.

332

rice and mushroom bake

Preparation time
10 minutes

Cooking time
40–45 minutes

Oven temperature
200°C (400°F), gas 6

Serves 4

Calories
415 per portion

2 tablespoons vegetable oil
1 large onion, sliced
250 g (8 oz) mushrooms sliced
250 g (8 oz) long-grain rice
1 teaspoon cumin powder
1 teaspoon mild chilli powder
1 teaspoon tomato purée
600 ml (1 pint) vegetable stock
75 g (3 oz) Cheddar cheese, grated
40 g (1½ oz) cornflakes

Heat the oil and cook the onion and mushrooms until softened, about 5 minutes. Add the rice and fry until golden brown. Stir in the spices, tomato purée and stock. Bring to the boil and stir once. Reduce the heat, cover the pan and simmer for 15–18 minutes, until the rice is tender and the liquid absorbed. Stir in half the grated cheese and transfer to an ovenproof casserole. Mix the remaining cheese with the cornflakes, sprinkle on top of the rice and bake in a moderately hot oven for 15–20 minutes, until golden brown.

■ COOK'S TIP

Parmesan and pecorino are both hard cheeses, suitable for grating. When young, they are eaten in chunks accompanied by white wine. Straw-coloured Parmesan is made from cows' milk and pecorino from ewes' milk.

■ COOK'S TIP

Cumin, with its distinctive pungent flavour, is a spice worth investigating both in whole and ground form. Popular in Mexico, North Africa and the Middle East, it is sold by specialist grocers and some supermarkets. Whole seeds keep their flavour longest and may be ground very easily in an electric coffee grinder.

rice salad gado gado

Preparation time
10 minutes, plus
30 minutes to cool

Cooking time
15–18 minutes

Serves 4

Calories
415 per portion

250 g (8 oz) long-grain rice
50 g (2 oz) mushrooms, halved
600 ml (1 pint) vegetable stock
125 g (4 oz) bean sprouts
2 tomatoes, skinned and quartered
2 hard-boiled eggs, quartered
FOR THE SAUCE
125 g (4 oz) salted peanuts
4 spring onions, chopped
1 tablespoon soy sauce
1 teaspoon chilli powder

Put the rice, mushrooms and stock into a covered pan, bring to the boil and simmer gently for 15–18 minutes, until the rice is cooked and all the liquid is absorbed. Allow to cool then mix in the bean sprouts, tomatoes and hard-boiled eggs.

Put all the remaining ingredients into a food processor or blender and purée thoroughly, adding enough water to make a smooth sauce. Pour over the rice salad and serve.

spiced rice and courgette salad

Preparation time
15 minutes, plus
chilling

Cooking time
40–45 minutes

Serves 4

Calories
530 per portion

250 g (8 oz) long-grain brown rice
1 teaspoon each turmeric, curry powder,
    ground cumin and coriander
600 ml (1 pint) water
125 g (4 oz) courgettes, thinly sliced
2 tablespoons wine vinegar
5 tablespoons groundnut oil
2 carrots, grated
1 onion, finely chopped
125 g (4 oz) salted peanuts
1 dessert apple, unpeeled, cored and
    chopped
salt

Place the rice into a saucepan with the spices and water. Bring to the boil then cover and simmer for 35–40 minutes, until the rice is tender and the liquid has been absorbed.

Meanwhile, blanch the courgettes in boiling salted water for 1 minute. Drain, refresh under cold running water and drain again. Turn the rice into a large salad bowl and stir in the vinegar, oil and salt to taste. Leave to cool slightly then add the courgettes, carrots, onion, peanuts and apple. Mix well and chill thoroughly before serving.

■ COOK'S TIP

Made from fermented soya beans, soy sauce is used as extensively in Chinese cookery as salt is in the West. Most commonly dark and pungently flavoured, a more delicate – yet very salty – light soy sauce is also available.

■ COOK'S TIP

Flavourless groundnut oil is a good choice for salad dressing, as it does not obscure the taste of other ingredients. If you want to cook with it, a pleasant flavour is imparted by first frying several slices of fresh root ginger or garlic in in.

335

vegetarian gumbo

Preparation time
10 minutes

Cooking time
20–25 minutes

Serves 4

Calories
280 per portion

4 tablespoons corn oil
25 g (1 oz) plain flour
1 large onion, chopped
4 celery sticks, chopped
1 small green pepper, cored, deseeded and
    chopped
250 g (8 oz) okra, sliced
1 x 400 g (13 oz) can tomatoes
300 ml (½ pint) vegetable stock
1 teaspoon Tabasco sauce
salt and pepper
375 g (12 oz) hot cooked brown rice
    (125 g/4 oz uncooked weight)

Place half the oil in a small, heavy-based saucepan and heat gently. Add the flour and cook over a low heat, stirring frequently until the roux becomes a rich brown colour, being careful not to let it burn.

In a large saucepan, heat the remaining oil and cook the onion until tender, about 5 minutes. Add the celery, green pepper and okra and sauté for 3 minutes. Stir the tomatoes, stock, Tabasco and the roux into the mixture and simmer, covered, for 10 minutes. Season to taste with salt and pepper and serve in individual bowls, topped with a portion of hot brown rice.

336

pasta pesto

Preparation time
15 minutes

Cooking time
12 minutes

Serves 4

Calories
600 per portion

375 g (12 oz) wholewheat caramelli
    shells, or other pasta shapes
75 g (3 oz) basil leaves
4 tablespoons olive oil
3 garlic cloves, crushed
50 g (2 oz) pine nuts or blanched slivered
    almonds
50 g (2 oz) Parmesan cheese, grated
25 g (1 oz) butter, softened
salt and pepper
grated Parmesan cheese, to serve

Cook the pasta in plenty of boiling salted water for about 12 minutes, or according to the directions on the packet, until just tender. Drain, refresh in hot water and drain again, tossing to ensure that no water is trapped inside the shells. Keep hot.

To make the sauce, blend the basil, oil, garlic and nuts in a food processor or blender. Remove the mixture to a bowl, beat in the cheese and butter and season with pepper.

Spoon the sauce over the hot pasta and serve at once, with grated Parmesan.

▩ COOK'S TIP

Corn oil, made from the sweetcorn (maize) plant is among the oils containing polyunsaturated fatty acids, desirable in the diet. Safflower, sunflower, and soya bean oil are others.

▩ COOK'S TIP

It is very easy to grow your own basil in a pot. Basil is excellent sprinkled on salads, particularly tomato ones.

337

mushroom pasta
with pine nuts

Preparation time 25 minutes	*1½ tablespoons vegetable oil*
	1 onion, sliced
Cooking time 40 minutes	*500 g (1 lb) flat open mushrooms, sliced*
	1–2 teaspoons green peppercorns
Serves 4	*1 tablespoon soy sauce*
	3 tablespoons water
Calories 480 per portion	*2 tablespoons double or whipping cream*
	375 g (12 oz) pasta shapes
	2 tablespoons pine nuts
	salt
	chopped parsley, to garnish

Heat 1 tablespoon oil in a medium saucepan and cook the onion for about 5 minutes. Add the mushrooms and cook for a further few minutes. Add the green peppercorns, soy sauce, water and salt to taste. Cover the pan and simmer gently for about 20 minutes. Remove the lid and cook quickly for 1 minute to reduce the liquid. Pour into a food processor or blender and blend very briefly, for just a few seconds. Return to the rinsed pan and stir in the cream.

Bring a large pan of salted water to the boil. Add the pasta and boil briskly for 10 minutes then drain.

Meanwhile, heat the remaining oil in a small saucepan and fry the pine nuts for 2 minutes until golden brown. Drain on kitchen paper. To serve, reheat the sauce without boiling and pour over the pasta. Sprinkle with the pine nuts and parsley.

■ COOK'S TIP

This mushroom sauce has a marvellous flavour. Use the flat dark mushrooms for the best flavour. Pine nuts or kernels can be bought in health food shops.

338

brown rice
and hazelnut salad

Preparation time 20–25 minutes	*175 g (6 oz) long-grain brown rice*
	pinch of salt
Cooking time 40 minutes	*75 g (3 oz) hazelnuts, chopped and toasted*
Serves 6–8	*1 red pepper, cored, deseeded and diced*
	6 spring onions, finely sliced
Calories 245–185 per portion	*3 celery sticks, sliced (optional)*
	50 g (2 oz) button mushrooms, sliced
	6 tablespoons French dressing
	3 tablespoons chopped parsley

Cook the rice in a saucepan of boiling water for 30–40 minutes, until tender. Rinse and drain well.

Place in a salad bowl with all the remaining ingredients. Add the dressing and toss thoroughly. Serve cold.

■ COOK'S TIP

Instead of the hazelnuts use toasted cashew nuts instead.

339

brown rice salad

Preparation time
10 minutes, plus
cooling

Cooking time
35 minutes

Serves 4

Calories
395 per portion

125 g (4 oz) long-grain brown rice
125 g (4 oz) shelled peas or sliced beans
125 g (4 oz) sweetcorn kernels
150 ml (¼ pint) Vinaigrette dressing
(made up of 6 tablespoons oil,
2 tablespoons vinegar, herbs and
salt and pepper)
1 red pepper, cored, deseeded and diced
50 g (2 oz) salted peanuts
1 small onion, grated
salt and pepper

Cook the rice in a saucepan of boiling salted water for 30 minutes or until tender. Add the peas or beans and sweetcorn and simmer for a further few minutes until just tender. Drain thoroughly.

Transfer to a bowl and add half of the dressing while the rice and vegetables are still hot. Toss well to mix, then leave to cool.

Add the remaining ingredients and dressing. Mix well. Taste and adjust the seasoning just before serving. Serve cold with other salad dishes.

340

macaroni special

Preparation time
5 minutes

Cooking time
20 minutes

Serves 4

Calories
570 per portion

250 g (8 oz) wholewheat macaroni
250 g (8 oz) frozen mixed vegetables
25 g (1 oz) butter
1 garlic clove, crushed
3 large tomatoes, skinned and chopped
250 g (8 oz) mushrooms, sliced
3 tablespoons chopped parsley (optional)
300 ml (½ pint) soured cream
50 g (2 oz) mozzarella cheese, coarsely
grated
4 tablespoons grated Parmesan cheese
4 slices of bread, crusts removed, cut into
triangles and toasted

Cook the macaroni in plenty of boiling water for about 5 minutes, then add the frozen mixed vegetables and cook for a further 7 minutes. Drain.

Melt the butter in a saucepan, cook the garlic for 1 minute, then stir in the tomatoes and mushrooms and cook for 3 minutes. Stir in the macaroni mixture, parsley, if using, soured cream and mozzarella and heat gently until the mixture is hot and the cheese just melting. Stir in the Parmesan cheese and serve immediately, garnished with the toast triangles.

■ COOK'S TIP

Brown rice has more protein than polished (white) rice. It also has traces of iron, calcium and vitamin B. When cooked it retains much of its bite and is therefore an ideal basis for salads.

■ COOK'S TIP

A soured cream equivalent may be achieved by adding a few drops of lemon juice to fresh double cream.

341

pasta with aubergines

Preparation time 35 minutes,	*500 g (1 lb) aubergines*
	250 g (8 oz) penne
Cooking time 25 minutes	*1 onion, chopped*
	2 garlic cloves, crushed
Serves 4	*4 tablespoons sunflower oil*
Calories 355 per portion	*1 teaspoon mustard powder*
	1 tablespoon tomato purée
	1 x 400 g (13 oz) can tomatoes
	½ teaspoon oregano
	1 tablespoon chopped parsley
	salt and pepper
	grated Parmesan cheese, to serve

Cut the aubergine into cubes, place in a colander and sprinkle with salt. Leave for 30 minutes to extract some of the bitter juices, rinse thoroughly and pat dry.

Cook the pasta in plenty of boiling salted water for 10–12 minutes or until just cooked. Drain and keep warm.

Meanwhile, cook the onion and garlic gently in the oil for 5 minutes until softened. Increase the heat, add the aubergines and cook, stirring, until lightly browned. Stir in the mustard, tomato purée, tomatoes and their juices, oregano, parsley and pepper to taste and simmer the mixture gently for 10 minutes until the aubergines are cooked, stirring occasionally. Pour the sauce over the pasta and serve at once, with Parmesan cheese.

342

spaghetti with walnut sauce

Preparation time 5 minutes	*500 g (1 lb) spaghetti*
	1 onion, chopped
Cooking time 20 minutes	*2 garlic cloves, crushed*
	1 tablespoon oil
Serves 4	*50 g (2 oz) mushrooms, sliced*
Calories 700 per portion	*75 g (3 oz) walnuts, finely chopped*
	1 bunch of watercress, chopped
	300 ml (½ pint) soured cream
	salt and pepper

Cook the spaghetti in plenty of boiling salted water for 10–12 minutes until just tender. Fry the onion and garlic in the oil for about 3 minutes until softened. Add the mushrooms and walnuts and cook for a further 3 minutes over a moderate heat. Remove the pan from the heat, stir in the watercress, soured cream and salt and pepper to taste. Reheat very gently. Do not allow the sauce to boil.

Drain the spaghetti and place in a warm serving dish. Pour the sauce over it and serve immediately.

■ COOK'S TIP

Be adventurous in selecting pasta shapes: rigatoni and mezze maniche (short sleeves) are other short, tubular pasta shapes; the latter, as its name suggests, is served with summer sauces in Italy.

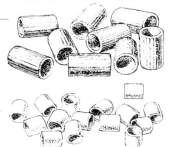

■ COOK'S TIP

To eat pasta at its best, remember to drain it while it is *al dente*, which means while it still has a bit of bite to it. Test the pasta and remove it from the heat before it has become completely soft and it will be cooked to perfection.

spinach noodles

Preparation time
10 minutes

Cooking time
15 minutes

Serves 2–3

Calories
780–520 per portion

250 g (8 oz) noodles
1 onion, chopped
50 g (2 oz) butter
250 g (8 oz) spinach, chopped
150 ml (¼ pint) natural yogurt
125 g (4 oz) low-fat soft cheese
1 teaspoon lemon juice
¼ teaspoon grated nutmeg
salt and pepper

Cook the noodles in boiling salted water for about 12 minutes until tender.

Meanwhile, cook the onion in the butter until soft, but not browned. Add the spinach and continue to cook for 2–3 minutes. Stir in the yogurt, cheese, lemon juice, nutmeg and salt and pepper to taste and stir over a low heat without boiling. Drain the noodles and add to the hot spinach sauce; toss well then serve immediately.

pasta with ratatouille sauce

Preparation time
15–20 minutes

Cooking time
35 minutes

Serves 4–6

Calories
500–335 per portion

1 large onion, chopped
1 garlic clove, crushed
500 g (1 lb) courgettes, sliced
1 large aubergine, diced
1 green pepper, cored, deseeded and diced
500 g (1 lb) tomatoes, skinned and chopped
1 tablespoon chopped oregano or basil
500 g (1 lb) pasta (spaghetti, noodles, etc.)
salt and pepper
1 tablespoon chopped parsley, to garnish
grated Parmesan cheese, to serve

Put all the ingredients, except the pasta, parsley and cheese in a large saucepan. Add enough water to cover the vegetables and cook gently for 30 minutes until the vegetables are tender and the juices have thickened slightly, stirring occasionally.

Meanwhile, cook the pasta in a large saucepan in plenty of boiling salted water until just tender (about 5 minutes for freshly made pasta and 15 minutes for dried). Drain and place in a warmed serving dish.

Taste the sauce and adjust the seasoning, then pour it over the pasta. Sprinkle with the parsley and grated Parmesan cheese. Serve hot.

■ COOK'S TIP

For special occasions, use a full-fat soft cheese such as Roulé, which is made with a blend of garlic and fine herbs.

■ COOK'S TIP

This dish makes a filling main course. It can also be served cold as a starter, without the pasta. Served in vol-au-vent cases, it makes an attractive party snack .

345

nutty ribbon pasta

Preparation time 5 minutes	*375 g (12 oz) tagliatini or tagliatelle* *300 ml (½ pint) single cream*
Cooking time 14–18 minutes	*2 large egg yolks* *4 dill sprigs, chopped*
Serves 4	*175 g (6 oz) salted peanuts, roughly* * chopped*
Calories 730 per portion	*salt and pepper* *chopped dill, to garnish*

Cook the pasta in boiling salted water for about 12–15 minutes, until tender but not soft.

Meanwhile, combine the cream, egg yolks, dill and pepper in a bowl. Stir in the peanuts.

Drain the pasta and return it to the pan, then immediately add the cream mixture. Heat gently for 2–3 minutes, stirring to mix thoroughly. Serve immediately.

346

pasta al pomodoro

Preparation time 10 minutes	*175 g (6 oz) pasta bows* *salt and pepper*
Cooking time 25 minutes	*2 tablespoons grated Parmesan cheese* FOR THE SAUCE
Serves 2	*1 small onion, finely chopped*
Calories 430 per portion	*125 g (4 oz) mushrooms, sliced* *1 teaspoon sunflower oil* *1 x 400 g (13 oz) can tomatoes* *1 tablespoon chopped basil (optional)* *salt and pepper*

Cook the pasta bows in a large pan of boiling salted water for 10–12 minutes. Drain and keep warm.

Meanwhile, sauté the onion and mushrooms in the oil for 5 minutes. Stir in the tomatoes and cook gently for 15 minutes until the sauce has reduced. Add the basil, if using, and simmer for a further 5 minutes. Season to taste and serve with the pasta bows, topped with Parmesan and pepper.

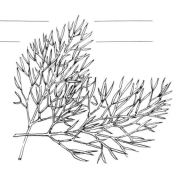

■ COOK'S TIP

Well known for its affinity with fish, dill deserves to be more widely used. It is especially delicious with eggs, so complements the eggs in this sauce.

■ COOK'S TIP

This simple dish is ideal for children, who enjoy it even more if it is made with tri-coloured pasta – plain, spinach and tomato-flavoured.

347

pasta with bolina cheese sauce

Preparation time 10 minutes	*300 g (10 oz) tagliatelle or pasta shells* *135 g (4½ oz) Danish Bolina cheese*
Cooking time 10–12 minutes	*25 g (1 oz) butter* *4 tablespoons single cream*
Serves 4	*2 tablespoons chopped parsley*
Calories 435 per portion	*salt and pepper*

Cook the pasta in a large pan of boiling salted water for 10–12 minutes, until just tender.

Meanwhile, place the cheese in a bowl. Break it up with a fork, add the butter and set over a pan of boiling water. Cook, stirring occasionally, until the cheese and butter have melted and blended together. Add the cream and parsley. Season to taste with salt and pepper and heat through.

Drain the cooked pasta and place on a heated serving dish. Pour the sauce over the pasta and turn gently with two forks to coat. Serve immediately with a mixed salad and crusty bread.

348

gratin of pasta

Preparation time 15 minutes	*125 g (4 oz) pasta shells* *25 g (1 oz) butter*
Cooking time 25 minutes	*25 g (1 oz) plain flour* *300 ml (½ pint) milk*
Serves 4	*125 g (4 oz) Cheddar cheese, grated*
Calories 380 per portion	*1 x 300 g (10 oz) packet frozen Country* * stir-fry vegetables*
	2 tablespoons chopped parsley
	2 hard-boiled eggs, sliced
	salt and pepper

Cook the pasta shells in a large saucepan of boiling salted water for 10–12 minutes, until just tender. Melt the butter, add the flour and cook for a minute. Remove from the heat and gradually stir in the milk. Return to the heat and bring to the boil, stirring continually until the sauce bubbles and thickens. Add the cheese, season to taste and leave to cool slightly.

Cook the stir-fry vegetables according to the packet instructions. Toss the cooked pasta shells in parsley and place in a flameproof serving dish. Sprinkle with the stir-fry vegetables and arrange the egg slices on top. Pour over the cheese sauce and brown under a hot grill, if preferred. Serve immediately.

■ COOK'S TIP

Using a big saucepan with plenty of boiling water to cook the pasta is important. The pasta swells and if it is too cramped it will tend to clog together in lumps. Adding a few drops of oil to the water helps to prevent this.

■ COOK'S TIP

Pasta shells (conchiglie) are available in a range of sizes and in both plain and wholemeal varieties. They are particularly good with chunky sauces like this one.

349

marrow lasagne

Preparation time 35 minutes	*1 kg (2 lb) whole marrow or squash*
	2 tablespoons olive oil
Cooking time 50 minutes	*1 large onion, chopped*
	4–6 cardamom pods
Oven temperature 200°C (400°F) gas 6	*2 teaspoons black peppercorns*
	1 teaspoon caster sugar
	250 g (8 oz) green lasagne, cooked
Serves 6	*250 g (8 oz) small round goats' cheese,*
Calories 300 per portion	* thinly sliced*
	2 tablespoons cornflour
	2 tablespoons milk
	450 ml (¾ pint) natural yogurt
	2 tablespoons grated Parmesan cheese
	salt

Scoop out the centre of the marrow or squash, peel and slice the flesh. Cook in boiling water for 15 minutes, or until soft. Drain and mash coarsely.

Heat 1 tablespoon oil in a large pan and cook the onion until soft. Extract the seeds from the cardamom pods and crush with the peppercorns. Stir the ground spices, onion and sugar into the marrow and season with salt. Brush the remaining oil over the base of a 20 x 28 cm (8 x 11 inch) ovenproof dish. Layer the lasagne, marrow and goats' cheese in the dish, ending with a layer of lasagne.

Mix the cornflour, milk and yogurt in a saucepan. Bring gently to the boil, stirring, and cook for 2–3 minutes. Pour over the lasagne and sprinkle with Parmesan. Bake in a preheated oven for about 35 minutes.

350

vegetable lasagne

Preparation time 10 minutes	*2 tablespoons oil*
	250 g (8 oz) French beans, chopped
Cooking time 1½ hours	*1 leek or onion, thinly sliced*
	1 x 400 g (13 oz) can tomatoes
Oven temperature 180°C (350°F) gas 4	*125 g (4 oz) lentils*
	300 ml (½ pint) water
	pinch of oregano
Serves 4	*500 g (1 lb) cream or curd cheese*
Calories 800 per portion using cream cheese	*2 eggs, beaten*
	125 g (4 oz) lasagne, cooked
	2 tablespoons chopped parsley
520 per portion using curd cheese	*2 tablespoons grated Parmesan cheese*
	salt and pepper

Heat the oil in a saucepan and fry the beans and leek or onion for 5 minutes. Season to taste with salt and pepper. Add the tomatoes, lentils, water and oregano and bring to the boil. Simmer for about 30 minutes or until the lentils are tender.

Mix together the cream or curd cheese and the eggs. Spread half the vegetable mixture in a 1.2 litre (2 pint) ovenproof dish and cover with one-third of the lasagne. Spread over half the cheese mixture, then cover with another layer of lasagne. Make a layer with the remaining vegetable mixture, cover with the remaining lasagne and finally the remaining cheese mixture. Sprinkle over the Parmesan and bake in a preheated oven for 40 minutes.

■ COOK'S TIP

Green or white cardamom pods have lots of tiny black seeds inside, which should be shiny and highly aromatic. Buy from Asian food stores.

■ COOK'S TIP

A very popular herb in Italy, oregano, like basil, perfectly complements the flavour of tomatoes. Aubergines and courgettes are also enhanced by its pronounced, aromatic flavour.

351

spinach lasagne

Preparation time
20 minutes

Cooking time
45 minutes

Oven temperature
200°C (400°F),
gas 6

Serves 4

Calories
530 per portion

500 g (1 lb) frozen spinach, defrosted and
  drained
¼ teaspoon grated nutmeg
25 g (1 oz) pecan nuts, chopped
40 g (1½ oz) butter
40 g (1½ oz) plain flour
600 ml (1 pint) milk
200 g (7 oz) mature Cheddar cheese,
  grated
½ teaspoon prepared English mustard
175 g (6 oz) wholewheat lasagne, cooked
salt and pepper
paprika, to garnish

Season the spinach with nutmeg and salt and pepper and stir in the nuts.

Melt the butter in a saucepan over a low heat, then add the flour. Cook for 2 minutes, stirring. Gradually add the milk and bring the sauce to the boil, stirring constantly. Simmer gently for 2–3 minutes. Add 175 g (6 oz) of the cheese and season with salt, pepper and mustard.

Layer the spinach and lasagne in an ovenproof dish. Top with the sauce and sprinkle with the reserved cheese. Bake near the top of a preheated moderately hot oven for 20–30 minutes until piping hot and brown on top.

Sprinkle with paprika and serve immediately.

352

courgette and cauliflower macaroni

Preparation time
30 minutes

Cooking time
20 minutes

Serves 4

Calories
605 per portion

250 g (8 oz) macaroni
250 g (8 oz) cauliflower, broken into
  small florets
250 g (8 oz) courgettes, finely chopped
salt
paprika, to garnish (optional)
FOR THE SAUCE
500 ml (¾ pint) milk
50 g (2 oz) plain flour
50 g (2 oz) margarine, cut up
175 g (6 oz) Cheddar cheese, grated
salt and pepper

Cook the macaroni in boiling salted water for 15 minutes, then drain. Cook the cauliflower in boiling salted water for 5 minutes, adding the courgettes for the final 2 minutes. Drain well and reserve 150 ml (¼ pint) of the water. Place the vegetables and macaroni in an ovenproof dish.

Whisk the milk, flour and margarine with the reserved vegetable water in a pan over low heat until boiling and thickened. Stir in most of the cheese with salt and pepper to taste. Pour over the macaroni, sprinkle with the remaining cheese and a little paprika, if using. Brown under a preheated moderate grill, then serve piping hot.

■ COOK'S TIP

A roasting tin is the best container to use for cooking lasagne as it gives the pasta sheets plenty of room. When cooked, lift each sheet from the water separately with a fish slice and place in a pan or bowl of warm water. Keep the lasagne sheets in the warm water until needed but no longer than necessary, as they can absorb too much water. No-need-to-precook lasagne works very well too, provided there is plenty of sauce.

■ COOK'S TIP

Chop a few sprigs of parsley and stir into the vegetable and macaroni mixture for additional flavour.

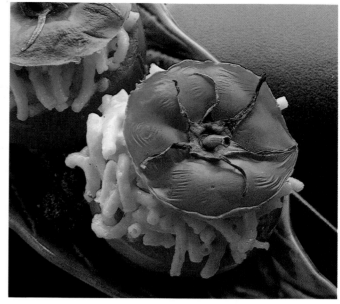

353

spinach ravioli

Preparation time 40 minutes	*250 g (8 oz) frozen chopped spinach,* *cooked and drained*
Cooking time 5 minutes	*125 g (4 oz) Cheddar cheese, grated* *25 g (1 oz) Parmesan cheese, grated*
Serves 4	*1 egg plus 1 yolk, beaten*
Calories 720 per portion	*¼ teaspoon grated nutmeg* *500 g (1 lb) strong plain flour* *5 eggs* *½ beaten egg mixed with 1 tablespoon* *water, for brushing* *salt and pepper*

Mix the spinach with the cheeses, whole egg and yolk, nutmeg and salt and pepper, cover and chill. Heap the flour on to a work surface and make a well in the centre. Break the 5 eggs into it and with a fork lightly beat them into the flour. Gradually work in all the flour. Use your hands to knead the soft dough for 10 minutes until it becomes satiny smooth. Rest the dough for 5 minutes, covered. Halve the dough and roll out each portion thinly to equal size rectangles. Brush one with a little of the beaten egg wash, and top with rows of teaspoons of stuffing, each about 2.5 cm (1 inch) apart. Cover with the second sheet of pasta. Press together around the stuffing. Using a pastry wheel, cut the dough into 2.5 cm (1 inch) squares. Sprinkle lightly with flour.

Have ready a large pan of boiling salted water, drop in the ravioli, bring back to the boil and cook for 5 minutes. Lift out with a slotted spoon and keep warm if cooked in two batches. Serve with tomato sauce (see Cook's Tip, recipe 88) and grated Parmesan cheese.

354

macaroni tomatoes

Preparation time 15 minutes	*4 beefsteak tomatoes* *2 teaspoons oil*
Cooking time 30 minutes	*1 small onion, finely chopped* *1 garlic clove, crushed*
Oven temperature 180°C (350°F) gas 4	*½ teaspoon mustard powder* *pinch of paprika* *2 drops of Tabasco sauce*
Serves 4	*125 g (4 oz) Cheddar cheese, grated*
Calories 255 per portion	*125 g (4 oz) macaroni, cooked and* *drained* *salt and pepper*

Cut a lid off the tomatoes, scoop out the centres to leave a thin wall of flesh in each one. Place the pulp in a small saucepan with the oil, onion, garlic, mustard, paprika, Tabasco and salt and pepper. Cover and cook over a low heat for 10 minutes until pulpy, then press through a sieve and mix with the cheese and macaroni. Divide the mixture between the tomatoes and place the lids on top. Bake for 15–20 minutes until the tomatoes are soft and the macaroni is beginning to brown. Serve at once.

■ COOK'S TIP

If you want to go Italian replace the Cheddar cheese in the filling with soft ricotta cheese. You will need to double the quantity to 250 g (8 oz). Made from whey, ricotta is lighter in flavour and texture than cream cheese, but not tangy like curd cheese. Italian food stores, delicatessens, or good delicatessen counters in supermarkets stock it.

■ COOK'S TIP

If you happen to grow rosemary in your garden, then snip off a sprig, chop finely and add to the tomato pulp and the other seasonings before cooking and sieving.

355

corsican cannelloni

Preparation time
15 minutes

Cooking time
55 minutes

Oven temperature
180°C (350°F)
gas 4

Serves 4

Calories
275 per portion

750 ml (1¼ pints) boiling water
½ teaspoon vegetable oil
8 sheets 'no-need-to-precook' lasagne
* verde*
250 g (8 oz) frozen Ratatouille mix
125 g (4 oz) frozen broad beans
2 teaspoons chopped mixed herbs
freshly ground black pepper
1 x 400 g (13 oz) can chopped tomatoes
125 g (4 oz) mature Cheddar cheese,
* grated, to serve*

Pour the boiling water into a suitably shaped large shallow oven-proof dish. Add a few drops of oil. Slide the sheets of lasagne into the dish and leave for 4–5 minutes to soften. Cook the ratatouille and beans in boiling water in a medium saucepan for about 10 minutes or until cooked. Drain well. Add the herbs and pepper to taste.

Lift out the lasagne sheets from the water and drain. Spread out on a clean working surface or large board. Divide the vegetable filling between the lasagne sheets then roll up the strips. Place the cannelloni in a shallow ovenproof dish and spoon the tomatoes over them. Cook in a moderate oven for 30 minutes. To serve, sprinkle with grated cheese and place under a preheated hot grill until brown.

356

tropical salad

Preparation time
15 minutes

Cooking time
5 minutes

Serves 4

Calories
475 per portion

300 g (10 oz) long-grain brown rice,
* cooked*
50 g (2 oz) dried coconut flakes
½ cucumber, unpeeled and cut into 1 cm
* (½ inch) cubes*
1 small ripe pineapple, peeled, cored and
* cut into 2.5 cm (1 inch) pieces*
2 tablespoons olive oil
1 teaspoon lemon juice
2 teaspoons olive oil for shallow frying
50 g (2 oz) whole blanched almonds
salt and pepper
pineapple leaves, to garnish

Put the rice, coconut, cucumber and pineapple into a bowl. Add the oil and lemon juice and a little salt and pepper. Taste and adjust the seasoning if necessary. Spoon the salad into a serving dish.

Heat the 2 teaspoons of oil in a small pan and quickly fry the almonds until golden brown. Scatter the almonds over the salad and garnish with the pineapple leaves.

■ COOK'S TIP

Cover the cannelloni with foil and freeze for up to 3 months. Reheat from frozen in a moderate oven (180°C/350°F/gas 4) for about 30 minutes, then top with the cheese and place under a hot grill to brown.

■ COOK'S TIP

To remove the centre core from a slice of pineapple, stamp out with a small plain pastry cutter.

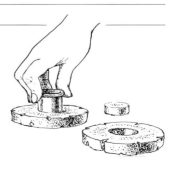

357

szechuan noodles

Preparation time 10 minutes, plus preparing the cucumber	½ cucumber, cut into 1 cm (½ inch) dice salt small bunch of radishes, trimmed 1 spring onion, trimmed
Cooking time 8 minutes	500 g (1 lb) fresh egg noodles or dried noodles
Serves 4	125 g (4 oz) bean sprouts 4 tablespoons groundnut oil
Calories 720 per portion	3–4 tablespoons crunchy peanut butter 1 teaspoon sesame oil 25 g (1 oz) salted peanuts, lightly crushed

Sprinkle the cucumber with salt and leave to drain for 15 minutes. Rinse and dry on kitchen paper. Slice a third of the radishes, leaving the remainder whole. Slice the spring onion diagonally.

Meanwhile, cook the fresh noodles for 1 minute in boiling salted water, then drain thoroughly. Cook dried noodles as directed on the packet. Blanch the bean sprouts in boiling water for 1 minute. Plunge into cold water, then drain thoroughly.

Fry the drained noodles quickly in 3 tablespoons of the groundnut oil, stirring constantly. Transfer to a hot serving plate. Put the remaining oil in a pan with the peanut butter and sesame oil and heat gently. Pour over the noodles and mix lightly.

Arrange the prepared ingredients attractively on top and serve. Serve the remaining radishes in a bowl.

358

rice and beans

Preparation time 10 minutes	250 g (8 oz) long-grain brown rice 750 (1½ pints) boiling water
Cooking time 40 minutes	3 tablespoons sunflower oil 1 tablespoon red wine vinegar
Serves 4	4 spring onions, chopped 1 x 425 g (14 oz) can red kidney beans
Calories 475 per portion	50 g (2 oz) button mushrooms, sliced 250 g (8 oz) tomatoes 4 tablespoons French dressing 50 g (2 oz) black olives salt and pepper chopped parsley, to garnish

Cook the rice in the water for 40 minutes or until cooked and the water absorbed. Mix together the oil, vinegar and salt and pepper. Fluff up the rice with a fork and stir in the spring onions and oil and vinegar dressing. Cool.

Mix together the kidney beans and mushrooms. Slice the tomatoes and pour over the French dressing. Stir in the olives and salt and pepper to taste.

On a large serving plate, arrange a circle of rice salad round the edge, a circle of bean salad inside, and the tomato mixture in the middle. Scatter over the parsley to garnish.

■ COOK'S TIP

Groundnut and sesame oil are used
in this recipe as they add a distinctive
flavour, favoured by the Chinese.

■ COOK'S TIP

The difference between black
and green olives is that the black
ones are ripe. Black olives vary
from plump and succulent to
small and wrinkly specimens.
You can sometimes sample them
before buying.

359
vegetable risotto

Preparation time 15 minutes	*4 tablespoons oil* *1 onion, chopped*
Cooking time 55–60 minutes	*175 g (6 oz) long-grain brown rice* *3 garlic cloves, crushed*
Serves 4	*500 ml (¾ pint) water* *1 teaspoon salt*
Calories 465 per portion	*2 celery sticks, thinly sliced* *1 red pepper, cored, deseeded and diced*

250 g (8 oz) button mushrooms, sliced
1 x 425 g (14 oz) can red kidney beans
3 tablespoons chopped parsley
1 tablespoon soy sauce
50 g (2 oz) cashew nuts, roasted
chopped parsley, to garnish

Heat 2 tablespoons oil in a pan, add the onion and cook until softened, about 5 minutes. Add the rice and 2 garlic cloves and sauté, stirring, for 2 minutes. Pour in the water, add the salt and bring to the boil. Cover and simmer gently for 35–40 minutes, until all the water has been absorbed and the rice is tender.

Heat the remaining oil in a large frying pan, add the celery and red pepper and cook for 5 minutes, until softened. Stir in the mushrooms and the remaining garlic and sauté for 3 minutes. Add the cooked rice, drained kidney beans, parsley, soy sauce and nuts. Cook, stirring to mix, until the beans are heated through. Garnish with parsley, and serve with a green salad.

■ COOK'S TIP

It is unnecessary to wash cultivated mushrooms, as well as being detrimental to their nutritional content. Simply wipe them with a clean, damp cloth before use.

360
creamy curried pasta

Preparation time 10 minutes	*250 g (8 oz) pasta shapes* *3 tablespoons olive oil*
Cooking time 15 minutes	*1 tablespoon white wine vinegar* *1 teaspoon chopped mint*
Serves 4	*1 onion, finely chopped* *4 tablespoons dry vermouth*
Calories 465 per portion	*2 teaspoons mild concentrated curry paste* *2 teaspoons apricot jam*

50 g (2 oz) slivered or flaked almonds, toasted
150 ml (¼ pint) soured cream
½ bunch of watercress, chopped
salt and pepper

Cook the pasta in plenty of boiling salted water for 10–12 minutes or until just tender. Drain.

Meanwhile, mix together the oil, vinegar, mint and salt and pepper to make a dressing. Pour over the hot pasta and leave until cold.

Place the onion and vermouth in a pan and bring to the boil. Simmer for 3 minutes, then leave to cool. Stir the curry paste and jam into the pasta mixture. Stir in the onion mixture. Turn the mixture into a serving dish and scatter the almonds on top. Mix together the soured cream and watercress and serve in a bowl with the salad.

■ COOK'S TIP

Choose small, chunky shapes, such as orecchiette, little ears, or conchiglie, shells, which provide ideal surfaces for the delicious dressing; or lumachine, little snakes, which trap the sauce like containers.

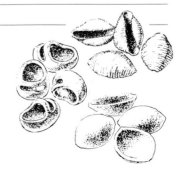

361

pumpkin and sage risotto

Preparation time 20 minutes	*2 tablespoons extra virgin olive oil* *1 large onion, finely chopped*
Cooking time 35–40 minutes	*1 garlic clove, chopped* *1–2 tablespoons chopped sage*
Serves 4	*375 g (12 oz) arborio rice*
Calories 260 per portion	*500 g (1 lb) pumpkin flesh, diced* *1 litre (1¼ pints) boiling vegetable stock* *25 g (1 oz) pine nuts, toasted* *25 g (1 oz) freshly grated vegetarian* *Parmesan cheese* *4 tablespoons milk* *pinch of freshly grated nutmeg* *salt and pepper*

Heat the oil in a large saucepan and fry the onion, garlic and sage for about 5 minutes until golden. Add the rice and pumpkin and stir-fry for 1 minute until the rice grains are well coated in the oil.

Add 150ml (¼ pint) of stock and simmer, stirring until absorbed. Continue to add the stock, a little at a time, stirring frequently, for about 25 minutes, until the rice is creamy and all the stock is absorbed.

Meanwhile, process the pine nuts, cheese, milk and nutmeg in a blender until smooth. Stir in the risotto, with the final addition of stock, and simmer for a further 5 minutes. Season to taste and serve at once.

362

fruit and nut pilaff

Preparation time 20 minutes, plus soaking	*75 g (3 oz) sultanas* *175 g (6 oz) dried fruit (apricots, apples,* *pears, etc.)*
Cooking time 40 minutes	*1 tablespoon sweet sherry* *75 g (3 oz) butter*
Oven temperature 190°C (375°F) gas 5	*1 onion, finely chopped* *250 g (8 oz) brown rice, cooked* *½ teaspoon ground allspice*
Serves 6	*50 g (2 oz) flaked almonds*
Calories 366 per portion	*salt and pepper*

Put the sultanas and dried fruit in a bowl, sprinkle with the sherry and cover with water. Leave to soak for 4 hours. Drain and chop the apricots, apples or pears.

Melt the butter in a frying pan, add the onion and fry until softened. Stir in the rice and allspice, then add salt and pepper to taste and mix well.

Fold in the fruit and almonds, then turn the mixture into a greased casserole. Bake in a preheated moderately hot oven for 30 minutes covered with a tight-fitting lid. Serve hot or cold.

■ COOK'S TIP

As a variation, use 500 g (1 lb)
of butternut squash instead of
pumpkin and substitute rosemary for
the sage.

■ COOK'S TIP

This sweet, spicy dish is packed with
protein, vitamins and minerals.
It is also high in fibre. Serve with a
crisp salad for a nutritious lunch.

363

spiced vegetables and rice

Preparation time
20 minutes

Cooking time
50 minutes

Serves 2

Calories
312 per portion

Suitable for vegans

1 tablespoon oil
1 leek, sliced
1 carrot, thinly sliced
1 onion, sliced
½ dessert apple, cored and chopped
½ teaspoon cumin seeds
½ teaspoon ground coriander
pinch of cayenne pepper
4–5 tablespoons vegetable stock
125 g (4 oz) brown rice
salt and pepper
chopped parsley, to garnish

Heat the oil in a saucepan, add the leek, carrot, onion and apple and cook gently, stirring, for 3 minutes. Add the cumin, coriander, cayenne and salt and pepper to taste. Continue to cook for 3 minutes, then stir in the stock. Cover and simmer for 10–15 minutes until the vegetables are tender but not soft.

Cook the rice in plenty of boiling salted water for 25–30 minutes or until tender. Drain and rinse with boiling water.

Stir the rice into the vegetables and heat gently for 5 minutes. Transfer to a warmed serving dish and garnish with parsley.

■ COOK'S TIP

Cumin is best bought in seed form and ground as needed. If bought ready-ground, get only a small quantity at a time and store in an airtight container.

364

tagliatelle verde with mushrooms

Preparation time
20 minutes

Cooking time
30 minutes

Serves 4

Calories
484 per portion

250–350 g (8–12 oz) tagliatelle verde
flat leaf parsley, to garnish
FOR THE SAUCE
1 onion, chopped
40 g (1½ oz) butter or margarine
1 garlic clove, crushed
350 g (12 oz) button mushrooms, wiped and sliced
300 m1 (½ pint) soured cream
freshly grated nutmeg
salt and pepper

First make the sauce. Fry the onion gently in 25 g (1 oz) butter or margarine for about 10 minutes until softened. Then add the garlic and mushrooms and cook quickly for 2–3 minutes. Add the soured cream, season with nutmeg, salt and pepper, then remove from the heat.

Half-fill a large saucepan with water and bring to the boil, then add the tagliatelle. Stir once, then leave the tagliatelle to cook, uncovered, for 10–15 minutes, until a piece feels tender but not soggy when you bite it. Drain immediately into a colander, then tip back into the still hot saucepan, add the rest of the butter or margarine and some salt and pepper. Stir for 1 minute until the fat has melted.

Quickly reheat the sauce, then tip the tagliatelle into a hot serving dish. Pour the sauce over the top and serve at once garnished with flat leaf parsley.

■ COOK'S TIP

Mushrooms are pretty full of moisture so they should not be soaked in water. A wipe with a damp cloth should be enough in way of preparation. Trim tough stalk ends if applicable and slice stalks and large caps for ease of cooking. Peeling should hardly ever be necessary.

365

savoury fried rice

Preparation time 10 minutes	*250 g (8 oz) brown rice*
	1 tablespoon olive oil
Cooking time 40 minutes	*125 g (4 oz) frozen sweetcorn*
	6 spring onions, chopped
Serves 4	*1 tablespoon soy sauce*
Calories 261 per portion	*salt and pepper*
Suitable for vegans	

Fill a large saucepan two-thirds full of water, add a teaspoonful of salt and bring to the boil. Add the rice, bring back to the boil and cook for about 30 minutes until the grains are tender, then drain.

Heat the olive oil in another saucepan and add the rice, corn and spring onions, stirring all the time. Continue to stir-fry for 3–4 minutes, until all the ingredients are heated through. Add the soy sauce, and taste for seasoning before serving.

366

spinach lasagne

Preparation time 20 minutes	*2 large onions, chopped*
	1 tablespoon olive oil
Cooking time 1 ¼ hours	*2 garlic cloves, crushed*
	2 x 400 g (13 oz) can tomatoes
Oven temperature 190°C (375°F) gas 5	*500 g (1 lb) packet frozen leaf spinach, thawed, or 1 kg (2 lb) fresh spinach, cooked, drained and chopped*
Serves 4	*350 g (12 oz) vegetarian cream cheese*
Calories 578 per portion	*125 g (4 oz) quick-cook lasagne*
	salt and pepper
	FOR THE TOPPING
	soft wholewheat breadcrumbs
	a little butter or margarine

Fry the onions in the oil for 5 minutes, then add the garlic and fry for a further 5 minutes, without browning. Purée 3 tablespoons of this onion mixture in a food processor or blender with the tomatoes and some salt and pepper to make a sauce.

Add the rest of the onion to the spinach, together with the cream cheese and salt and pepper to taste. Put a layer of the spinach mixture into the bottom of a shallow ovenproof dish and cover with a layer of lasagne then half the tomato sauce. Repeat the layers, ending with the sauce. Sprinkle breadcrumbs all over the top of the lasagne and dot with butter or margarine. Bake, in a preheated oven, uncovered, for 50–60 minutes. If more convenient, this dish can cook for 1½–2 hours at a lower temperature, 150°C (300°F) gas 2.

■ COOK'S TIP

As a variation, stir in 50 g (2 oz) bean sprouts before serving. Alternatively, serve with Tofu with bamboo shoots and carrots (see recipe 411).

■ COOK'S TIP

This dish can be varied by adding more cheeses: 50 g (2 oz) grated Parmesan can be added to the spinach mixture, and 175–250 g (6–8 oz) mozzarella can be sliced and layered with the lasagne, spinach mixture and sauce, for a richer (more fattening!) version.

367

two-cheese lasagne

Preparation time 20 minutes	*300 ml (½ pint) skimmed milk*
	1 small onion stuck with 4 cloves
Cooking time about 55 minutes	*20 g (¾ oz) butter*
	20 g (¾ oz) plain flour
Oven temperature 190°C (375°F) gas 5	*250 g (8 oz) runner beans, sliced*
	150 g (5 oz) green or wholemeal quick cook lasagne
Serves 4	*250 g (8 oz) vegetarian cottage cheese, sieved*
Calories 318 per portion	*2 tablespoons chopped parsley*
	1 garlic clove, crushed
	150 ml (¼ pint) natural yogurt
	1 medium egg
	3 tablespoons grated Parmesan cheese
	salt and pepper

Put the milk into a saucepan with the onion. Bring to the boil and leave to stand, off the heat, for 15 minutes. Melt the butter in a another pan and stir in the flour; cook for 1 minute. Gradually stir in the strained milk and cook until thickened. Season to taste with salt and pepper.

Cook the beans, then drain and reserve the cooking liquid.

Put one-third of the lasagne into a greased ovenproof dish; thin the white sauce with a little of the bean cooking liquid, and spoon half over the lasagne. Top with the beans, and then with a second layer of lasagne. Mix the cottage cheese with the parsley and garlic, spread over the lasagne and top with the remaining sauce. Arrange the remaining lasagne on top. Beat the yogurt with the egg and Parmesan; spoon over the top of the lasagne. Bake in a preheated oven for about 45 minutes.

■ COOK'S TIP

Mild-tasting cottage cheese is made from skimmed milk curds which have been washed and rinsed. Being very low in fat, it is popular with slimmers.

368

tomato tagliatelle

Preparation time 20 minutes	*500 g (1 lb) fresh red tagliatelle*
	2 tablespoons vegetable oil
Cooking time 25 minutes	*15 g (½ oz) soft margarine*
	2 onions, sliced
Serves 4	*2 garlic cloves, crushed*
	500 g (1 lb) courgettes, thinly sliced
Calories 506 per portion	*1 green pepper, cored, deseeded and sliced*
	2 large tomatoes, skinned and chopped
	250 g (8 oz) button mushrooms, sliced
	2 tablespoons chopped parsley
	cheese topping (see Cook's Tip)
	salt and pepper
	oregano sprigs, to garnish

Cook the tagliatelle in lightly salted water for about 5 minutes, or until it is just tender. Drain the pasta, run hot water through it to prevent it from becoming sticky, and drain it again. Return to the pan and keep warm.

To make the sauce, heat the oil and margarine in a saucepan and fry the onions over moderate heat for 3 minutes, stirring once or twice. Add the garlic, courgettes and green pepper and fry for 3 minutes. Add the tomatoes and mush rooms, stir well, cover the pan and simmer for 10 minutes, or until the vegetables are just tender. Season with salt and pepper and stir in the parsley.

Turn the tagliatelle into a warmed serving dish, pour on the sauce and toss. Spoon the cheese topping into the centre, garnish with oregano sprigs and serve at once.

■ COOK'S TIP

To make the cheese topping, mix together 150 g (5 oz) low-fat vegetarian cottage cheese (sieved), 25 g (l oz) vegetarian Cheddar cheese (grated), 2 tablespoons chopped parsley and 2 tablespoons natural yogurt. Season to taste.

369

pasta with rich tomato sauce

370

vegetarian chilli with brown rice

Preparation time
25 minutes

Cooking time
30 minutes

Serves 3–4

Calories
391–293 per portion

Suitable for vegans using soya margarine

25 g (1 oz) butter or soya margarine
1 large onion, sliced
1 garlic clove, crushed
750 g (1½ lb) ripe tomatoes, skinned and chopped
1 tablespoon tomato purée
2 teaspoons caster or granulated sugar
2 tablespoons fresh marjoram
150 ml (¼ pint) vegetable stock
250 g (9 oz) wholemeal pasta shells
Crunchy dressing (see Cook's Tip)
salt and pepper

Melt the butter or soya margarine in a pan and fry the onion and garlic for about 7 minutes until cooked but not brown. Add the tomatoes, tomato purée, sugar, marjoram, stock and salt and pepper. Half cover the pan and simmer gently for 25 minutes.

Remove the lid and increase the heat for 2–3 minutes to reduce the sauce. It should have a thick, rich consistency. Keep the sauce hot.

Meanwhile, cook the pasta. Bring a large pan of salted water to the boil, add the pasta and cook for about 15 minutes, until just tender.

Drain the pasta thoroughly, turn into a warm serving dish, spoon the hot sauce over it, and top with the crunchy dressing. Serve immediately.

Preparation time
20 minutes, plus soaking

Cooking time
30 minutes (2 hours for dried beans)

Serves 4

Calories
269 per portion

Suitable for vegans

175 g (6 oz) dried red kidney beans or 2 x 425 g (14 oz) cans red kidney beans
1 onion, chopped
1 green pepper, cored, deseeded and chopped
1 tablespoon olive oil
1 garlic clove, crushed
400 g (13 oz) can tomatoes
150 g (5 oz) cooked green lentils (see Cook's Tip, recipe 371)
½–1 teaspoon chilli powder
1 teaspoon mild paprika
sugar
250 g (8 oz) brown rice, cooked
salt and pepper

If using dried kidney beans, soak for 6–8 hours then drain. Cover with fresh water, boil hard for 10 minutes, then simmer gently for 1¼–1½ hours, until tender.

Fry the onion and pepper in the oil in a large saucepan for 10 minutes, then add the garlic and tomatoes. Drain the red kidney beans and the lentils and add to the tomato mixture. Flavour with the paprika and chilli powder, sugar, salt and pepper to taste. Simmer for 10–15 minutes, taste for seasoning and serve with the brown rice.

■ COOK'S TIP

To make the Crunchy dressing, brown 25 g (l oz) sunflower seeds in 10 g (¼ oz) butter or soya margarine. Stir in 25 g (l oz) wholemeal breadcrumbs. Shake the pan over the heat until the breadcrumbs are brown.

■ COOK'S TIP

Always fast-boil kidney beans for at least 10 minutes of the cooking time to dispel harmful toxins, then lower the heat to a gentle boil.

371

spaghetti with lentil bolognese sauce

Preparation time 20 minutes, plus cooking the lentils	*250–350 g (8–12 oz) spaghetti*
	15 g (½ oz) butter or soya margarine
	pepper
Cooking time 45 minutes	FOR THE SAUCE
	250 g (8 oz) cooked whole green lentils (see Cook's Tip)
Serves 4	*2 onions, chopped*
Calories 604 per portion	*2 tablespoons oil*
	2 garlic cloves, crushed
Suitable for vegans using soya margarine	*2. celery sticks, chopped*
	2 carrots, finely diced
	2 tablespoons tomato purée
	salt and pepper

First prepare the sauce. Drain the lentils, keeping the liquid. Fry the onions in the oil for 5 minutes, then add the garlic, celery and carrots. Simmer, covered, for 15 minutes, until tender. Stir in the lentils, tomato purée, salt and pepper and a little of the reserved liquid to make a thick, soft consistency. Simmer for about 10 minutes, adding more liquid if necessary.

Half-fill a large pan with water, add 1 teaspoon of salt and bring to the boil. Add the spaghetti and simmer for about 10 minutes, until just tender. Drain the spaghetti, then return to the saucepan with the butter or soya margarine and pepper.

Make sure the spaghetti is hot, then turn it on to a hot serving dish and pour the sauce on top. Hand round grated cheese separately.

■ COOK'S TIP

Green lentils do not need presoaking. Simply rinse, place in a pan, cover with water and bring to the boil. Simmer gently for about 40 minutes until tender.

372

spiced brown rice with broccoli

Preparation time 20 minutes	*15 g (½ oz) butter or soya margarine*
	1 onion, finely sliced
Cooking time 30–40 minutes	*175 g (6 oz) long-grain brown rice*
	450 ml (¾ pint) vegetable stock
Serves 2	*175 g (6 oz) broccoli, trimmed*
Calories 623 per portion	*1 tablespoon olive oil*
	50 g (2 oz) pine nuts
Suitable for vegans using soya margarine	*salt and pepper*
	½ teaspoon garam masala (optional)

Melt the butter or soya margarine and fry the onion until golden. Add the rice and fry gently for 2–3 minutes. Pour in the stock and bring to the boil, then cover the pan, lower the heat and simmer gently for 35–40 minutes until the rice is cooked but still slightly chewy, and all the stock has been absorbed.

About 15 minutes before the rice is cooked, prepare the broccoli. Cut the heads into thin strips lengthways. Heat the olive oil in a large frying pan and stir-fry the broccoli for about 10 minutes. If you like the broccoli soft rather than slightly crisp, cover the pan for part of the time. This will create steam which will soften it further.

When the broccoli is cooked to your taste add the pine nuts to the pan and stir-fry until they are lightly browned. Stir in the cooked rice, adding black pepper and a little salt if necessary. Spoon into a serving dish, sprinkle lightly with garam masala (if liked) and serve immediately.

■ COOK'S TIP

Although bright green broccoli looks attractive, several other vegetables could be used for this recipe: courgettes, mushrooms or peppers, for instance.

373

spaghetti with three herb sauce

Preparation time
15 minutes

Cooking time
about 12 minutes

Serves 4

Calories
325 per portion

3 tablespoons chopped parsley
1 tablespoon chopped tarragon
2 tablespoons chopped basil
1 tablespoon olive oil
1 large garlic clove, crushed
4 tablespoons vegetable stock
2 tablespoons dry white wine
375 g (12 oz) wholemeal spaghetti
salt and pepper

Put the parsley, tarragon, basil, olive oil, garlic, vegetable stock, white wine and salt and pepper to taste into a food processor or blender and purée until smooth.

Cook the spaghetti in a large pan of boiling, salted water until just tender; test a strand from time to time, as wholemeal spaghetti takes longer to cook than the standard variety (about 12 minutes in total).

Drain the spaghetti and heap in a warmed bowl. Pour over the herb sauce and toss well. Serve with a crisp salad.

374

peperonata with wholemeal noodles

Preparation time
20–25 minutes

Cooking time
20 minutes

Serves 4

Calories
315 per portion

3 tablespoons olive oil
2 large onions, thinly sliced
1 large garlic clove, crushed
2 red peppers, cored, deseeded and cut into strips
2 green peppers, cored, deseeded and cut into strips
500 g (1 lb) tomatoes, skinned, deseeded and chopped
1 tablespoon chopped basil
175 g (6 oz) wholemeal noodles
salt and pepper
basil sprigs, to garnish

Heat 2 tablespoons olive oil in a deep frying pan. Add the onions and garlic and cook very gently until the onions soften. Add the peppers, tomatoes, basil and salt and pepper to taste. Cover and cook gently for 10 minutes. Remove the lid from the pan and cook over a fairly high heat until most of the moisture has evaporated. Keep warm.

Meanwhile, cook the noodles in plenty of boiling salted water until just tender. Drain the noodles thoroughly and toss in the remaining olive oil. Add salt and pepper to taste.

Divide the noodles among 4 serving plates and spoon the hot peperonata over the top. Garnish with sprigs of basil and serve immediately as a light main course with a salad.

■ COOK'S TIP

Don't just stick to spaghetti, there is a wide range of other pastas suited to this sauce. Try tubular rigatoni, curled fusilli, shells, or the large bows called farfalle.

■ COOK'S TIP

Peperonata is a classic summer dish, combining the best of the summer produce – peppers, tomatoes and basil. Use fresh wholemeal noodles if you can find them; these will take about 8–10 minutes to cook.

375
spring green and rice mould

Preparation time	750 g (1½ lb) spring greens
20 minutes	3 medium eggs
Cooking time	4 tablespoons natural yogurt
about 50 minutes	6 tablespoons cooked brown rice
Oven temperature	50 g (2 oz) grated Parmesan cheese
180°C (350°F)	pinch of ground nutmeg
gas 4	1 tablespoon chopped chives
Serves 4	salt and pepper
Calories	watercress and parsley sprigs, to garnish
173 per portion	

Wash the greens and shake dry; discard any tough stalk pieces. Shred the greens coarsely and put them into a saucepan with just enough boiling water to cover the base of the pan; cover and cook gently until they are just tender.

Drain the greens thoroughly, pressing to extract as much excess moisture as possible; blend to a purée.

Mix the purée with the remaining ingredients. Transfer to a greased 900 ml (1½ pint) mould.

Stand the mould in a roasting tin and add sufficient hot water to come half-way up the sides; cover the top of the mould with a circle of lightly greased foil.

Bake in a preheated oven for 45 minutes, until the mould is set. Allow to stand for 2–3 minutes, then carefully turn out on to a plate. Garnish with watercress and parsley.

■ COOK'S TIP

A cheese mill, a cylindrical enclosed grater, is useful for Parmesan. The cheese is stored in it and the lid is turned to grate it straight on to the food.

376
mung bean and fresh herb risotto

Preparation time	175 g (6 oz) mung beans, soaked for
15 minutes, plus	2 hours in cold water
soaking	15 g (½ oz) butter or soya margarine
Cooking time	1½ tablespoons vegetable oil
about 50 minutes	1 large onion, chopped
Serves 4	250 g (8 oz) long-grain brown rice
Calories	750 ml (1¼ pints) hot vegetable stock
327 per portion	3 tablespoons chopped mixed herbs
Suitable for vegans	(parsley, thyme, basil, mint)
using soya margarine	salt and pepper
	2 tablespoons pumpkin seeds, to garnish

Drain and rinse the beans.

Using a large pan with a well-fitting lid, heat the butter or soya margarine and 1 tablespoon of the oil and fry the onion for 3 minutes, then stir in the beans and rice. Pour on the hot stock and bring to the boil. Cover the pan, lower the heat and simmer gently for 40 minutes until the beans and rice are tender and all the stock has been absorbed.

Add the herbs, salt and pepper and gently fork them through the mixture. Spoon the risotto into a warm serving dish and keep warm.

Fry the pumpkin seeds rapidly in the remaining oil for 30 seconds (take care, as they jump about in the heat) then sprinkle over the risotto. Serve hot.

■ COOK'S TIP

Pumpkin seeds are dull green, oval shaped and flat. They come from fully matured ripe pumpkins and are widely available from health food shops. Rich in iron and vitamin C, they also contain a high amount of protein

suppers
and snacks

Choose a super-speedy snack when you are in a hurry – a gratin or bake for a satisfying supper dish; both are highly nutritious making it easy to maintain a healthy life-style. The recipes in this chapter make good use of a large number of storecupboard items, as well as fresh ingredients, including vegetables, herbs, cheeses and eggs.

potato jackets with soured cream dip

Preparation time 10 minutes	*5 large potatoes, scrubbed and dried*
Cooking time 1½–1¾ hours	*150 ml (¼ pint) soured cream*
Oven temperature 190°C (375°F) gas 5	*1 tablespoon snipped chives*
	salt and pepper
	vegetable oil, for frying
Serves 4	
Calories 306 per portion	

Prick the potatoes with a fork and bake in a preheated oven for about 1¼ hours until tender.

Meanwhile, prepare the dip. Mix the soured cream with the chives and salt and pepper to taste. Spoon into a bowl, cover and chill in the refrigerator.

When the potatoes are cooked, leave to cool for a few minutes then cut each one lengthways into 4. Scoop out most of the potato, leaving just a thin layer next to the skin.

Pour vegetable oil into a small pan to a depth of 7.5 cm (3 inches). There is no need to use a large deep-fryer.

Heat the oil to 180–190°C (350–375°F) or until a cube of bread browns in 30 seconds.

Fry 4–5 potato skins at a time for about 2 minutes until brown and crisp. Lift from the oil with a slotted spoon and drain on kitchen paper. Keep the skins hot in the oven while the remaining skins are cooking. Serve with the chilled dip.

■ COOK'S TIP

These golden, crisp potato skins are an American speciality. Use the insides of the potatoes for Colcannon (recipe 203) or as topping for a vegetable pie.

vegetable kebabs

Preparation time 30 minutes, plus marinating	*36 small button mushrooms, wiped*
	1 aubergine, cut into chunks, sprinkled with salt, left for 30 minutes, then rinsed and drained
Cooking time 15 minutes	*1 red or green sweet pepper, cored, deseeded and cut into strips*
Serves 6	*24 baby pickling onions or 2 onions, cut into chunks*
Calories 129 per portion	*6 small courgettes, cut into thick slices*
Suitable for vegans using soya margarine	FOR THE MARINADE
	3 tablespoons Dijon mustard
	3 garlic cloves, crushed
	3 tablespoons dark brown sugar
	3 tablespoons soy sauce
	3 tablespoons olive oil
	1½ teaspoons salt

Thread the vegetables on to 12 skewers then mix together the marinade ingredients. Put the skewers flat on a non-metallic tray or a plate. Spoon the marinade over them, turning the skewers to make sure that all the vegetables are coated with the mixture. Leave to marinate for at least 1 hour, basting occasionally.

Cook the kebabs on a barbecue or under a preheated hot grill for 10–15 minutes, until the vegetables are tender. Serve the kebabs on a bed of special rice (see Cook's Tip) with the remaining marinade served separately in a small jug.

■ COOK'S TIP

For special rice, put 300 g (10 oz) brown rice and 50 g (2 oz) wild rice in a pan with 900 ml (1½ pints) vegetable stock. Cook the rice for 40–45 minutes until tender. Add 25 g (l oz) butter or soya margarine, some chopped herbs and stir over a low heat until well coated. Season and serve.

379

wild mushroom feuilleté

Preparation time 30 minutes	*375 g (12 oz) flaky pastry (not containing animal fat)*
Cooking time 15 minutes	FOR THE FILLING *15 g (½ oz) butter or margarine*
Oven temperature 200°C (400°F) gas 6	*500 g (1 lb) white button mushrooms, sliced* *375 g (12 oz) oyster mushrooms, sliced*
Serves 4	*300 ml (½ pint) soured cream* *300 ml (½ pint) single cream*
Calories 693 per portion	*1 garlic clove, crushed* *salt and pepper* *lemon twists, to garnish*

Roll out the pastry to a thickness of about 3 mm (⅛ inch) and cut out 6 six 7.5 cm (3 inch) circles and six 5 cm (2 inch) ones. Put the circles on a baking sheet and bake in a preheated oven for 10–12 minutes, until puffed up and golden brown.

Meanwhile, melt the butter or margarine and fry the button mushrooms and oyster mushrooms for 5 minutes, until tender. Remove the mushrooms with a slotted spoon and boil the remaining liquid rapidly until reduced to 1 tablespoon. Add the mushrooms, soured and single cream, garlic and salt and pepper.

To serve, place the large pastry circles on a warmed individual plates, with a serving of the mushroom mixture and cover with one of the smaller pastry circles. Garnish with a twist of lemon and serve with fresh vegetables (see Cook's Tip).

380

cauliflower ramekins

Preparation time 20–25 minutes	*1 small cauliflower* *3 tablespoons wholemeal breadcrumbs*
Cooking time about 30 minutes	*2 tablespoons natural yogurt* *1 tablespoon chopped dill*
Oven temperature 190°C (375°F) gas 5	*2 medium eggs, separated* *2 tablespoons grated Parmesan cheese* *1 teaspoon ready-made pesto sauce*
Serves 4	*salt and pepper*
Calories 100 per portion	*dill sprigs, to garnish*

Trim the leaves and base stalk from the cauliflower (reserve and use for soup). Divide the cauliflower into florets and cook in boiling, salted water until just tender. Drain the cauliflower well and mash to a purée.

Put the purée into a pan and stir over a gentle heat for 1–2 minutes; this will allow some of the excess moisture to evaporate.

Mix the purée with the breadcrumbs, yogurt, dill, egg yolks and half the Parmesan cheese, pesto sauce and salt and pepper to taste. Whisk the egg whites until stiff but not dry then fold lightly but thoroughly into the cauliflower mixture.

Spoon into 4 greased ramekin dishes then sprinkle with the remaining Parmesan cheese. Bake in a preheated oven for about 15–20 minutes, until puffed and lightly golden. Serve piping hot, garnished with dill sprigs.

■ COOK'S TIP

Serve this dish with such vegetables as steamed or boiled baby new potatoes, broccoli florets, carrots cut into matchsticks and mangetout.

■ COOK'S TIP

Dill is an aromatic, sweet herb which has the useful property of having a calming effect on the stomach, helping to ease the pangs of indigestion.

broccoli with egg cream sauce

Preparation time 10 minutes	*375–425 g (12–14 oz) broccoli spears* *600 ml (1 pint) boiling water*
Cooking time 20 minutes	*salt* *pinch of grated nutmeg*
Serves 4	FOR THE SAUCE
Calories 214 per portion	*150 ml (¼ pint) double cream* *2 medium egg yolks, beaten* *1 tablespoon chopped parsley* *white pepper*

Remove the leaves from the broccoli and trim the spears. Place the broccoli spears in a pan with the water, a pinch of salt and the nutmeg. Bring to the boil, then lower the heat, cover and cook for about 8–10 minutes. Drain thoroughly, reserving 150 ml (¼ pint) of the cooking liquid.

To make the sauce, place the reserved cooking liquid in a small pan, stir in the cream and bring to just below boiling point. Add the egg yolks, stirring constantly. Add the parsley and salt and pepper to taste.

Pour the egg cream sauce over the broccoli and leave to stand in a warm place for about 5 minutes before serving.

▓ COOK'S TIP

Broccoli stalks should be firm and crisp and the leaves vigorous. Trim the ends of sprouting broccoli, cut off any tough or damaged stalks, then remove any bruised or wilted leaves. Rinse in cold running water then peel the stalk from below the flower head to the end.

This allows the stalk and delicate head to cook in the same time.

cauliflower crumble

Preparation time 20 minutes	*1 cauliflower, broken into florets* *2 tablespoons oil*
Cooking time 40 minutes	*4 tablespoons wholemeal flour* *350 ml (12 fl oz) milk*
Oven temperature 190°C (375°F) gas 5	*1 x 350 g (11½ oz) can sweetcorn, drained* *2 tablespoons chopped parsley* *125 g (4 oz) mature vegetarian Cheddar* * cheese, grated*
Serves 4	*salt*
Calories 453 per portion	FOR THE TOPPING *50 g (2 oz) wholemeal flour* *25 g (1 oz) margarine* *25 g (1 oz) porridge oats* *25 g (1 oz) chopped almonds*

Cook the cauliflower in boiling salted water for 5 minutes. Drain, reserving the water.

Heat the oil in the same pan and stir in the flour. Remove from the heat, add the milk, stirring until blended. Add 150 ml (¼ pint) of the reserved cooking liquid, bring to the boil and cook for 3 minutes, until thickened. Stir in the sweetcorn, parsley and half the cheese. Gently fold in the cauliflower and turn into a 1.5 litre (2½ pint) ovenproof dish.

To make the topping, place the flour in a bowl and rub in the margarine until the mixture resembles fine breadcrumbs. Add the oats, almonds and the remaining cheese. Sprinkle the topping over the vegetable mixture and bake in a preheated oven for 30 minutes, until golden brown and crisp.

▓ COOK'S TIP

Instead of using cauliflower, try a mixture of different vegetables. Carrots, green beans, broccoli, swede or parsnip all make interesting alternatives. Add some sesame seeds to the topping for extra protein.

383

deep-dish salad bowl

Preparation time
30 minutes

Serves 2

Calories
211 per portion

4 lettuce leaves, shredded
125 g (4 oz) cold cooked potato, diced
4 tablespoons mayonnaise or soured
*   cream, or a mixture of both*
125 g (4 oz) bean sprouts (see Cook's Tip)
1 tablespoon olive oil
1 tablespoon wine vinegar
2 tomatoes, chopped
10 cm (4 inch) piece of cucumber, cubed
2 tablespoons raisins
1 large carrot, finely grated
1 raw beetroot, peeled and finely grated
salt and pepper
salad cress or watercress, or garnish

Put the shredded lettuce in the bottom of two deep dishes or soup bowls. Mix the potato with half the mayonnaise, soured cream or mixture; season with salt and pepper, then spoon into the bowls.

Mix the bean sprouts with oil, vinegar and salt and pepper to taste. Put the bean sprouts on top of the potatoes, followed by the tomatoes, cucumber, raisins, grated carrot and beetroot. Spoon the remaining mayonnaise, soured cream or mixture on top of the beetroot and sprinkle with some salad cress or watercress. Serve immediately.

384

courgette fritters

Preparation time
30 minutes

Cooking time
20 minutes

Oven temperature
110°C (225°F)
gas ¼

Serves 4

Calories
284 per portion

5 small courgettes, about 300 g (10 oz)
FOR THE BATTER
125 g (4 oz) wholemeal self-raising flour
1 medium egg
1 tablespoon vegetable oil
2 teaspoons vinegar
150 ml (5 fl oz) milk
vegetable oil, for frying
salt and pepper
Stilton dip (see Cook's Tip)

Trim the courgettes and cut them into short sticks about 5 cm (2 inches) long and 5 mm (¼ inch) wide. Dry on kitchen paper.

To make the batter, put the flour, egg, oil, vinegar and half the milk into a basin with salt and pepper to taste. Whisk to a thick paste then gradually whisk in the rest of the milk.

Pour the vegetable oil into a small pan to a depth of about 7.5 cm (3 inches). Heat the oil to 180–190°C (350–375°F) or until a cube of bread browns in 30 seconds.

Dip each piece of courgette into the batter, allowing any excess to run back into the bowl, and fry in small batches until puffy and golden (about 3 minutes per batch). Lift out with a slotted spoon, drain on kitchen paper, and keep hot on a serving dish in the preheated oven until you have completed the frying.

To serve, sprinkle the fritters lightly with salt and serve hot with the Stilton dip.

■ COOK'S TIP

To sprout beans, select clean, whole seeds of any variety except kidney beans. Soak in cold water, drain and place in a large glass jar. Cover with muslin and secure with a rubber band. Twice a day, pour cold water through the muslin, then drain it off. The seeds should sprout in 4–5 days.

■ COOK'S TIP

To make the Stilton dip, mix 4 tablespoons mayonnaise and 4 tablespoons natural yogurt. Fold in 50 g (2 oz) crumbled vegetarian Stilton. Season with pepper.

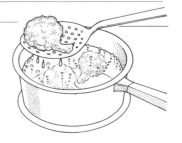

385

colourful beetroot salad

Preparation time 30 minutes	*600–750 g (1¼–1½ lb) beetroot* *1 fennel bulb, cut into julienne strips*
Cooking time 1½ hours	*1 apple, cored and chopped* *1 onion, sliced into rings*
Serves 4	*150 g (5 oz) natural yogurt*
Calories 251 per portion	*4 tablespoons double cream* *1 teaspoon creamed horseradish* *pinch of sugar* *1 tablespoon chopped hazelnuts* *1–2 medium hard-boiled eggs* *salt* *fennel sprigs, to garnish*

Scrub the beetroot under running water. Place the beetroot in a large saucepan and cover with boiling water. Add a pinch of salt and bring back to the boil. Lower the heat and cook gently for about 1½ hours until tender.

Rinse the beetroot under cold water and leave to cool slightly. Peel, then slice, thinly. Place in a large serving bowl. Add the fennel, apple and onion and toss well to mix.

To make the dressing, beat the yogurt with the cream, horseradish, sugar and hazelnuts. Pour over the beetroot salad and toss well to mix.

Cut the hard-boiled eggs into quarters and arrange on top of the salad. Garnish with fennel sprigs, if liked.

■ COOK'S TIP

For a quicker recipe, buy ready-cooked beetroot. Choose ones that haven't been cooked with vinegar as they are too sharp for this dish.

386

health club sandwiches

Preparation time 25 minutes	*8 slices rye or wholemeal bread* FOR THE TOPPINGS
Serves 4	*175 g (6 oz) low-fat soft vegetarian cheese*
Calories 250 per fruity sandwich 210 per vegetable sandwich	*75 g (3 oz) currants* *1 teaspoon grated lemon rind* *50 g (2 oz) dried dates, stoned and* * chopped* *2 dessert apples, peeled, cored and sliced* *1 tablespoon lemon juice* *1 kiwifruit, peeled and sliced* *4 mint sprigs, to garnish* *150 g (5 oz) cottage cheese, sieved* *25 g (1 oz) vegetarian Cheddar, grated* *2 tablespoons snipped chives* *salt and pepper* *2 carrots, grated* *50 g (2 oz) button mushrooms, sliced* *1 tablespoon French dressing* *2 medium hard boiled eggs, sliced*

Cut the crusts from the bread. Beat the soft cheese and stir in the currants, lemon rind and dates. Spread 4 of the bread slices with this mixture. Toss the apple slices in the lemon juice, then arrange them on the sandwich base, followed by the kiwifruit. Garnish with mint sprigs.

Beat the sieved cottage cheese, then beat in the grated cheese and chives, season with salt and pepper and spread over the remaining bread slices. Sprinkle over the grated carrot and press it lightly into the cheese. Toss the mushroom slices in the dressing and arrange them with the egg slices over the carrot topping.

■ COOK'S TIP

Add chopped walnuts or hazelnuts to the low-fat soft cheese for a delicious crunch. Try using vegetarian Stilton instead of Cheddar for the vegetable sandwich.

387

nutburgers in soft baps

Preparation time
20 minutes

Cooking time
25 minutes

Serves 4

Calories
895 per portion

Suitable for vegans
using soya margarine

2 onions, chopped
2 celery sticks, finely diced
125 g (4 oz) butter or soya margarine
2 tablespoons mixed herbs
2 tablespoons wholemeal flour
300 ml (½ pint) vegetable stock
2 tablespoons soy sauce
2 teaspoons yeast extract
500 g (1 lb) mixed nuts: almonds, Brazil
*   nuts, walnuts, cashew nuts, finely*
*   chopped*
250 g (8 oz) soft wholemeal breadcrumbs
dried breadcrumbs, to coat (see Cook's
*   Tip)*
olive oil, for shallow-frying
salt and pepper

Fry the onions and celery in the butter or soya margarine for 10 minutes, browning them lightly. Add the herbs, stir for 1 minute, then mix in the flour and cook for a further 1–2 minutes. Pour in the vegetable stock and stir until thickened. Add the soy sauce, yeast extract, nuts, breadcrumbs and salt and pepper to taste.

Allow the mixture to cool, then form into 12 flat burgers about 1 cm (½ inch) thick, and coat with dry breadcrumbs. Cook in an oiled frying pan over a gentle heat for 5 minutes on each side. Serve in soft burger baps, with chutney and pickles as required.

388

radicchio salad supreme

Preparation time
30 minutes

Serves 4

Calories
199 per portion

1 head of radicchio
3–4 tomatoes, cut into wedges
125 g (4 oz) vegetarian Camembert
*   cheese, cubed*
1 teaspoon prepared English mustard
125 ml (4 oz) whipping cream
1 tablespoon chopped parsley
½ onion, chopped
salt and pepper

Remove the outer leaves from the radicchio and keep to one side for garnish. Separate the heart, tearing the larger leaves into pieces. Place in a sieve, rinse and drain thoroughly. Place in a mixing bowl. Add the tomatoes and cheese and mix well.

To make the dressing, beat the mustard with the cream, half the parsley and salt and pepper to taste. Fold in the onion and pour over the salad. Toss lightly and leave to stand for a few minutes to allow the flavours to develop.

Line a salad bowl with the reserved radicchio leaves and fill with the salad. Sprinkle with the remaining parsley.

■ COOK'S TIP

Dried breadcrumbs are best for coating food before frying. Make fresh crumbs and let them dry out in a very cool oven until crisp. Keep in an airtight container.

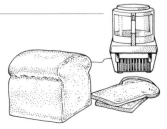

■ COOK'S TIP

Radicchio is an attractive, red, crinkly lettuce. Its slightly bitter leaves make an excellent, although expensive, salad ingredient. Radicchio is a good source of vitamin C.

389

blinis

Preparation time	125 g (4 oz) buckwheat or plain
10 minutes, plus	wholemeal flour
standing	125 g (4 oz) plain white flour
Cooking time	½ teaspoon salt
20 minutes	2 teaspoons Easy Bake yeast
Serves 6	1 medium egg, separated
Calories	1 tablespoon vegetable oil
180 per portion	300 ml (½ pint) tepid milk
	a selection of toppings (see Cook's Tip)
	watercress sprigs, to garnish (optional)

Put the flours, salt, yeast, egg yolk and oil into a bowl. Pour in the tepid milk and mix to a thick smooth batter. Cover and leave to stand for 1 hour. The surface of the batter should be puffy and covered with bubbles.

Whisk the egg white and fold into the batter. The mixture is now ready for use.

Heat a lightly oiled griddle or frying pan over a steady heat. Drop 2 tablespoons of batter into the pan and cook for 3 minutes until tiny holes appear over the surface. Turn the pancake and cook the other side for 2 minutes. Cook 3–4 blinis at a time. When ready put them between the layers of a clean tea towel, folded on a plate over a pan of boiling water. There should be 16–20.

To serve, arrange 2–3 warm blinis with one or more of the chosen toppings on individual plates and garnish with sprigs of watercress if liked.

390

wheat-filled pittas

Preparation time	250 g (8 oz) wholewheat grains, covered
20 minutes, plus	with cold water and soaked for 6–8
soaking and cooling	hours or overnight
Cooking time	2 tablespoons red wine vinegar
1¼ hours	2 tablespoons olive oil
Serves 4	1 onion, red if possible, sliced
Calories	2 tablespoons chopped parsley or
333 per portion	coriander
Suitable for vegans	2 tomatoes, skinned and chopped
	1 head of radicchio or a small lettuce,
	separated into leaves
	wholemeal pitta bread
	salt and pepper
	watercress sprigs, to garnish

Drain the wheat, then put it into a saucepan and cover with fresh water. Bring to the boil and simmer for 1¼ hours. Drain and cool.

Put the red wine vinegar into a bowl with the olive oil and add the wheat, onion, parsley or coriander, tomatoes and a little salt and pepper to taste. Spoon the mixture into warm wholemeal pitta bread with the radicchio or lettuce leaves. Garnish with watercress sprigs.

■ COOK'S TIP

Suggested toppings: cottage cheese with radish and cress; soured cream with chopped pecan nuts; mozzarella with stuffed olives; sliced tomatoes with soured cream.

■ COOK'S TIP

These hearty sandwiches make a delicious main course. Other fillings: endive and sliced tomatoes, cucumber and salad cress or thinly sliced courgettes and watercress. If wholemeal pitta bread is unobtainable, split and fill large wholemeal baps.

391

cream cheese toasts

Preparation time
10 minutes

Serves 6

Calories
389 per portion

175 g (6 oz) vegetarian cream cheese
1 small beetroot, cooked or uncooked
1 tablespoon finely chopped parsley
2 hard-boiled egg yolks
pinch of turmeric
1 packet of Melba toast (about 30 pieces),
  or see Cook's Tip, recipe 56
FOR THE GARNISHES
shelled pistachio nuts
salted cashew nuts
mashed hard-boiled egg yolk
small parsley sprigs

Divide the cream cheese into three equal portions and put them into separate bowls. Add a very little mashed or finely grated beetroot to one bowl; then beat the chopped parsley into another portion and finally mash the egg yolk until it is smooth and stir this into the third portion of cream cheese, together with the turmeric. Pipe or spread these mixtures on the Melba toast. Top each one with a pistachio nut, cashew nut, parsley or other garnish as desired.

392

jacket potatoes with pesto

Preparation time
15–20 minutes

Cooking time
1¼ hours

Oven temperature
190°C (375°F)
gas 5

Serves 4

Calories
320 per portion

4 baking potatoes, about 200 g
  (7 oz) each
40 g (1½ oz) butter
2 teaspoons pesto sauce
generous pinch of grated nutmeg
4 tablespoons chopped cooked spinach
salt and pepper

Scrub the potatoes and dry them with kitchen paper. Prick each one several times with a fork or fine skewer. Wrap each potato in foil, put into a preheated oven and bake for about 1¼ hours, or until cooked.

Melt the butter, stir in the pesto sauce and nutmeg and salt and pepper to taste.

Remove the potatoes from the oven and cut a thin horizontal slice from the top of each one. Fluff up the potato and make a slight well in the centre. Spoon in a little of the pesto butter, and then a spoonful of spinach. Top with the remaining pesto-flavoured butter. Pull up the foil over each filled potato and return to the oven for a further 10 minutes. Serve as a light meal.

■ COOK'S TIP

Watching the calories? Use a low-fat curd or cream cheese instead and go easy on the nuts to garnish. Although high in protein, they are also high in fat.

■ COOK'S TIP

Instead of pesto butter, stir in some garlic and herb cream cheese or grated vegetarian Cheddar. Serve with a large fresh salad for a filling lunch or supper snack.

393

courgette fritters with tzatziki

Preparation time
10 minutes, plus standing and chilling

Cooking time
2–3 minutes

Serves 4

Calories
335 per portion

500 lb (1 lb courgettes)
25 g (1 oz) polenta
25 g (1 oz) plain flour
1 egg, lightly beaten
vegetable oil, for deep-frying
salt and pepper
FOR THE TZATZIKI
125 g (4 oz) natural yogurt
1 garlic clove, crushed
1 tablespoon chopped mint
125 g (4 oz) cucumber, peeled, grated and
*   squeezed dry*

First make the tzatziki. Place all the ingredients in a small bowl and stir well until evenly combined. Set aside for 30 minutes for the flavours to infuse.

Cut the courgettes into thin slices about 5 mm (¼ inch) thick. Mix the polenta and flour in a large bowl with plenty of salt and pepper. Dip the courgettes, first into the egg and then into the polenta, to coat evenly.

Put about 10 cm (4 inches) oil in a deep heavy-based saucepan and heat to 180–190°C (350–375°F) or until a cube of bread browns in 30 seconds. Fry the courgette slices in batches for 2–3 minutes until crisp and golden. Drain on kitchen paper and serve hot with the tzatziki to dip.

394

aubergines au gratin

Preparation time
45 minutes

Cooking time
20 minutes

Oven temperature
220°C (425°F)
gas 7

Serves 4

Calories
290 per portion

2 large aubergines, cut into large cubes
3 tomatoes, sliced
1 courgette, sliced
1 bunch mixed herbs (e.g. parsley, basil,
*   rosemary), chopped*
150 ml (¼ pint) double cream
2 eggs, beaten
15 g (½ oz) butter
1 garlic clove, halved
2 tablespoons dry white breadcrumbs
salt and pepper

Sprinkle the aubergines with salt, place them in a colander and leave to drain for about 30 minutes. Rinse and wipe dry with kitchen paper.

Arrange alternate layers of aubergine, tomato and courgette in a greased ovenproof dish. Sprinkle with the chopped herbs. Mix the cream with the eggs and add salt and pepper to taste. Pour over the vegetable mixture.

Melt the butter in a small saucepan, add the garlic and fry for a few minutes until golden brown. Remove and discard the garlic. Add the breadcrumbs to the garlic-flavoured butter and cook for 1–2 minutes. Sprinkle over the vegetables in the dish. Cook in a preheated oven for 12–15 minutes, or until golden brown. Serve hot.

■ COOK'S TIP

Use half Greek yogurt and half natural yogurt for a more creamy tzatziki. If wished, the fritters can be made in advance and reheated in a hot oven, 200°C (400°F) gas 6, for 10 minutes until crisp.

■ COOK'S TIP

Individual garlic cloves vary enormously in size. When a recipe calls for 1 garlic clove, choose one about the size of the top joint on your little finger.

395

red pepper macaroni cheese

Preparation time
20 minutes

Cooking time
20 minutes

Serves 4

Calories
740 per portion

25 g (1 oz) butter
25 g (1 oz) plain flour
750 ml (1¼ pints) milk
½ teaspoon prepared English mustard
large pinch of cayenne
¼ teaspoon grated nutmeg
1 red pepper, cored, deseeded, cut into
    1 cm (½ inch) dice and blanched
250 g (8 oz) mature Cheddar cheese,
    grated
175 g (6 oz) wholemeal macaroni, cooked
2 tablespoons chopped parsley
salt and pepper
12 triangles wholemeal bread, fried,
    to garnish

Melt the butter in a large saucepan over a low heat, then add the flour. Cook for 2 minutes, stirring. Gradually add the milk and bring to the boil, stirring constantly. Simmer for 2–3 minutes.

Add the mustard, cayenne, nutmeg, red pepper, 200 g (7 oz) of the cheese and salt and pepper to taste. Add the macaroni and parsley, and heat through.

Transfer the macaroni to a flameproof dish, top with the remaining cheese and grill to brown. Garnish with the toast triangles and serve.

396

crumbly nut roast

Preparation time
30 minutes

Cooking time
about 1¼ hours

Oven temperature
220°C (425°F)
gas 7

Serves 4

Calories
535 per portion

40 g (1½ oz) butter
1 onion, chopped
1 celery stick, trimmed, scrubbed and
    chopped
250 g (8 oz) mixed nuts (walnuts, Brazils
    and hazelnuts in equal quantities),
    coarsely chopped
3 large tomatoes, skinned and chopped
175 g (6 oz) fresh wholemeal
    breadcrumbs
1 teaspoon mixed dried herbs
¼ teaspoon chilli powder
2 eggs, lightly beaten
salt and pepper

Oil a 500 g (1 lb) loaf tin and line the base with oiled greaseproof paper. Melt the butter in a large saucepan and fry the onion and celery gently for 5 minutes without browning. Add the nuts, tomatoes, breadcrumbs, mixed herbs, chilli powder and salt and pepper. Add the eggs and mix to a fairly soft consistency, then taste and adjust the seasoning if necessary.

Spoon the mixture into the prepared tin, cover with oiled foil and bake in a preheated hot oven for 50–60 minutes, or until set.

Ease off the foil and run a knife around the sides of the tin. Turn the loaf out on to a warm dish and serve with salad and buttered pasta, if liked.

■ COOK'S TIP

To add extra flavour, place a few tomato slices and some chopped fried onion on the base of the dish before adding the macaroni cheese.

■ COOK'S TIP

The uncooked nut roast mixture can be prepared up to 8 hours in advance and kept covered.

courgette gratin

Preparation time
20 minutes

Cooking time
45 minutes

Oven temperature
180°C (350°F)
gas 4

Serves 4

Calories
320 per portion

2 tablespoons oil
2 onions, sliced
1 garlic clove, crushed
375 g (12 oz) courgettes, sliced
1 tablespoon chopped parsley
1 teaspoon chopped thyme
4 large tomatoes, skinned and sliced
25 g (1 oz) margarine
25 g (1 oz) wholemeal flour
300 ml (½ pint) milk
125 g (4 oz) Cheddar cheese, grated
1 tablespoon fresh wholemeal
   breadcrumbs
salt and pepper

Heat the oil in a pan and cook the onions until softened. Add the garlic, courgettes, herbs and salt and pepper to taste, and cook for 5 minutes, stirring occasionally. Put half the mixture into an ovenproof dish and top with tomatoes, then spread the remaining mixture on top.

Melt the margarine in a saucepan over a low heat, then add the flour. Cook for 2 minutes, stirring. Gradually add the milk and bring the sauce to the boil, stirring constantly. Simmer gently for 2–3 minutes. Add half of the cheese and salt and pepper to taste, then pour over the courgettes. Sprinkle with the breadcrumbs, then the remaining cheese. Bake in a preheated oven for 30 minutes until golden.

leek, potato and coriander bake

Preparation time
15 minutes

Cooking time
1¼ hours

Oven temperature
200°C (400°F)
gas 6

Serves 4

Calories
315 per portion

500 g (1 lb) leeks, trimmed and washed
1 kg (2 lb) small potatoes, scrubbed and
   diced
1 tablespoon oil
25 g (1 oz) butter
1 teaspoon black peppercorns
2 teaspoons coriander seeds
1 teaspoon sea salt

Slice the leeks into 1.5 cm (¾ inch) rings and cut the potatoes into 1 cm (½ inch) slices.

Put the oil and butter into a large shallow roasting tin and place in the oven until the butter is just melted. Add the leeks and potatoes, turning them over several times to coat them with the oil and butter. Crush the peppercorns with the coriander seeds in a mortar.

Put the crushed peppercorns and coriander in a small bowl and add the salt. Sprinkle evenly over the potatoes and leeks and stir through.

Cover the tin tightly with foil. Bake in a preheated oven for 45 minutes. Remove the foil, turn the potatoes and leeks over and put the tin back near the top of the oven for a further 30 minutes until brown. Serve hot.

■ COOK'S TIP

To skin tomatoes, cut a cross in the base of each one, place them in a bowl and pour on freshly boiling water. Leave for 30–60 seconds, depending on ripeness, then drain and peel off the skins which should slide off easily.

■ COOK'S TIP

If you do not have a pestle and mortar, put the coriander seeds and peppercorns between 2 double sheets of kitchen paper or greaseproof paper and crush firmly with a rolling pin.

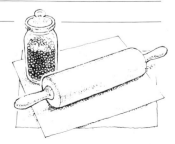

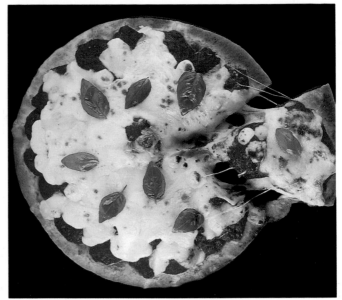

399

provençal eggs

Preparation time 10 minutes	2 tablespoons oil 1 large onion, thinly sliced
Cooking time 25 minutes	1 garlic clove, crushed 1 red pepper, cored, deseeded and sliced
Oven temperature 190°C (375°F) gas 5	250 g (8 oz) courgettes, sliced ½–1 tablespoon chopped oregano 1 x 400 g (13 oz) can tomatoes
Serves 4	a few drops of Tabasco sauce
Calories 235 per portion	4 eggs 50 g (2 oz) Cheddar cheese, grated salt and pepper

Heat the oil in a large saucepan, add the onion and garlic and cook for about 5 minutes until softened. Add the red pepper and courgettes and cook for a further 5 minutes. Stir in the oregano, the tomatoes and their juices, Tabasco and salt and pepper to taste and heat through.

Pour the mixture into a shallow ovenproof dish. Make four hollows in the mixture and break an egg into each one. Sprinkle the cheese over the eggs. Bake in a preheated oven for 12–15 minutes or until the eggs are just set. Serve hot.

■ COOK'S TIP

Tabasco sauce gets its name from the part of Mexico which produced the peppers from which it was originally made. The peppers are pulped, salted and matured for 3 years, then mixed with distilled vinegar. After it has been clarified, the sauce is bottled. It keeps very well. A fiery relish, a few drops are sufficient to impart a pleasing flavour.

400

pizza margherita

Preparation time 35 minutes, plus rising and proving	FOR THE DOUGH 250 g (8 oz) strong plain flour 1 teaspoon salt
Cooking time 30 minutes	5 g (¼ oz) fresh yeast 150 ml (¼ pint) lukewarm water
Oven temperature 220°C (425°F) gas 7	FOR THE TOPPING 1 tablespoon oil 1 large onion, chopped
Serves 4	1 garlic clove, crushed
Calories 360 per portion	1 x 400 g (13 oz) can tomatoes, chopped if liked 125 g (4 oz) mozzarella cheese, sliced salt and pepper basil leaves, to garnish

To make the dough, put the flour and salt into a bowl. Blend the fresh yeast with the water until dissolved, then add to the flour and mix to a firm dough. Knead on a lightly floured surface for 10 minutes. Put the dough into a warm, greased bowl, cover with greased polythene and leave in a warm place until doubled in size.

Heat the oil in a saucepan. Add the onion and garlic and fry until soft. Add the tomatoes and season with salt and pepper. Knead the dough for 2 minutes, roll to a 23 cm (9 inch) circle and place on a greased baking sheet. Top with the tomato mixture and mozzarella slices. Leave to rise in a warm place for 15 minutes. Bake in a preheated oven for 20–25 minutes. Garnish with basil leaves.

■ COOK'S TIP

Instead of fresh yeast use 1 teaspoon dried yeast. To prepare dried yeast dissolve ¼ teaspoon sugar in the water, sprinkle in the yeast and set aside until frothy.

401

potato and courgette omelette

Preparation time 5 minutes	*500 g (1 lb) potatoes, grated* *2 tablespoons olive oil*
Cooking time 20 minutes	*250 g (8 oz) courgettes, coarsely grated* *1 garlic clove, crushed*
Serves 4	*6 eggs, beaten*
Calories 300 per portion	*few drops of Tabasco sauce* *salt and pepper*

Place the potatoes in a sieve and press out the excess moisture. Heat the oil in a large frying pan, add the potatoes and fry quickly until browned and almost cooked, about 10 minutes. Add the courgettes and garlic and cook gently for 5 minutes. Stir in the eggs, Tabasco and salt and pepper and cook gently until just set, about 5 minutes.

Remove the pan from heat, cut the omelette into wedges and serve hot with a mixed salad.

402

cauliflower omelettes

Preparation time 5 minutes	*½ cauliflower, cut into florets* *2 tablespoons double cream*
Cooking time 45 minutes	*pinch of grated nutmeg* *1 egg yolk*
Serves 4	*1 tablespoon grated Parmesan cheese*
Calories 310 per portion	*2 teaspoons chopped basil* *6 eggs* *oil, for frying* *75 g (3 oz) Emmental cheese, grated* *salt* FOR THE GARNISH *tomato wedges* *parsley sprigs*

Place the cauliflower florets in medium saucepan. Add boiling water to cover and a pinch of salt. Bring to the boil, then lower the heat and cook for about 20 minutes.

Drain the cauliflower and blend in a food processor or pass through a fine sieve. Add the cream, nutmeg, egg yolk, Parmesan cheese and basil, mixing well.

Beat the eggs with a little salt. Heat a little oil in a frying pan. When hot, add one quarter of the egg mixture and cook for 2–3 minutes or until set. Spread with one quarter of the cauliflower purée, fold over to enclose the purée and sprinkle generously with one quarter of the Emmental cheese. Place under a preheated hot grill until the cheese melts. Keep the omeletter warm while making three more omelettes in the same way. Garnish with the tomatoes and parsley sprigs and serve.

■ COOK'S TIP

Accompany each omelette with a simple side salad of tomato and basil, served with a vinaigrette dressing enlivened by a splash of soy sauce.

■ COOK'S TIP

The oil should be very hot before the omelette mixture is added to the pan. Immediately turn down the heat (eggs toughen at high temperatures) and, as the omelette begins to cook, draw the sides towards the centre with a spatula.

403

stuffed pancakes

Preparation time 50 minutes	FOR THE BATTER *125 g (4 oz) plain flour* *pinch of salt*
Cooking time about 1 hour	*1 egg, plus 1 yolk, beaten* *300 ml (½ pint) milk*
Oven temperature 200°C (400°F) gas 6	*1 tablespoon vegetable oil* *50 g (2 oz) lard or oil, for frying* FOR THE FILLING
Serves 5	*10 small leeks, trimmed, slit and washed*
Calories 705 per portion	FOR THE SAUCE *75 g (3 oz) butter or margarine* *75 g (3 oz) plain flour* *1 litre (1¾ pints) milk* *salt and pepper* *150 g (5 oz) Parmesan cheese, grated*

To make the batter, place all the ingredients in a food processor and blend until smooth. Use to make 10 pancakes (see Cook's Tip). Set the leeks in a steamer over a pan of boiling water. Cover and cook for 10 minutes until tender. Set aside.

To make the sauce, melt the butter or margarine in a saucepan over a low heat, then add the flour. Cook for 2 minutes, stirring. Gradually add the milk and bring the sauce to the boil, stirring constantly. Simmer gently for 2–3 minutes. Season with salt and pepper. Cool a little and add 125 g (4 oz) of the cheese.

Place 2 leeks and a little of the sauce on each pancake. Roll up and arrange in a greased ovenproof dish. Pour over remaining sauce and sprinkle with the remaining cheese. Bake in a preheated oven for 25–30 minutes.

404

frittata

Preparation time 15 minutes	*25 g (1 oz) butter* *4 eggs, beaten*
Cooking time 7 minutes	*300 g (10 oz) spinach, cooked and lightly* *chopped,*
Serves 2	*3 firm tomatoes, skinned and roughly* *chopped*
Calories 310 per portion	*125 g (4 oz) cooked potatoes, diced, or* *75 g (3 oz) cooked brown rice* *salt and pepper* *½–1 tablespoon chopped sage* *few drops of Tabasco sauce*

Heat half the butter in a large frying pan until sizzling. Pour in the beaten eggs and stir-fry for a few seconds. Allow the eggs to settle in the pan and then distribute the spinach, tomatoes and potatoes or rice evenly over the surface. Sprinkle with salt, pepper, sage and Tabasco sauce. Cook gently for about 4 minutes until the underside is set and golden brown. Gently lift the edge with a fish slice to check. When the underside is done, tip out the frittata out on to a large plate so that the cooked side is on top.

Add the remaining butter to the pan and melt, coating the base. Slice the frittata back into the pan and cook on the other side for about 3 minutes. Cut into quarters and serve hot or cold.

■ COOK'S TIP

For good pancakes, use a frying pan that does not stick. Grease with oil, heat slowly until very hot, then pour in a little batter. Tilt the pan to cover the base, cook to set then turn the pancake and brown the second side.

■ COOK'S TIP

Butter burns more readily than oil and must be carefully watched while melting. To alleviate this problem, use a mixture of butter and oil when frying the fritatta.

405

aubergine galette

Preparation time 50 minutes	*2 large aubergines*
	150 ml (¼ pint) olive oil
Cooking time 1 hour 10 minutes	*1 onion, chopped*
	1 garlic clove, crushed
Oven temperature 180°C (350°F) gas 4	*500 g (1 lb) tomatoes, skinned and chopped*
	1 egg
Serves 4	*250 g (8 oz) ricotta or curd cheese*
Calories 460 per portion	*1 tablespoon sesame seeds, toasted*
	salt and pepper
	crusty wholemeal bread, to serve

Slice the aubergines, sprinkle with salt and leave in a colander for at least 30 minutes. Rinse well and dry on kitchen paper.

Heat 2 tablespoons of the oil in a frying pan and cook the onion until softened. Add the garlic and tomatoes and simmer, uncovered, for 5–7 minutes.

Mix the egg with the ricotta or curd cheese, adding salt and pepper to taste. Heat the remaining oil in a frying pan and cook the aubergine slices on both sides until golden. Drain on absorbent kitchen paper.

Arrange a layer of overlapping aubergine slices on the base and sides of an 18 cm (7 inch) springform cake tin. Cover with half the tomato mixture, then top with half the cheese mixture. Repeat the layers, finishing with aubergine. Cover with foil and bake in a preheated moderate oven for 40–50 minutes. Turn out on to a hot serving dish and sprinkle with the sesame seeds. Serve with wholemeal bread.

406

spinach and potato patties

Preparation time 15 minutes	*1 tablespoon oil*
	1 onion, chopped
Cooking time 20 minutes	*1 garlic clove, crushed*
	250 g (8 oz) frozen chopped spinach, defrosted and drained
Serves 4	*500 g (1 lb) potatoes, boiled and mashed*
Calories 450–340 per portion	*¼ teaspoon grated nutmeg*
	125 g (4 oz) Cheddar cheese, grated
	wholemeal flour for coating
	oil, for shallow-frying
	salt and pepper
	watercress sprigs, to garnish

Heat the oil in a pan and cook the onion and garlic until softened. Squeeze the spinach dry and add to the pan with the potato, nutmeg, cheese and salt and pepper to taste. Mix thoroughly.

Shape the mixture into eight balls, using dampened hands, and flatten slightly. Place some flour in a plastic bag, add the patties one at a time and shake to coat completely.

Fry the patties in hot oil for 2 minutes on each side until golden brown. Garnish with watercress and serve with salad and crusty bread.

■ COOK'S TIP

Toast sesame seeds under the grill or in a dry frying pan for 3–4 minutes, shaking the pan continuously.

■ COOK'S TIP

The peppery flavour of mineral-rich watercress is the perfect foil for these patties.

407

cheesy banana muffins

Preparation time 5 minutes	*4 wholemeal muffins, split in half and* *toasted*
Serves 4	*butter, for spreading*
Calories 210 per portion	*a little yeast extract, for spreading* *(optional)* *75 g (3 oz) low-fat hard cheese, grated* *a little cress* *1 banana, thinly sliced*

Lightly spread the muffins with butter and spread four halves with yeast extract, if liked. Top the yeast-spread muffins with cheese, a sprinkling of cress and a few banana slices. Replace the muffin tops and serve at once with fresh salad ingredients.

408

tofu cakes

Preparation time 15 minutes	*375 g (12 oz) tofu* *6 spring onions, chopped*
Cooking time 10–15 minutes	*2 tablespoons chopped parsley* *3 tablespoons finely chopped walnuts*
Serves 4	*125 g (4 oz) fine wholemeal* *breadcrumbs*
Calories 210 per cake	*2 tablespoons grated Parmesan cheese* *oil, for shallow-frying* *salt and pepper*

Mix the tofu with the spring onions, parsley, nuts, breadcrumbs and Parmesan. Season to taste with salt and pepper. Knead by hand to bind together. Shape the mixture into eight round cakes.

Heat the oil for shallow-frying and fry the cakes in batches until light golden brown, turning once. Drain on absorbent kitchen paper and keep hot while frying the remainder.

Serve with a crisp salad.

■ COOK'S TIP

For a school lunchbox treat, use bread rolls (untoasted) instead of muffins, wrapping them in foil to keep the filling in place. Add a tangerine as a thirst-quencher.

■ COOK'S TIP

Caper cream sauce goes well with these tofu cakes. Simply stir 1 tablespoon chopped capers and 1 teaspoon tomato purée into 150 ml (¼ pint) soured cream or fromage frais and serve as an accompaniment.

409
crunchy tofu

Preparation time
15 minutes, plus chilling

Cooking time
10–15 minutes

Serves 4

Calories
280 per portion

500 g (1 lb) tofu
4 tablespoons plain flour
grated nutmeg
1 egg, beaten
75–125 g (3–4 oz) dry white breadcrumbs
900 ml (1½ pints) oil, for deep-frying
salt and pepper
FOR THE SAUCE
1 large garlic clove, crushed
2 tablespoons tomato purée
4 tablespoons chopped herbs
150 ml (¼ pint) double cream, lightly
   whipped
FOR THE GARNISH
watercress sprigs
lemon wedges

Cut the tofu into slices. Mix the flour, nutmeg and salt and pepper to taste. Coat the tofu in the seasoned flour, beaten egg and breadcrumbs. Cover and chill for 1 hour.

Mix the ingredients for the sauce and chill until required.

Heat the oil for deep frying to 190° (375°F). Fry the tofu until crisp and golden, then drain on absorbent paper. Garnish with watercress and lemon wedges and serve piping hot with the chilled sauce.

410
savoury waffles

Preparation time
10 minutes

Cooking time
20–25 minutes

Makes 10–12

Calories
195–160 per waffle

125 g (4 oz) wholemeal flour
2 teaspoons baking powder
pinch of salt
50 g (2 oz) fine oat flakes
2 eggs, separated
50 g (2 oz) butter or margarine
300 ml (½ pint) milk
FOR THE TOPPING
250 g (8 oz) ricotta cheese
2 tablespoons toasted sunflower seeds
1 tablespoon sesame seeds
4 tomatoes, chopped
4 spring onions, chopped

Mix together the flour, baking powder and salt and stir in the oats. Combine the egg yolks with the butter or margarine and the milk, blending well. Make a well in the dry ingredients, pour in the milk mixture and beat until well blended. Whisk the egg whites until stiff and fold them into the batter.

Prepare a waffle iron, following the manufacturer's instructions. Pour in just enough batter to cover the plates, close the iron and cook quickly for 2 minutes or until the waffle is golden and crisp. Use the rest of the batter in the same way.

To make the topping, lightly mix all the ingredients together. To serve, place a generous spoonful of savoury cheese topping on each waffle.

■ COOK'S TIP

Tofu makes a creamy salad dressing. Simply mash 150 g (5 oz) tofu with 2 tablespoons vegetable oil, 1 tablespoon cider vinegar, 1 teaspoon minced onion and salt and pepper to taste.

■ COOK'S TIP

The oats in these waffles add valuable fibre and a delicious flavour. Buckwheat flakes may be used instead.

411

chinese-style tofu

Preparation time 10 minutes	*1 x 250 g (8 oz) can bamboo shoots, drained*
Cooking time 12 minutes	*375 g (12 oz) tofu* *4 tablespoons oil*
Serves 4	*1 garlic clove* *175 g (6 oz) mangetout, trimmed*
Calories 250 per portion	*4 tablespoons soy sauce* *2 tablespoons roasted sesame seeds*

Slice, then shred the bamboo shoots. Cut the tofu into 5 mm (¼ inch) thick slices.

Heat the oil in a wok or large frying pan and crush the garlic into it. Add the tofu and fry the slices until crisp and golden, then remove them from the wok with a slotted spoon and drain on kitchen paper.

Add the mangetout and bamboo shoots to the wok and stir-fry for 5 minutes. Sprinkle the soy sauce and sesame seeds over them. Return the tofu to the wok and cook for a further minute then serve. A rice dish makes the ideal accompaniment.

412

tofu with leeks

Preparation time 15 minutes, plus marinating	*325 g (11 oz) tofu, cubed* *4 tablespoons soy sauce* *1 tablespoon dry sherry*
Cooking time 20 minutes	*1½ tablespoons wholemeal flour* *2 tablespoons oil*
Serves 4	*250 g (8 oz) leeks, thinly sliced* *1 garlic clove, finely chopped*
Calories 155 per portion	*125 ml (4 fl oz) vegetable stock* *1 red pepper, cored, deseeded and diced* *2 tablespoons chopped parsley* *white pepper* *gomasio, for sprinkling*

Place the tofu in a bowl. Pour over the soy sauce and sherry and marinate for at least 30 minutes.

Drain the tofu, reserving the marinade, and coat in the flour. Heat the oil in a frying pan and fry the tofu until brown and crisp, stirring frequently. Remove and keep hot.

Add the leeks and garlic to the pan and fry them over a moderate to high heat until coated in oil. Add the stock and reserved marinade. Bring to the boil, cover and simmer for 5–7 minutes.

Season the sauce to taste with pepper. Arrange the tofu on the vegetables and serve sprinkled with red pepper, parsley and gomasio.

■ COOK'S TIP

Tofu, or bean curd, is made from ground, soaked soya beans – it is a sort of soya cheese. It is tasteless on its own and has a texture which is reminiscent of a chilled custard. However, it is high in food value (protein) and can be seasoned and flavoured in any number of dishes. You can buy tofu in health food stores and Chinese supermarkets. Traditionally used in Chinese cooking, it is also used in lots of vegetarian dishes.

■ COOK'S TIP

Salt substitute, gomasio or sesame salt, is available from health food stores. To make your own, simply grind 4–5 parts roasted sesame seeds with one part salt. Gomasio will keep in an airtight container for up to 2–3 weeks.

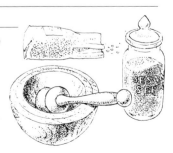

413

sunflower snacks

Preparation time 20 minutes	*125 g (4 oz) sunflower seeds, ground*
Cooking time 10–12 minutes	*125 g (4 oz) fresh wholemeal breadcrumbs*
Serves 4	*2 tablespoons grated Parmesan cheese*
Calories 285 per portion	*1 garlic clove, crushed*
	1 large egg, lightly beaten
	about 50 g (2 oz) wholemeal flour
	oil, for deep-frying
	salt and pepper

Mix together the ground sunflower seeds, breadcrumbs, Parmesan, a little salt and pinch of pepper in a bowl. Stir in the garlic, then add the beaten egg and mix well to bind the ingredients together.

Using floured hands, roll the mixture into small balls. Season the flour with salt and pepper and sprinkle on a plate. Dip each ball into the flour to coat thoroughly.

Heat the oil for deep-frying and fry the balls, in batches, until crisp and golden. Drain on kitchen paper.

414

nutty fruit salad

Preparation time 10 minutes	*2 dessert apples, cored and chopped*
Serves 2	*2 celery sticks, chopped*
Calories 210 per portion	*2 tablespoons sultanas*
	8 walnut halves, chopped
	50 g (2 oz) drained canned red kidney beans
	4 tablespoons natural yogurt
	shredded crisp lettuce leaves
	2 kiwifruit, sliced, to decorate

Mix the apples, celery, sultanas, walnuts and kidney beans, then coat with the yogurt.

Serve on a bed of shredded lettuce and kiwifruit slices. This salad is idea for a packed lunch.

■ COOK'S TIP

Serve these irresistible morsels as a cocktail party snack. Supply plenty of cocktail sticks with which to spear them.

■ COOK'S TIP

Kiwifruit came originally from China and are now largely grown in New Zealand, hence the name. They are rich in vitamin C. Peel before cutting in slices or wedges to reveal their pretty interior.

415

walnut dip

Preparation time 15 minutes, plus chilling	*375 g (12 oz) Lancashire cheese, grated*
	150 ml (¼ pint) single cream
	3 tablespoons milk
Serves 6	*4 spring onions, chopped*
Calories 350 per portion	*salt and pepper*
	125 g (4 oz) walnuts, finely chopped

Pound the cheese with the cream until very well mixed, then beat in the milk, onions, reserving a few rings for garnish if liked, and salt and pepper until creamy. Add the walnuts, spoon into a dish and chill for 1 hour before serving. Plain biscuits or toast, celery and crisp apples make good accompaniments.

416

hummus

Preparation time 5 minutes, plus soaking	*250 g (8 oz) chickpeas, soaked overnight*
	150 ml (¼ pint) tahini
Cooking time 2¼ hours	*3 garlic cloves, roughly chopped*
	juice of 1–2 lemons
Serves 8–10	*salt and pepper*
	FOR THE GARNISH
Calories 210–170 per portion	*1 tablespoon olive oil blended with 1 teaspoon paprika*
	2 teaspoons chopped parsley

Drain the chickpeas, place them in a saucepan and cover with cold water. Bring to the boil, cover and boil rapidly for 10 minutes, then simmer gently for 1½–2 hours, until soft; the time will vary depending on the age and quality of the chickpeas. Drain, reserving 300 ml (½ pint) of the liquid.

Place the chickpeas in a food processor or blender, add all the remaining ingredients and season with salt and pepper to taste. Add some of the reserved cooking liquid and blend to a soft creamy paste.

Turn into a shallow serving dish, drizzle over the blended oil and sprinkle with the parsley. Serve with pitta bread.

■ COOK'S TIP

A white cheese with a crumbly texture, Lancashire has a mild flavour which develops as it matures. It is an excellent cheese for toasting.

■ COOK'S TIP

This is a tasty starter which is easy to make. It will keep for up to a week, covered, in the refrigerator.

417

tofu and avocado spread

Preparation time
10 minutes, plus chilling

Serves 2

Calories
320 per portion

250 g (8 oz) silken tofu
1 ripe avocado
2 tablespoons mayonnaise
½ teaspoon salt
1 teaspoon lemon juice
2 teaspoons finely chopped onion
4 drops of Tabasco sauce
a little cayenne

Break up the tofu with a fork. Halve the avocado, remove the stone and scoop out all the flesh. Mash the flesh and add to the tofu together with the mayonnaise, salt, lemon juice, onion, Tabasco and cayenne to taste. Mix well and chill for about 1 hour. Serve with toast or wholewheat bread or rolls.

418

breakfast special

Preparation time
10 minutes

Serves 8

Calories
250 per portion

250 g (8 oz) rolled oats
50 g (2 oz) wheatgerm
125 g (4 oz) small dried apricots, chopped
175 g (6 oz) sultanas
50 g (2 oz) walnuts, roughly chopped
½ pear (per portion), peeled, cored and grated
brown sugar or honey, optional
milk or natural yogurt to serve

Mix together the cereals, dried fruit and nuts. Store in an airtight container. To serve, add grated pear to each portion, sprinkle with sugar or honey and serve with milk or yogurt.

■ COOK'S TIP

What a combination! Protein-rich tofu and vitamin-packed avocado. With wholemeal bread providing carbohydrate, this makes a well-balanced meal.

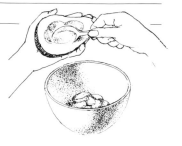

■ COOK'S TIP

Seasonal fruits make a juicy addition: fresh peach slices, cherry halves, raspberries and strawberries are among the naturally sweet possibilities.

419

spiced muesli

Preparation time	*250 g (8 oz) rolled oats*
5 minutes	*250 g (8 oz) barley flakes or kernels,*
Makes	*sesame and sunflower seeds, bran and*
575 g (1¼ lb) muesli	*wheatgerm, mixed according to taste*
Calories	*2 teaspoons cinnamon*
360 per 100 g (4 oz)	*1 teaspoon grated nutmeg*
	grated rind of 1 lemon
	50 g (2 oz) mixed nuts, chopped
	50 g (2 oz) seedless raisins and coarsely
	chopped dried fruit (apples, apricots,
	dates, figs), mixed according to taste

Put the oats in a large mixing bowl, then stir in all the remaining ingredients.

Store the muesli in a tin or another suitable airtight container and use as required. Serve with brown sugar or honey and milk, cream or yogurt. Seasonal fresh fruit may be added, if liked.

420

hazelnut toasts

Preparation time	*1 tablespoon nutri-grain cereal (rye and*
5 minutes	*oats with hazelnuts)*
Cooking time	*1 tablespoon cottage cheese*
3–4 minutes	*½ small tomato, skinned and chopped*
Serves 1	*2 mushrooms, chopped*
Calories	*pinch of dried mixed herbs*
136 per portion	*1 slice wholemeal bread, toasted*

Mix together the cereal, cottage cheese, tomato, mushrooms and mixed herbs. Spread this over the slice of toast, making sure it comes right to the edge. Heat under a moderate grill and cook until the topping is golden brown. Serve hot.

■ COOK'S TIP

To get a good muesli base, make with a mixture of different grains and seeds. Bran is dry, wheatgerm has a strong flavour and sesame seeds are dry, so use sparingly.

■ COOK'S TIP

For children, cut the bread into fancy shapes using large biscuit cutters.

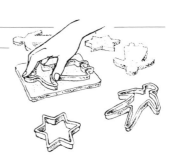

desserts

The final impression of a meal is made by the dessert, so always bear in mind the preceding courses when choosing a dessert. Follow a light main course with a substantial treat, like Gourmet Bread and Butter Pudding or Chestnut Roulade. On the other hand, a light dessert such as Nectarine Brulée provides the perfect refreshing finish to a heavier main course. Whatever you decide upon, this chapter will provide the inspiration for the finishing touch.

iced orange cups

Preparation time 25 minutes, plus freezing Serves 4 Calories 225 per portion	*2 oranges* *50 g (2 oz) caster sugar* *125 ml (4 fl oz) whipping cream* *125 ml (4 fl oz) thick Greek yogurt* *50 g (2 oz) raisins* *2 glacé cherries, chopped* *1 tablespoon brandy*

Using a small sharp knife, cut the oranges in half with zig-zag cuts. Scoop out the flesh with a teaspoon and press it through a sieve to extract the juice. Mix the juice with the sugar. Whip the cream until thick, then fold in the yogurt and orange juice. Pour into a shallow container and freeze until set 2.5 cm (1 inch) in from the edges.

Meanwhile, macerate the raisins and cherries in the brandy.

Turn the frozen mixture into a cold bowl and whisk to remove any large lumps. Stir in the raisin mixture and pour into the orange shells. Set these on a tray with absorbent kitchen paper underneath to keep them steady. Return to the freezer until firm, about 2 hours.

nectarine brulée

Preparation time 15 minutes Cooking time 15 minutes Serves 6 Calories 230 per portion	*500 g (1 lb) nectarines, stoned and sliced* *4 tablespoons orange liqueur, plus extra* * to flavour fruit* *350 ml (12 fl oz) soured cream* *pinch of grated nutmeg* *1 teaspoon vanilla essence* *125 g (4 oz) soft light brown sugar*

Cover the nectarines with water in a saucepan. Bring to the boil, then poach gently for 5–10 minutes or until soft. Drain and transfer to a flameproof casserole. Stir in a little of the orange liqueur for flavour.

Beat together the soured cream, nutmeg, vanilla and the remaining orange liqueur until blended. Spoon the mixture over the nectarine slices then scatter the brown sugar over the top in a thick layer. Grill under a preheated hot grill for a few minutes until the sugar caramelizes. Serve immediately.

■ COOK'S TIP

Pack a crumpled piece of greaseproof paper around the oranges to make quite certain that they do not fall over in the freezer.

■ COOK'S TIP

Use fresh apricots, peaches or pineapple instead of nectarines. Double cream can be used instead of soured cream. Replace the nutmeg with cinnamon and the orange liqueur with rum, if preferred.

apricot and orange glories

Preparation time
20 minutes, plus setting

Serves 4

Calories
245 per portion

2 x 185 g (6½ oz) cans apricot halves in fruit juice
1 orange jelly tablet (see Cook's Tip)
150 ml (¼ pint) boiling water
300 ml (½ pint) natural yogurt
2 tablespoons clear honey
4 fresh cherries with stalks

Drain the juice from the apricots and make up to 300 ml (½ pint) with water. Reserve 4 apricot halves and slice the remainder. Dissolve the jelly tablet in the boiling water then stir in the fruit juice. Pour into a shallow container and chill until set.

Turn out the jelly on to a wet work surface and chop it into small dice with a wet knife. Mix together the yogurt and honey, then layer the jelly, yogurt and apricot slices in 4 individual tall glasses. Top each one with an apricot half, hollow side up, and add a cherry as a final touch.

fruit baskets

Preparation time
30 minutes, plus standing and chilling

Cooking time
10 minutes

Oven temperature
180°C (350°F) gas 4

Serves 4

Calories
315 per portion

125 g (4 oz) plain flour
125 g (4 oz) icing sugar
3 egg whites
few drops of orange essence
25 g (1 oz) flaked almonds
1 ripe pear, cored and sliced
a little lemon juice
FOR THE SAUCE
2 slices fresh pineapple, peeled, cored and chopped
125 ml (4 fl oz) pineapple juice
1–2 drops yellow food colouring
125 ml (4 fl oz) natural yogurt
FILLING AND DECORATION
375 g (12 oz) seasonal fruit
1 tablespoon icing sugar

Sift the flour and icing sugar, then beat in the egg whites until smooth. Leave to stand for 1–2 hours. Stir in the orange essence and almonds.

Mark four 18 cm (7 inch) circles on baking sheets lined with nonstick baking parchment. Spread the batter in the marked circles. Cook in a preheated oven for 8 minutes until pale golden. Allow to cool for about a minute, then ease off the baking sheets with a palette knife and mould (see Cook's Tip).

Simmer the pineapple juice and colouring for 2 minutes then blend in a food processor or blender. Chill for 1 hour then mix in the yogurt. Place each basket on a pool of pineapple sauce. Fill and decorate the biscuit baskets as shown.

▪ COOK'S TIP

Vegetarian table jelly crystals are available in 100 g (3½ oz) tubs. To use, place the powdered crystals in a large bowl, pour in 200 ml (⅓ pint) boiling water, stir briskly, then add the fruit juice. Proceed as in the recipe above.

▪ COOK'S TIP

Shaping the biscuits: cut a fine slice off 4 oranges, so they stand well. Grease with oil thencarefully slide a biscuit off the tray and lift over an orange. Press gently and flute the edges. Lift off when cold.

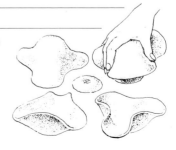

425

crunchy pear layer

Preparation time
10–15 minutes

Cooking time
35 minutes

Oven temperature
180°C (350°F)
gas 4

Serves 4

Calories
305 per portion

*500 g (1 lb) cooking pears, peeled, cored
and quartered*
3 tablespoons water
1–2 teaspoons ground ginger
150 g (5 oz) demerara sugar
50 g (2 oz) butter
50 g (2 oz) fresh breadcrumbs
150 ml (¼ pint) single cream, to serve

Cook the pears gently in the water with the ginger and 50 g (2 oz) of the sugar until tender. Slice one of the poached pear quarters and reserve for decoration.

Melt the butter in a frying pan and fry the breadcrumbs with the remaining sugar until crisp. Layer the pears and crunchy crumbs in a buttered ovenproof dish, finishing with a layer of crumbs.

Bake in a moderate oven for 30 minutes and serve hot or cold. Decorate with the reserved pear slices and serve with a jug of cream.

426

winter fruit compote

Preparation time
15 minutes, plus
soaking

Cooking time
30 minutes

Oven temperature
190°C (375°F)
gas 5

Serves 4

Calories
305 per portion

250 g (8 oz) dried apricots
125 g (4 oz) stoned dried prunes
600 ml (1 pint) unsweetened orange juice
2 oranges
125 g (4 oz) raisins
2 small bananas, thickly sliced
natural yogurt, to serve

Place the apricots and prunes in a bowl and pour over the orange juice. Cover and leave to soak overnight.

Using a serrated knife, peel the oranges and remove all the pith. Cut in between the membranes to separate the orange segments. Stir into the fruit mixture with the raisins and bananas and turn into an ovenproof dish. Cover and cook in a preheated oven for about 30 minutes. Serve warm with natural yogurt.

■ COOK'S TIP

Use crushed ginger biscuits instead of the breadcrumbs, or try hazelnut biscuits for a delicious combination of flavours.

■ COOK'S TIP

The fruit may be plumped in a microwave oven, if preferred. Combine the apricots, prunes, raisins and orange juice in a bowl, cover lightly and cook for 5 minutes on Full power. Cool slightly before adding the oranges and bananas.

427

plum flapjack crumble

Preparation time
15 minutes

Cooking time
30 minutes

Oven temperature
180°C (350°F)
gas 4

Serves 4

Calories
380 per portion

1 kg (2 lb) plums, halved and stoned
5 tablespoons apple juice
125 g (4 oz) rolled oats
50 g (2 oz) soft brown sugar
1 teaspoon mixed spice
50 g (2 oz) unsalted peanuts, roughly
  chopped
50 g (2 oz) polyunsaturated margarine,
  melted
Greek yogurt or vanilla ice cream,
  to serve (optional)

Place the plums in a covered pan with the apple juice and cook gently for about 10 minutes, until starting to soften. Transfer the plums with their juices to a greased 1.8 litre (3 pint) ovenproof dish.

Mix together the oats, sugar, mixed spice and peanuts in a bowl. Add the margarine and mix thoroughly. Spread evenly over the top of the plums, pressing down lightly with the back of a spoon. Bake in a preheated oven for 20 minutes, until the topping is crunchy and golden brown. Serve hot with thick Greek yogurt or vanilla ice cream, if liked.

428

carnival figs

Preparation time
15 minutes, plus
chilling

Serves 4

Calories
135 per portion

8 fresh figs
1 x 300 ml (½ pint) soured cream
4 tablespoons crème de cacao
grated chocolate or fig slices, to decorate

Place the figs in an ovenproof bowl, pour over boiling water to cover and leave for 1 minute. Drain thoroughly and peel off the skins. Cut each fig into quarters and place in a serving bowl.

Combine the soured cream and crème de cacao and pour over the figs. Decorate with grated chocolate or fig pieces or slices. Chill for at least 1 hour before serving.

■ COOK'S TIP

Instead of cooking fruits in sugar syrup, try using natural juices, as in this recipe. The edible leaves of herbs such as apple-scented geranium may be added to give a subtle flavour and fragrance.

■ COOK'S TIP

Try using orange curaçao
instead of crème de cacao,
and decorate with grated
orange rind.

429

orange russe

Preparation time
30 minutes, plus setting

Serves 6

Calories
350 per portion

about 21 sponge fingers
grated rind and juice of 2 oranges
1 teaspoon lemon juice
2 teaspoons agar-agar or 3 teaspoons
  powdered gelatine
150 g (5 oz) blue Brie cheese
125 g (4 oz) curd cheese
50 g (2 oz) caster sugar
2 egg whites
150 ml (¼ pint) whipping cream
few strips of blanched orange rind,
  to decorate

Base-line an 18 cm (7 inch) loose-bottomed cake tin. Trim the sponge fingers to 7.5 cm (3 inches) in length. Stand the fingers, trimmed side downwards and sugar side out, around the edges of the tin (see Cook's Tip).

Heat the orange and lemon juices to just below boiling. Add the agar-agar and stir until dissolved. Set aside to cool. Thinly de-rind the blue Brie. Beat with the curd cheese, sugar and orange rind until smooth. Gradually add the cooled gelatine mixture. Leave until on the point of setting.

Whisk the egg whites until stiff but not dry, then whip the cream until it holds its shape. Fold just over half the cream into the setting cheese mixture, then add the egg whites. Pour into the biscuit-lined tin and level the surface. Refrigerate until set.

Remove from the tin to serve and decorate with the reserved cream and strips of blanched orange rind.

430

st clement's cheesecake

Preparation time
30 minutes, plus chilling

Cooking time
5 minutes

Serves 8–10

Calories
390–315 per portion

75 g (3 oz) unsalted butter
175 g (6 oz) digestive or gingernut
  biscuits, crushed
FOR THE FILLING
2 eggs, separated
50 g (2 oz) caster sugar
375 g (12 oz) low-fat cream cheese,
  lightly creamed
150 ml (¼ pint) whipping cream, lightly
  whipped
1 x 135 g (4¾ oz) packet lemon jelly
200 ml (7 fl oz) boiling water
TO DECORATE
1 large orange, peeled and segmented
1 small lemon, peeled and segmented
mint sprig

Lightly grease a 20 cm (8 inch) loose-bottomed cake tin. Melt the butter in a saucepan, mix in the crushed biscuits and press on to the base of the tin. Chill. Beat together the egg yolks and sugar until very thick and pale. Fold in the cheese and cream. Dissolve the jelly in the boiling water. Cool, then stir into the cheese mixture. Whisk the egg whites stiffly, and fold into the mixture. Pour over the biscuit base and chill until firm.

Remove the cheesecake from the tin and decorate as shown.

■ COOK'S TIP

If the sponge fingers slither sideways in the tin, stand them upright and secure each to the tin with a tiny knob of butter.

■ COOK'S TIP

When you are making cakes and biscuits it is worth having the butter at room temperature before you start. The best way to achieve this quickly is to put it in the microwave, on high, for a couple of seconds.

431

spiced sultana cheesecake

Preparation time
30 minutes

Cooking time
1 hour

Oven temperature
180°C (350°F)
gas 4

Serves 8–10

Calories
330–265 per portion

FOR THE BASE
50 g (2 oz) caster sugar
75 g (3 oz) butter
1 egg
125 g (4 oz) self-raising flour
½ teaspoon cinnamon
½ teaspoon mixed spice
FOR THE TOPPING
250 g (8 oz) cottage cheese, sieved
250 g (8 oz) low-fat soft cheese
2 eggs, separated
grated rind and juice of 2 lemons
50 g (2 oz) caster sugar
2 tablespoons cornflour
150 ml (¼ pint) low-fat double cream
50 g (2 oz) sultanas

Beat together the sugar and butter until creamy. Stir in the egg, flour and spices. Mix to a soft dough, press into the base of a greased 20–25 cm (8–10 inch) round loose-bottomed tin.

Beat together the cheeses, egg yolks, lemon rind and juice, caster sugar and cornflour. Whip the cream until its holds it shape and fold into the cheese mixture. Whisk the egg whites until stiff and add to the mixture, with the sultanas. Spoon over the base. Bake in a preheated oven for about 1 hour, until the centre is firm to the touch. Partly cool in the tin and then remove to cool completely. Serve chilled.

■ COOK'S TIP

Thick and creamy mandarin yogurt
may be used instead of the
double cream if preferred. The
cheesecake will not be quite so
light, but it will taste delicious.

432

danish apple pudding

Preparation time
15–20 minutes, plus
cooling

Cooking time
25–30 minutes

Serves 4

Calories
455 per portion

625 (1¼ lb) cooking apples, peeled, cored
and sliced
75 g (3 oz) butter
sugar, to taste
75 g (3 oz) granulated sugar
125 g (4 oz) white breadcrumbs
TO DECORATE
150 ml (¼ pint) whipping or double
cream, whipped
redcurrant jelly (optional)

Place the apples in a saucepan with a small amount of water and cook gently until soft. Mash with a fork, adding 25 g (1 oz) of the butter and sugar to taste. Leave to cool completely.

Melt the remaining butter in a saucepan. Add the granulated sugar and the breadcrumbs. Cook gently for 20–25 minutes, stirring frequently, until the crumbs are golden. Cool completely.

Arrange alternate layers of apple and crumb mixture in a glass serving bowl, finishing with a layer of crumbs. Decorate the apple pudding with the whipped cream, and top with teaspoons of redcurrant jelly if wished.

■ COOK'S TIP

To prevent the breadcrumbs
from becoming soggy, serve
this traditional Danish cake as
soon as it is assembled.

433

pavlova

Preparation time
30 minutes, plus
cooling

Cooking time
1 hour

Oven temperature
150°C (300°F)
gas 2, then 140°C
(275°F) gas 1

Serves 6

Calories
360 per portion

FOR THE MERINGUE
3 egg whites
200 g (7 oz) light soft brown sugar
1 teaspoon cornflour
1 teaspoon white wine vinegar
1 teaspoon vanilla essence
FOR THE FILLING
150 g (5 oz) blue Brie cheese
300 ml (½ pint) double or whipping
  cream
500 g (1 lb) fresh fruit

Draw a 23 cm (9 inch) circle on a piece of nonstick baking parchment then place this paper, pencil side down, on a baking sheet.

Whisk the egg whites until very stiff and dry. Gradually whisk in the sugar. Mix together the cornflour, vinegar and vanilla and whisk into the meringue mixture. Turn on to the prepared baking sheet and spread inside the marked circle, making a slight wall around the edge. Place in a preheated oven and immediately turn down the heat to the lower temperature. Bake for 1 hour then turn off the heat and leave the meringue to cool in the oven, preferably overnight.

Thinly derind the cheese, place in a bowl and beat until soft. Lightly whip the cream, add to the cheese and whisk until stiff. Prepare the fruit, reserve some for decoration and pile the remainder into the meringue case. Cover completely with the cream and decorate.

434

hot spiced peaches

Preparation time
10 minutes

Cooking time
15–20 minutes

Oven temperature
180°C (350°F) gas 4

Serves 4

Calories
112 per portion

4 large ripe fresh peaches
grated rind of 1 lemon
¼ teaspoon ground cinnamon
2 tablespoons clear honey
15 g (½ oz) unsalted butter

First skin the peaches. Dip them one at a time into boiling water and the skins will slide off very easily. Cut each peach in half and twist to separate the halves, then remove the stone.

Arrange the peach halves cut side up in an ovenproof dish. Sprinkle with the lemon rind and cinnamon then spoon the honey over the top.

Place a dot of butter in the cavity of each peach, cover the dish and bake for about 20 minutes, until the peaches are tender and juicy.

■ COOK'S TIP

The mixture of cheese and cream in the topping adds a new dimension to this most popular of dinner party desserts. Assemble as near to the time of serving as possible for best results.

■ COOK'S TIP

A delightful late summer pudding. Serve the peaches hot from the oven with cream. If peaches are not available, look for fresh nectarines instead.

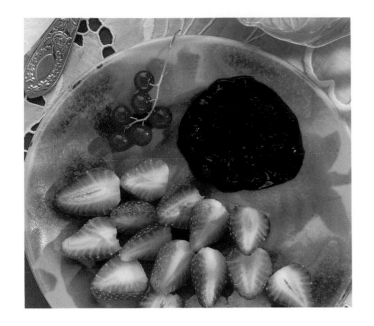

435

strawberries with blackcurrant sauce

Preparation time 25 minutes plus cooling	*250 g (8 oz) fresh blackcurrants, stems removed*
Cooking time 5 minutes	*2 tablespoons clear honey* *3 tablespoons red wine*
Serves 4	*375 g (12 oz) ripe strawberries, hulled and halved*
Calories 75 per portion	*small sprigs of fresh redcurrants, to decorate*

Put the trimmed blackcurrants into a pan with the honey and red wine; stir well then simmer gently until the natural fruit juices are released (about 5 minutes).

Blend the lightly cooked blackcurrants and their liquid in a food processor until fairly smooth; the sauce should still have some texture. Allow to cool.

Arrange the halved strawberries in small decorative dishes and spoon the blackcurrant sauce beside them. Decorate with clusters of fresh redcurrants.

436

cherry cobbler

Preparation time 25 minutes	*2 tablespoons orange juice* *40 g (1½ oz) light muscovado sugar*
Cooking time 50 minutes	*1 bay leaf* *1 kg (2 lb) dessert cherries, pitted*
Oven temperature 200°C (400°F) gas 6	FOR THE COBBLER DOUGH *250 g (8 oz) wholemeal self-raising flour* *1 teaspoon baking powder*
Serves 6	*salt* *pinch of grated nutmeg*
Calories 320 per portion	*50 g (2 oz) soft margarine* *40 g (1½ oz) demerara sugar* *1 teaspoon grated orange rind* *2 tablespoons orange juice* *1 egg, beaten* *100 m1 (3½ fl oz) natural yogurt*

Put the orange juice, sugar and bay leaf into a frying pan and stir over low heat until the sugar has dissolved. Add the cherries, reserving a few for decoration, and simmer for about 10 minutes, shaking the pan frequently, until they are just tender. Turn the cherries into a baking dish and discard the bay leaf.

Make the cobbler dough (see Cook's Tip).

Roll out the dough on a lightly floured board until it is 2 cm (¼ inch) thick. Use a heart-shaped biscuit cutter to cut out the dough. Arrange the scone shapes over the fruit, brush with milk and sprinkle on a little sugar.

Bake the pudding in a preheated oven for 35 minutes or until the topping is well risen and golden brown. Serve hot.

■ COOK'S TIP

This is an ideal dessert for slimmers and is rich in vitamin C. For a treat, try serving it with a scoop of Strawberry and yogurt ice (see recipe 449).

■ COOK'S TIP

To make the cobbler dough, mix the dry ingredients together, rub in the margarine, stir in the sugar and grated orange rind, then the orange juice, egg and yogurt. Shape the mixture into a ball in the mixing bowl and knead lightly.

437

strawberries with cointreau

Preparation time	750 g (1½ lb) small ripe strawberries,
10 minutes, plus macerating	hulled and washed
	2–3 tablespoons fruit sugar
Serves 4	3 tablespoons Cointreau or other orange
Calories	liqueur
121 per portion	thin strips of rind from 1 large, well-scrubbed orange

Put the strawberries into a bowl and sprinkle with the fruit sugar and Cointreau. Add the orange rind, stir gently, then cover and leave to macerate for 1 hour. Serve on individual plates, with the macerating liquid spooned over the strawberries.

438

green fruit pudding

Preparation time	10 large slices wholemeal bread, crusts
25 minutes, plus chilling	removed
	4–5 tablespoons clear honey
Cooking time	375 g (12 oz) gooseberries, topped and
20 minutes	tailed
Serves 6	375 g (12 oz) greengages, stoned and
Calories	roughly chopped
190 per portion	2 small cooking apples, peeled, cored and thinly sliced
	few mint or scented geranium leaves, to decorate
	chilled Greek yogurt, to serve

Line a greased 1.2 litre (2 pint) bowl or pudding basin with bread, cutting and fitting it to ensure there are no gaps.

Melt the honey in a large frying pan over low heat. Add all the fruit, reserving a few gooseberries for decoration. Shake the pan and simmer gently for about 12–15 minutes, until the fruit is quite tender.

Spoon a little of the juice over the bread, then pour in the fruit to fill the lined bowl. Cover the top with the remaining bread, taking great care to fit it closely and neatly around the rim. Cover the bowl with a saucer that just fits inside the rim then weigh it down with a large filled can or something equally large and heavy. Chill the pudding overnight.

To serve, run a knife around the edge of the pudding and unmould it on to a flat serving plate. Decorate the pudding with the reserved gooseberries and geranium leaves and serve it cold, cut into wedges, with chilled Greek yogurt.

■ COOK'S TIP

Serve this dessert with Greek yogurt or some thin shortbread biscuits.

■ COOK'S TIP

This is an autumn version of a traditional summer pudding. For summer pudding, use strawberries, raspberries, redcurrants and blackcurrants.

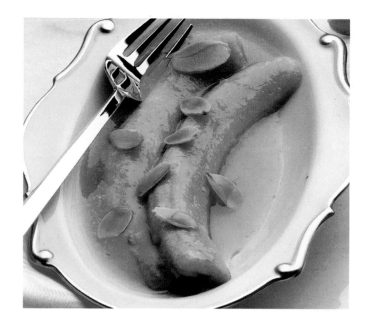

439

bananas flambé

Preparation time	4 *medium bananas, halved lengthways*
3–4 minutes	50 *g (2 oz) butter, melted*
Cooking time	50 *g (2 oz) light brown sugar*
3–4 minutes	4 *tablespoons brandy*
Serves 4	*flaked almonds, toasted, to decorate*
Calories	
295 per portion	

Fry the bananas in the melted butter until they are golden and just tender.

Sprinkle in the sugar and stir carefully to coat the fruit. Stir in the brandy. Bring to the boil. Immediately set it alight, using a long taper, and, once the flames have died, serve sprinkled with a few flaked almonds.

440

grape cheesecake

Preparation time	175 *g (6 oz) wholemeal biscuits, crushed*
20 minutes	75 *g (3 oz) butter or margarine, melted*
Cooking time	500 *g (1 lb) curd or cream cheese*
1½ hours	150 *ml (¼ pint) natural yogurt*
Oven temperature	4 *tablespoons clear honey*
160°C (325°F)	50 *g (2 oz) Demerara sugar*
gas 3	4 *medium eggs*
Serves 6	2 *tablespoons ground almonds*
Calories	1 *teaspoon vanilla extract or essence*
555 per portion	FOR THE TOPPING
	150 *ml (¼ pint) soured cream*
	125 *g (4 oz) each black and green grapes,*
	halved and deseeded
	3 *tablespoons clear honey*

To make the crust, mix together the biscuit crumbs and melted butter or margarine. Spoon into the bottom of a 20 cm (8 inch) loose-bottom or spring-clip flan tin. Press down firmly.

Put the filling ingredients into a bowl and beat together until smooth and creamy. Pour on to the crumb crust and spread evenly. Bake the cheesecake in a preheated oven for 1–1¼ hours until firm in the centre. Remove the crumb crust from the oven and carefully spoon the soured cream on top, gently levelling it with a knife. Turn off the heat but put the cheesecake back in the still-warm oven for 15–20 minutes.

When cold, lift the cheesecake out of the tin. Arrange the grapes on top. Put the honey into a small saucepan and heat, then spoon or brush it over the grapes. Leave to cool before serving.

■ COOK'S TIP

Use a frying pan, not a deep-sided pan to flambé the fruit. It will be easier – and safer – to set the brandy alight from the side of the pan, not over the top.

■ COOK'S TIP

If a loose-bottomed tin is not available, grease and line a 20 cm (8 inch) deep cake tin and place double thickness foil strips in a cross to lift out the cheesecake when set.

441

tropical fruits in sherry

Preparation time 10 minutes, plus macerating **Serves 4** **Calories** 118 per portion Suitable for vegans	*1 papaya (pawpaw)* *2 kiwifruit* *2 small bananas* *1 tablespoon lemon juice* *150 ml (¼ pint) medium or dry sherry* *mint sprigs, to decorate*

Using a sharp knife, peel the papaya, cut it in half and scrape out the black seeds. Cut the flesh into long slices and put them into a small bowl. Peel the kiwifruit, cut them into slices and add to the bowl of papaya slices.

Peel the bananas and cut them into slices. Put into another bowl and sprinkle with the lemon juice to stop them discolouring. Add the bananas to the other fruits and pour the sherry over them. Cover the bowl and leave to macerate for 2 hours in the refrigerator.

Spoon the fruits carefully into 4 glasses, adding a little of the sherry to each one. Decorate with mint sprigs and serve.

442

apricot fool

Preparation time 10 minutes, plus chilling **Cooking time** 30 minutes **Serves 4** **Calories** 218 per portion	*250 g (8 oz) dried apricots, covered with boiling water, soaked overnight, then simmered for 20–30 minutes until tender* *275 g (9 oz) thick Greek yogurt* *honey or fruit sugar, to taste* *a few toasted flaked almonds*

Purée the apricots in a food processor or blender. Mix with the yogurt. Sweeten to taste with honey or fruit sugar. Spoon into individual glasses or bowls and chill in the refrigerator. Sprinkle with toasted almonds before serving.

■ COOK'S TIP

Papayas are large, greeny-yellow pear-shaped fruits with an orange flesh. The dark seeds should be discarded. Buy when just beginning to soften.

■ COOK'S TIP

Instead of dried apricots, try using prunes, peaches or pears. Prunes will add a sweet taste, so will not need added sugar. Instead of almonds, try hazelnuts.

443

pears with fresh raspberry sauce

Preparation time
about 20 minutes,
plus cooling

Cooking time
10 minutes

Serves 4

Calories
120 per portion

4 large firm pears
300 ml (½ pint) orange juice
1 bay leaf
small piece of cinnamon stick
1 tablespoon clear honey
250 g (8 oz) fresh raspberries

Peel, halve and core the pears. Place them in a saucepan with the orange juice, bay leaf, cinnamon stick and honey. Cover the pan and simmer gently for 10 minutes.

Turn the pear halves over in their cooking liquid. Cover the pan and leave them to cool in their liquid.

Blend the raspberries in a food processor or blender until smooth; add sufficient of the pear cooking liquid to give a thin coating consistency.

Arrange the drained pear halves in a shallow serving dish and trickle over the prepared sauce.

444

greengage fool

Preparation time
30 minutes, plus
chilling

Cooking time
10–15 minutes

Serves 4

Calories
85 per portion

500 g (1 lb) ripe fresh greengages
juice of 1 orange
150 ml (¼ pint) skimmed milk
15 g (½ oz) cornflour
sugar or artificial sweetener, to taste
4 tablespoons natural yogurt
halved orange slices, to decorate

Put the greengages into a saucepan with the orange juice; cover the pan and simmer gently until the fruit is just tender. Remove all the stones and leave the fruit to cool.

Blend 2 tablespoons of the milk with the cornflour. Heat the remaining milk in a pan and then stir into the cornflour paste. Return to the saucepan and stir over a gentle heat until the sauce has thickened. Add a little sugar or sweetener to taste.

Cool the sauce and then mix it with the cooled greengages. Stir in the yogurt.

Spoon the fool into stemmed glass dishes and chill for 2 hours before serving. Garnish each portion with a halved orange slice.

■ COOK'S TIP

Spoon the raspberry sauce on to individual serving plates; trickle a little natural yogurt on top, and arrange the pear halves carefully on top. Calories per portion 135.

■ COOK'S TIP

This is a low-fat fool, ideal for slimmers. Instead of the sauce, stir in 150 ml (¼ pint) thick Greek yogurt or lightly whipped double cream for a richer dessert.

445
fruit and nut crumble

Preparation time 15 minutes, plus soaking	*175 g (6 oz) dried apricots*
	125 g (4 oz) dried pitted prunes
	125 g (4 oz) dried figs
Cooking time 35–45 minutes	*50 g (2 oz) dried apples*
	600 ml (1 pint) apple juice
Oven temperature 200°C (400°F) gas 6	*175 g (6 oz) wholemeal flour*
	75 g (3 oz) margarine
Serves 6	*50 g (2 oz) dark soft brown sugar, sifted*
	50 g (2 oz) hazelnuts, chopped
Calories 452 per portion	*Greek yogurt, to serve*

Place the dried fruits in a glass bowl with the apple juice and leave overnight. Transfer to a saucepan and simmer for 10–15 minutes, until softened. Turn into an ovenproof dish.

Place the flour in a bowl and rub in the margarine until the mixture resembles breadcrumbs. Stir in the sugar and hazelnuts, then sprinkle over the fruit.

Bake in a preheated oven for 25–30 minutes. Serve with some Greek yogurt.

446
iced stuffed apples

Preparation time 35 minutes, plus freezing	*2 cooking apples, peeled, cored and sliced*
	4 tablespoons lemon juice
Cooking time 5–6 minutes	*2 tablespoons brandy*
	2 medium egg yolks
Serves 4	*3 tablespoons natural yogurt*
	4 red or green dessert apples
Calories 60 per portion	*1 medium egg white*
	2 tablespoons sultanas

Stew the cooking apples with half the lemon juice in a covered pan until they are tender. Beat in the brandy and egg yolks then leave to cool.

Mix the yogurt with the cooked apple purée; pour into a shallow container and freeze until firm around the edges.

Cut a thin slice from the stalk end of each dessert apple, about 1 cm (½ inch) thick, and reserve for lids. Carefully hollow out the centre flesh and core, leaving a shell about 5 mm (¼ inch) thick. Brush inside with the remaining lemon juice.

Tip the semi-frozen apple mixture into a bowl and beat until smooth.

Whisk the egg white until stiff but not dry; fold lightly but thoroughly into the apple mixture, together with the sultanas. Spoon the apple mixture into the hollow apples, and replace the lids. Open freeze until firm.

■ COOK'S TIP

As a topping variation, use toasted chopped almonds instead of the hazelnuts, or stir in freshly grated coconut. Use soya margarine in the topping for a vegan version.

■ COOK'S TIP

Remove the frozen filled apples from the freezer a few minutes before serving to allow the centres to soften slightly. Sprinkle with a little cinnamon if desired.

447

yogurt knickerbocker glory

Preparation time	275 g (9 oz) thick Greek yogurt
10 minutes, plus chilling	300 ml (½ pint) raspberry yogurt, preferably with real fruit
Serves 4	2 large bananas, sliced
Calories	50 g (2 oz) chopped hazelnuts
290 per portion	

Layer the Greek yogurt, raspberry yogurt and banana attractively in four deep glasses, putting some of the banana slices down the sides of the glasses. Sprinkle the chopped nuts on top. Chill until ready to serve.

448

date and apple shortcake

Preparation time	FOR THE NUT PASTRY
25 minutes	75 g (3 oz) margarine
Cooking time	40 g (1½ oz) dark soft brown sugar
25 minutes	125 g (4 oz) wholemeal flour
Oven temperature	75 g (3 oz) Brazil nuts, ground
190°C (375°F) gas 5	egg white
	1 tablespoon chopped Brazil nuts
Serves 8	FOR THE FILLING
Calories	3 tablespoons apple juice
250 per portion	500 g (1 lb) dessert apples, peeled
	125 g (4 oz) dates, stoned and chopped
	1 teaspoon ground cinnamon
	150 ml (¼ pint) double cream, whipped

Beat the margarine and sugar until softened. Stir in the flour and ground Brazil nuts and mix to a firm dough. Turn on to a floured surface and knead lightly until smooth. Divide the dough in half and roll each piece into a 20 cm (8 inch) round. Place on a baking sheet. Brush one with egg white and sprinkle with the nuts.

Bake in a preheated moderately hot oven for 10–15 minutes, until golden. Cut the nut-covered round into 8 sections while warm. Transfer both rounds to a wire rack to cool.

Place the apple juice in a pan and slice the apples into it. Cover and cook gently for about 10 minutes, stirring from time to time, until just soft. Add the dates and cinnamon. Cool.

Spread the apple filling over the whole shortcake round, cover with the cream and the cut top.

■ COOK'S TIP

Try using strawberry or mandarin yogurt instead of raspberry. Add some fresh fruit to complement the yogurt, if available.

■ COOK'S TIP

Instead of Brazil nuts, use hazelnuts or almonds. Curd or cream cheese could be used instead of cream. Mix with a little milk and sugar for a creamy texture.

449

strawberry and yogurt ice

Preparation time	*125 g (4 oz) caster sugar*
25 minutes, plus	*300 ml (½ pint) water*
freezing	*375 g (12 oz) fresh strawberries*
Cooking time	*300 ml (½ pint) strawberry yogurt*
10 minutes	*1 medium egg white*
Serves 4	*150 ml (¼ pint) double cream*
Calories	
363 per portion	

Put the sugar and water into a small pan and heat gently to dissolve the sugar, then boil rapidly until the thread stage is reached (see Cook's Tip). Leave to cool.

Reserve 4 strawberries for decoration, slice the rest and put into a food processor or blender or with the syrup. Blend for a few seconds then pour into a bowl. Stir the yogurt into the strawberries and pour into a 1.2 litre (2 pint) freezer container. Freeze for about 2 hours, stirring once or twice, until mushy, then spoon into a large mixing bowl.

Beat the egg white until stiff. Whisk the cream until it forms soft peaks, and beat the strawberry mixture until smooth. There is no need to wash your whisk if you keep to this order.

With a metal spoon fold the egg white and cream into the strawberry mixture until blended. Pour into the container and freeze for about 3 hours until the ice cream is setting round the edges. Spoon into a bowl and whisk until smooth and light. Pour back into the container, cover and freeze for at least 6 hours. Serve decorated with the reserved strawberries.

■ COOK'S TIP

When boiling sugar syrup, the thread stage temperature is 107°C (225°F), on a sugar boiling thermometer. To test without a thermometer remove a little of the syrup with a small spoon and allow it to fall from the spoon on to a dish. The syrup should form a fine thread.

450

mango sorbet with cardamom sauce

Preparation time	*2 large ripe mangoes, halved, peeled,*
20 minutes, plus	*stones removed and flesh cut into*
freezing	*even-sized chunks*
Serves 4	*2 medium egg whites*
Calories	*a few pistachio nuts, shelled and chopped,*
129 per portion	*to decorate*
	FOR THE SAUCE
	1 teaspoon cardamom pods
	3 tablespoons clear honey
	3 tablespoons orange juice

Put the mango flesh in a food processor or blender and purée until smooth. It should make about 600 ml (1 pint). Put the purée into a freezer container and freeze until firm round the edges.

Whisk the egg whites until stiff. Add the cold mango purée to the egg whites a little at a time, continuing to whisk. Put the mixture back into the freezer and freeze until firm.

Meanwhile. make the sauce. Crush the cardamom pods and remove the black seeds. Crush the seeds as finely as you can. Then mix with the honey and orange juice. Cover and leave for at least 30 minutes for the flavours to blend.

Just before serving, strain the sauce. Remove the sorbet from the freezer 30 minutes before it is required. Serve in individual bowls with the cardamom sauce and a few chopped pistachio nuts on top.

■ COOK'S TIP

The mango is a rich source of vitamins A and C. If the fruit is not ripe when purchased, keep it in a warm temperature for a few days to ripen before use.

melon ice cream

Preparation time
20–25 minutes, plus freezing

Serves 4

Calories
65 per portion

1 medium melon (Ogen or Charentais)
300 ml (½ pint) natural yogurt
sugar or artificial sweetener (optional)
small melon balls, to decorate

Halve the melon and scoop out all the seeds. Put the melon flesh into a food processor or blender, and blend until smooth.

Mix the melon purée with the yogurt and add sugar or artificial sweetener to taste, if using. Transfer the melon and yogurt mixture to a shallow container, and freeze until firm.

Serve the melon ice cream in scoops, decorated with the small melon balls.

raspberry and pistachio ice cream

Preparation time
20–25 minutes, plus freezing

Serves 4

Calories
720 per portion

375 g (12 oz) fresh raspberries, washed
175 g (6 oz) sugar or clear honey
450 ml (¾ pint) whipping cream
125 g (4 oz) pistachio nuts, chopped

Blend then sieve the raspberries to remove the pips and make a smooth purée. Add the sugar or honey. Whip the cream until it is thick, then fold in the raspberry purée. Pour the mixture into a freezer container and freeze until half-frozen. Stir well and add most of the pistachio nuts, reserving a few for decoration. Return the ice cream to the freezer and freeze until solid.

Remove the ice cream from the freezer 30 minutes before serving. Spoon into individual bowls and sprinkle with the chopped pistachio nuts.

■ COOK'S TIP

For a richer, creamier dessert, use Greek yogurt or double cream instead of the natural yogurt. Try adding chopped crystallized ginger for a delicious spicy flavour.

■ COOK'S TIP

Any combination of fruit and nuts can be used for this recipe. Try blackcurrants with hazelnuts, or strawberries or apricots with almonds.

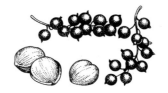

apple and raisin pie

Preparation time
25 minutes, plus chilling

Cooking time
30–40 minutes

Oven temperature
200°C (400°F)
gas 6

Serves 6

Calories
418 per portion

300 g (10 oz) wholemeal flour
150 g (5 oz) margarine
4–5 tablespoons iced water
1 teaspoon sesame seeds, to finish
Greek yogurt or whipped cream, to serve
FOR THE FILLING
750 g (1½ lb) dessert apples, peeled, cored
  and thinly sliced
2 tablespoons light soft brown sugar
1 teaspoon ground cinnamon
4 cloves
50 g (2 oz) raisins

Place the flour in a bowl and rub in the margarine until the mixture resembles fine breadcrumbs. Stir in enough water to mix to a dough. Turn on to a floured surface, knead lightly until smooth, then divide in half. Roll out one piece thinly and use to line a shallow 20 cm (8 inch) pie dish.

Layer the apples with the sugar, spices and raisins in the pastry case. Brush the pastry rim with water.

Roll out the remaining pastry and use to cover the pie. Seal and pinch the edges well, then trim off any surplus pastry with a sharp knife. Make a hole in the centre of the pie and chill for 20 minutes.

Brush the pastry with water and sprinkle with the sesame seeds. Bake in a preheated moderately hot oven for 30–40 minutes, until golden. Serve warm or cold with thick Greek yogurt or whipped cream.

■ COOK'S TIP

The juice from the apples in this dish raisins will plump up the raisins. You could also add some chopped dates and reduce the amount of sugar used.

sliced figs with lemon sauce

Preparation time
15–20 minutes

Serves 6

Calories
110 per portion

8 plump ripe figs
2 tablespoons lemon juice
150 ml (¼ pint) unsweetened apple purée
  (see Cook's Tip)
grated rind of ½ lemon
3 tablespoons natural yogurt
sugar or artificial sweetener, to taste
1 tablespoon chopped pistachio nuts
6 twists of lemon rind, to decorate
  (optional)

Cut each fig into 4 wedges. (Alternatively, the figs can be sliced, provided they are not too soft.) Sprinkle the cut figs with the lemon juice.

Mix the apple purée with the lemon rind and yogurt; add sugar or artificial sweetener to taste and half the chopped pistachios.

Spoon a pool of the lemon and pistachio sauce on to each of 6 small plates and arrange the pieces of fig decoratively on top.

Sprinkle with the remaining pistachio nuts and decorate with twists of lemon rind, if liked.

■ COOK'S TIP

To make apple purée, peel and core a large cooking apple, such as a Bramley. Immediately place it in a saucepan with a little water and simmer until soft.

455

pear and ginger pie

Preparation time 20 minutes	*250 g (8 oz) plain flour or 100 per cent* *wholemeal flour*
Cooking time 30 minutes	*125 g (4 oz) butter or margarine* *3 tablespoons cold water*
Oven temperature 200°C (400°F) gas 6	FOR THE FILLING *1 teaspoon ground ginger* *750 g (1½ lb) ripe dessert pears, peeled,*
Serves 4–6	*cored and sliced*
Calories 480–320 per portion	*2 tablespoons muscovado sugar* *milk, to glaze*

Sift the flour into a bowl, adding the bran left behind in the sieve. Rub in the fat with your fingertips until the mixture looks like breadcrumbs, then mix in the water to make a dough. Roll out half of the pastry on a floured board and use to line a 20–23 cm (8–9 inch) pie plate. Sprinkle the ginger over the pastry, making sure that it is well distributed, then put the pears on top of the pastry and sprinkle with the sugar.

Roll out the rest of the pastry and use it to make a crust for the pie. Trim the pastry and crimp the edges of the pie with a fork. Make two or three holes for steam to escape and brush with milk.

Bake in a preheated oven for about 30 minutes, until the pastry is crisp and lightly browned. If the pears make a great deal of liquid, simply pour this off after you have cut the first slice of pie.

■ COOK'S TIP

This is a pleasant change from the classic apple pie but you could replace the pears with the same quantity of cooking apples, also peeled, cored and sliced.

456

ginger creams

Preparation time 15 minutes	*150 ml (¼ pint) whipping cream, lightly* *whipped*
Serves 6	*300 ml (½ pint) natural yogurt*
Calories 198 per portion	*75 g (3 oz) ginger nut biscuits, finely* *crushed*
	25 g (1 oz) crystallized or stem ginger, *chopped*
	pieces of crystallized or stem ginger, *to decorate*

Stir together the cream, yogurt and biscuits, then fold in the chopped ginger.

Spoon into individual glasses. Top each serving with pieces of ginger and serve with crisp biscuits.

■ COOK'S TIP

To crush the ginger biscuits, put them between sheets of greaseproof paper and press a rolling pin over them. Do not reduce them to a powder.

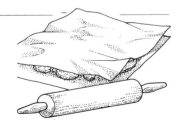

457

chestnut roulade

Preparation time 30 minutes, plus cooling	*50 g (2 oz) wholemeal flour* *1 tablespoon cocoa powder* *4 eggs, separated*
Cooking time 20 minutes	*150 g (5 oz) caster sugar* *icing sugar to sprinkle*
Oven temperature 160°C (325°F), gas 3	FOR THE FILLING *50 g (2 oz) raisins* *175 g (6 oz) chestnut purée*
Serves 6	*25 g (1 oz) soft brown sugar*
Calories 285 per portion	*120 ml (4 fl oz) thick Greek yogurt* *pinch of ground cinnamon*

Sift the flour with the cocoa powder, adding any bran left in the sieve. Whisk the egg whites until stiff, then whisk in half the sugar. Whisk the egg yolks with the remaining sugar in a large bowl until thick and pale, about 5 minutes. Carefully fold in first the flour mixture then the whisked egg whites. Turn into a greased and lined 23 x 30 cm (9 x 12 inch) Swiss roll tin. Shake the tin gently to level the mixture and cook in a moderate oven for 20 minutes, until firm to the touch.

Turn out on to a large sheet of greaseproof paper dusted with icing sugar and discard the lining paper. Roll up from one short end, rolling the clean greaseproof paper with the roulade, and leave until cold.

Beat together the raisins, chestnut purée and soft brown sugar. Fold in the yogurt and cinnamon. Carefully unroll the roulade and spread evenly with the filling. Reroll and dust with icing sugar.

458

fruity yule pudding

Preparation time 25 minutes	*125 g (4 oz) self-raising wholemeal flour* *125 g (4 oz) fresh wholemeal breadcrumbs*
Cooking time 3–4 hours, plus 2 hours on the day of serving	*1 teaspoon mixed spice* *1 teaspoon ground cinnamon* *1 teaspoon grated nutmeg*
Serves 8	*125 g (4 oz) polyunsaturated margarine* *75 g (3 oz) light soft brown sugar*
Calories 295 per portion	*2 eggs, beaten* *1 dessert apple, peeled, cored and grated* *1 carrot, grated* *250 g (8 oz) raisins* *grated rind and juice of 1 orange*

Mix together the flour, breadcrumbs and spices. Beat the margarine with the sugar for about 5 minutes, until soft and light, then beat in the eggs, apple, carrot, raisins and orange rind and juice. Stir in the flour mixture until evenly blended.

Press lightly into a greased 1.2 litre (2 pint) pudding basin and cover with double thickness greaseproof paper, tied down securely. Steam for 3–4 hours, topping up the water as necessary, then for a further 2 hours on the day of serving.

■ COOK'S TIP

Before rolling up the just-cooked roulade, trim off any crusty edges with a sharp knife. This will make rolling much easier.

■ COOK'S TIP

Dried and fresh fruit replaces much of the sugar in this light Christmas pudding – an ideal alternative for the health and weight conscious.

459

choux ring

Preparation time 45 minutes	*300 ml (½ pint) water*
Cooking time 40–45 minutes	*125 g (4 oz) butter* *150 g (5 oz) plain flour* *3–4 eggs, lightly beaten*
Oven temperature 220°C (425°F) gas 7, then 190°C (375°F) gas 5	*300 ml (½ pint) double cream* *1 tablespoon sweet sherry* *1 x 250 g (8 oz) can sweetened chestnut purée*
Serves 8	*a little cocoa powder*
Calories 435 per portion	

Make the choux pastry, using the first four ingredients and following the instructions in the Cook's Tip below. Transfer to a piping bag fitted with a large nozzle.

Dampen a large baking sheet and pipe a 25 cm (10 inch) circle of paste on it. Pipe another circle immediately inside. Bake for 10 minutes at the higher setting, then reduce the temperature and cook for a further 35–40 minutes, until well puffed, crisp and brown. Split the choux ring in half immediately it is removed from the oven. Leave to cool.

Whip the cream and sherry together and fold into the chestnut purée. Spread the choux base with the chestnut cream and cover with the choux top. Dust with cocoa powder.

460

pear flan

Preparation time 25 minutes, plus chilling	FOR THE PASTRY *125 g (4 oz) plain flour* *1 teaspoon ground cinnamon*
Cooking time 45 minutes	*50 g (2 oz) butter, softened* *25 g (1 oz) walnuts, ground* *25 g (1 oz) caster sugar*
Oven temperature 190°C (375°F) gas 5	*1 egg yolk* *2 teaspoons cold water* *icing sugar, to sprinkle*
Serves 4	FOR THE FILLING *2 x 300 g (10 oz) cans pear quarters in fruit juice*
Calories 350 per portion	*1 tablespoon each currants, sultanas and chopped lemon rind* *1 tablespoon cornflour* *1 tablespoon lemon juice*

Sift the flour and cinnamon into a bowl, rub in the butter then stir in the walnuts and sugar. Bind with the egg yolk and water. Chill for 30 minutes.

Drain the pear juice into a pan and add the currants, sultanas and lemon peel. Bring to the boil and simmer for 5 minutes. Mix the cornflour and lemon juice and stir into the mixture. Cook, stirring, until thickened.

Roll out the pastry to line a 19 cm (7½ inch) flan tin, reserving the trimmings. Prick the pastry and bake blind in a moderately hot oven for 15 minutes (see Cook's Tip, recipe 177). Fill the pastry case with the pears and thickened juice; top with a pastry lattice and bake for a further 20 minutes. Dust with icing sugar when cool.

■ COOK'S TIP

To make choux pastry, heat the water and butter gently until the fat melts, then bring to a rapid boil. Off the heat, immediately add all the flour. Beat vigorously, return to the heat and continue beating until the mixture forms a ball which leaves the sides of the pan clean. Cool to lukewarm, beat in enough egg to give a piping consistency, then beat until glossy.

■ COOK'S TIP

There are three ways to make a pastry lattice: the pastry slats may simply be placed on top of the filling with all the horizontal slats underneath and the vertical ones on top; for a woven lattice the top slats are threaded under and over the bottom ones to give a basketweave effect; and in the twisted lattice the slats are turned to give an even more decorative appearance.

461

orchard tart

Preparation time 25 minutes	FOR THE PASTRY *125 g (4 oz) plain flour*
Cooking time 35–40 minutes	*50 g (2 oz) concentrated butter, softened* *50 g (2 oz) ground hazelnuts*
Oven temperature 200°C (400°F) gas 6	*25 g (1 oz) soft brown sugar* *1 egg, beaten* FOR THE FILLING
Serves 6	*4 large pears, peeled, cored and chopped*
Calories 355 per portion	*2 cm (¾ inch) piece of fresh root ginger,* * peeled and chopped* *2 tablespoons clear honey* *125 g (4 oz) demerara sugar* *3 tablespoons water* *4 dessert apples, peeled, cored and halved*

Place the flour in a mixing bowl and add the concentrated butter; rub in until it forms very fine crumbs. Add the hazelnuts and sugar then bind with the egg. Roll out to line a 20 cm (8 inch) loose-bottomed flan tin.

Place the pears in a pan with the ginger, honey, sugar and water and cook over a moderate heat for 5 minutes. Remove the pears with a slotted spoon, drain well and place in the flan case, crushing them slightly.

Slice the apple halves almost through but keeping in shape and arrange rounded side up over the flan. Reduce the pan juices until thick enough to coat then spoon over the apples.

Bake the tart in a preheated moderately hot oven for 30 minutes and serve warm with cream.

462

gourmet bread and butter pudding

Preparation time 15 minutes	*8 large slices white or granary bread* *50 g (2 oz) concentrated butter, melted*
Cooking time 30–40 minutes	*50 g (2 oz) demerara sugar* *½ teaspoon mixed spice*
Oven temperature 180°C (350°F) gas 4	*125 g (4 oz) sultanas* *2 eggs, beaten* *1 teaspoon vanilla essence*
Serves 4	*450 ml (¾ pint) milk*
Calories 455 per portion	*1 tablespoon sherry (optional)*

Remove the crusts and cut the bread into fingers or desired shapes for one large (1.15 litre/2 pint) pudding or four individual (300 ml/½ pint) puddings.

Brush a little melted butter inside the ovenproof dishes and cover the base with bread. Mix the sugar, spice and sultanas together and sprinkle half over the bread, drizzle with a little of the melted butter and repeat the layers finishing with bread and melted butter. Beat the eggs, vanilla, milk and sherry together and carefully pour over. Bake in a moderate oven for 30–40 minutes until set.

■ COOK'S TIP

To slice the apples evenly without cutting right through place the halves, cut side down, on a work surface in front of a thin chopping board. Use a large knife held horizontally so that the board halts the descending blade.

■ COOK'S TIP

The texture and flavour of this updated old favourite will be even better if the pudding is allowed to stand for 1 hour before cooking.

463

blackberry and apple crumble

Preparation time
15 minutes

Cooking time
35–40 minutes

Oven temperature
190°C (375°F)
gas 5

Serves 4

Calories
350 per portion

250 g (8 oz) blackberries
500 g (1 lb) cooking apples, peeled, cored
*   and thinly sliced*
25 g (1 oz) unrefined sugar (golden
*   granulated or molasses)*
FOR THE CRUMBLE
125 g (4 oz) wholemeal flour
75 g (3 oz) polyunsaturated margarine
50 g (2 oz) fruit'n'fibre cereal, lightly
*   crushed*
15 g (½ oz) unrefined sugar

Mix together the fruit and sugar and place in a 1.2 litre (2 pint) ovenproof dish.

Put the flour into a mixing bowl and rub in the fat. Stir in the cereal and sugar. Spread this topping evenly over the fruit and bake in a preheated moderately hot oven for 35–40 minutes, until the crumble is crisp and the fruit soft. Serve warm with custard.

464

autumnal pudding

Preparation time
20 minutes, plus
chilling and setting

Cooking time
10 minutes

Serves 4

Calories
225 per portion

oil, for brushing
8 thin slices wholewheat bread
150 ml (¼ pint) apple juice
50 g (2 oz) granulated sugar
juice of ½ lemon
2 dessert apples, peeled, cored and sliced
1 dessert pear, peeled, cored and sliced
75 g (3 oz) blackberries
pinch of ground cinnamon
1½ teaspoons agar-agar or 2 teaspoons
*   powdered gelatine*
6 tablespoons water
fresh fruit, to decorate
FOR THE SAUCE
250 g (8 oz) blackberries
3 tablespoons icing sugar
juice of ½ lemon

Brush the insides of four individual pudding basins with oil. Cut the bread into circles and fingers to line them.

Stir the apple juice, sugar and lemon juice over low heat until dissolved. Add the apple and pear slices and poach gently for 4 minutes. Stir in the blackberries and cinnamon. Leave to cool.

In a small saucepan, dissolve the agar-agar in the cold water, then bring to the boil, stirring constantly. Add to the cooled fruits. Spoon into the basins and chill.

Poach the sauce ingredients gently, purée in a food processor or blender and serve with the puddings, as shown. Decorate with seasonal fruit.

■ COOK'S TIP

All berry fruits taste good with a crumble topping. Try cranberries, loganberries, tayberries or raspberries, varying the quantity of sugar as required.

■ COOK'S TIP

Agar-agar, which is derived from seaweed, is the preferred setting agent for many vegetarians. If using gelatine, dissolve it in a little water in a basin over a saucepan of hot water. Stir frequently.

baking

Home-baked cakes and breads are irresistible and their commercial counterparts cannot compete for texture and flavour. Among the teatime treats in this chapter are imaginative teabreads, such as Plum Teabread and Banana and Honey Teabread, moist cakes – fruity, spicy and nutty – the exotic Brazilian Ginger Bran Bread and Cheese and Pineapple Scones. Make any occasion special with these tempting recipes.

465
fruit tartlets

Preparation time
20 minutes, plus cooling and chilling

Cooking time
20–25 minutes

Oven temperature
190°C (375°F) gas 5

Makes 6 medium or 12 small tartlets

Calories
630 per medium tartlet

375 g (12 oz) plain flour
1 egg
250 g (8 oz) butter or margarine
1 tablespoon caster sugar
FOR THE FILLING
50 g (2 oz) caster sugar
3 egg yolks
2 tablespoons cornflour
300 ml (½ pint) milk
2–4 drops vanilla essence

Line and grease six 10 cm (4 inch) or twelve 5–7.5 cm (2–3 inch) tartlet tins. Sift the flour and salt into a large bowl. Make a well in the centre, drop in the egg and butter, and knead to form a soft, pliable dough. Wrap the dough and chill for 30 minutes. Roll out and use to line the tins. Prick the bases and bake blind (see Cook's Tip, recipe 177) in a preheated oven for 10–15 minutes. Remove the beans and greaseproof paper and bake for a further 5–10 minutes.

Mix together the sugar, egg yolks and cornflour. Heat the milk in a saucepan just to boiling point, cool slightly, then whisk into the egg mixture, return to the pan and slowly bring to the boil. Cover the surface of the mixture with dampened paper to cool. Fill the tartlets with the cold pastry cream and fruit.

■ COOK'S TIP

To prevent oxidisation or drying out, warm some jam or marmalade flavoured with either lemon juice or liqueur, sieve and brush carefully over the fruit.

466
bakewell tart

Preparation time
25 minutes

Cooking time
20–25 minutes

Oven temperature
180°C (350°F) gas 4

Serves 4

Calories
900 per portion

75 g (3 oz) plain flour
50 g (2 oz) wholemeal flour
25 g (1 oz) icing sugar
125 g (4 oz) margarine
25 g (1 oz) All-Bran cereal, crushed
1 egg
5 tablespoons jam
icing sugar, for dusting
FOR THE FILLING
125 g (4 oz) brown sugar
125 g (4 oz) margarine
2 eggs
1 teaspoon vanilla essence
125 g (4 oz) fresh breadcrumbs
125 g (4 oz) All-Bran cereal
50 g (2 oz) flaked almonds

Sift the flours and icing sugar together, adding any bran in the sieve to the mixture. Cut the margarine into small pieces and rub in until the mixture resembles fine breadcrumbs. Stir in the cereal and egg and mix to a dough. Knead lightly, cover and chill.

To make the filling, cream together the sugar and margarine until light and fluffy. Gradually beat in the eggs. Stir in the vanilla essence, breadcrumbs, cereal and almonds until well mixed.

Roll out the dough to line a 20 cm (8 inch) round, loose-bottomed cake tin. Spread the jam over the dough. Top with the filling and bake in a preheated oven for 20–25 minutes or until the pastry is crisp and the filling set. Cool the tart for 10 minutes, remove from the tin and dust the top with icing sugar. Serve warm or cold.

■ COOK'S TIP

For a more elaborate effect, like that shown in the photograph, reserve one third of the pastry, roll out the base thinly, then roll out the reserved pastry, cut into strips for the lattice and arrange over the filling. Decorate the tart by spooning a little glacé icing into the holes in the lattice. Add chopped cherries and nuts.

467

cheese scone ring

Preparation time 15 minutes	*250 g (8 oz) self-raising flour* *1 teaspoon baking powder*
Cooking time 15–20 minutes	*50 g (2 oz) butter* *50 g (2 oz) Danish Blue cheese*
Oven temperature 200°C (400°F) gas 6	*about 150 ml (¼ pint) milk*
Makes 8 scones	
Calories 180 per scone	

Sift the flour with the baking powder into a large bowl. Rub in the butter until the mixture resembles fine breadcrumbs. Crumble the cheese into this mixture and rub in. Using a fork, mix in enough milk to make a soft, but not sticky dough. Knead lightly.

Divide the mixture into eight equal pieces and shape each piece into a ball. Place one ball in the centre of a well buttered 20 cm (8 inch) cake tin and arrange the remainder around the edge so that they are just touching. Brush with milk to glaze. Bake in a preheated moderately hot oven for approximately 15–20 minutes, or until well risen and golden brown.

468

passion cake

Preparation time 30 minutes	*175 g (6 oz) plain flour* *1 teaspoon bicarbonate of soda*
Cooking time 1¼ hours	*1 teaspoon baking powder* *1 teaspoon ground cinnamon*
Oven temperature 160°C (325°F) gas 3	*1 teaspoon mixed spice* *½ teaspoon salt*
Makes 1 cake	*2 large oranges* *175 g (6 oz) light soft brown sugar*
Total calories 4835	*3 eggs* *175 g (6 oz) butter, melted* *250 g (8 oz) carrots, grated* *125 g (4 oz) walnuts, chopped* FOR THE TOPPING *125 g (4 oz) cream cheese* *50 g (2 oz) unsalted butter, softened* *grated rind of 1 orange* *125 g (4 oz) icing sugar, sifted* *15 g (½ oz) walnuts, chopped to decorate*

Sift together the first six ingredients. Pare the rind of half of one of the oranges. Cut into thin strips and blanch in boiling water. Grate the remaining orange rind.

Beat the sugar, eggs and grated orange rind. Beat in the melted butter then mix in the carrots, walnuts and flour mixture. Pour into a lined and greased 18 cm (7 inch) square or 20 cm (8 inch) round cake tin. Bake in a preheated moderate oven for about 1¼ hours, until firm to the touch. Cool in the tin for 5 minutes, then cool on a wire rack.

Beat the topping ingredients together, spread over the cake and decorate as shown.

■ COOK'S TIP

This is delicious on its own, served split and buttered, or with a sweet or savoury filling. At teatime spread with blackcurrant or apricot jam, and for a lunch snack, fill with sliced cucumber and slim wedges of Danish Blue cheese.

■ COOK'S TIP

This lovely moist cake is almost irresistible. For a vanilla passion cake, substitute 1 teaspoon vanilla essence for the orange rind in the cake and omit the orange rind in the topping.

469

carrot and orange cake alabama

Preparation time
20 minutes

Cooking time
30–35 minutes

Oven temperature
180°C (350°F)
gas 4

Makes 15 squares

Calories
250 per square

175 g (6 oz) brown sugar
175 ml (6 fl oz) groundnut oil
3 eggs, beaten
250 g (8 oz) carrots, finely grated
125 g (4 oz) raisins
75 g (3 oz) peanuts, chopped
175 g (6 oz) self-raising wholemeal flour
1 teaspoon bicarbonate of soda
1 teaspoon ground cinnamon
1 teaspoon finely grated orange rind
150 ml (¼ pint) double cream, whipped
1–2 tablespoons chopped peanuts, to decorate

Mix together the sugar, oil and eggs in a large bowl. Stir in the carrots, raisins and peanuts. Mix the flour with the bicarbonate of soda, cinnamon and orange rind. Add to the bowl and mix lightly.

Turn into a greased and lined 18 x 25 cm (7 x 10 inch) oblong tin and bake in a moderate oven for 30–35 minutes, until firm to the touch.

Cool in the tin for 5 minutes, then turn out and cool completely on a wire rack. Cut into squares, then top with whipped cream and peanuts to serve.

470

blackcurrant nut cake

Preparation time
15 minutes

Cooking time
40–45 minutes

Oven temperature
180°C (350°F)
gas 4

Makes 1 loaf

Total Calories
2610

150 g (5 oz) plain flour
2 teaspoons baking powder
½ teaspoon salt
75 g (3 oz) All-Bran or Bran Buds cereal
125 g (4 oz) butter
75 g (3 oz) sugar
2 eggs
150 ml (¼ pint) natural yogurt
125 g (4 oz) chopped nuts
125 g (4 oz) blackcurrants, fresh, frozen or canned

Line and grease a 1 kg (2 lb) loaf tin. Sift together the flour, baking powder and salt. Stir in the cereal. Cream the butter and sugar together until light and fluffy. Gradually beat in the eggs. Stir in the yogurt and then the flour mixture until just combined. Lightly stir in the nuts and blackcurrants (well drained, if canned).

Spoon the mixture into the loaf tin and bake in a preheated oven for 40–45 minutes. Insert a skewer in the centre of the cake; if it comes out clean the loaf is cooked.

Cool the cake for about 10 minutes before removing from the tin. Place on a wire rack to cool completely.

■ COOK'S TIP

In the USA, where this cake originated, it is traditional to serve it with a cream cheese topping. Beat 175 g (6 oz) cream cheese until soft and light and gradually add 500 g (1 lb) icing sugar and 1 teaspoon vanilla essence. Beat in enough milk to give a spreading consistency, cover the cake and watch the calories climb!

■ COOK'S TIP

This is the perfect cake for a picnic. Slice it just before setting out, reassemble the slices in the tin in which it was cooked. Overwrap in foil and pack it in a picnic hamper or cooler.

471

apple and almond layer cake

Preparation time
20 minutes

Cooking time
1½ hours

Oven temperature
160°C (325°F)
gas 3

Makes 1 cake

Total calories
3190

150 g (5 oz) soft margarine
2 large eggs, beaten
250 g (8 oz) golden granulated sugar
1 teaspoon almond essence
250 g (8 oz) self-raising flour, sifted
1½ teaspoons baking powder
375 g (12 oz) cooking apples, peeled,
*   cored and sliced*
25 g (1 oz) flaked almonds

Place the margarine, eggs, sugar, almond essence, flour and baking powder in a bowl and beat thoroughly until well combined. Alternatively use a mixer or food processor.

Spread half the cake mixture in the base of a greased 20 cm (8 inch) loose-bottomed cake tin. Cover with the sliced apples and put the remaining cake mixture on top of the apples in blobs. Sprinkle over the flaked almonds and bake in a preheated moderately hot oven for about 1½ hours, until evenly golden and the edges shrink away from the sides of the tin. Turn out and cool on a wire rack.

■ COOK'S TIP

This is especially delicious served warm with whipped cream for dessert, though equally good as a lovely teatime cake.

472

californian christmas cake

Preparation time
30 minutes, plus
macerating the fruit

Cooking time
2–2¼ hours

Oven temperature
160°C (325°F)
gas 3

Makes 1 cake

Total calories
4650

375 g (12 oz) raisins
50 g (2 oz) glacé cherries, quartered
50 g (2 oz) dried apricots, chopped
3 tablespoons sherry
175 g (6 oz) margarine
175 g (6 oz) light soft brown sugar
3 eggs, beaten
50 g (2 oz) ground almonds
50 g (2 oz) almonds, chopped
few drops of almond essence
250 g (8 oz) self-raising wholemeal flour
1 teaspoon mixed spice
whole nuts, for topping
clear honey, to glaze

Soak the fruit in the sherry for 1 hour. Beat together the margarine and sugar until fluffy, beat in the eggs, then stir in the fruit mixture, ground and chopped almonds and almoind essence. Fold in the flour and spice.

Turn into a greased and double-lined 20 cm (8 inch) round cake tin and smooth the top. Arrange rows of nuts over the top of the cake to completely cover it and bake in a preheated moderate oven for 2–2¼ hours, until firm to the touch and a skewer inserted in the centre of the cake comes out clean.

Cool in the tin for 30 minutes, then turn out, remove the paper and cool on a wire rack. When cold, brush the cake with melted honey and fasten a ribbon around the side.

■ COOK'S TIP

The easiest way to quarter the cherries and chop the apricots is to use clean kitchen scissors, frequently dipping the blades in a jug of hot water.

473

spiced tea bread

Preparation time 10 minutes, plus macerating the fruit	*175 g (6 oz) mixed dried fruit* *grated rind and juice of ½ orange* *1 teaspoon mixed spice*
Cooking time 1¼ hours	*1 teaspoon ground cinnamon* *freshly made tea*
Oven temperature 180°C (350°F) gas 4 then 160°C (325°F) gas 3	*175 g (6 oz) self-raising flour* *50 g (2 oz) wholemeal flour* *2 teaspoons baking powder* *50 g (2 oz) caster sugar*
Makes 500 g (1 lb) loaf	*1 egg, beaten* *4 tablespoons oil*
Total calories 2005	*1 tablespoon chopped nuts*

Place the fruit, orange rind and spices in a bowl. Make the orange juice up to 150 ml (¼ pint) with tea and stir into the fruit. Cover and leave to macerate overnight.

Line and grease a 500 g (1 lb) loaf tin. Mix the dry ingredients in a bowl. Beat in the egg, oil and macerated fruit mixture. Pour into the prepared tin and sprinkle the nuts on top. Bake in a preheated oven at the hotter temperature for 45 minutes, then reduce the temperature for a further 30 minutes, or until bread is firm and a skewer comes out clean.

Leave the bread for 5 minutes in the tin, then transfer to a wire rack to cool.

474

banana and walnut loaf

Preparation time 20 minutes	*125 g (4 oz) soft margarine* *175 g (6 oz) light muscovado sugar*
Cooking time 1 hour	*2 ripe bananas* *2 eggs*
Oven temperature 180°C (350°F) gas 4	*250 g (8 oz) self-raising flour* *1 teaspoon baking powder*
Makes 1 loaf	*50 g (2 oz) walnuts, chopped* *2 tablespoons milk*
Total calories 2790	

Cream the margarine with the sugar until soft and light. Mash the bananas and mix in well. Break the eggs into the mixture and beat well. Gently fold in the sifted flour and baking powder, then stir in the walnuts and milk. Turn into a lined and greased 1 kg (2 lb) loaf tin and bake in a moderate oven for 1 hour, until well risen and golden brown. Turn out and cool on a wire rack. Serve sliced, spread with butter if liked.

■ COOK'S TIP

If a cake or loaf such as this one begins to brown too much before it is fully cooked, cover loosely with a piece of foil.

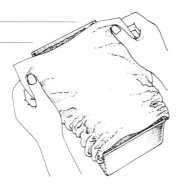

■ COOK'S TIP

This is a great favourite with children and so easy to make that even a relatively young child could attempt it with adult supervision.

475

brazilian ginger bran bread

Preparation time
20 minutes, plus macerating the fruit

Cooking time
1¼ hours

Oven temperature
180°C (350°F)
gas 4

Makes 18 slices

Calories
145 per slice

125 g (4 oz) sultanas
125 g (4 oz) raisins
125 g (4 oz) currants
125 g (4 oz) glacé cherries, washed, dried and halved
175 g (6 oz) dark brown sugar
200 ml (7 fl oz) strong black coffee
1 large egg
125 g (4 oz) cottage cheese, sieved
50 g (2 oz) bran
200 g (7 oz) plain flour
2 teaspoons ground ginger
½ teaspoon bicarbonate of soda

Soak the fruits and sugar in the coffee for 2 hours. Base-line and grease a deep 20 cm (8 inch) square cake tin.

Beat the egg and cottage cheese into the fruit mixture. Stir in all the remaining ingredients, mixing thoroughly.

Pour into the prepared tin and bake in a preheated oven for 1¼ hours until well-risen and firm.

Cool in the tin for 5 minutes then transfer to a wire rack to cool completely. Serve sliced, spread with butter.

476

plum teabread

Preparation time
30 minutes

Cooking time
1¼ hours

Oven temperature
190°C (375°F)
gas 5

Makes 12 slices

Calories
180 per slice

250 g (8 oz) cottage cheese
175 g (6 oz) light soft brown sugar
2 large eggs
50 g (2 oz) walnuts, chopped
175 g (6 oz) plums, stoned
250 g (8 oz) self-raising flour

Line and thoroughly grease a 900 g (2 lb) loaf tin.

Sieve the cottage cheese into a bowl and beat in the sugar. Add the eggs and walnuts. Reserve two plums and chop the rest. Stir in the chopped plums and flour into the mixture and spoon into the prepared tin.

Bake the bread in a preheated oven for 30 minutes. Press four plum halves as decoration along the centre of the loaf and bake for a further 45 minutes, covering the bread with foil if it over-browns, until cooked through.

Transfer to a wire rack to cool and serve sliced, spread with butter.

■ COOK'S TIP

Instead of spreading the slices of bread with butter, try using a light cream cheese. The flavours are wonderfully complementary.

■ COOK'S TIP

For a more elaborate decoration on the top of this loaf, use almonds to transform each inverted plum half to a sunburst.

banana and honey teabread

Preparation time 20 minutes	200 g (7 oz) self-raising flour
Cooking time 1¼–1½ hours	¼ teaspoon bicarbonate of soda pinch of salt 75 g (3 oz) butter
Oven temperature 180°C (350°F) gas 4	50 g (2 oz) soft brown sugar 175 g (6 oz) sultanas 125 g (4 oz) walnuts, chopped
Makes 1 large loaf	2 bananas, peeled
Total calories 2830	2 tablespoons clear honey 2 eggs

Line and grease a 900 g (2 lb) loaf tin. Sift together the flour, soda and salt into a large bowl. Rub in the butter until the mixture resembles fine breadcrumbs. Stir in the sugar, sultanas and walnuts.

Mash the bananas in a bowl. Add the honey and eggs and whisk together. Add to the dry ingredients and mix well.

Pour into the prepared loaf tin and level the surface with the back of a metal spoon. Bake in a preheated moderate oven for 1¼–1½ hours, or until a warmed skewer inserted into the centre comes out clean.

Allow the teabread to cool in the tin for 5 minutes. Then turn on to a wire rack, remove lining paper and cool completely. Serve sliced and buttered.

apricot bars

Preparation time 20 minutes	175 g (6 oz) butter, softened
Cooking time 25–30 minutes	175 g (6 oz) soft brown sugar 250 g (8 oz) plain flour, sifted
Oven temperature 180°C (350°F) gas 4	½ teaspoon bicarbonate of soda 125 g (4 oz) rolled oats ½ teaspoon salt
Makes 18	15 g (½ oz) butter, melted
Calories 125 per bar	1 x 300 g (10 oz) can apricot halves, drained grated rind of 1 lemon caster sugar, to decorate

Beat the softened butter in a bowl with the sugar. Mix in the flour, bicarbonate of soda, oats and salt. Brush a 20 x 30 cm (8 x 12 inch) tin with the melted butter and spread over half the crumb mixture. Chop the apricots and mix with the lemon rind. Spread on to the crumb base and cover with the remaining mixture.

Cook the cake in a preheated moderate oven for 25–30 minutes then cut into bars and leave to cool in the tin. Before serving, sprinkle over a little caster sugar.

■ COOK'S TIP

It is important to preheat the oven for at least 15 minutes before baking a cake. If the temperature is too low, the texture of the cake is liable to be coarse.

■ COOK'S TIP

To soften the butter, cut it into large cubes and place it in a bowl with cold (room temperature) water to cover. Allow to stand for a few minutes, then pour off water.

479

date and cinnamon scones

Preparation time	250 g (8 oz) plain wholewheat flour
20 minutes	4 teaspoons baking powder
Cooking time	2 teaspoons cinnamon
15 minutes	pinch of salt
Oven temperature	50 g (2 oz) butter or margarine
220°C (425°F)	50 g (2 oz) muscovado sugar
gas 7	75 g (3 oz) dates, stoned and chopped
Makes 10–12	175 ml (6 fl oz) milk and water mixed
Calories	extra flour for rolling out
101–84 per portion	

Sift the flour, baking powder and cinnamon and salt into a bowl, adding any bran left in the sieve. Rub in the fat, then add the sugar, dates and milk. Mix to a dough, then turn it out on to a floured board and knead gently for 1–2 minutes; the consistency will be sticky and soft.

Place the dough on a lightly floured board and roll or pat out to a thickness of 2 cm (¾ inch). Cut out the scones using a 5 cm (2 inch) round cutter. Put the scones on a baking sheet and bake in a preheated oven for 10–15 minutes, until risen and firm. Cool on a wire rack. Serve warm.

480

walnut soda bread

Preparation time	500 g (1 lb) wholewheat flour
15 minutes	2 teaspoons baking powder
Cooking time	1 teaspoon salt
40 minutes	1 tablespoon light muscovado sugar
Oven temperature	75 g (3 oz) chopped walnuts
190°C (375°F)	300 ml (½ pint) natural yogurt
gas 5	water, to mix
Makes 1 x 18 cm	2 tablespoons milk
(7 inch) round loaf	2 tablespoons cracked wheat
Calories	
215 per average slice	

Sift the flour, baking powder and salt into a mixing bowl and stir in the sugar and walnuts. Stir in the yogurt and sufficient water to make a firm dough.

Knead the dough lightly in the bowl until it is smooth and free from cracks. Shape the dough into a round about 18 cm (7 inches) in diameter and place it on a greased baking sheet. Mark the top into 4 segments. Brush the top with milk and sprinkle with the cracked wheat.

Bake the loaf in a preheated oven for 40 minutes, or until it is well risen and firm and sounds hollow when tapped underneath. Cool on a wire rack.

■ COOK'S TIP

Vary the the flavour of the scones by using other spices, fruits and nuts. Try raisin and ginger scones, replacing the cinnamon with ground ginger and the dates with raisins.

■ COOK'S TIP

As nuts are high in fat, they tend to go rancid quickly. Store in airtight jars either in a cool, dry cupboard or the frefrigerator. Nuts are also best freshly cracked.

481

figgy scone bread

Preparation time
20 minutes

Cooking time
25 minutes

Oven temperature
200°C (400°F)
gas 6

**Makes 1 x 20 cm
(8 inch) round
scone**

Calories
200 per piece

175 g (6 oz) wholewheat flour
1 teaspoon baking powder
pinch of salt
25 g (1 oz) light muscovado sugar
50 g (2 oz) fine oatmeal
75 g (3 oz) soft margarine
125 g (4 oz) dried figs, finely chopped
about 150 ml (¼ pint) skimmed milk
2 tablespoons clear honey, melted

Sift the flour, baking powder and salt into a mixing bowl, tip in any bran remaining in the sieve and stir in the sugar and oatmeal. Using a fork, beat in the margarine and stir in the figs and just enough milk to form a soft dough. Knead the dough lightly until it is smooth.

Press the dough into a greased 20 cm (8 inch) round tin and mark into 6 wedges. Brush the top with honey.

Bake in a preheated oven for 25 minutes, or until the scone is well risen and golden brown. Cool the scone partly in the tin, then turn out on to a wire rack.

482

wheatgerm, honey and raisin muffins

Preparation time
15 minutes

Cooking time
20 minutes

Oven temperature
180°C (350°F)
gas 4

Makes 12

Calories
108 per portion

butter, for greasing
125 g (4 oz) wheatgerm
2 teaspoons baking powder
pinch of salt
75 g (3 oz) raisins
4 tablespoons clear honey
50 g (2 oz) butter or margarine, melted
2 small eggs, beaten
about 6 tablespoons milk

Grease a bun or muffin tin with butter. Put the wheatgerm, baking powder, salt and raisins into a bowl, then add the honey, butter or margarine and eggs. Mix until blended, then stir in enough milk to make a fairly soft mixture, which drops heavily from the spoon when you shake it.

Put heaped tablespoons of the mixture into the bun tin, dividing the mixture between twelve sections. Bake in a preheated oven for 15–20 minutes, until the muffins have puffed up and feel firm to a light touch. Serve warm.

■ COOK'S TIP

This bread is good served warm. Spread it with cottage cheese for a calcium-rich snack. Add 50 g (2 oz) chopped walnuts to the dough for extra protein.

■ COOK'S TIP

These muffins contain the goodness of wheatgerm and raisins and are quick and easy to make. Serve them warm from the oven with a fresh fruit salad.

483

honey teacakes

Preparation time
30 minutes, plus
standing and rising

Cooking time
25 minutes

Oven temperature
220°C (425°F)
gas 7

Makes 8

Calories
300 per portion

125 g (4 oz) wholewheat flour
1 teaspoon light muscovado sugar
1 tablespoon dried yeast
175 ml (6 fl oz) tepid skimmed milk
FOR THE DOUGH
350 g (12 oz) wholewheat flour
pinch of salt
50 g (2 oz) soft margarine
3 tablespoons clear honey, melted
75 g (3 oz) chopped hazelnuts
1 medium egg, beaten
Glaze (see Cook's Tip)

Mix together the flour, sugar and dried yeast, pour on the milk and mix to a smooth batter. Set aside in a warm place for about 15 minutes until the mixture is frothy.

To make the dough, sift the flour and salt, rub in the margarine, and stir in the honey, nuts and egg. Pour on the yeast batter mixture and mix until the dough leaves the sides of the bowl. Turn out the dough on to a lightly floured board and knead for about 10 minutes, or until it is smooth and pliable.

Shape the dough into a ball, return it to the bowl and cover with a piece of oiled polythene. Leave it in a warm place for about 45 minutes, or until it has doubled in size.

Knead the dough and divide it into 8 pieces. Shape into rounds and place them well apart on two baking sheets.

Bake the teacakes in a preheated oven for 20 minutes, or until they sound hollow when tapped underneath. Brush with the glaze and return to the oven for 2–3 minutes.

■ COOK'S TIP

For an easy, tasty glaze for the teacakes, mix together 1 tablespoon each light muscovado sugar and skimmed milk.

484

carrot cake

Preparation time
25 minutes, plus
cooling

Cooking time
1 hour 10 minutes

Oven temperature
180°C (350°F)
gas 4

**Makes 1 x 18 cm
(7 inch) round cake**

Total calories
3094

250 g (8 oz) light soft brown sugar
175 ml (6 fl oz) vegetable oil
2 medium eggs
125 g (4 oz) plain wholemeal flour
1 teaspoon ground cinnamon
1 teaspoon bicarbonate of soda
150 g (5 oz) coarsely grated carrots
Jam topping (see Cook's Tip)
50 g (2 oz) chopped walnuts

Line an 18 cm (7 inch) round cake tin with nonstick silicone paper or greaseproof paper. Use a fixed-base tin as the mixture has almost a pouring consistency.

Put the sugar into a mixing bowl and using an electric whisk gradually whisk in the oil, then whisk in the eggs one at a time. Mix together the flour, cinnamon and bicarbonate of soda and stir into the egg mixture, then add the carrots. Beat all the ingredients together with a wooden spoon then pour into the prepared cake tin.

Place the tin in the centre of a preheated oven and bake for about 1 hour 10 minutes until the cake is risen and firm to the touch. Remove the cake from the oven, let it stand in the tin for 3 minutes, then turn out on to a wire rack, peel off the paper and leave to cool.

Brush the topping generously over the top of the cooled cake and immediately sprinkle over the walnuts. The glaze will set very quickly.

■ COOK'S TIP

To make the jam topping: boil together for 2–3 minutes 2 tablespoons apricot jam and 1 tablespoon lemon juice. Prepare 50 g (2 oz) chopped walnuts.

485

orange marmalade ring

Preparation time
20 minutes

Cooking time
1 hour 5 minutes

Oven temperature
160°C (325°F)
gas 3

**Makes 1 x 23 cm
(9 inch) cake ring**

Calories
310 per piece
(of 10)

250 g (8 oz) wholewheat flour
pinch of salt
2 teaspoons baking powder
1 teaspoon ground cinnamon
50 g (2 oz) light muscovado sugar
8 tablespoons low-sugar orange
  marmalade, chopped
grated rind and juice of 1 orange
175 ml (6 fl oz) vegetable oil
2 medium eggs
150 g (5 oz) seedless raisins
2 tablespoons honey, melted, to glaze
orange rind strands, to decorate

Sift the flour, salt, baking powder and cinnamon into a bowl and tip in any bran remaining in the sieve. In another bowl mix together the sugar, marmalade, orange rind, orange juice and oil and beat in the eggs. Gradually beat in the flour mixture, and stir in the raisins.

Turn the mixture into a greased and floured 23 cm (9 inch) metal ring mould. Bake in a preheated oven for 1 hour and 5 minutes, or until the cake is well risen and firm.

Leave the cake to cool a little in the ring, then turn it out on to a wire rack. Brush it with the melted honey while it is still warm. Cool the cake completely, then wrap it in foil.

486

fruit and nut cake

Preparation time
20 minutes, plus
chilling

Cooking time
5 minutes

**Makes 1 x 1 kg
(2 lb) cake**

Total calories
3915

250 g (8 oz) digestive biscuits, coarsely
  crumbled
175 g (6 oz) candied peel, chopped
175 g (6 oz) glacé cherries, chopped
125 g (4 oz) raisins
125 g (4 oz) shelled Brazil nuts, chopped
1 teaspoon ground mixed spice
3 tablespoons sherry
3 tablespoons black treacle
125 g (4 oz) plain chocolate, broken into
  pieces
FOR THE DECORATION
shelled Brazil nuts
glacé cherries, halved

Lightly grease a 1 kg (2 lb) loaf tin and line with greased greaseproof paper.

Mix the crumbled biscuits with the candied peel, cherries, raisins, nuts and mixed spice.

Place the sherry, black treacle and chocolate in a bowl. Stand the bowl over a saucepan of gently simmering water and stir until all the ingredients have melted. Stir the melted ingredients into the biscuit and fruit mixture, and mix thoroughly together.

Pour into the prepared loaf tin and spread the surface level. Cover with a piece of greased greaseproof paper. Chill until the cake is quite firm. Turn out and decorate with Brazil nuts and glacé, cherries. Slice to serve.

■ COOK'S TIP

For a really moist cake, leave to mature for a few days, wrapped in foil and stored in an airtight container. It will keep well in this way for up to one week.

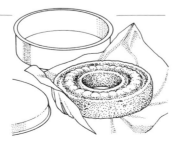

■ COOK'S TIP

The usual red glacé cherries, being dyed with cochineal, are not strictly vegetarian. Choose natural glacé cherries instead. Health food shops and supermarkets sell them.

vegetarian mince pies

Preparation time
30 minutes

Cooking time
10 minutes

Oven temperature
200°C (400°F)
gas 6

Makes 24

Calories
130 per portion

125 g (4 oz) each currants, raisins and sultanas
50 g (2 oz) cooking dates, chopped
50 g (2 oz) candied peel
50 g (2 oz) glacé cherries, chopped
50 g (2 oz) flaked almonds
1 ripe banana, chopped
4 tablespoons brandy or whisky
½ teaspoon each ground ginger, grated nutmeg, mixed spice
FOR THE PASTRY
500 g (1 lb) wholewheat flour
250 g (8 oz) butter or margarine
10–12 teaspoons cold water

To make the mincemeat, simply mix all the ingredients together.

Lightly grease a shallow bun or muffin tin. Sift the flour and salt into a bowl, tipping in any bran left in the sieve. Add the butter or margarine, and rub into the flour with your fingertips until the mixture resembles breadcrumbs. Add the water, then press the mixture together to make a dough.

Roll out the dough on a lightly-floured board, then cut out 12 cm (4¾ inch) circles and 10 cm (4 inch) circles using round cutters. Press one of the larger circles gently into each section of the bun or muffin tin, then put a heaped teaspoon of mincemeat into each one and cover with the smaller pastry circles. Press down firmly at the edges, make a hole in the top for steam to escape, then bake for about 10 minutes, until the pastry is lightly browned. Leave to cool in the tin.

■ COOK'S TIP

This mincemeat can be stored for a week in a covered bowl in the refrigerator, but doesn't keep in the same way as ordinary mincemeat because of the lack of sugar. There is enough mincemeat here to fill about 36 pies in all.

christmas carrot cake

Preparation time
30 minutes, plus soaking

Cooking time
1¼ hours

Oven temperature
180°C (350°F)
gas 4

Serves 16

Calories
300 per slice

175 g (6 oz) sultanas
4 tablespoons whisky
250 ml (8 fl oz) corn oil
125 g (4 oz) molasses sugar
3 large eggs
1 tablespoon cocoa powder
250 g (8 oz) plain wholemeal flour
1 teaspoon cinnamon
½ teaspoon grated nutmeg
½ teaspoon allspice
½ teaspoon salt
1½ teaspoons baking powder
1½ teaspoons bicarbonate of soda
250 g (8 oz) carrots, finely grated
75 g (3 oz) walnuts, finely chopped
Icing (see Cook's Tip)

Soak the sultanas in the whisky for 1 hour or more. Line a loose-bottomed 20 cm (8 inch) cake tin with nonstick silicone, or greased and floured greaseproof paper.

Beat together the oil and sugar, adding the eggs one at a time. (At this stage the mixture looks very odd, but don't worry.) Still beating, add the cocoa powder, flour, spices, salt, baking powder and bicarbonate of soda.

Mix in the carrots, the sultanas and the whisky, and the nuts. Tip the mixture into the cake tin. Bake in a preheated oven for about 1¼ hours; a warmed skewer will come out clean when the cake is cooked. Allow the cake to cool in the tin. When it is quite cold, spread over the icing.

■ COOK'S TIP

To make the icing, work 50 g (2 oz) icing sugar into 375 g (12 oz) low-fat soft cheese. Add the finely grated rind of half a lemon. Spread the icing over the top of the cake.

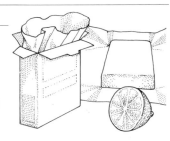

489

chocolate biscuit squares

Preparation time
15–20 minutes, plus chilling

Makes 9

Calories
329 per biscuit

175 g (6 oz) plain chocolate
50 g (2 oz) butter or margarine
250 g (8 oz) digestive biscuits
grated rind of 1 orange
125 g (4 oz) sultanas
50 g (2 oz) natural glacé cherries, chopped
icing sugar, sifted, to decorate

Melt the chocolate and butter in a heatproof bowl over a pan of hot water. Remove from the heat.

Put the biscuits in a polythene bag and crush with a rolling pin. Add to the chocolate mixture with the orange rind, sultanas and chopped cherries. Mix well and press into an 18 cm (7 inch) square tin. Mark into 9 squares.

Chill well then cut into squares. Sprinkle with a little icing sugar before serving.

490

marzipan and apple pies

Preparation time
35 minutes, plus chilling

Cooking time
20 minutes

Oven temperature
220°C (425°F)
gas 7

Makes 20 pies

Calories
184 per portion

375 g (12 oz) wholemeal self-raising flour
pinch of salt
250 g (8 oz) hard vegetable margarine, from the freezer
scant 7 tablespoons water
2 tablespoons vegetable oil
300 g (10 oz) Bramley apples, peeled, cored and coarsely chopped
125 g (4 oz) bought marzipan, cut into 5 mm (¼ inch) cubes
milk, for brushing

To make the pastry, put the flour and salt into a bowl. Grate the margarine straight into the flour, dipping the grater into the bowl now and again to free the flakes of margarine. Distribute the margarine gently through the flour, using a round-bladed knife, then add the water and oil. Mix to a fairly firm dough then put into a polythene bag and chill for 1 hour.

Mix the apples and marzipan in a bowl. Roll out the pastry quite thinly on a lightly floured surface. Cut out 40 rounds using a 7 cm (3 inch) fluted cutter.

Line 20 small tartlet tins with half the rounds, and spoon the filling into them, packing it in well. Brush both sides of the remaining rounds with milk and put them on top of the tartlets in the tin. Press the edges together to seal.

Bake near the top of a preheated oven for 15–20 minutes until golden brown. Lift carefully from the tin and leave to cool slightly on a wire rack. Serve warm or cold.

■ COOK'S TIP

If preferred, omit the glacé cherries and increase the quantity of sultanas in these biscuits.

■ COOK'S TIP

These tempting little pies make the perfect vegetarian alternative to traditional mince pies. Sprinkle them with a little demerara sugar before baking, if liked.

491

american bran muffins

Preparation time
10 minutes

Cooking time
15 minutes

Oven temperature
200°C (400°F)
gas 6

Makes 24

Calories
106 per muffin

4 tablespoons oil
75 g (3 oz) soft dark brown sugar
75 g (3 oz) golden syrup
2 medium eggs, beaten
250 ml (8 fl oz) milk
50 g (2 oz) bran
75 g (3 oz) seedless raisins
125 g (4 oz) self-raising flour
1 teaspoon baking powder
½ teaspoon bicarbonate of soda
½ teaspoon salt

Place the oil, sugar, syrup, beaten eggs and milk in a large bowl. Mix thoroughly with a fork.

Add the bran and raisins and sift in the flour, baking powder, bicarbonate of soda and salt. Stir very lightly until the ingredients are just mixed.

Spoon the mixture into paper cake cases or greased bun tins a scant two-thirds full.

Bake in a preheated oven for 15 minutes, until well risen and firm to the touch. Serve warm, split in half and buttered.

492

treacle and sultana flapjacks

Preparation time
10 minutes

Cooking time
40 minutes

Oven temperature
160°C (325°F)
gas 3

Makes 12

Calories
213 per biscuit

150 g (5 oz) butter
75 g (3 oz) Barbados or molasses sugar
1–2 tablespoons black molasses
50 g (2 oz) sultanas
250 g (8 oz) jumbo or rolled oats
grated rind and juice of ½ lemon

Melt the butter in a saucepan. Stir in the sugar and molasses. Add the sultanas, oats and lemon rind and juice and mix well. Press into a greased 25 x 20 cm (10 x 8 inch) tin.

Bake in a preheated oven for 40 minutes. Allow to cool for 10 minutes, then cut into bars. Leave the flapjacks in the tin until completely cold.

■ COOK'S TIP

Unlike traditional British muffins, American muffins are deep and have a cake-like texture. Bake them in bun tins or in individual paper cases.

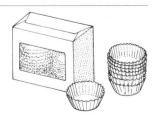

■ COOK'S TIP

Try currants instead of sultanas in these flapjacks. If molasses is unavailable, use black treacle or golden syrup instead.

493

peanut cookies

Preparation time
10 minutes

Cooking time
12 minutes

Oven temperature
180°C (350°F)
gas 4

Makes 12

Calories
95 per cookie

50 g (2 oz) butter, softened
50 g (2 oz) soft brown sugar
50 g (2 oz) salted peanuts, roughly
  chopped
½ teaspoon mixed spice
75 g (3 oz) self-raising flour
1 tablespoon orange juice

Cream the butter and sugar together until light and fluffy, then stir in the peanuts, mixed spice, flour and orange juice to form a soft, not sticky, dough.

Break the mixture into 12 equal-sized pieces and roll each one into a ball. Place well apart on greased baking sheets, flattening them slightly with a fork. Bake in a preheated oven for 10–12 minutes or until firming. Leave on the cookies on the baking sheets until they are firm enough to transfer to a wire rack to cool completely.

494

muesli squares

Preparation time
10 minutes

Cooking time
20 minutes

Oven temperature
180°C (350°F)
gas 4

Makes 18

Calories
120 per biscuit

3 tablespoons honey
125 g (4 oz) butter
50 g (2 oz) soft light brown sugar
50 g (2 oz) chopped mixed nuts
125 g (4 oz) porridge oats
25 g (1 oz) desiccated coconut
50 g (2 oz) sesame seeds

Place the honey, butter and sugar in a saucepan. Heat gently until the butter has melted and the sugar has dissolved. Stir in the nuts, oats, coconut and sesame seeds.

Press the mixture evenly into a greased 28 x 18 cm (11 x 7 inch) shallow oblong tin. Bake in a preheated oven for 20 minutes, until golden brown.

Cool for 5 minutes in the tin, then cut into squares. Leave in the tin to cool completely.

■ COOK'S TIP

Mixed spice usually includes
cinnamon, cloves and nutmeg,
but Jamaica pepper or
coriander may also be added.

■ COOK'S TIP

For a delicious variation, melt
125 g (4 oz) plain chocolate and
dip one side of each cold square
into it. Sit the squares on a wire
rack to let the chocolate harden.

495

crispy crackles

Preparation time
10 minutes, plus cooling

Cooking time
3 minutes

Makes 16

Calories
57 per biscuit

50 g (2 oz) butter or margarine
2 tablespoons golden syrup
50 g (2 oz) drinking chocolate powder, sifted
50 g (2 oz) cornflakes

Melt the butter and golden syrup over a low heat. Remove from the heat and stir in the drinking chocolate powder and cornflakes, mixing well so that the cornflakes are well coated in the chocolate syrup mixture.

Spoon into paper cases, set on a baking sheet, and leave to cool. They will set on cooling.

496

nut flapjacks

Preparation time
5 minutes

Cooking time
40 minutes

Oven temperature
160°C (325°F)
gas 3

Makes 12

Calories
215 per flapjack

125 g (4 oz) vegetable margarine
4 tablespoons golden syrup
75 g (3 oz) soft brown sugar
250 g (8 oz) rolled oats
75 g (3 oz) walnuts, chopped
grated rind of 1 orange
¼ teaspoon salt
FOR THE DECORATION
fromage frais (optional)
orange slices (optional)

Grease a 19 cm (7½ inch) square shallow tin.

Put the margarine and syrup in a saucepan and melt over a low heat. Remove the pan from the heat and stir in the sugar, oats, walnuts, orange rind and salt until well mixed.

Turn the mixture into the prepared tin and bake in a pre-heated oven for 40 minutes or until it is just starting to bubble at the edges.

Leave to cool for 4 minutes to firm up slightly then cut into squares and leave until stiff enough to lift out on to a wire rack to cool completely. Decorate as shown if liked.

■ COOK'S TIP

Use plain corn flakes for this recipe, not ones with added chopped nuts, honey or sugar. Or try using a different cereal.

■ COOK'S TIP

Coconut makes a very good addition to these flapjacks. Reduce the amount of oats by 75 g (3 oz) and substitute desiccated coconut.

497

blue cheese loaf

Preparation time 20 minutes	*125 g (4 oz) self-raising wholemeal flour*
	125 g (4 oz) self-raising flour
Cooking time 1 hour	*½ teaspoon baking powder*
	1 teaspoon mustard powder
Oven temperature 190°C (375°F) gas 5	*½ teaspoon salt*
	50 g (2 oz) butter
	125 g (4 oz) Danish Blue cheese
Makes 1 loaf	*2 celery sticks, finely chopped*
	50 g (2 oz) walnuts, chopped
Total calories 1865	*1 large egg*
	125 ml (4 fl oz) milk
	sesame seeds or poppy seeds (optional)

Sift the flours, baking powder, mustard and salt into a mixing bowl, adding any bran left in the sieve. Rub in the butter until the mixture resembles fine breadcrumbs. Crumble the cheese and rub it in. Mix in the celery and walnuts. Beat the egg and milk together, add to the dry ingredients and mix well to make a fairly stiff consistency.

Spoon the mixture into a lined and greased 500 g (1 lb) loaf tin. Level the top and sprinkle with sesame or poppy seeds, if liked. Bake in a preheated moderately hot oven for 1 hour, or until well browned. When cooked, a skewer inserted into the centre of the loaf will come out clean.

Cool the loaf in the tin for 5 minutes, then turn out on to a wire rack, remove the lining paper and cool completely.

Serve warm or cold, sliced and spread with butter.

498

caraway rolls

Preparation time 25–30 minutes, plus rising and proving	*25 g (1 oz) fresh yeast or 15 g (½ oz)* *dried yeast (see Cook's Tip)*
	1 teaspoon sugar
Cooking time 20 minutes	*250 ml (8 fl oz) lukewarm water*
	15 g (½ oz) butter or margarine
Oven temperature 230°C (450°F) gas 8	*500 g (10 oz) strong white bread flour*
	50 g (2 oz) bran flakes, crushed
Makes 8	*1 teaspoon caraway seeds*
	½ teaspoon salt
Calories 120 per roll	

Blend the fresh yeast and sugar with a little of the water to form a smooth paste. Add the remaining water. Leave until frothy.

Rub the butter or margarine into the flour and stir in the bran flakes, caraway seeds and salt. Add the yeast mixture and mix well to form a soft dough. Knead for about 10 minutes. Place the dough in a bowl and cover loosely with a large oiled plastic bag or clingfilm. Leave in a warm place until doubled in size.

Turn the dough on to a floured surface and knead for a further 45 minutes. Shape into eight rolls, place on a greased baking tray and leave in a warm place until doubled in size.

Brush with a little milk and bake in a preheated oven for about 20 minutes.

■ COOK'S TIP

To cook in your microwave, turn the loaf mixture into a 900 ml (1½ pint) oblong dish. Microwave on full power for 12 minutes then leave to stand for 10 minutes before cooling on a wire rack.

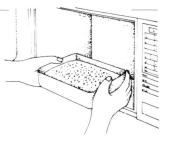

■ COOK'S TIP

If using dried yeast, you will need 15 g (½ oz). Sprinkle the dried yeast over the water, stir in the sugar and leave for about 10 minutes until frothy.

499

savoury cheese
flowerpot bread

Preparation time
30 minutes, plus
rising

Cooking time
45 minutes

Oven temperature
200°C (400°F)
gas 6

Makes 1 x 675 g
(1½ lb) flowerpot
loaf

Total calories
1680

375 g (12 oz) strong wholemeal flour
¼ teaspoon salt
15 g (½ oz) butter
1 sachet easy-blend dried yeast
25 g (1 oz) walnuts, chopped
125 g (4 oz) low-fat hard cheese, finely
* grated*
75 g (3 oz) celery, chopped
150 ml (¼ pint) warm water
beaten egg, to glaze
1 tablespoon kibbled wheat

Mix the flour and salt together. Rub in the butter and stir in the
yeast. Thoroughly mix in the walnuts, cheese and celery. Add the
water to make a dough and knead for 10 minutes. Place in a large
bowl, covered with a lightly oiled plastic bag, and leave to rise in
a warm place until doubled in size – about 2 hours.

Knock back, knead and shape to fit a well greased unused
flowerpot measuring about 15 cm (6 inches) in depth and width.
Cover with plastic again and leave to rise for about 1 hour.

Glaze with beaten egg and sprinkle with kibbled wheat. Bake
in a preheated oven for 45 minutes until golden. The bottom of
the bread should sound hollow when tapped. Leave to cool on a
wire rack. Serve sliced, lightly spread with butter.

500

cheese and
pineapple scones

Preparation time
20 minutes

Cooking time
15 minutes

Oven temperature
200°C (400°F)
gas 6

Makes 12 scones

Calories
145 per scone

300 g (10 oz) wholemeal flour
4 teaspoons baking powder
pinch of salt
65 g (2½ oz) butter
50 g (2 oz) low-fat hard cheese, finely
* grated*
1 x 250 g (8 oz) can crushed pineapple,
* drained*
3 tablespoons milk
1 large egg, beaten
milk, to glaze

Mix together the flour, baking powder and salt. Rub in the butter until the mixture resembles fine breadcrumbs. Stir in the
cheese and pineapple. Bind to a dough with the milk and egg.

Roll out 1 cm (½ inch) thick and cut out twelve 6 cm (2½ inch)
rounds. Place on a greased baking sheet. Brush with milk and
bake for about 15 minutes, until well risen and golden. Cool on a
wire rack. Serve split, spread with butter and pineapple jam.

■ COOK'S TIP

Season the flowerpot before use by
brushing the inside very thoroughly with oil.
Place the empty pot in a moderately hot
oven (200°C/400°F/gas 6) for 15 minutes.
Allow to cool completely before use.

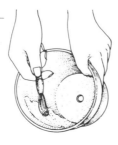

■ COOK'S TIP

Baking powder loses its potency if
stored for a long time. If dubious
about that tin at the back of the
cupboard, sprinkle 1 teaspoon of the
baking powder into a little hot water.
It should fizz enthusiastically.

index